SECOND DICTIONARY OF ACRONYMS & ABBREVIATIONS

PUBLISHER'S NOTE

This book is a supplement to Eric Pugh's
A dictionary of acronyms and abbreviations,
second edition 1970; it does not cumulate any of
the material therein, but does update it in many
cases.

ERIC PUGH

ALA

SECOND DICTIONARY OF ACRONYMS & ABBREVIATIONS

More abbreviations in management, technology and information science

ARCHON BOOKS & CLIVE BINGLEY

Library of Congress Cataloging in Publication Data
Pugh, Eric.
  Second dictionary of acronyms & abbreviations.
  " This book is a supplement to Eric Pugh's A dictionary
of acronyms and abbreviations, second edition 1970."
  1. Technology—Abbreviations. 2. Management—
Abbreviations. 3. Information science—Abbreviations.
4. Acronyms. I. Pugh, Eric. A dictionary of
acronyms & abbreviations. II. Title.
T8.P82   601'.48   74-4271
ISBN 0-208-01354-7

FIRST PUBLISHED 1974 BY CLIVE BINGLEY LTD
THIS EDITION SIMULTANEOUSLY PUBLISHED IN THE USA
BY ARCHON BOOKS, AN IMPRINT OF THE SHOE STRING PRESS, INC,
995 SHERMAN AVENUE, HAMDEN, CONNECTICUT 06514
PRINTED IN GREAT BRITAIN
© ERIC PUGH 1974

This second volume contains another 10,000 entries. Again it must be stressed that some of the acronyms listed are registered trade names and care should be taken in their use.

One explanation, which covers both volumes, may be helpful; it concerns the word ' PROGRAM ' which is the accepted standard term relative to software in computer data processing. However, because of the variance in the usage of this word in the USA, I have used ' PROGRAMME ' to cover data processing; ' PROGRAM ' has only been used when it covers proceedings, or projects, undertaken by institutions, etc. in the USA.

Once again I am pleased to acknowledge the support inherent in the continuing interest shown by S G Berriman and A J Walford.

Most of all I am indebted to my wife. Her inexhaustible patience over many years and typing of most of the manuscript have made this volume possible. The work has been a joint venture in every respect and we dedicate it to Barbara and Sandra.

Teddington, Middlesex   ERIC PUGH
November 1973

CONTENTS

A

A	prefix to numbered: dated series of Aircraft Bolts Standards issued by BSI (letter is sometimes preceded by a number)
A / C A S P	Air Conditioning Analytical Simulation Package
A & A E E	Aeroplane and Armament Experimental Establishment (MOD)
A A	Anti-Aircraft
	Atomic Absorption
A A A	American Academy of Allergy (USA)
	American Arbitration Association (USA)
	Anti-Aircraft Artillery
A A A F	Association Aeronautique et Astronautique de France (France) (Aeronautic and Astronautic Association of France)
A A A S - H A C	American Association for the Advancement of Science, Herbicide Assessment Commission (USA)
A A A S A	Association for the Advancement of Agricultural Sciences in Africa (Ethiopia)
A A B B	American Association of Blood Banks (USA)
A A B F S	Amphibious Assault Bulk Fuel System
A A B N C P	Advanced Airborne National Command Post (USAF)
A A B P	Australian Association of Business Publications (Australia)
A A C	Alaskan Air Command (USAF)
	Average Annual Cost
A A C C	Airport Associations Co-ordinating Committee
	American Association of Cereal Chemists (USA)
	American Association of Clinical Chemists (USA)
A A C C H	American Association for Child Care in Hospital (USA)
A A C I A	American Association for Clinical Immunology and Allergy (USA)
A A C O	Arab Air Carriers Organization
A A C P	Advanced Airborne Command Post (USAF)
	American Association of Colleges of Pharmacy (USA)
A A C R	American Association for Cancer Research (USA)
A A C S	Advanced Automatic Compilation System
A A C T	American Academy of Clinical Toxicology (USA)

7

A A C U	American Association of Clinical Urologists (USA)
A A D C	All-Application Digital Computer
A A D B	Army Air Defense Board (US Army)
A A D S	American Association of Dental Schools (USA)
A A E	prefix to dated-numbered series of reports issued by Department of Aeronautical and Astronautical Engineering, Illinois University (USA)
A A E E	Aeroplane and Armament Experimental Establishment (MOD)
A A E E R	Aerophysics and Aerospace Engineering Research Report
A A F I F	Automated Air Facility Information File (of DMAAC (USDOD))
A A F P	American Academy of Family Physicians (USA)
A A F R A	Association of African Airlines
A A G	Association of American Geographers (USA)
A A H	Advanced Armed *or* Attack Helicopter
A A H S	American Aviation Historical Society (USA)
A A I	American Association of Immunologists (USA)
A A I I	Association for the Advancement of Invention and Innovation (USA)
A A L	Association of Assistant Librarians
A A L A S	American Association for Laboratory Animal Science (USA)
A A L C	Amphibious Assault Landing Craft
A A L L	American Association of Law Libraries (USA)
A A M	Arma Aerea de la Marina (Spain) (Naval Air Force)
A A M C	Association of American Medical Colleges (USA)
A A M F	Association Aeromedicale de France (France) (Aeromedical Association of France)
A A M R D L	Army Air Mobility Research and Development Laboratory (US Army)
A A M W	American Association of Medical Writers (USA)
A A N	American Academy of Neurology (USA)
A A N C P	Advanced Airborne National Command Post (USAF)
A A N I	Arkticheskii i Antarkticheskii Nauchno Issledovatel'skiy Institut (USSR) (Arctic and Antarctic Scientific Research Institute)
A A O	American Academy of Optometry (USA)
A A O M	American Academy of Occupational Medicine (USA)

A A O O	American Academy of Ophthalmology and Oto-laryngology (USA)
A A P	American Academy of Psychoanalysis (USA)
	American Association of Pediatrics (USA)
A A P A	Advertising Agency Production Association
	Australian Asphalt Pavement Association (Australia)
A A P M R	American Academy of Physical Medicine and Rehabilitation (USA)
A A P S	Automated Astronomic Positioning System
A A P S P	Advanced Automotive Power Systems Program (of NAPCA (USA))
A A P S S	American Academy of Political and Social Science (USA)
A A R	prefix to numbered series of Aircraft Accident Reports issued by NTSB (USA)
A A R L S	Arkansas Association of Registered Land Surveyors (USA)
A A R R O	Afro-Asian Rural Reconstruction Organization (India)
A A R S	Aerospace Rescue and Recovery Service (of Military Airlift Command (USAF))
A A R V	Aerial Armoured Reconnaissance Vehicle
A A S	Advanced Administrative System
	American Antiquarian Society (USA)
	Atomic Absorption Spectrophotometry
	Atomic Absorption Spectroscopy
A A S E	Department of Aerophysics and Aerospace Engineering, Mississippi University (USA)
A A S L	American Association of School Librarians (USA)
A A S L H	American Association for State and Local History (USA)
A A S T	American Association for the Surgery of Trauma (USA)
A A T	Air Abrasive Trimming
A A T M S	Advanced Air Traffic Management Systems
A A T S	Committee on the Application of Aerospace Technology to Society (of AIAA (USA))
A A T T	American Association for Textile Technology (USA)
A A U	American Association of Universities (USA)
A A U P	American Association of University Professors (USA)

1*

A A U T A	Australasian Association of University Teachers of Accountancy (Australia)
A A V A	Army Audio Visual Agency (US Army)
A A W S A	Addis Ababa Water and Sewerage Authority (Ethiopia)
A B	Aktiebolaget (Limited Company)
A B A	American Blasting Association (USA)
	Australian Booksellers Association (Australia)
	Azobenzenearsonate
A B A C U S	Architecture and Building Aids Computer Unit, Strathclyde (Strathclyde University)
	Automatic, Block-schematic Advanced Control User-oriented System
A B A E	Advisory Board of Accountancy Education
A B A G	Association of Bay Area Governments (USA)
A B C	Advanced-Booking Charter
	America, Britain, Canada
	Anchored By Cassini
	Antigen-Binding Capacity
	Associated Builders and Contractors (USA)
	Automatic Bar and Chucking
A B C C	Atomic Bomb Casualty Commission
A B C F R C	Auke Bay Coastal Fisheries Research Center (of NMFS (USA))
A B C P	Associacao Technica Brasileira de Celulose e Papel (Brazil) (Brazilian Technical Association for Pulp and Paper)
A B E	Arithmetic Building Element
A B E S	Air Breathing Engine System
A B F M	Association of Business Forms Manufacturers (USA)
A B L C	Association of British Launderers and Cleaners
A B L E	Acquisition Based on Consideration of Logistic Effects (a project of USAF)
	Asymptotically Best Linear Estimate
A B L S	*Atlas* (*Chemical Industries*) Biomedical Literary System
A B L V	Air-Breathing Launch Vehicle
A B M	Apogee Boost Motor
	Associacao Brasileira de Metais (Brazil) (Brazilian Association for Metals)
A B M A	American Brush Manufacturers Association (USA)
A B M D A	Army Ballistic Missile Defense Agency (US Army)
A B O	Apparent Body Orientation

A B O I	Association of British Oceanological Industries
A B P	Accounting Principles Board (of AICPA (USA))
A B P A	Australian Book Publishers Association (Australia)
A B P C	Association of British Pewter Craftsmen
A B R	prefix to numbered series of Australian Navy Books of Reference
A B R A C E	Associacao Brazileira de Computadores Electronicos (Brazil) (Brazilian Association for the Use of Electronic Computers)
A B R A L O C	Acoustic Beacon Ranging and Location
A B R C	Advisory Board of the Research Councils
A B S	Adaptive Braking System American Bureau of Shipping (USA)
A b s	Analysis by Synthesis
A B S T E C H	American Bureau of Shipping Worldwide Technical Services (USA)
A B T A P L	Association of British Theological and Philosophical Libraries
A B T M	Association of British Transport Museums
A B T O A D	Air Blast Time-of-Arrival Detector
A B U	Ahmadu Bello University (Nigeria)
A C	Adaptive Control Asphaltic Concrete
A C A	Air Cushion Aircraft American College of Apothecaries (USA) American Cryptogram Association (USA) Association of Consulting Architects Australian Consumer Association (Australia) Australasian Corrosion Association (Australia)
A C A A P S	Advisory Committee on Advanced Automotive Power Systems (USA)
A C A C T	Associate Committee on Air-Cushion Technology (of NRC (Canada))
A C A F	Aero-Club Air France (France)
A C A M	Augmented Content-Addressed Memory
A C A M P S	Automated Communications And Message Processing System
A C A P	Aviation Consumer Action Project (USA)
A C A S S	Association of Chartered Accountants Students Societies
A C B	Assam Carbon Black

A C C	Adjustable Chain Clutch
	Administrative Committee on Co-ordination (of UN)
	American College of Cardiology (USA)
	Annual Capital Charge
	Antarctic Circumpolar Current
	Associated Cement Companies (India)
	Average Correlation Coefficients
A C C A	Air Charter Carriers Association
A C C C	Advisory Committee to the Canada Centre for Inland Waters (Canada)
A C C E S S	Access Characteristics Estimation System
	Air Canada Cargo Enquiry and Service System
	Argonne (*National Laboratory*) Code Center Exchange and Storage System
A C C G	American Committee for Crystal Growth (USA)
A C C O R D D	informal association of Regional Dissemination Centers (of NASA (USA))
A C C P	American College of Chest Physicians (USA)
A C C R	Annual Cost of Capital Recovery
A C C R A	Australian Chart and Code for Rural Accounting (Australia)
A C D	Admiralty Chart Datum
	American College of Dentists (USA)
A C D P I	Association for a Competitive Data Processing Industry (USA)
A C D P S	Automated Cartographic, Drafting and Photogrammetric System
A C E	Association for Centrifuge Enrichment
	Audit, Control and Evaluation
	Automatic Clutter-Eliminator
	Average Cumulative Error
A C E C	American Consulting Engineers Council (USA)
A C E M B	Annual Conference on Engineering in Medicine and Biology
A C E P	American College of Emergency Physicians (USA)
A C E R	Australian Council for Educational Research (Australia)
A Cer S	American Ceramic Society (USA)
A C E S	Advanced Concept Escape System
A C F	Air Cushion Ferry
A C G	Activated Charcoal Granules
	American College of Gastroenterology (USA)

A C G R	Associate Committee on Geotechnical Research (of NRC (Canada))
A C G S	Aerospace Cartographic and Geodetic Service (USAF) (disbanded 1972)
A C I	Alloy Casting Institute (a division of SFSA (USA))
A C I C	Aeronautical Chart and Information Center (USAF) (now Defense Mapping Agency Aerospace Center)
A C I C A F E	Association du Commerce et de l'Industrie du Cafe dans la C.E.E. (Association of the Coffee Trade and Industry in the European Economic Community)
A C I D	Acceleration, Cruising, Idling, Deceleration
A C I L	American Council of Independent Laboratories (USA)
A C I M G A	Associazione Costruttori Italiani Macchine Grafiche e Affini (Italy) (Italian Association of Manufacturers of Machinery and Equipment for the Graphic Arts and Allied Trades)
A C I M I T	Associazione Costruttori Italiani di Macchinario per l'Industria Tessile (Italy) (Italian Association of Machinery Manufacturers for the Textile Industry)
A C I M S	Aircraft Component Intensive Management System (US Army)
A C I P	Advisory Committee on Immunization Practices (of Center for Disease Control (USA))
A C I R	Advisory Commission on Intergovernmental Relations (USA)
	Automotive Crash Injury Research
A C I R L	Australian Coal Industries Research Laboratories (Australia)
A C J M S	Air Corporations Joint Medical Service (of BEA and BOAC)
A C L	Association for Computational Linguistics (USA)
	Association of Cinema Laboratories (USA)
A C L A M	American College of Laboratory Animal Medicine (USA)
A C L D	Association for Children with Learning Disabilities (USA)
A C L O S	Automatic Command to Line Of Sight
A C L S	Automatic Carrier Landing System
	Aircraft Carrier Landing System

A C M C	Agricultural and Construction Machinery Council (of SAE (USA))
A C M E	Association of Consulting Management Engineers (USA)
A C M R	Air Combat Manoeuvring Range (USN)
A C M S	Australasian Conference on the Mechanics of Structures and Materials
A C O N D A	Activities Committee on New Directions for the ALA (American Library Association (USA))
A C O R N	Automatic Coder of Report Narrative
A C P	Accomplishment/Cost Procedure
	Acyl-Carrier Protein
	Allied Communications Publication
	American College of Psychiatrists (USA)
A C P A	Association of Computer Programers and Analysts (USA)
A C P M	American College of Preventive Medicine (USA)
A C P R	Annular Core Pulse Reactor
A C P S	Attitude-Control Propulsion System
A C Q S	Association of Consultant Quantity Surveyors
A C R	Active Cavity Radiometer
	American College of Radiology (USA)
A C R E	Advanced Chemical Rocket Engineering program (of NASA (USA) and USDOD)
A C R M	Air Cushion Rig Mover
	American Congress of Rehabilitation Medicine (USA)
A C R O D A B A	Acronym Data Base
A C S	Accelerated Climatic Simulator
	Adhesive Component System
	American Cancer Society (USA)
	American College of Surgeons (USA)
	Association of Consultant Surveyors
	Association of Consulting Scientists
	Automatic Control System
A C S A	Aerocargo SA (Mexico)
	Army Communications Systems Agency (US Army)
A C S A P	Automated Cross Section Analysis Programme
A C S I	American Ceramic Society, Incorporated (USA)
	Assistant Chief of Staff for Intelligence (US Army)
A C S I M	Accelerated Constrained Simplex technique
A C S R	Aluminium Conductors, Steel-Reinforced

A C S T	Advisory Council on Science and Technology (Australia)
A C S T I S	Advanced Circular Scan Thermal Imaging System
A C T	Actuarial Programming Language
	Advance Corporation Tax
	Advanced Concept Train
	Air Cushion *or* Cushioned Transporter
	Anti-Comet Tail
	Automated Contingency Translator
A C T A	Association de Coordination Technique Agricole (France) (Association for the Coordination of Agricultural Techniques)
A C T D	Automatic Telephone Call Distribution
A C T H	Adrenocorticotropic Hormone
A C T I O N	Accepting Challenges of Today In Our New-world
A C T I S	Auckland Commercial and Technical Information Service (New Zealand)
A C T I V E	Advanced Computer Training In a Versatile
A C T U	Environment
	Australian Council of Trade Unions (Australia)
A C U	Association of Commonwealth Universities
	Avionic Control Unit
A C U T A	Association of College and University Telecommunications Administrators (USA)
A D	prefix to dated-numbered series of reports issued by Airdrop Engineering Laboratory (of NLABS (US Army)
	prefix to numbered series of reports issued through Defense Documentation Center (USDOD) and usually sold by NTIS (USA)
A D A	Adenosine Deaminase
	Airborne Data Automation
	American Dietetic Association (USA)
	Automated Differential Agglutination
	Automated Dispensing Analyzer
A D A M	Advanced Data Access Method
A D A P	Airport Development Aid Program (of FAA (USA))
A D A P S	Armament Delivery Analysis Programming System
	Automated Design And Packaging Service

A D A P S O	Association of Data Processing Service Organizations (USA)
A D A P T S	Air-Delivered Anti-Pollution Transfer System
	Analogue/Digital/Analogue Process and Test System
A D A S	Agricultural Development and Advisory Service (of MAFF)
	Auxiliary Data Annotation Set
A D A T E	Automatic Digital Assembly Test Equipment
A D A W S	Action Data Automation and Weapon System
A D C	Agricultural Development Corporation (Korea)
	Agricultural Development Corporation (Pakistan)
	Areas of Deeper Convection
A D C A	Australian Department of Civil Aviation (Australia)
A D C C P	Advanced Data Communication Control Procedures (of ANSI (USA))
A D C S	Association of District Council Surveyors
A D D	Airstream Direction Detector
	Ascent Descent Director
A D D A S	Airborne Digital Data Acquisition System
A D D S	Advanced Deep Diving Submersible
A D E L A	Atlantic Community Development Group for Latin America
A D E P A	Association pour le Developpement de la Production Automatisee (France) (Association for the Development of Automated Production)
A D E S	Automated Data Entry System
A D H	Alaska Department of Highways (USA)
A D I	Acceptable Daily Intake
	Alternating Direction Implicit
	Alternating Direction Iterative
A D I C E P	Association de Directeurs de Centres Europeens de Plastiques (Association of Directors of European Plastics Associations)
A D I S	Association for Development of Instructional Systems (USA)
	Attitude Director Indicator System
	Automated Data Interchange Systems (a panel of ICAO)
A D I S P	Automated Data Interchange Systems Panel (of ICAO)
A D L	Automatic Data Logger

A D M	Adaptive Delta Modulation
	Aid in Decision Making
	Atomic Demolition Munition
A D M A R C	Agricultural Development and Marketing Corporation (a government agency) (Malawi)
A D N	Adiponitrile
A D O C	Air Defence Operations Centre
A D O I T	Automatically Directed Outgoing Intertoll Trunk test circuit
A D P	Ammonium Dihydrogen Phosphate
A D P A C S	Automated Data Processing and Communications Service (of GSA (USA))
A D P R E P	Automatic Data Processing Resource Estimating Procedures
A D Q C	Almost Difference Quasiternary Code
A D R	Accelerated Depreciation Range
	Accord European Relative au Transport International des Marchandises Dangereuses par Route (European Agreement on the International Transport of Dangerous Goods by Road)
	Automatical Digital Relay
A D R E P P	Aircraft Accident Data Reporting Panel (of ICAO)
A D R E S	Aircraft Data Recording Evaluation System
	Army Data Retrieval Engineering System (US Army)
A D R I	Automatic Dead-Reckoning Instrument
A D S	Advanced Diving System
	Advanced Dosimetry System
	Air Data System
	Aircraft Development Services (of FAA) (USA)
A D S A T I S	Australian Defence Science and Technology Information Service (of Department of Supply and Department of the Army (Australia))
A D S E	Alternative Delivery Schedule Evaluator
A D S E L	Address Selective
A D S G	Alternative Delivery Schedule Generator
A D S I D	Air-Delivered Seismic Intrusion Detector
A D S M	Air Defence Suppression Missile
A D S O L	Analysis of Dynamical Systems On-line
A D S T A R	Automatic Document Storage And Retrieval
A D S T E E L	Automated Drafting System - Structural Steel Detailing
A D T	Average Daily Traffic

A D T E C	ABMDA Data Processing Testbed and Evaluation Center (US Army)
A D T U	Automatic Digital Test Unit
A D V	Arbeitsgemeinschaft Deutscher Verkehrsflughafen (Germany)
A D V I C E	Analytical Determination of the Values of Information to Combat Effectiveness
A D V I S E R	Airborne Dual-channel Variable Input Severe Environmental Recorder/Reproducers
A D W S	Automatic Digital Weather Switch
A E	Acousto-Electric
	prefix to numbered-lettered series of reports issued by Department of Aeronautical Engineering, Indian Institute of Science (India)
	prefix to numbered series of reports issued by Department of Aerospace Engineering, Cincinnati University (USA)
	Atomic Emission
	Auroral Electrojet Magnetic Activity Index
A E A I	Association of Engineers and Architects in Israel (Israel)
A E B	Atomic Energy Bureau (Japan)
A E C	Association des Enducteurs, Calandreurs et Fabricants de revetements de sols plastiques de la C.E.E.
	Atomic Energy Commission (India)
	Atomic Energy Committee (New Zealand)
A E C T	Association for Educational Communications and Technology (USA)
A E D	Aerodynamic Equivalent Diameter
	Association of Equipment Distributors (USA)
A E D C A P	Automated Engineering Design Circuit Analysis Programme
A E D E	Aircraft Economic Design Evaluation
A E D P S	Automated Engineering Documentation Preparation System
A E D S	Advanced Electric Distribution System
A E E C	Airlines Electronics Engineering Council (USA)
A E E F	Association Europeenne des Exploitation Frigorifiques (European Association for Refrigeration Development)
A E E P	prefix to series of reports issued by Department of Aerospace Engineering and Engineering Physics, Virginia University (USA)

A E E P	Association of European Engineering Periodicals
A E I	Associazione Elettrotecnica ed Elettronica Italiana (Italy) (Italian Electrotechnical and Electronics Association)
A E I H	Association Europeenne des Industries de l'Habillement (European Association of Clothing Manufacturers)
A E K	Atomenergikommissionen (Denmark) (Atomic Energy Commission)
A E L C	Accident-Experience Learning Curve
A E M	Acoustic Emission Monitor
A E N	Affaiblissement Equivalent pour la Nettete (Articulation Reference Equivalent)
A E O	Acousto-Electric Oscillator
A E P S	Advanced Extra-vehicular Protective System
A E R A	American Education Research Association (USA)
A E R C A B	Aircrew Escape/Rescue System Capability
A E R D	Agricultural Engineering Research Division (of ARS (USDA))
A E R I	Atomic Energy Research Institute (Korea)
A E R O	Air Education and Recreation Organization
	prefix to dated/numbered series of reports issued by Department of Aeronautics, London University
A E R O D E S A	Aeronaves del Ecuador SA (Ecuador)
A E R O S	Aeronomy Satellite
A E R O S A T	Aeronautical Services Satellite
A E R T E L	Association Europeenne Rubans, Tresses, Tissus Elastiques (European Association for Ribbons, Braid, Elastic Textiles)
A E S	Architectural Engineering System
	Artificial Earth Satellite
A E S A	Aerolineas el Salvador SA (Panama)
A E S O P	Automated Engineering and Scientific Optimization Programme
A E T	Acoustic Emission Testing
	Automatic Exchange Tester
A E T E	Aerospace Engineering Test Establishment (of the Canadian Armed Forces)
A E T F A T	Association pour l'Etude Taxonomique de la Flore d'Afrique Tropicale (Germany) (Association for the Taxonomic Study of Tropical Africa Flora)
A E U	Asia Electronics Union (Japan)

A E V S	Automatic Electronic Voice Switch
A E W	Admiralty Experiment Works (MOD)
A F	Atomic Fluorescence
A F - E S	prefix to dated-numbered and lettered series of Environmental Surveys issued by USAF
A F A	Army Finance Association (US Army)
A F A A	Air Force Audit Agency (USAF)
A F A E P	Association of Fashion, Advertising and Editorial Photographers
A F A R	Azores Fixed Acoustic Range (a research project of the Defence Research Group of NATO)
A F C	Automatic Fare Collection
A F C A	Atom Fluorescence for Chemical Analysis
A F C A C	African Civil Aviation Commission
A F C E N T	Allied Forces Central Europe (of NATO)
A F C M R	Armed Forces Central Medical Registry (School of Aerospace Medicine (USAF))
A F C R L - P S R P	USAF Cambridge Research Laboratories - Physical Sciences Research Paper
A F C S	Auxiliary Flight Control System
A F D A	Abstract Family of Deterministic Acceptors
A F D A A	Air Force Data Automation Agency (USAF)
A F D B S	Association Francaise des Documentaires et des Bibliothecaires Specialises (France) (French Association of Documentalists and Special Librarians)
A F D C	Automatic Formation Drone Control
A F D E C	Association of Franchised Distributors of Electronic Components
A F D L	Abstract Family of Deterministic Languages
A F D S	Autopilot Flight Director System
A F E B	Armed Forces Epidemiological Board (USA)
A F E C I	Association des Fabricants Europeens de Chauffe-bains et Chauffe-eau Instantanes au Gaz (Association of Manufacturers of Gas Water Heaters)
A F E T R	Air Force Eastern Test Range (USAF)
A F F	Auditory-Flutter Fusion
A F F F	Aqueous Film-Forming Foam
A F F S C E	Air Forces Flight Safety Committee Europe
A F F T	Auditory-Flutter Fusion Threshold
A F G W C	Air Force Global Weather Central (USAF)
A F I	American Film Institute (USA)

A F I N E	Association Francaise pour l'Industrie Nucleaire d'Equipment (France) (French Association for the Nuclear Equipment Industry)
A F I S A	Aero Fletes Internacionales SA (Panama)
A F I S C	Air Force Inspection and Safety Center (USAF)
A F I T A E	Association Francaise d'Ingenieurs et Techniciens de l'Aeronautique et de l'Espace (France) (French Association of Aeronautical and Space Engineers and Technicians (now part of AAAF)
A F L C - O A	Air Force Logistics Command - Operations Analysis Office (USAF)
A F N O R T H	Allied Forces Northern Europe (of NATO)
A F O	Advanced File Organization
A F O S I	Air Force Office of Special Investigations (USAF)
A F P	Abstract Family of Processors
	Associative File Processor
A F P C S	Automatic Flight Path Control System
A F P G	Abelian Finitely Presented Group
A f P U	African Postal Union
A F R	Abstract Family of Relations
	Air/Fuel Ratio
A F R C	Area Frequency Response Characteristic
A F R I D	Automatic Fuze Radiograph Inspection Device
A F S	Aeronautical Fixed Service
	American Fertility Service (USA)
	Atomic Fluorescence Spectroscopy
A F S C F	Air Force Satellite Control Facility (USAF)
A F S C P	Air Force System Command Pamphlet (series issued by USAF)
A F S C R	Air Force Systems Command Regulation (series issued by USAF)
A F S I G	Air Force Surveys In Geophysics (USAF)
A F S O U T H	Allied Forces Southern Europe (of NATO)
A F T I	Advanced Fighter Technology Integration
A G	Aktiengesellschaft (Limited Company)
	Alternate Gradient
	Anti-Globulin
A G A	Abrasive Grain Association (USA)
	Australian Gas Association (Australia)
A G A R D - L S	AGARD (of NATO) Lecture Series
A G A R Dograph	prefix to numbered series of monographs issued by AGARD (of NATO)
A G A S S	Automated Geomagnetic Airborne Survey System
A G D	Agar Gel Diffusion

A G D T	Advisory Group on Data Transmission (of NEDO)
A G I P A C	*Agie* (A.G. fur Industrielle Elektronic (Switzerland)) Interactive Programming and Calculations
A G L	Automated Group Learning
A G M C	Aerospace Guidance and Metrology Center (USAF)
A G P A	American Group Psychotherapy Association (USA)
A G R I S	International Information System for the Agricultural Sciences and Technology (of FAO (UN))
A G S	Acoustic Guidance Sonar
	Aircraft General Standards (issued by SBAC)
A G S D	Advisory Group on Systems Definitions (of the Post Office and telecommunications industry)
A G T	Aircraft-derivative Gas Turbine
A G W N	Additive Gaussian White Noise
A H A	American Heart Association (USA)
	American Hospital Association (USA)
	Area Health Authority
A H F I T B	Agricultural, Horticultural and Forestry Industry Training Board
A H H	Aryl Hydrocarbon Hydroxylase
A H I	Approach, Horizon Indicator
A H I R S	Australian Health Information and Research Service (Australia)
A H M E	Association for Hospital Medical Education (USA)
A H P	Association for Humanistic Psychology (USA)
A H R S	Attitude and Heading Reference System
A H S B	Authority Health and Safety Branch (UKAEA) (now Authority Safety and Reliability Directorate)
A H S P	Association for High Speed Photography
A H U	Anti-Halation Undercoat
A I	Airborne Intercept *or* Interception
	Air-India (India)
	Articulation Index
	Artificial Intelligence
	Asphalt Institute (USA)
	Attitude Indicator
A I A	Abrasive Industries Association
	Anti-Icing Additive
	Association of International Accountants
	Associazione Italiana delle Industrie Aerospaziali (Italy) (Italian Aerospace Industry Association)
A I A C	Air Industries Association of Canada (Canada)
A I B D	Association of International Bond Dealers

A I C	American Institute of Chemists (USA)
	Association Internationale Cybernetique (Belgium) (International Cybernetic Association)
	Association Internationale de la Couleur (International Colour Association)
	Automatic Iris Control
A I C / I N T	Aerodynamic Influence Coefficients with Interference
A I C C F	Association Internationale des Congres des Chemins de Fer (International Railway Congress Association)
A I C D	Accelerated Individual and Company Development
A I C E	American Institute of Consulting Engineers (now part of ACEC (USA))
A I C M A	Association Internationale des Constructeurs de Materiel Aerospatial (International Association of Aerospace Material Manufacturers)
A I C S	Advanced Interior Communication System
	Association of Independent Computer Specialists
	Automated Industrial Control System
	Automatic Inlet Control System
A I D	Agency for International Development (of State Department (USA))
	Analogue Interface Device
	Attached Inflatable Decelerator
	Automatic Information Distribution
	Automatic Interaction Detection
A I D A	Australian Industries Development Association (Australia)
A I D A P S	Automatic Inspection, Diagnostic And Prognostic Systems
A I D A S	Advanced Instrumentation and Data Analysis System
A I D D	Auckland Industrial Development Division (of DSIR (New Zealand))
A I D E	Automated Integrated Design and Engineering
A I D J E X	Arctic Ice Dynamics Joint Experiment (a project of Canada and USA)
A I D S	Acoustic Intelligence Data System
	Advanced Impact Drilling System
	Advanced Interactive Display System
	Advanced Interconnection Development System
	All-purpose Interactive Debugging System

A I D S	American Institute for Decision Sciences (USA) Automated Information Dissemination System
A I E P	Association Internationale des Usagers d'Embranchements Particuliers (International Association of Users of Private Branch Railway Sidings)
A I F	Arbeitsgemeinschaft Industrieller Forschungsvereinigungen (Germany) (Association of Industrial Research Organisations)
A I F S T	Australian Institute of Food Science and Technology (Australia)
A I G	Architects in Industry Group Association Internationale Geodesie (France) (International Association of Geodesy)
A I H A	American Industrial Hygienists Association (USA)
A I I C	Association Internationale des Interpretes de Conference (France) (International Association of Conference Interpreters)
A I I H P H	All India Institute of Hygiene and Public Health (India)
A I I M H	All India Institute of Mental Health (India)
A I I P M R	All India Institute of Physical Medicine and Rehabilitation (India)
A I L - S S T	American Industry and Labor for the Super-Sonic Transport (USA) (a committee)
A I L S	Advanced Integrated Landing System
A I L S A	Aerospace Industrial Life Sciences Association (USA)
A I M	Aerothermodynamic Integration Model Asian Institute of Management (Philippines) Association pour les Applications de l'Informatique a la Medecine (France) (Association for the Application of Data Processing to Medicine)
A I M - T W X	Abridged *Index Medicus* via the Teletypewriter Exchange Network (of NLM (USA))
A I M C	Association of Internal Management Consultants (USA)
A I M E	AUTODIN Interface in a Multiprogramming Environment
A I M E X	Symposium and Exhibition of Advanced Industrial Measurement and Control
A I M M P E	American Institute of Mining, Metallurgical and Petroleum Engineers (USA)
A I M O	All-India Manufacturers Organisation (India)

A I M S	Airborne Integrated Maintenance System
	Air Traffic Control Radar System, Identification Friend or Foe, Military Identification System
	American Institute of Merchant Shipping (USA)
	Arbat (Consultants) Interactive Multi-user System
	Arlington Inventory Management System
A I N	American Institute of Nutrition (USA)
A I N S	Area-Inertial Navigation System
A I N S E	Australian Institute of Nuclear Science and Engineering (Australia)
A I O	Action Information Organization
	Arecibo Ionospheric Observatory (Puerto Rico)
A I P	Anti-Inflammatory Protein
A I P C	Association Internationale des Palais de Congress (International Association of Congress Centres)
A I P C E E	Association des Industries du Poisson de la C.E.E. (Association of the Fish Industries of the European Economic Community)
A I P H	Association Internationale des Producteurs de l'Horticulture (International Association of Horticultural Producers)
A I P M A	All-India Plastics Manufacturers Association (India)
A I P U	Associative Information Processing Unit
A I R	Airworthiness (a committee of ICAO)
	All-India Radio (India)
	Asociacion Interamericana de Radiodifusion (USA) (Inter-American Broadcasting Association)
A I R A C	Aeronautical Information Regulation and Control
A I R A P T	Association International pour l'Advancement de la Recherche et de la Technologie aux Haute Pressions (International Association for the Advancement of Research and Technology of High Pressures)
A I R C	Airworthiness Committee (of ICAO)
A I R C O	Air-line Industrial Relations Conference (USA)
A I R E A	American Institute of Real Estate Appraisers (USA)
A I R L O R D	Airline Load Optimisation, Recording and Display
A I R M E C	Association Internationale pour la Recherche Medicale et les Echanges Culturels (France) (International Association for Medical Research and Intellectual Exchanges)

A I R P A P	Air Pressure Analysis Programme
A I R S	Airport Information Retrieval System
A I R T R A N S	Intra-Airport Transportation System
A I S	Abbreviated Injury Scale
	Air System Interrogator
	Association Internationale de la Savonnerie et de la Detergence (Belgium) (International Association of Soap and Detergents Manufacturers)
A I S E	Average Integral Square Error
A I S G	Accountants International Study Group (of the three chartered institutes of the United Kingdom, the Canadian Institute of Chartered Accountants, and the AICPA (USA))
A I T	Acoustic Impact Technique *or* Test
	Alliance Internationale de Tourisme (Switzerland) (International Alliance for Tourism)
	Asian Institute of Technology (Thailand)
A I T F A	Association des Ingenieurs et Techniciens Francaise des Aeroglisseurs (France) (Association of French Air Cushion Vehicle Engineers and Technicians)
A I T U C	All-India Trades Union Congress (India)
A I U	Association Internationale des Universites (International Association of Universities)
A I V	AMETS Instrumentation Vehicle
A I W	Auroral Infrasonic Wave
A J I S	Automated Jail Information System (County of Los Angeles (USA))
A J P C	Accountants Joint Parliamentary Committee
A K E S	Automatic Kinetic Enzyme System
A L	Aeronomy Laboratory (of ESSA (USA)) now (of NOAA (USA))
A K E B	Aktiengesellschaft fur Kernenergie Beteiligungen (Switzerland)
A L A	American Logistics Association (USA)
	Austral Lineas Aereas (Argentina)
A L A L C	Asociacion Latinoamericana de Libre Comercio (Latin-America Free Trade Association)
A L A R M	Alerting Long Range Airborne Radar for MTI (Moving Target Indicator)
A L A T	Aviation Legere de l'Armee de Terre (France) (Light Aviation Wing of the French Army)
A L A W	Advanced Light Anti-tank Weapon
A L B O	Automatic Line Build-Out

A L C A S A	Aluminio del Caroni SA (Venezuela)
A L E	Automatic Line Equalization
	Aviazione Leggera Esercito (Italy) (Army Air Corps)
A L E C	Analysis of Linear Electronic Circuits
A L E R T	Alcohol Level Evaluation Roadside Test
	All-Africa Leprosy and Rehabilitation Training Centre (Ethiopia)
	Automated Law Enforcement Reporting Technique
A L F A	Automatic Line Fault Analysis
A L F C	Automatic Load-Frequency Control
A L G	Antilymphocyte Globulin
A L G S	Approach and Landing Guidance System
A L I	Air-Launched Interceptor
A L I A	Association of Lecturers in Accountancy
A L I M D	Association of Life Insurance Medical Directors (USA)
A L I T	Automatic Line Insulation Test
A L L	Acute Lymphoblastic Leukaemia
A L L C	Association of Literary and Linguistic Computing
A L L D	Airborne Locator Laser Designator
A L M	Airfield Landing Mat
A L M S	Air-Lift Management System (USAF)
	Automated Logic Mapping System
A L M S A	Automated Logistics Management Systems Agency (US Army)
A L O H A	Additive Links On-line Hawaii Area System (of Hawaii University)
A L O I T	Association of Library Officers-in-Training (Australia)
A L O R S	Advanced Large Object Recovery System
A L P C	Army Logistics Policy Council (US Army)
A L P H A	Army Materiel Command Logistics Program - Hardcore Automated (US Army)
	Automatic Lector Position Handwriting machine
A L P S P	Association of Learned and Professional Society Publishers
A L R C	Anti-Locust Research Centre (now merged into Centre for Overseas Pest Research of the Overseas Development Administration of the Foreign and Commonwealth Office)
A L S	Advanced Logistics System (of AFLC (USAF))
	Amyotrophic Lateral Sclerosis

A L S	Automated Library System
	Azimuth Laying Set
A L S C	Automatic Level and Slope Control
A L S E	*Apollo* Lunar Sounder Experiment
A L S E R	Axle-Load Survey Recorder
A L S R C	*Apollo* Lunar Sample Return Container
A L T	Accelerated-Life Testing
A L T A	American Land Title Association (USA)
	American Library Trustees Association (USA)
	Association of Local Transport Airlines (USA)
A L U	Advanced Logical Utility
	Arithmetic and Logic Unit
A L V R J	Air-launched, Low-Volume, Ramjet-powered
A M	Airlock Module
A M / M D A	Airlock Module and Multiple Docking Adapter
A M - M E M O	prefix to numbered series of Memoranda issued by Aviation Medicine Branch, Department of Civil Aviation (Australia)
A M A	Adhesives Manufacturers Association
	Aerospace Medical Association (USA)
	Automobile Manufacturers Association (USA)
A M A - M T R	Automatic Message Accounting-Magnetic Tape Recording
A M A D	Activity Median Aerodynamic Diameters
A M A P I	Association of Medical Advisers in the Pharmaceutical Industry
A M C	Acceptable Means of Compliance (series issued by ICAO)
	Auto-Manual Centre
A M C A P	Advanced Microwave Circuit Analysis Programme
A M C P	prefix to numbered series of Army Materiel Command Pamphlets (US Army)
A M C P S C C	Army Materiel Command Packaging, Storage and Containerization Center (US Army)
A M C R	Army Materiel Command Regulations (US Army)
A M C S	prefix to numbered series of reports issued by Division of Applied Mathematics and Computer Science, University of Virginia (USA)
A M D	prefix to numbered series on Atomic Molecular Data issued by ASTM (USA)
	Avions Marcel Dassault (France)
A M D A	Advanced Manoeuvring Demonstration Aircraft

A M D R S	Automatic Mobile Director and Reporting System
A M E	Acoustic-magneto-electric
A M E A M S	Adaptive Multibeam Experiment for Aeronautical and Maritime Services
A M E S	Air Medical Evacuation System
	Automated Medical Examination System
	Automatic Message Entry System
A ME S A	Ateliers Mecaniques et Electrotechniques SA (Switzerland)
A M H T S	Automated Multiphasic Health Testing and Services
A M I	Advanced Manned Interceptor
	Aeronautica Militare Italiana (Italy) (Military Air Force)
	Alternate Mark Inversion
	Average Mutual Information
A M I C E E	Asociacion Mexicana de Ingenieros en Comuni- caciones Electricas y Electronica (Mexico) (Mexican Association of Electrical and Electro- nic Communication Engineers)
A M I C S	Aircraft Maintenance Irregularity Control Sys- tem
A M I F	Automated Map Information File (of Defense Mapping Agency Aerospace Center (USDOD))
A M I L	A Microprogramming Language
A M I S	Airport Management Information System
A M L	Acute Myelogenous Leukaemia
	Algebraic Manipulation Language
	Amplitude Modulated Link
A M M A	Australian Margarine Manufacturers Association (Australia)
A M M E	Automated Multi-Media Exchange
A M M S	Automated Multi-Media Switch
A M M T	Automated Multi-Media Terminal
A M O S	Adjustable Multi-class Organizing System
	Automatic Meteorological Observing Station
A M O S S	Adaptive Mission-Oriented Software System
A M P S	Automatic Message Processing System
A M R G	Air Management Research Group (of OECD)
A M R L	Applied Mechanics Research Laboratory (Uni- versity of Texas (USA))
A M R R D C	Army Manpower Resources Research and Devel- opment Center (US Army) (now ARI (US Army))

A M R V	Astronaut Manoeuvring Research Vehicle
A M S	prefix to series of numbered/lettered series of reports issued by Department of Aerospace and Mechanical Sciences, Princeton University (USA)
	Aerospace Material Specification (numbered/ lettered series issued by SAE (USA))
	Agricultural Marketing Service (of USDA)
A M S A T	Radio Amateur Satellite Corporation (head-quarters in USA)
A M S E C	Analytical Method for System Evaluation and Control
A M S O	Association of Market-Survey Organisations
A M S R	Automated Microform Storage and Retrieval
A M S T	Advanced Medium STOL Transport
A M S U S	Association of Military Surgeons in the United States (USA)
A M T D A	Agricultural Machinery and Tractor Dealers Association
A M T E G	Australian Metal Trades Export Group (Australia)
A M T I C P	Asociacion Mexicana de Tecnicos de las Industrias de la Celulosa y del Papel (Mexican Technical Association of the Pulp and Paper Industries)
A M U	Aligarh Muslim University (India)
A M U X	Avionics Multiplex System
A M V	Avian Myeloblastosis Virus
A M W A	American Medical Writers Association (USA)
AN SSR	Akademiya Nauk SSR (Academy of Sciences of the USSR)
A N A	American Nurses Association (USA)
A N A B A	Asociacion Nacional de Bibliotecarios, Archiveros y Arquelogos (Spain) (National Association of Librarians, Archivists and Archeologists)
A N A C O M	Analogue Computer
A N A C O N D A	Analytical Control and Data
A N A L I T	Analysis of Automatic Line Insulation Tests
A N B	Ambient Noise Buoy
A N C B	Association Nationale des Comptables de Belgique (Belgium) (National Association of Accountants of Belgium)

A N C C	Associazione Nazionale per il Controllo della Combustione (Italy) (National Association for the Inspection of Combustion Equipment)
A N C I	Associazione Nazionale Calzaturifici Italiani (Italy) (Italian National Association of Footwear Manufacturers)
An C O	An Chomhairle Oiluna (Eire) (Industrial Training Authority)
A N C O L D	Australian National Committee on Large Dams (Australia)
A N C S	Association Nationale des Clubs Scientifiques (France) (National Association of Scientific Clubs)
A N D A S	Automatic Navigation and Data Acquisition System
A N D E S	Aerolineas Nacionales del Ecuador SA (Ecuador)
A N D I N	Associazione Nazionale di Ingeneria Nucleare (Italy) (National Association of Nuclear Engineering)
A N D S	Automated Newspaper Delivery System
A N F I A	Associazione Nazionale fra Industrie Automobilistiche (Italy) (National Association for the Automobile Industry)
A N F I M A	Associazione Nazionale fra i Fabbricanti Imballaggi Metalici ed Affini (Italy) (National Association for the Manufacture of Metal Containers and Allied Industries)
A N G L F N	Angle Function
A N G U S	A Navigable General Purpose Underwater Surveyor
A N I E	Associazione Nazionale Industrie Elettrotechniche ed Elettroniche (Italy) (National Association for the Electrotechnical and Electronics Industry)
A N I M A	Associazione Nazionale Industria Meccanica Varia ed Affine (Italy) (National Association of Mechanical Engineering and Allied Industries)
A N I R C	Annual National Information Retrieval Colloquium (USA)
A N I S A	Anglo Naval e Industrial SA (Spain)
A N L P	Alpha-Numeric Logic Package
A N P A	American Newspaper Publishers Association (USA)
A N P A / R I	American Newspaper Publishers Association/ Research Institute (USA)

A N P U E P	Association Nationale des Proprietaires et Usagers d'Embranchements Particuliers (France) (National Association of Owners and Users of Private Branch Railway Sidings)
A N R A O	Australian National Radio Astronomy Observatory (Australia)
A N R P C	Association of Natural Rubber Producing Countries (Malaysia)
A N S	Astronomical Netherlands Satellite
A N S I M	Analogue Simulator
A N S S R	Aerodynamically Neutral Spin Stabilized Rocket
A N S W E R	Algorithm for Non-Synchronized Waveform Error Reduction
A N T	Assessment of New Techniques (a scheme operated by the Wiring Regulations Committee of IEE)
	Autonomous Navigation Technology
A N T A R E S	Antenna Tracking Altitude, Azimuth and Range by Electronic Scan
A N T E L	Administracion Nacional de Telecomunicaciones (El Salvador) (National Telecommunications Administration)
A N T E L C O	Administracion Nacional de Telecommunicaciones (Paraguay) (National Telecommunications Administration)
	Administracion Nacional de Telecomunicaciones (Peru) (National Telecommunications Administration)
A N U - P	Australian National University, Research School of Physical Sciences (Australia)
A N W E S	Association of Naval Weapon Engineers and Scientists (USA)
A N Z U S	Australia, New Zealand, United States
A O	Argon-Oxygen
A O A	American Optometric Association (USA)
	American Orthopsychiatric Association (USA)
	Ascending Order Arrangement
A O A A	Amino-oxy-acetic acid
A O C	Attitude and Orbit Control
A O C R	Advanced Optical Character Reader
	Advanced Optical Character Recognition
A O C S	American Oil Chemists Society (USA)
A O D	Argon-Oxygen Decarburization
	Auriculo-Osteodysplasia

A O E L	Advanced Ocean Engineering Laboratory (Scripps Institution of Oceanography) (USA)
A O G A	Alaska Oil and Gas Association (USA)
A O H	Acid Open Hearth
A O I	Acousto-Optical Imaging
A O L	Atlantic Oceanographic Laboratories (of NOAA (USA))
A O M L	Atlantic Oceanographic and Meteorological Laboratories (of ERL (NOAA) (USA))
A O N B	Areas of Outstanding Natural Beauty
A O O S Y	Automatic Orbital Operations System for Satellites and Space Probes
A O P U	Asian-Oceanic Postal Union (Philippines)
A O Q S	Acousto-Optic Q-Switch
A O R B	Aviation Operational Research Branch (of CAA)
A O S	Advanced Operating System
	American Ophthalmological Society (USA)
A O T	Alignment Optical Telescope
A O T C	Associated Offices Technical Committee (of several insurance companies)
A O T T	Automatic Outgoing Trunk Test
A O V	Analysis Of Variance
A P	prefix to numbered series of publications issued by Air Programs Office (of EPA (USA))
	Anomalous Propagation
	Armour Piercing
	prefix to numbered series of reports on Atmospheric Physics issued by School of Physics and Astronomy, Minnesota University (USA)
A P - H C	Armour Piercing Hard Core
A P (S E)	Armour Piercing (Special Effects)
A P A	American Pharmaceutical Association (USA)
	American Photoplatemakers Association (USA)
	Association for the Prevention of Addiction
	Association of Professional Architects (replaced by ACA)
A P A A	Automotive Parts and Accessories Association (USA)
A P A C	Asphalt-Plastic-Asphalt-Chip
A P A C H E	Accelerator for Physics and Chemistry of Heavy Elements
	Application Package for Chemical Engineers
A P A C S	Airborne Position and Attitude Camera System

A P A I S	Australian Public Affairs Information Service (of the National Library of Australia)
A P A T	Auxiliary Propelled Anti-Tank Gun
A P B	Accounting Principles Board (of AICPA (USA)) Antiphase Boundary
A P C	Agricultural Prices Commission (India) American Power Conference (USA) Approach Power Compensator Automatic Peripheral Control Automatic Potential Control
A P C L	Atmospheric Physics and Chemistry Laboratory (of NOAA (USA))
A P C M	Adaptive Pulse Code Modulator
A P C O	Air Pollution Control Office (of EPA (USA)) (now Air Programs Office)
A P C O M	International Symposium on the Application of Computer Methods in the Mineral Industry
A P C P	Aquatic Plants Control Program (of Athens College (USA))
A P C S	Approach Power Compensator System Attitude and Pointing Control System
A P D	Amplitude Probability Distribution Approach Progress Display Avalanche Photo-Diode
A P D C	Ammonium Pyrrolidene Dithiocarbamate
A P E A	Association of Professional Engineers, Australia (Australia) Australian Petroleum Exploration Association (Australia)
A P E O	Association of Professional Engineers of Ontario (Canada)
A P E X	Advanced Purchase Excursion
A P F A	American Production Finishers Association (USA)
A P F S D	Armour-Piercing, Fin-Stabilized, Discarding Sabot
A P G	Aberdeen Proving Ground (of US Army) Azimuth Pulse Generator
A P H A	Australian Pneumatic and Hydraulic Association (Australia)
A P H B	American Printing House for the Blind (USA)
A P H E	Armour-Piercing High Explosive
A P H I S	Animal and Plant Health Inspection Service (of USDA)

A P I	Armour Piercing Incendiary
	Automated Pronunciation Instructor
A P I - T	Armour Piercing Incendiary-Tracer
A P L	Aero Propulsion Laboratory (USAF)
	Applications Programming Language
	Association of Photographic Laboratories
A P L / J H U - T P R	Applied Physics Laboratory, Johns Hopkins University - Transportation Programs Report
A P L E T	Association for Programmed Learning and Educational Technology
A P L I C	Association of Population/Family Planning Libraries and Information Centers (USA)
A P L L	Automatic Phased-Locked Loop
A P M	Academy of Psychosomatic Medicine (USA)
	Automatic Plugging Meter
A P M C	Automatic Permanent Magnetic-field Compensator
A P M I	American Powder Metallurgy Institute (USA)
A P O	Air Programs Office (of EPA (USA))
	Australian Post Office (Australia)
A P O A	Arctic Petroleum Operators Association
A P O L	Aerospace Program-Oriented Language
A P P	Aggregate Production Planning
	Air Pollution Potential
A P P A	Artificial Pilot Phased Array
A P Q I	Associacao Portuguesa para a Qualide Industrial (Portugal) (Portuguese Association for Quality Control)
A P R A C	Air Pollution Research Advisory Committee (of CRC and EPA (USA))
A P R I L	Aquaplaning Risk Indicator for Landings
A P R I S	*Alcoa* (Aluminum Company of America) Picturephone Remote Information System
A P R T	Adenine Phosphoribosyltransferase
A P R U	Applied Psychology Research Unit (Medical Research Council)
A P S	American Psychosomatic Society (USA)
	Ascent Propulsion System
	Australian Psychological Society (Australia)
	Auxiliary Propulsion System
A P S A	Ammunition Procurement and Supply Agency (US Army)
	Association for the Psychiatric Study of Adolescents

A P S T	Association of Professional Scientists and Technologists
A P S T R A T	Aptitude Strategies
A P T	Advanced Pilot Training
	Armour Piercing Tracer
	Automatically Programmed Tooling
	Automatic Position Telemetering
A P T A	American Physical Therapy Association (USA)
	Asian Pineapple Traders Association
A P T D	prefix to numbered series issued by Air Programs Office (of EPA (USA))
A P T E	Automatic Production Test Equipment
A P T I	Automatic Print Transfer Instrument
A P T I C	Air Pollution Technical Information Center (of EPA (USA))
A P U	After Power Unit
	Applied Psychology Unit (of Medical Research Council)
A P X	L'Atelier de Construction de Puteaux (of Groupement Industriel des Armements Terrestres (France))
A Q A D	Aeronautical Quality Assurance Directorate (MOD (PE))
A Q A P	prefix to series of Allied Quality Assurance Publications issued by NATO
A R	Advisory Report
	Aspect Ratio
A R A	Aircraft Rescue Association
A R A A V	Armoured Reconnaissance Airborne Assault Vehicle
A R A C	Aerospace Research Applications Center (cooperative unit of NASA, Indiana University, and industry (USA))
	Array Reduction Analysis Circuit
A R A E N	Appareil de Reference pour la determination de l'Affaiblissement Equivalent pour la Nettete (Reference Apparatus for the Determination of AEN)
A R A P T	*Atlantic Research* Automatic Position Telemetering
A R B	Air Registration Board (absorbed into CAA, 1972)
A R B E D	Acieries Reunies de Burbach-Eich-Dudelange (Luxembourg)
A R B S	Angle Rate Bombing System

A R C	Addiction Research Center (of NIMH (USA))
	Aeronautical Research Committee (of CSIR (India))
	Aeronautical Research Council (MOD (PE))
	Agricultural Refinance Corporation (India)
A R C H I	Asociacion de Radiodifusoras de Chile (Chile)
A R C M	Agricultural Research Council of Malawi (Malawi)
A R C O	*Alitalia* Reservation and Communication System
A R C S	Automated Revenue Collection System
	Automated Ring Code System
	Automatic Recognition of Continuous Speech
A R D C	Aberdeen Research and Development Center (of APG (US Army))
A R D I S O	Army Research and Development Information Systems Office (US Army)
A R D S	Advance Remote Display System
A R E	Asymptotic Relative Efficiency
	Atelier de construction de Roanne (of Groupement Industriel des Armements Terrestres (France))
A R E A	Association of Records Executives and Administrators (USA)
A R E L E M	Arithmetic Element
A R E P S	Advanced Reconnaissance Electrically Propelled Spacecraft
A R E S	Advanced Research Electro-magnetic Simulator
A R G	Akron Rubber Group (USA)
A R G E	Arbeitsgemeinschaft Meerestechnik (Germany) (an ocean engineering consortium)
A R G S	Anti-Radar Guidance Sensor
A R I	Animal Research Institute (Ghana)
	Army Research Institute for the Behavioral and Social Sciences (US Army)
	Automated Readability Index
A R I S	Automated Reactor Inspection System
A R L	Aeronautical and Astronautical Research Laboratory, Ohio State University (USA)
	Aeronautical Research Laboratories (of Department of Supply (Australia))
	Air Resources Laboratory (of ESSA (USA)) (now of ERL (NOAA))
	Applied Research Laboratories, Texas University (USA)

A R L	Association of Research Libraries (USA)
A R L B	Automatic Radio Location Beacon
A R M	Accelerated Relaxation Method
	Ampex Replacement Memory
	Anhysteretic Remanent Magnetisation
A R M A	Auto-Regressive Moving Average
A R M A D A	Aircraft Reliability, Maintainability, Availability Design Analysis
A R M M S	Automatically Reconfigurable Modular Multi-processor System
A R M S C O R	Armaments Development and Production Corporation (South Africa)
A R M S P A N	*Argonne* (*National Laboratory* (USAEC)) Multi-channel Stored Program Analyzer
A R N	Atmospheric Radio Noise
A R O - D	Army Research Office - Durham (US Army) (now Army Research Office)
A R O M	Alterable Read-Only Memory
A R P	Aerospace Recommended Practice (series issued by SAE)
	Analogous Random Process
A R P A C	Agricultural Research Policy Advisory Committee (USA)
A R P A N E T	ARPA (USDOD) Computer Network
A R P S	Association of Railway Preservation Societies
	Australian Royal Photographic Society (Australia)
A R S	Absolute Radiation Scale
	Atelier de construction de Rennes (of Groupement Industriel des Armaments Terrestres (France))
A R T	Animated Reconstruction of Telemetry
A R T A D S	Army Tactical Data Systems (US Army)
A R T E	Admiralty Reactor Test Establishment (MOD) (now Royal Naval Nuclear Propulsion Test and Training Establishment)
A R T I	Acoustic Ray Trace Indicator
A R T S	Audio Response Time-shared System
A R U	Architecture Research Unit (University of Edinburgh)
	Astrophysics Research Unit (of Science Research Council)
A R V	Advanced Aerial Armed Reconnaissance Vehicle
	Armoured Recovery Vehicle

A S	prefix to dated-numbered series of reports issued by Division of Aeronautical Sciences, University of California (USA)
	Airports Service (of FAA (USA))
	Auger Spectroscopy
A S A	Advertising Standards Authority
	American Society of Agronomy (USA)
	American Society of Anesthesiologists (USA)
	American Sociological Association (USA)
	American Subcontractors Association (USA)
	Anti-Static Additive
	Australian Society of Accountants (Australia)
	Automatic Separation System
A S A C	Asian Standards Advisory Committee
A S A I H L	Association of Southeast Asian Institutes of Higher Learning
A S A M	American Society for Abrasive Methods (USA)
A S A P	Alcohol Safety Action Program (of NHTSA (USA))
	As Soon As Possible (software for data processing)
	Automatic Spooling with Asynchronous Processing
A S A R C	Army Systems Acquisition Review Council (US Army)
A S A S	*Atkins (Research and Development)* Stress Analysis System
A S A T	Arbeitsgemeinschaft fur Satellitentragersysteme (Germany)
A S B C	American Society of Biological Chemists (USA)
A S B C A	Armed Services Board of Contract Appeal (USA)
A S B U	Arab States Broadcasting Union
A S C	Adaptive Speed Control
	Advanced Scientific Computer
	American Society for Cybernetics (USA)
	American Society of Cytology (USA)
	American Society of Consulting Arborists (USA)
A S C A	Association for Scientific Cooperation in Asia
A S C C	American Society of Concrete Constructors (USA)
	Australian Society of Cosmetic Chemists (Australia)
A S C H	American Society of Clinical Hypnosis (USA)
A S C M	Association of Ships Compositions Manufacturers (now part of PMAGB)

A S C M S	American Society of Contemporary Medicine and Surgery (USA)
A S C O G	Association of South Central Oklahoma Governments (USA)
A S C O M	Arvi Satellite Communication Project (India)
A S C S	Agricultural Stabilization and Conservation Service (USDA)
A S C S - A P	ASCS (USDA) - Aerial Photography Specification
A S C V D	Atherosclerotic Cardiovascular Disease
A S D A	Accelerate-Stop Distance Available
A S D B	Asian Development Bank (of ECAFE) (Philippines)
A S D C	Aeronomy and Space Data Center (of NOAA (USA)) (now part of National Geophysical and Solar Terrestrial Data Center)
A S D M	Association of Steel Drum Manufacturers
A S E	Active Seismic Experiment
	Anisotropic Stress Effect
	Association of Senior Engineers (USA)
	Association Suisse des Electriciens (Switzerland)
A S E A	Arizona State Electronics Association (USA)
A S E A N	Association of South East Asian Nations (Philippines, Indonesia, Thailand, Singapore, Malaysia)
A S E C N A	Agence pour la Securite de la Navigation Aerienne en Afrique et a Madagascar (Agency for Air Traffic Control in Africa and to Madagascar)
A S E P	American Society for Experimental Pathology (USA)
A S E S A	Armed Services Electro-Standards Agency (USDOD)
A S F	Advanced Simulation Facility (Missile Command (US Army))
	Alternative Salient Futures
A S F I T	Anisotropic Source Flux Iteration Technique
A S G E	American Society for Gastrointestinal Endoscopy (USA)
A S G W	Air-to-Surface Guided Weapon
A S H	American Society of Hematology (USA)
A S H A	American Social Health Association (USA)
	American Speech and Hearing Association (USA)
A S I	American Society of Indexers (USA)
	Asian Statistical Institute (Japan)
	Astronomy Society of India (India)
	United States of America Standards Institute (now ANSI (USA))

A S I A	Association Suisse de l'Industrie de l'Aviation (Switzerland)
A S I C	Association Scientifique Internationale du Cafe (International Scientific Association of Coffee)
A S I D I C	Association of Scientific Information Dissemination Centers (USA)
A S I L	Associazione Italiana di Studio del Lavoro (Italy) (Italian Work Study Association) Asymptotic Stability In the Large
A S I M	American Society of Internal Medicine (USA)
A S I N	Agricultural Services Information Network (of National Agricultural Library (USA))
A S I N E L	Asociacion de Investigacion Industrial Electrica (Spain) (Electrical Industry Research Association)
A S I O	Australian Security Intelligence Organisation (Australia)
A S I P	Aircraft Structural Integrity Program (USAF)
A S I W P C A	Association of State and Interstate Water Pollution Control Administrators (USA)
A S L	Antenna Systems Laboratory (University of New Hampshire (USA))
A S M A	Aerospace Medical Association (USA) Alaska State Medical Association (USA)
A S M D	Anti-Ship Missile Defence Asian Society for Manpower Development
A S M E	Association for the Study of Medical Education
A S M O	Arab Organisation for Standardisation and Metrology
A S M P	Aerospace Medical Panel (of AGARD (NATO))
A S O	Airborne Science Office (Ames Research Center (of NASA (USA))) American Society for Oceanography (USA) (merged into Marine Technology Service) Anisotropic Spin-Orbit
A S O S	American Society of Oral Surgeons (USA)
A S O V A C	Asociacion Venezolana para el Avance de la Ciencia (Venezuela) (Venezuelan Association for the Advancement of Science)
A S P	*Apollo* Simple Penetrometer
A S P A	Automatic Systems Pressure Alarms
A S P E	Alabama Society of Professional Engineers (USA) American Society of Plumbing Engineers (USA)

2*

A S P E T	American Society for Pharmacology and Experimental Therapeutics (USA)
A S P F	Australian Society of Perfumers and Flavourists (Australia)
A S P I	Advanced Propulsion Subsystem Integration
A S P O	American Society of Plumbing Officials (USA)
A S P R S	American Society of Plastic and Reconstructive Surgery (USA)
A S R	*Admiralty* Standard Range
	Analogue Shift Register
A S R D I	Aerospace Safety Research and Data Institute (of
A S R L	NASA (USA))
	Average Sample Run Length
A S R M	American Society of Range Management (USA)
A S R S	Automatic Seat Reservation System
	Automatic Storage and Retrieval System
A S S	Atelier de chargement de Salbris (of Groupement Industriel des Armements Terrestres (France))
A S S A S S I N	Agricultural System for Storage And Subsequent Selection of Information
A S S B R A	Association Belge des Brasseries (Belgium) (Belgian Association of Breweries)
A S S C	Accounting Standards Steering Committee (of the English, Irish and Scottish Institutes of Chartered Accountants, the Association of Certified Accountants and the Institute of Cost and Management Accountants)
A S S E S S	Airborne Science/Shuttle Experiment System Simulation
A S S I S T	Award Scheme for Science, Industry and School-Teaching (of Science Research Council)
A S S O C O M	Association of Chambers of Commerce (South Africa)
A S S O G O M M A	Associazione Nazionale fra le Industrie della Gomma (Italy) (National Association of the Rubber Industry)
A S S O P O M A C	Association des Obtèneurs de la Pomme de Terre des Pays de la C.E.E. (Association of Potato Growers of the Countries of the European Economic Community)
A S S O R T	Automatic System for Selection Of Receiver and Transmitter
A S S R S	Adaptive Step Size Random Search

A S S T	Azienda di Stato per i Servizi Telefonici (Italy) State Telephone Service Undertaking)
A S S U C	Association des Organizations Professionelles du Commerce des Sucres pour les Pays de la C.E.E. (Association of the Sugar Industry for the Countries of the European Economic Community)
A S T	Advanced Supersonic Technology Apparent Sidereal Time Apparent Solar Time
A S T A	Adaptive Search and Track Array Aviation Systems Test Activity (US Army)
A S T A C	Assembly Science and Technology Advisory Council (of California Assembly General Research Committee (USA))
A S T A N O	Astilleros y Talleres del Noroeste (Spain)
A S T F	Aeropropulsion System Test Facility (USAF)
A S T I	Automated System for Transport Intelligence
A S T P	Aging and Surveillance Test Programme *Apollo-Soyuz* Test Programme
A S T R A	Astronomical and Space Techniques for Research on the Atmosphere (a project at the University of Washington (USA))
A S T R A L	Automatic System of Telecommunications and Reservations for *Aer Lingus* (Eire)
A S T R A P	Application of Space Techniques Relating to Aviation Panel (of ICAO)
A S T R O	America's Sound Transportation Review Organisation (USA)
A S T R O S	Automated Shell Theory for Rotating Structures
A S T S	Air to Surface Transport System Association of Scientific and Technical Societies (South Africa)
A S T T	Action Speed Tactical Teacher
A S V	Air-to-Surface Vessel
A S V A B	Armed Services Vocational Aptitude Battery (USDOD)
A S W	Acoustic Surface-Wave
A S W B L P	Armed Services Whole Blood Processing Laboratory (USDOD)
A S W O T	Anti-Submarine Warfare Opposed Transit
A S Z	American Society of Zoologists (USA)
A S Z D	American Society for Zero Defects (USA)
A T	Autotransformer

A T A	Atlantic Treaty Association
A T A R	Association des Transporteurs Aeriens Regionaux (France) (Association of Regional Air Carriers)
A T B	Acetyle Tetrabromide
	Ampere-turn Balance Detector
A T C	Adiabatic Toroidal Compressor
	Advanced Thermodynamic Cycle
	Agence Transcongolaise des Communications (Congo)
	Automated Technical Control
A T C A C	Air Traffic Control Advisory Committee (USA)
A T C A P	Army Telecommunications Automation Program (US Army)
	Automatic Thyristor Circuit Analysis Programme
A T C D	Automatic Telephone Call Distribution
A T C E U	Air Traffic Control Evaluation Unit
A T D	Armoured Tank Destroyer
	Articulotrochanteric Distance
A T D A	Australian Telecommunications Development Association (Australia)
A T D L	Air Resources Atmospheric Turbulence and Diffusion Laboratory (of NOAA (USA))
A T D M	Asynchronous Time-Division Multiplexing
A T E	Atelier de fabrication de Toulouse (of Groupement Industriel des Armaments Terrestres (France))
A T E C	Automated Technical Control
	Automated Test Equipment Complex
A T E G G	Advanced Turbine Engine Gas Generator (a project of the USAF)
A T E N	Association Technique pour la production et l'utilisation de l'Energie Nucleaire (France) (Nuclear Energy Technology Association)
A T E S A	Aero Taxis Ecutorianas SA (Ecuador)
A T E T	Advanced Technology Experimental Transport
A T E V	Approximate Theoretical Error Variance
A T F	Amorphous Thin Film
A T F B	Alcohol, Tobacco, Firearms Bureau (of the Department of the Treasury (USA))
A T F C	Automatic Traffic-Flow Control
A T F E	Advanced Thermal Control Flight Experiment
A T G	Adaptive Threshold Gate
A T G W	Anti-Tank Guided Weapon
A T H	Automatic Attitude Hold

44

A T I	Aero Trasporti Italiani (Italy)
	Australian Textile Institute (Australia)
A T I F A S	Associazione Tessiture Italiano Artificiali e Sintetiche (Italy) (Italian Association for Weaving Artificial and Synthetic Fabrics
A T I G S	Advanced Tactical Inertial Guidance System
A T I P	Association Technique de l'Industrie Papetiere (France) (Technical Association of the Paper Industry)
A T I R A	Ahmedabad Textile Industry's Research Association (India)
A T L A S	group of European Airlines (Air France, Iberia, Lufthansa, Alitalia, and Sabena)
A T L B	Air Transport Licensing Board (absorbed into CAA, 1972)
A T L D	Air-Transportable Loading Dock
A T L S	Air Transport LORAN C System
A T M	Air Traffic Management
	Association of Teachers of Mathematics
A T M A C	Air Traffic Management Automated Centers (US Army)
A T M S S	Automatic Telegraph Message Switching System
A T N	Aid-to-Navigation buoys
A T O L S	Automatic Testing On-Line System
A T O M I C	Automated Train Operation by Minicomputer
A T P	prefix to numbered-dated series of publications on Agricultural Trade Policy issued by FAS (USDA)
A T P M	Association of Teachers of Preventive Medicine (USA)
A T R	*Admiralty* Test Rating
	Air-Turbo-Rocket
A T R A C	Angle Tracking Computer
A T R L	Anti-Tank Rocket Launcher
A T S	Air-to-Surface
	Air Traffic Service (FAA (USA))
	American Thoracic Society (USA)
	Anti-Thymocyte Serum
	Atelier de construction de Tarbes (of Groupement Industriel des Armaments Terrestres (France))
	Atomiteknillinen Seura-Atomtekniska Sallskapet (Finland) (Nuclear Society)
	Automated Telemetry System

A T S	Automatic Train Stopping
A T S D	Airborne Traffic and Situation Display
A T S J E A	Automatic Test System for Jet Engine Accessories
A T S M	Advanced Tactical Stand-off Missile
A T S O	Association of Transportation Security Officers (USA)
A T S S	Augmented Target-Screening Subsystem
	Automatic Telegraph - Sub System
A T S T M - L I B	Office of Administration and Technical Services - Libraries Branch (of NOAA (USA))
A T T	Advanced Technology Transport
A T T I T B	Air Transport and Travel Industry Training Board
A T T O	Avalanche Transit-Time Oscillator
A Tu S	Antitumour Serum
A T V	All-Terrain Vehicle
	Automatic Ticket Vendor
A U A	Argonne Universities Association (USA)
A U C E T	Association of University Chemical Education Tutors
A U D	Asynchronous Unit Delay
A U P E L F	Association des Universites Partiellement ou Entierement de Lange Francaise (Association of Partially or Wholly French Language Universities)
A U R I	Angkatan Udari Republik Indonesia (Indonesia) (Military Air Force)
A U S	prefix to numbered series of Austenitic Cast Irons
A U S T R I A T O M	Interessengemeinschaft fur Nukleartechnik (Austria)
A U T	Assembly Under Test
A U T O M A T	Automatic Methods And Times
A U T O M E X	Automatic Message Exchange
A U T O N E T	Automatic Network Display Programme
A U T O P O L	Automatic Programming Of Lathes
A U T O S P O T	Automatic System for Positioning Tools
A U T O S T R A D	Automated System for Transportation Data (USDOD)
A U X I N I	Empresa Auxiliar de la Industria (Spain)
A U X R C	Auxiliary Recording Control Circuit
A V A B	Automatic Vending Association of Britain
A V A D S	Autotrack Vulcan Air Defence System
A V A T I	Asphalt Vinyl and Asbestos Tile Institute (USA)
A V D S	Articulated Vehicle Dynamic Simulator

A V E N S A	Aerovias Venzolanas SA (Venezuela)
A V G A S	Aviation Gasoline
A V H	Alexander von Humboldt-Stiftung (Germany) (Alexander von Humboldt Foundation)
A V I	Adjustable Voltage Inverter
	Automatic Vehicle Identification
A V I A C O	Aviacion y Comercia (Spain)
A V I A N C A	Aerovias Nacionales de Colombia (Colombia)
A V L	Automatic Vehicle Location
A V M	Automatic Vehicle Monitoring
A V O I D	Avionic Observation of Intruder Danger
A V O S	Acoustic Valve Operating System
A V P	Anti-Viral Protein
A V R S	Audio Video Recording System
A V T	Added Value Tax
A W A	Antique Wireless Association (USA)
A W C L S	All-Weather Carrier Landing System
A W C S	Airborne Weapons Control System
A W D A T S	Artillery Weapon Data Transmission System
A W D R E Y	Atomic Weapon Detection, Recognition and Yield
A W G C	Australian Woolgrowers and Graziers Council (Australia)
A W G N	Additive White Gaussian Noise
A W I	American Watchmakers Institute (USA)
	Architectural Woodwork Institute (USA)
A W M P F	Australian Wool and Meat Producers Federation (Australia)
A W R C	Australian Water Resources Council (Australia)
A W R E	Atomic Weapons Research Establishment (UKAEA) (transferred from UKAEA to MOD, 1973)
A W R S	Airborne Weather Reconnaissance System
A W S	Automatic Warning System
A W S G	Army Work Study Group (of AWSO (MOD))
A W S O	Army Work Study Organisation (MOD)
A W T M S	All-Weather Topographic Mapping System
A W W S	Automated Want/Warrant System (Los Angeles Police Department (USA))
A X M	Acetocycloheximide
A Z B N	Azobisisobutyronitrile
A Z H D - E P D	Arizona Highway Department, Environment Planning Division (USA)

47

B

B A A	British Acetylene Association (merged into BCGA, 1971)
	British Association of Accountants and Auditors
B A A A	British Association of Accountants and Auditors
B A A L	British Association for Applied Linguistics
B A A P C D	Bay Area (San Francisco (USA)) Air Pollution Control District
B A B	British Airways Board
B A B S	British Association for Brazing and Soldering
B A B W	Beratender Ausschuss fur Bildungs-und Wissenschaftspolitik (Germany) (Advisory Commission for Education and Science Policy)
B A C	Blood Alcohol Concentration
B A C A T	Barge Aboard Catamaran
B A C C I	Beton Arme, Constructions Civiles et Industrielles (France)
B A C E	Basic Aircraft Check-out Equipment
B A C E A	British Airport Construction and Equipment Association
B A C S	Bankers Automated Clearing Services
B A E	Bureau of Agricultural Economics (Australia)
B A F A	British Accounting and Finance Association
B A F S	British Academy of Forensic Sciences
B A I E	British Association of Industrial Editors
B A K	Bundesassistentkonferenz (Germany) (Federal University Assistants Conference)
B A L	Blood Alcohol Level
B A L A R E	Buoyancy Actuated Launch and Retrieval Elevator
B A L M	Block And List Manipulator
B A L T H U M	Balloon Temperature and Humidity
B A M A	British Aerosol Manufacturers Association
B A M A C	British Automobile Manufacturers Association in Canada
B A M B I	Bayesian Analysis Modified By Inspection
B A N S D O C	Bangladesh National Scientific and Technical Documentation Centre (Bangladesh)
B A P C	British Aircraft Preservation Council
B A P E	Balloon Atmospheric Propagation Experiment
B A P M & R	British Association of Physical Medicine and Rheumatology (now British Association for Rheumatology and Rehabilitation)

B A P N	Beta-amino Propionitrile
B A P S	Beam And Plate System
B A P T A	Bearing And Power Transfer Assembly
B A R I T T	Barrier-Injection and Transit-Time
B A R R	British Association for Rheumatology and Re-habilitation
B A R S	*Bell (Telephone Laboratories)* Audit Relate System
B A S	*Bell (Telephone Laboratories)* Audit System
	Building Advisory Service (of NFBTE)
B A S C	British Aerial Standards Council
B A S E	Brokerage Accounting System Elements
B A S E E F A	British Approvals Service for Electrical Equipment in Flammable Atmospheres (of DTI)
B A S I C / P T S	BASIC Paper Tape System
B A S I S	*Batelle (Memorial Institute (USA))* Automated Search Information System for the Seventies
B A S O P S	Base Operating Information System (US Army)
B A S P	British Association for Social Psychiatry
B A S S	*Kailash M. Bafna* Stacker Simulator
B A S Y S	Building Aid System
B A T	Bureau of Apprenticeship and Training (Department of Labor (USA))
Bau - B G	Bau-Berufsgenossenschaft (Germany) (State Insurance Organisation for Building)
B A U A	British Aircraft Users Association
B B B S	Bang-Bang-Bang Surfaces
B B C	Black Body Cavity
B B D	Bucket Brigade Device
B B E A	Brewery and Bottling Engineers Association (now merged with PPA)
B B M A	British Brush Manufacturers Association
	Building Board Manufacturers Association
B B O L	Building Block Oriented Language
B B S P	Balloon-Borne Solar Pointer
B C	Ballistic Coefficient
B C A	Bilderberg Continuum Atmosphere
B C B	British Consultants Bureau
B C C	British Cryogenics Council
B C C L	Bharat Coking Coal Limited (India) (government owned)
B C D P	Bubble Chamber Data Processing
B C E C A	British Chemical Engineering Contractors Association

B C E M	Bureau of Community Environmental Management (of HEW (USA))
B C F	Bureau of Commercial Fisheries (of NOAA (USA)) (now NMFS)
B C G A	British Compressed Gases Association
B C I P P A	British Cast Iron Pressure Pipe Association
B C M A	British Council of Maintenance Associations
B C N	Biomedical Communication Network
B C P L	Basic Combined Programming Language
B C P M A	British Chemical Plant Manufacturers Association (now merged with TIPA)
B C P M M A	British Ceramic Plant and Machinery Manufacturers Association
B C P S	Beam - Candle-Power - Seconds
B C R A	British Cave Research Association
B C R S	Bar-Code Reader/Sorter
B C S	Basic Court System
	Bounded Cellular Space
	British Calibration Service (of DTI)
	British Cartographic Society
B C S O C	Binary Convolutional Self-Orthogonal Code
B C U R A	British Coal Utilisation Research Association (disbanded 1971)
B D	Butadiene
B D A	British Dietetic Association
B D C	Binary-Differential Counter
	Bureau of Domestic Commerce (of Department of Commerce (USA))
B D F	Backwards Differentiation Formulas
	Box-car Doppler Filter
B D I	Base-Diffusion Isolation
B D M A	Benzl Dimethyl Amine
B D S A	Business and Defense Services Administration (of Dept of Commerce (USA)) (now Bureau of Domestic Commerce)
B D S M	Base Depot Stockage Model
B E	Beryllium
B E A	Basic Electric Arc
	Blue Etch-Anodize or Anodizing
	British European Airways (now part of British Airways)
	Burroughs Extended ALGOL

B E A B	British Electrical Approvals Board for Domestic Appliances (now British Electrotechnical Approvals Board for Household Appliances)
B E A M	Bidders Early Alert Message (a service of the National Small Business Association (USA))
B E A M A	British Electrical and Allied Manufacturers Association now split into: —
	a) Association of Manufacturers Allied to the Electrical and Electronics Industry
	b) Power Generation Association
	c) Rotating Electrical Machines Association
	d) BEAMA Transmission and Distribution Association
	e) Electrical and Electronic Insulation Association
	f) Control and Automation Manufactures Association
	g) Electrical Installation Equipment Manufacturers Association
	h) Welding Manufacturers Association
	i) Process Heating Plant Manufacturers Association
B E A M S	Base Engineer Automated Management System (USAF)
B E A S T	*Brookings (Institute* (USA)) Economics And Statistical Translator
B E B	British Export Board
B E C	Boron Electron Centre
B E C C R	British Empire Cancer Campaign for Research (now Cancer Research Campaign)
B E C S M	British Electric Conduit Systems Manufacturers (now British Electrical Systems Association)
B E E F	Business and Engineering Enriched FORTRAN
B E I R	Advisors Committee on the Biological Effects of Ionizing Radiations (of NAS/NRC (USA))
B E L	Bharat Electronics Limited (India) (government owned)
B E L L R E L	*Bell (Telephone) Laboratories* Library Real-time Loan
B E M S	Bakery Equipment Manufacturers Society (merged with PPA)
B E N S	Bounded Error Navigation System
Be O	Beryllium Oxides

B E O	Bureau d'Etudes Oceanographiques (France) (Oceanography Research Bureau)
B E P I	Bureau d'Etudes et de Participations Industrielles (Morocco) (Industrial Development Bureau)
B E R S A F E	*Berkeley (Nuclear Laboratories* (CEGB)) Stress Analysis Finite Elements
B E S A	British Electrical Systems Association
B E S O	British Executive Service Overseas (sponsored by CBI, DTI, and The Institute of Directors)
B E S R L	Behavioral Science Research Laboratory (now Behavior and Systems Research Laboratory of ARI (US Army))
B E S T	Basic Executive Scheduler and Timekeeper
B E T	Balanced-Emitter Transistor
B E T A	Basic English for Testing Applications
B E V	Bovine Enterovirus
B F	Beam-Foil
B F C	Braking Force Coefficient
B F E C	British Food Export Council
B F I	Battlefield Interdiction
	British Film Institute
B F I A	British Flower Industry Association
B F L	Betonforskningslaboratoriet (Sweden) (Concrete Research Laboratory)
B F M F	British Footwear Manufacturers Federation
B F P D D A	Binary Floating Point Digital Differential Analyzer
B F P R	Binary Floating Point Resistor
B F P S A	British Fire Protection Systems Association
B F R P	Boron Fibre Reinforced Plastics
B G R G	British Geomorphological Research Group (now Geomorphological Study Group of the Institute of British Geographers)
B H A B	British Helicopter Advisory Board
B H E L	Bharat Heavy Electricals Limited (India) (government owned)
B H M E	Bureau of Health Manpower Education (of NIH (USA))
B H U	Banaras Hindu University (India)
B I A	British Insurance Association
B I A C	Business and Industry Advisory Committee (of OECD)
B I A S	Battlefield Illuminator Airborne System

B I B	Balanced Incomplete Block
	Bibliography
B I B O	Bounded-Input Bounded-Output
B I C - C I D	Bureau of International Commerce, Commercial Intelligence Division (USA)
B I C E P S	Basic Industrial Control Engineering Programming System
B I C T A	British Investment Casters Technical Association
B I F	Banded Iron Formation
B I F O R E	Binary Fourier Representation
B I G F E T	Bipolar Insulated-Gate Field-Effect Transistor
B I I T	Blood Incubation *or* Inoculation Infectivity Test
B I M	Blade Inspection Method
B I M A	British Industrial Marketing Association
B I M A C S	Blood Bank Information and Management Control System
B I M C O	Baltic and International Maritime Conference
B I M L	Bureau International de Metrologie Legale (of (OIML) (International Bureau of Legal Metrology)
B I N G O	Business International Non-Governmental Organisation
B I O M O D	Biological Modelling
B I P	Balloon Interrogation Package
	Binary Image Processor
	Bitumen Product
B I P E	Bureau d'Information et de Previsions Economiques (France) (Bureau for Information and Economic Forecasting)
B I P M	Bureau International des Poids et Mesures (International Bureau of Weights and Measures) (France)
B I R P I	Bureaux Internationaux Reunis pour la Protection de la Propriete Intellectuelle (United International Bureaux for the Protection of Intellectual Property) (now WIPO)
B I S	Bureau of Information Science
	Business Information Systems
B I S C U S	Business Information System/Customer Service
B I S R A	British Iron and Steel Research Association (now the Corporate Laboratories of the British Steel Corporation)

B I S R A - P E	prefix to series of reports issued by the Plant Engineering Department of BISRA
B I S S	Base and Installation Security System (an organization of ESD (USAF))
	Bioisolator Suit Systems
B I T E	Benthic Inflatable Toolstore Enclosure
B I T M	Birla Industrial and Technological Museum (India)
B J A	British Jewellers Association
B J C C	British Junior Chambers of Commerce
B J C G	British Joint Corrosion Group (of Iron and Steel Institute, Society of Chemical Industry, Institute of Metals, Institute of Metal Finishing, Institution of Corrosion Technology)
B J T	Bi-polar Junction Transistor
B K D	Bilateral Kinaesthetic Differences
B L	The British Library
B L A D E S	*Bell (Telephone) Laboratories* Automatic Design System
B L A R D	Boat Launching and Recovery Device
B L C M P	Birmingham Libraries Co-operative Mechanisation Project
B L E A C H	Babel Language Editing And Checking
B L E T	Bureau of Libraries and Educational Technology (USOE) (now Bureau of Libraries and Learning Resources)
B L E V E	Boiling Liquid-Expanding Vapour Explosion
B L H A	British Linen Hire Association
B L I P	Boundary Layer Instrument Package
	Brookhaven (National Laboratory) (USAEC) LINAC Isotope Producer
B L I S S	Basic List-oriented Information Structures System
B L L	British Library Lending Division of the British Library (the division formed by merging the National Central Library and National Lending Library for Science and Technology in 1973)
B L L R	Bureau of Libraries and Learning Resources (USOE)
B L O C	*Booth Library* On-line Circulation system (Eastern Illinois University (USA))
B L O D I - G	Block Diagram Graphics
B L P E S	British Library of Political and Economic Science (of London School of Economics and Political Science)

B L S	Bureau of Labor Statistics (USDL)
B L S G M A	British Lampblown Scientific Glassware Manufacturers Association
B L T C	Bottom Loading Transfer Cask
B L U E	Best Linear Unbiased Estimate
B M	Bromine-Methanol
	Bureau of Mines (Department of the Interior (USA))
B M B	Barium Metaborate
B M B W	Bundesministerium fur Bildung und Wissenschaft (Germany) (Federal Ministry for Education and Science)
B M C	Bulk Moulding Compound
B M C C	British Metal Castings Council
B M C S	Bureau of Motor Carrier Safety (of FHWA (USA))
B M D C	Biomedicinska Dokumentationscentralen (Sweden) (Biomedical Data Centre)
B M F S A	British Metal Finishing Suppliers Association
B M F T	Bundesministerium fur Forschung und Technologie (Germany) (Federal Ministry for Research and Technology
B M L	British Museum Library (now part of The British Library)
B M L D	Binaural Masking Level Difference
B M O	Bonding Molecular Orbitals
B M P R	Bimonthly Progress Report
B M R	Bureau of Mineral Resources (Australia)
B M R A	Basic Multi-Role Avionics
B M S	Breathing Metabolic Simulator
B M S A	British Metals Sinterings Association
B M S P	British Modal Speaking Position
B M V	Basic Minute Values
B M W F	Bundesminsterium fur Wissenschaftliche Forschung (Germany) (Federal Ministry of Scientific Research)
B N	Belgonucleaire (Belgium)
B N A	Biblioteca Nacional de Angola (Angola) (National Library of Angola)
	Bureau des Normes de l'Automobile (France) (Bureau of Automobile Standards)
	Bureau of National Affairs (USA)
B N B	British National Bibliography (now part of The British Library)

B N C O E	British National Committee on Ocean Engineering
B N D C	British Nuclear Design and Construction Limited (partly State owned)
	Bulk Negative Differential Conductivity
B N D D	Bureau of Narcotics and Dangerous Drugs (Department of Justice (USA))
B N E C	British National Export Council (now BOTB)
B N F	British Nuclear Forum
	British Nuclear Fuels Limited (a State corporation)
B N F L	British Nuclear Fuels Limited (a State corporation)
B N L	Berkeley Nuclear Laboratories (of CEGB)
B N M	Bureau National de Metrologie (France) (National Metrology Bureau)
B N M A	British Non-wovens Manufacturers Association
B N P	Banque Nationale de Paris (France)
B O A C	British Overseas Airways Corporation (now part of British Airways)
B O B	Bureau of the Budget (USA) (now Office of Management and Budget)
	Bureau of Biologics (FDA (USA))
B O C A	Building Officials Conference of America (USA) (now Building Officials and Code Administrators International)
B O C S	Bisynchronous Oriented Communications System
B O D S	British Oceanographic Data Service (of NIO)
B O F A D S	Business Office Force Administration Data System
B O H C	Boron-Oxygen Hole Centre
B O I	Board of Investments (Philippines)
B O L O V A C	Bolometric Voltage and Current
B O M	Bureau of Mines (Department of the Interior (USA))
B O M E X	Barbados Oceanographic and Meteorological Experiment (of NOAA) (USA)
B O M P	Bill Of Material Processor
B O M S	Base Operations Maintenance Simulator
B O R	Bureau of Operating Rights (of CAB (USA))
B O R D	Book Order and Record Document
B O S R	prefix to series of Reports issued by Bureau of Safety (of CAB (USA))

B O S S	Biased Optimal Steering Selector
	Broad Ocean Scoring System
B O S T C O	Boston (USA) Standardized Components
B O S T I D	Board on Science and Technology for International Development (of National Academy of Sciences (USA))
B O T	Board of Trade (disbanded 1970)
B O T B	British Overseas Trade Board
B O T E X	British Office for Trainee Exchange
B O T G I	British Overseas Trade Group for Israel
B P & B M A	British Paper and Board Makers Association
B P A	Bisphenol A
	British Parachute Association
	British Parking Association
	Bush Pilots Airways (Australia)
B P C	Blast-furnace Portland Cement
B P C A	British Pest Control Association
B P D A	Bibliographic Pattern Discovery Algorithm
B P E G	British Photographic Export Group
B P F	Blade-Passing Frequency
B P I A	British Photographic Importers Association
B P I C S	British Production and Inventory Control Society
B P L	Betapropiolactone
	Business Planning Language
B P M E	Branching Process with Markovian Environments
B P M M A	British Paper Machinery Makers Association
B P O	Benzoyl Peroxide
B P O C	British Post Office Corporation (State owned)
B P P	Boundary Phase Plasticity
B P R	Bonded Particle Rolling
B P R E	Branching Process with Random Environments
B P R S	Brief Psychiatric Rating Scale
B P S	British Psychological Society
	Bureau of Product Safety (of FDA (USA))
B Q A	Benzoquinone Acetic Acid
B R	prefix of numbered series of Books of Reference issued by MOD (Navy Department)
B R A B	Building Research Advisory Board (of NAS/NRC (USA))
B R A C A N	submarine telephone cable between Brazil and the Canary Islands
B R A I L L E	Balanced Resource Allocation Information for Logical Lucid Evaluation
B R A N D Y	Boron Recovery and Electrodialysis

B R B	Ballistic Recoverable Booster British Railways Board
B R C M A	British Radio Cabinet Makers Association
B R D	Binary Rate Divider
B R D T	Bayesian Reliability Demonstration Tests
B R E	Building Research Establishment (of DOE)
B R E L	British Rail Engineering Limited (state owned)
B R H	Bureau of Radiological Health (of FDA (USA))
B R H/D E P	Bureau of Radiological Health, Division of Electronics Products (of FDA (USA))
B R H / D E R	Bureau of Radiological Health, Division of Environmental Radiation (of FDA (USA))
B R H / D M R E	Bureau of Radiological Health, Division of Medical Radiation Exposure (of FDA (USA))
B R H / N E R H L	Bureau of Radiological Health, North Eastern Radiological Health Laboratory (of FDA (USA))
B R H / O R O	Bureau of Radiological Health, Office of Regional Operations (of FDA (USA))
B R H / S E R H L	Bureau of Radiological Health, South-Eastern Radiological Health Laboratory (of FDA (USA))
B R H / S W R H L	Bureau of Radiological Health, South-Western Radiological Health Laboratory (of FDA (USA))
B R I G H T P A D	*British Rail* Interactive Graphical Aid To Production And Design
B R L T	Basic Reference Lottery Ticket
B R M	Binary Rate Multiplier
B R O M	Bipolar Read-Only Memory
B R P A	British Radiological Protection Association
B R P M	Bureau de Recherches et de Participations Minieres (Morocco) (Mining Research and Development Bureau)
B R R I	Building and Road Research Institute (Ghana)
B R S	Building Research Station (now part of the Building Research Establishment (DOE))
B R U C E	Buffer Register Under Computer Edict
B S A	British Society of Audiology
B S A B	Byggandets Samordning (Sweden) (Building Co-ordination Centre)
B S A M	Basic Sequential Access Method
B S A P	British Society of Animal Production
B S B G	Binnenschiffahrts - Berufsgenossenschaft (Germany) (Inland Waterways Authority)
B S C	Binary Synchronous Communications British Society of Cinematographers

B S C A	Binary Synchronous Communications Adapter
B S C C	British-Swedish Chamber of Commerce
	British Society for Clinical Cytology
B S C S	Binary Synchronous Communication System
B S D	British Society of Dowsers
B S E S	Building Services Engineering Society
B S F C	Brake Specific Fuel Consumption
B S I A	British Security Industry Association
B S I R A	British Scientific Instrument Research Association (now known as the SIRA Institute)
B S L	Bokaro Steel Limited (India) (government owned)
B S L S S	" Buddy " Secondary Life Support System
B S N	Barium Sodium Niobate
B S O	Business Statistics Office
B S O E A	British Stationery and Office Equipment Association
B S P A	British Sports Photographers Association
B S P L	Behavioral Science Programming Language
B S R	Bacteria Survival Ratio
B S S	prefix to numbered Building Science Series issued by Building Research Division, National Bureau of Standards (USA)
B S S C	Bit Synchronizer/Signal Conditioner
B T	Benzotriazole
	Butanthiol
B T A M	Basic Telecommunications Access Method
B T A N Z	British Trade Association of New Zealand (New Zealand)
B T B	Bus Tie Breaker
B T B M F	British Tin Box Manufacturers Federation
B T C	British Technical Council of the Motor and Petroleum Industries
B T E	Bureau of Transport Economics (Australia)
B T I	Board of Trade and Industries (South Africa)
B T I A	British Tar Industry Association
B T P S	Body Temperature, Pressure, and Saturation
B T R	Blood Transfusion Reactions
B T S D	Basic Training for Skill Development
B T T A	British Thoracic and Tuberculosis Association
B T V	Buoyancy Transport Vehicle
B T Z	Benzotriazole
B U D R	Bromodeoxyuridine
B U D S	Building Utility Design System
B U E	Built-Up-Edge

B U F C	British Universities Film Council
B U G	Basic Update Generator
B U G S	*Brown University* (USA) Graphics System
B U N	Blood Urea Nitrogen
B U T E C	British Underwater Test and Evaluation Centre (MOD)
B V H	Biventricular Hypertrophy
B W E T P A	British Water and Effluent Treatment Plant Association
B W M D F	British Work-Measurement Data Foundation
B W P A	British Women Pilots Association
B W S T M A	British Welded Steel Tube Manufacturers Association
B W T A	British Wood Turners Association

C

C	prefix to numbered: dated series of Aircraft Ground Service Connections issued by BSI
C - S I T	Committee on Social Implications of Technology (of IEEE (USA))
C - V - P	Cost-Volume-Profit
C & M S	Consumer and Marketing Service (USDA) (title changed to Agricultural Marketing Service in 1972)
C / P L S E L	Clothing and Personal Life Support Equipment Laboratory (of Natick Laboratories (US Army))
C / S C S C	Cost/Schedule Control Systems Criteria
C A	Catecholamine
	Cellulose Acetate
	prefix to numbered series of Civil Aviation publications issued by Civil Aviation Authority (previously issued by Board of Trade and later by DTI)
	Complex Angle
C A - H Y - B D	California State, Division of Highways, Bridge Department (USA)
C A (Aust)	Institute of Chartered Accountants in Australia (Australia)
C A A	Civil Aviation Authority
	Commonwealth Association of Architects
C A A C	Civil Aviation Administration of China (China)
C A A D	Computer-Aided Architectural Design
C A B	Civil Aeronautics Board (USA) (now merged into the National Transportation Safety Board)
	Computer Aided Building
C A B A S	Computerized Automated Blood Analysis System
C A B E I	Central American Bank for Economic Integration
C A B L E	Computer Assisted *Bay Area* (San Francisco (USA)) Law Enforcement
C A B O	Council of American Building Officials (USA)
C A C	Carbon-Arc Cutting
	Commonwealth Association of Architects
	Computer Acceleration Control
C A C A	Computer Aided Circuit Analysis
C A C A C	Civil Aircraft Control Advisory Committee
C A C A S	Civil Aviation Council of Arab States
C A C C I	Committee on the Application of Computers in the Construction Industry

C A C H E	Computer Aids for Chemical Engineering Education (of Committee of the National Academy of Engineering (USA))
C A C S	Comprehensive Airport Communications System
C A C T O S	Computation And Trade-Off Study
C A C T Q	Citizens Advisory Committee on Transportation Quality (USA)
C A D	Cartridge Activated Device
	Cartridge Actuated Device
	Circulatory Assist Device
	Civil Aviation Department (India)
C A D - E	Computer-Aided Design and Engineering
C A D A	Computer Assisted Distribution and Assignment
C A D A P S O	Canadian Association of Data Processing Service Organisations (Canada)
C A D A S	Computerized Automatic Data Acquisition System
C A D A V R S	Computer-Assisted Dial Access Video Retrieval System
C A D C	Computer-Aided Design Centre (of DTI)
C A D C O M	Computer-Aided Design for Communications
C A D E P	Computer Assisted Description of Patterns
C A D I C S	Computer Aided Design of Industrial Cabling Systems
C A D L I C	Computer-Aided Design of Linear Integrated Circuits
C A D O P C A R T	Computer Aided Design of Printed Circuit Artwork
C A D P I N	Customs Automated Data Processing Intelligence Network (Bureau of Customs (USA))
C A D S	Conversational Analyzer and Drafting System
C A E D M	Community/Airport Economic Development Model
C A E M	Cargo Airline Evaluation Model
C A E N D	Centro Argentino de Ensayos no Destructivos de Materiales (Argentine) (Centre for Non-Destructive Testing of Materials)
C A F	Canadian Armed Forces (Canada)
C A F B	Chemically Active Fluidised Bed
C A F C	Computed Automatic Frequency Control
C A F E	Computer-Aided Film Editor
C A F E A - I C C	Commission on Asian and Far Eastern Affairs - International Chamber of Commerce

C A F I	Commercial Advisory Foundation in Indonesia (Indonesia)
C A F S	Content Addressed File System
C A F U	Civil Aviation Flying Unit (of DTI)
C A G A C	Civil Aviation General Administration of China (China)
C A G C	Continuous-Access Guided Communication
C Ag M	Commission for Agricultural Meteorology (of WMO (UN))
C A I	Computer-Administered Instruction
	Concrete Association of India (India)
C A I - T M	prefix to numbered series of Technical Memoranda issued by Florida State University, Computer Assisted Instruction Center (USA)
C A I - T R	prefix to numbered series of Technical Reports issued by Florida State University, Computer Assisted Instruction Center (USA)
C A I C	Computer Assisted Indexing and Classification
C A I N	Cataloguing and Indexing System (of National Agricultural Library (USA))
C A I N S	Computer Aided Instruction System
C A I R	Counter-measures Airborne Infra-Red
C A I R S	Central Automated Inventory and Referral System (of USDOD)
C A I S	Canadian Association for Information Science (Canada)
C A K E	Computer Assisted Keyboard Evaluator
C A L	Cornell Aeronautical Laboratory (USA) (changed name to Calspan Corporation and became a for-profit organisation in 1972)
C A L D	Computer Assisted Logic Design
C A L L	Computerized Ambulance Location Logic
	Current Awareness - Library Literature
C A L M	Continuously Advancing Longwall Mining
C A L S	Connecticut Association of Land Surveyors (USA)
C A L T E C H	California Institute of Technology (USA)
C A L U S	Centre for Advanced Land Use Studies (College of Estate Management) (University of Reading)
C A M	Calculated Access Method
	Cartographic Automatic Mapping
	Cellulose Acetate Membrane
	Chorioallantoic Membrane
	Computer Assessment of Media
	Continuous Air Monitor

63

C A M A	Civil Aviation Medical Association (USA)
	Computer Aided Mathematical Analysis
	Control and Automation Manufacturers Association
C A M A C	Computer Aided Measurement And Control
	Computer Aided Monitoring And Control
C A M C	Canadian Association of Management Consultants (Canada)
C A M D S	Chemical Agent Munitions Dispersal System
C A M I	Civil Aeromedical Institute (of FAA (USA))
C A M P	Computer Aided Maintenance Project (of the British Post Office)
	Continuous Air Monitoring Project (of NAPCA (USA))
	Controls And Monitoring Processor
	Co-operative African Microform Project (administered by Center for Research Libraries, Chicago (USA))
C A M P R A D	Computer Assisted Message Preparation Relay And Distribution
C A M P U S	Computerized Analytical Methods in Planning University System
C A M S	Coastal Anti-Missile System
	Control of Aircraft Maintenance and Servicing
	Crew and Administrative Management System
C A M S P E K	Chemical Analysis by Microwave Spectroscopy
C A N	Centro Administrativo Nacional (Colombia)
	Committee on Aircraft Noise (of ICAO)
	Her Majesty's Customs Assigned Number
C A N / S D I	Canadian Selective Dissemination of Information (by National Library of Canada and the National Science Library)
C A N B E R	submarine telephone cable between Canada and Bermuda
C A N C A M	Canadian Congress of Applied Mechanics
C A N C E R	Computer Analysis of Nonlinear Circuits Excluding Radiation
C A N E	Chemical Applications of Nuclear Explosions
C A N S I M	Canadian Socio-Economic Information Management System
C A N T A T	submarine telephone cable between Scotland and Canada
C A N T O T	Computer Analysis of Troubles on Trunk Circuits

C A N W E C	Canadian National Committee of the World Energy Conference (Canada)
C A O C S	Carrier Aircraft Operational Compatibility System
C A O C S - M O D 2	Carrier Aircraft Operational Compatibility System - Model 2
C A O G	Central Association of Obstetricians and Gynecologists (USA)
C A P	Centre Aeroporte de Toulouse (of DTAT (France))
	Civil Air Publications (numbered series issued by Civil Aviation Authority) (previously issued by the Board of Trade and later by DTI)
	Commonwealth Association of Planners
	Communications Analysis Package
	Computer Assisted Placement
	Control Anticipation Parameter
	Crew Assignment Programme
C A P A	Central Airborne Performance Analyser
	Conference of Asian and Pacific Accountants
	Corrosion And Protection Association
C A P A C	Cathodic Protection by Automatically Controlled Impressed Current
C A P A R S	Computer Aided Placement And Routing System
C A P C O M	Capsule Communications
C A P E	Consortium for the Advancement of Physics Education (Kansas-Missouri region of the USA)
C A P E R	Cost of Attaining Personnel Requirements
C A P I C S	Computer Aided Processing of Industrial Cabling Systems
C A P I T B	Chemical and Allied Products Industry Training Board
C A P L I N	Computer Assisted Physics Laboratory Instruction (a project of Indiana University (USA))
C A P P	Computer Aided Part Planning
C A P R I	Computer Aided Personal Reference Index
	Centre d'Application et de Promotion des Rayonnements Ionisants (of Commissariat a l'Energie Atomique (France))
C A P S	Costs and Productivity Scheme (of the Road Haulage Association)
	Co-operative Awards in Pure Science (of the Science Research Council)
C A P S R	Cost Account Performance Status Report
C A R A D	Computer Aided Reliability And Design

C A R B	California (USA) Air Resources Board
C A R B I N E	Computer Automated Real-time Betting Information Network
C A R C	Commercial Aircraft Requirements Committee
C A R D	Civil Aeronautics Research and Development Policy Study (of DOT and NASA (USA))
C A R D A	Computer Aided Reliability Data Analysis
C A R D S	Computer Aided Reliability Data System
C A R E	Computer-Aided Reliability Estimation
C A R E - S O M	Coordinated Accident Rescue Endeavor - State of Mississippi (a state project on highway emergency medical services) (USA)
C A R E S	Computation And Research Evaluation System
C A R E T S	Central Atlantic Regional Ecological Test Site (a project of the Geological Survey and NASA (USA))
C A R F	Canadian Amateur Radio Federation (Canada)
C A R I A C	Cardboard Illustrative Aid to Computation
C A R I R I	Caribbean Industrial Research Institute (Trinidad)
C A R I S	Constant Angle Reflection Interference Spectroscopy
C A R L	Code Analysis Recording by Letters
C A R O T	Centralized Automatic Reporting On Trunks
C A R P	Comprehensive Aerial Rainfall Programme
C A R S	Central Agricultural Research Station (Somalia)
	Community Antenna Relay Service (USA)
	Computer Aided Routing System
	Computer Audit Retrieval System
C A R T	Containerized Automated Rail-Highway Transportation
	Continuous Air Resistance Tester
	Command, Arming, Recording and Timing
C A R T A	Contouring Analysis Random Triangular Algorithm
C A S	Calibrated Air Speed
	Canadian Anaesthetists Society (Canada)
	Canadian Cooperative Applications Satellite (cooperation between Canadian Department of Communications and NASA (USA))
	Close Air Support
	Commission for Atmospheric Sciences (of WMO (UN))
	Computer Arts Society

C A S	Cooperative Applications Satellite (co-operation between France and the USA)
C A S - C	Cooperative Applications Satellite C (co-operation between Canada and NASA (USA))
C A S / P W I	Collision Avoidance System/Pilot Warning Indicator
C A S A	Cooperative Applications Satellite (co-operation between France and NASA (USA))
C A S A P S	*Computer Applied Systems* (USA) Accounts Payable System
C A S C A D E	Computer Aided System for Circuit Analysis and Design
C A S C A I D	Careers Advisory Service Computerised Aid
C A S D	Computer Aided System Design
C A S E	Committee on the Atlantic Salmon Emergency
C A S H	Computer Aided System Hardware
C A S I N G	Cross-linking by Activated Species of Inert Gases
C A S L E	Commonwealth Association of Surveying and Land Economy
C A S M	Close Air Support Missile
C A S O	Computer Assisted System Operation
C A S P A R	Cushion Air System Parametric Assessment Rig
C A S P E R	*Clarkson's* Automatic System for Passenger and Agent Reservations
C A S S	Chartered Accountant Students Society
	Combat Area Surveillance System
	Computer Automatic Scheduling System
	Computerized Algorithmic Satellite Scheduler
	Copper Accelerated Acetic Acid Salt Spray
	Crab-Angle Sensing System
C A S T	Centre d'Actualisation Scientifique et Technique (France)
	Computer Applications and Systems Technology
C A S T L E	Computer Assisted System for Theater Level Engineering (US Army)
C A S W S	Close Air Support Weapon System
C A T	Capillary Agglutination Test
	Computer of Average Transients
	Crack Arrest Temperature
C A T A	Canadian Air Transportation Administration (Canada)
C A T A L Y S T	Computer Assisted Teaching And Learning System

C A T C	College of Air Traffic Control
C A T C H	Character Allocated Transfer Channel
C A T E	Computer Assisted Traffic Engineering
	Convair Automatic Test Equipment
C A T E D	Centre d'Assistance Technique et de Documentation du Batiment et des Travaux Publique (France) (Centre for Technical Assistance and Documentation for Building and Public Works)
C A T N I P	Computer Assisted Technique for Numerical Index Preparation
C A T O	Civil Air Traffic Operations
C A T R A L A	Car and Truck Renting and Leasing Association (USA)
C A T S	Centre for Advanced Television Studies
	Computer Aided Trouble-shooting
C A T T S	Computer-Aided Training in Troubleshooting
C A T V	Cable Telecommunication and Video
	Cable Television
C A V U	Ceiling and Visibility Unlimited
C A W	Carbon-Arc Welding
	Common Aerial Working
C A W C	Central Advisory Water Committee
C A Z R I	Central Arid Zone Research Institute (India)
C B	Citizen's Band radio service (USA)
C B A E	Commonwealth Board of Architectural Education
C B A S	City and Borough Architects Society
C B C	Cannabichromene
C B C C	Canada - British Columbia Consultative Board (Canada)
C B D	Cannabidiol
C B E U S	Center for Business Economics and Urban Studies (Lehigh University (USA))
C B I	Chesapeake Bay Institute (Johns Hopkins University (USA))
C B I S	Computer-Based Information System
C B L	Cannabicyclol
	Chesapeake Biological Laboratories (University of Maryland (USA))
C B M	Centre Scientifique et Technique de la Brasserie, de la Malterie et des industries connexes (Belgium) (Scientific and Technical Centre for the Brewing, Malting and Related Industries)

C B M P E	Council of British Manufacturers of Petroleum Equipment (name now changed to Council of British Manufacturers and Contractors serving the Petroleum and Process Industries)
C B N	Cannabinol
	Cubic Boron Nitride
C B O S S	Count, Back Order, and Sample Select
C B P C	Canadian Book Publishers Council (Canada)
C B R	Centre for Business Research (Manchester Business School, University of Manchester)
C B R M	Charger-Battery-Regulator Module
C B T	Center for Building Technology (of NBS (USA))
C B T U	Connecticut Board of Title Underwriters (USA)
C B W	Chemical and Biological Weapons
C C	Chemurgic Council (USA)
	Closure-Covering
	Colon Classification
	Constant Current
C C A	Central Computer Agency (of the Civil Service Department)
	Chemical Coaters Association (USA)
	Customer Cost Analysis
C C A I A	California Council of the American Institute of Architects (USA)
C C A P	Culture Centre of Algae and Protozoa (of the Natural Environment Research Council)
C C B S	Center for Computer-based Behavioral Studies (California University (USA))
C C B V	Compound Correlated Bivariate Poisson
C C C R	Co-ordinating Committee for Cancer Research (of Joint Cancer Research Campaign, Imperial Cancer Research Fund and Medical Research Council)
C C D	Carbonate Compensation Depth
	Charged-Coupled Device
	Circumscribing Circle Diameter
	Conference of the Committee on Disarmament
	Copolymer Composition Distribution
C C E	Council of Construction Employers (USA)
C C E N	Comision Chilena de Energia Nuclear (Chile) (Chilean Nuclear Energy Commission)
C C E P	Coordinating Committee for Earthquake Prediction (Japan)

C C E S P	Coordinating Committee of Engineering Society Presidents (USA)
C C F	Commutated Capacitor Filter
	Compressed Citation File
	Crown Competition Factor
C C F F	Critical Colour Flicker Frequency
C ch E N	Comision Chilena de Energia Nuclear (Chile) (Chilean Nuclear Energy Commission)
C C I	Chambre de Commerce Internationale (International Chamber of Commerce)
	Cotton Corporation of India (India)
	Cotton Council International
C C I G	Cold Cathode Ion Gauge
C C I I W	Canadian Council of the International Institute of Welding (Canada)
C C I P	Continuously Computed Impact Point
C C I S	Common Channel Inter-office Signalling
C C I W	Canada Centre for Inland Waters (Canada)
C C L	Coating and Chemical Laboratory (US Army)
C cl	Commission for Climatology (of WMO (UN))
C C L O	Coordinating Council of Library Organizations (USA)
C C M	Cuban Cane Molasses
C C M A	Contract Cleaning and Maintenance Association
C C M I S	Commodity Command Management Information System (US Army)
C C M M	Complete Correlation Matrix Memory
C C M S	Committee of the Challenges of Modern Society (of North Atlantic Council (NATO))
	Computer Centre Management System
C C N	Cloud Condensation Nuclei
	Companhia Comercio e Navegacao (Brazil)
C C N R	Current-Controlled Negative Resistance
C C O H	Corrosive Contaminants, Oxygen and Humidity
C C O P	Committee for Co-ordination of Joint Prospecting for Mineral Resources in Asian Offshore Areas (of ECAFE)
C C P	Conditional Command Processor
C C P A	Court of Customs and Patent Appeals (USA)
C C P C	Communications Computer Programming Center (of AFCS (USAF))
C C P E	Canadian Council of Professional Engineers (Canada)

C C R	Circulation Control Rotor
	Computer-Controlled Retrieval
C C R I	Comite Consultatif de Recherche en Informatique (France) (Advisory Committee for Data Processing)
C C R L	Cement and Concrete Reference Laboratory (of ASTM and NBS (USA))
C C R P	Continuously Computed Release Point
C C S	Canadian Ceramic Society (Canada)
	Cold Crank Simulator
	Countryside Commission for Scotland
	Coupled-Cavity Structure
C C S A	Common-Controlled Switching Arrangement
C C S O C	Character-error Correcting Convolutional Self-Orthogonal Code
C C S S	Conversational Computer Statistical System
C C S T	Center for Computer Sciences and Technology (of NBS (USA))
C C T	Centre-Cracked Tension
	Comite Consultatif de Thermometrie (Consultative Committee on Thermometry)
	Common Customs Tariff (of EEC)
	Continuous Cooling Transformation
C C T A	Canadian Cable Television Association (Canada)
C C T U	Comite de Coordination des Telecommunications (of CNET (France)) (Committee for the Co-ordination of Telecommunications)
C C T V	Closed-circuit Cable Television
C C U	Central Capabilities Unit (of the Cabinet Office)
	Central Computer Unit (of NPL (DTI))
C C U A P	Computer Cable Upkeep Administrative Programme
C C V	Control Configured Vehicle
C C V S	COBOL Compiler Validation System
C C W	Counter Clockwise
C D	Capacitor Discharge
	Certificate of Deposit
C D A	Canadian Department of Agriculture (Canada)
	Compania Dominicana de Aviacion (Dominican Republic)
	Cool Dehumidified Air
	Copper Development Association (USA)
C D A P	Community Development Action Plan
C D C	Canadian Dairy Commission (Canada)

C D C	Center for Disease Control (of PHS (HEW) (USA))
	Commonwealth Development Corporation
	Computer Display Channel
	Cryogenic Data Center (of NBS (USA))
C D C E C	Combat Developments Command Experimentation Center (US Army)
C D C I N T A	Combat Developments Command Intelligence Agency (US Army)
C D E C	Combat Developments Experimentation Command (US Army)
C D E E	Canadian Defence Education Establishment (of DRB (Canada))
C D F	Critical Demulsification Temperature
	Cumulative Distributive Function
C D I C P	Centrul de Documentare al Industriel Chimice si Petroliere (Romania) (Documentation Centre for the Chemical and Oil Industries)
C D I C S	Centralised Dealer Inventory Control System
C D L	Centrala Drift Ledningen (Sweden) (Central (Power) Operating Board)
	Computer Design Language
C D M	Centrul de Documentare Medicala (Romania) (Medical Documentation Centre)
	Code-Division Multiplexing
C D M A	Code Division Multiple Access
C D M L S	Commutated Doppler Microwave Landing System
C D P	Common Depth Point
C D P I	Centro de Desarrollo y Productividad Industrial (Guatemala) (Centre for Development and Industrial Productivity)
C D P I R S	Crash Data Position Indicator Recorder Subsystem
C D R	Constant Dose Range
C D R I	Central Drug Research Institute (India)
C D S	Case Data System
	Central Dynamic Store
	Centrul de Documentara Stiintifica (Romania) (Scientific Documentation Centre)
	Comprehensive Display System
	Computerized Documentation Service (of UNESCO)
	Construction Differential Subsidy
C D S O	Commonwealth Defence Science Organisation

C D S U	Computer and Data Systems Unit (of the Central Statistical Office)
C D U	Capacitor Discharge Unit
C D V T P R	Centre de Documentation du Verre Textile et des Plastiques Renforces (France) (Documentation Centre of Glass Fibre and Reinforced Plastics)
C E	Compacted Earth
	Composition Exploding
	prefix to lettered/numbered/dated series of reports issued by Control Engineering Department of BISRA
C E (P V)	Ministry of Technology Committee of Enquiry on Pressure Vessels
C E A	Canadian Electrical Association (Canada)
	Carcinoembryonic Antigen
	Centres d'Etudes Architecturales (Belgium) (Architecture Research Centre)
	Commissariat a l'Energie Atomique (Belgium) (Atomic Energy Commission)
	Commodity Exchange Authority (of USDA)
	Compania Ecutoriana de Aviacion (Ecuador)
	Consejo Estatal de Azucar (Dominican Republic) (State Sugar Council)
	Cost-Effectiveness Analysis
C E A D I	Coloured Electronic Attitude and Direction Indicator
C E A M	Centre d'Experiences Aerienne Militaire (France) (Military Aircraft Test Centre)
C E A O	Communaute Economique et Douaniere de l'Afrique de l'Ouest (Economic and Customs Community of West Africa)
C E B E D A I R	Centre Belge d'Etudes et de Documentation de l'Air (Belgium) (Belgian Centre for the Study and Documentation of Air)
C E C	Centicycle
	Ceramic Educational Council (USA)
	Cholesteryl Erucyl Carbonate
	Circular Exhaust Cloud
	Consejo Economico Centroamericana (of CACM) (Central American Economic Council)
	Consulting Engineers Council (USA) (now part of ACEC)

3*

C E C	Council for Exceptional Children (USA)
C E C / P A	Consulting Engineers Council of Pennsylvania (USA)
C E C C	CENEL Electronic Components Committee
C E C E	Committee for European Construction Equipment (Belgium)
C E C E P	Corps of Engineers (US Army), Colorado Citizens Coordinating Committee on Environmental Planning
C E C L A	Comite Especial Coordinador Latinoamericano (Special Co-ordination Commission of Latin America)
C E C R I	Central Electro-Chemical Research Institute (India)
C E D A C	Computer Energy Distribution and Automated Control
C E D A R	Computer-aided Environmental Design Analysis and Realisation
C E D B	Central Engineering and Design Bureau (India)
C E D E P	Centre Europeen d'Education Permanente
C E D I F	Compagnie Europeene pour le Developpement Industriel et Financier (Belgium)
C E D I M O M	Centre Europeen pour le Developpement Industriel et la Mise en valeur de l'Outre-Mer
C E D O	Centre for Educational Development Overseas
C E D O C O S	Centre de Documentation sur les Combustibles Solides (Belgium) (Documentation Centre on Solid Fuels)
C E E I A	Communications Electronics Engineering Installation Agency (US Army)
C E E I A - W H	CEEIA (US Army) - Western Hemisphere
C E E P	Centre Europeen de l' Entreprise Publique (European Centre of Public Sector Organizations) (of EEC)
C E F	Centrifugal - Electrostatic - Focused
C E F A C E F	Comite Europeen des Fabricants d'Appareils de Chauffage en Fonte
C E F I C	Conseil Europeen des Federations de l'Industrie Chimique (European Council of Industrial Chemistry Federations) (Switzerland)
C E F R A C O R	Centre Francais de la Corrosion (France) (French Corrosion Centre)
C E G	Centre d'Etudes de Gramat (of DTAT (France))

C E I R	Comite Europeen de l'Industrie de la Robinetterie (European Committee for the Brass-founding and Finishing Industry)
C E L	Centre d'Essais des Landes (France) (Test Centre for Weapons, Missiles and Launchers)
	Compagnie d'Energetique Lineaire (France)
	Conversational Extensible Language
	Corporate Engineering Laboratory (of the British Steel Corporation)
C E L A	Committee for Exports to Latin America (of BNEC) (amalgamated into CELAC, 1971)
C E L A C	Committee for Exports to Latin America and the Caribbean (of BNEC)
C E L N U C O	Comite Europeen de Liaison des Negociants et Utilisateurs de Combustibles (European Liaison Committee of Merchants and Users of Fuels)
C E L P A	Centro Espacial de Lanzamientos para la Prospeccion Atmosferica (Argentine)
C E L T E	Constructeurs Europeens de Locomotives Thermiques et Electriques (European Diesel and Electric Locomotive Manufacturers Association)
C E L T I C	Cell Transport Integral Calculation
C E M	Centre d'Essais de la Mediterranee (of DRME) (France)
	Communications - Electronics - Meteorology
C E M A	Canadian Electrical Manufacturers Association (Canada)
	Catering Equipment Manufacturers Association
	Centre d'Etudes Marine Avancees (France) (now merged with COCEAN)
	Channel Electron Multiplier Array
C E M A C	Committee of European Associations of Manufacturers of Active Electronic Components
C E M B U R E A U	Cement Statistical and Technical Organization (France)
C E M I	Conseil Europeen pour la Marketing Industriel (European Council for Industrial Marketing)
C E M I S	Client-Employee Management Information System
C E M S	Centre d'Etude de la Meteorologie Spatiale (France) (Centre for Space Meteorology Studies)
C E N	Comite Europeen de Normalisation (France) (European Committee for Standardisation)

C E N A	Centre d'Experimentation de la Navigation Aerienne (France) (Air Navigation Experimental Centre)
C E N E L	Comite Europeen de Coordination des Normes Electrotechniques (European Committee for the Co-ordination of Electrotechnical Standards)
C E N E L E C	European Organization for Electrotechnical Standardisation
C E N E T	Centro Nacional de Electronica y Telecomunicaciones (Chile) (National Centre for Electronics and Telecommunications)
C E N I P	Centro Nacional de Productividad (Peru) (National Centre for Productivity)
C E N L	Community Equivalent Noise Level
C E N P H A	Centro Nacional de Pesquisas Habitacionais (Brazil) (National Housing Research Council)
C E N S A	Committee of European National Shipowners Associations
C E N T A G	Central Army Group (of AFCENT (NATO))
C E N T E C	Gesellschaft fur Centrifugentechnik (Germany) (a company—shareholders are the United Kingdom, Federal Republic of Germany and the Netherlands)
C E N T I	Centre pour le Traitement de l'Informatique (France)
C E N U S A	Centrales Nucleaires SA (Spain)
C E O C	Colloque Europeen des Organismes de Controle (a group of independent European inspecting organizations)
C E P	Centre d'Essais des Propulseurs (France) (Aerospace Engines Test Centre)
	Chain Elongation Proteins
	Complementary Even Parity
	Confederation Europeenne d'etudes Phystosanitaires (France) (European Confederation for Plant Protection Research)
	Concentrated Employment Program (USA)
	Council on Economic Priorities
C E P A	Civil Engineering Program (ADP) Association (USA))
C E P A C C	Chemical Education Planning and Coordinating Committee (of American Chemical Society (USA))

C E P E	Compagnie d'Electronique et de Piezo-Electricite (France)
C E P E X	Controlled Ecosystem Pollution Experiment (a joint project of American, British and Canadian scientists)
C E P M	Centre d'Exploitation Postal Metropolitain (France) (French Postal Department)
C E P S	Cornish Engines Preservation Society (now absorbed into The Trevithick Society)
C E Q	Council on Environmental Quality (of the Executive Office of the President (USA))
C E R	prefix to dated-numbered-lettered series of reports issued by Colorado State University, Department of Civil Engineering (USA) Conditioned Emotional Response
C E R A F E R	Centre National d'Etudes Techniques et de Recherches Technologiques pour l'Agriculture, l'Equipement Rural et les Forets (France) (National Centre for Technical Studies and Technological Research for Agriculture, Rural Equipment and Forests)
C E R C I	Compagnie d'Etudes et de Realisations de Cybernetique Industrielle (France)
C E R E	Centre d'Etudes et de Recherches de Environnement (Belgium) (Centre for Environmental Study and Research)
C E R I	Centre d'Etudes et de Recherches en Informatique (Algeria) (Data Processing Study and Research Centre)
C E R L	Central Electricity Research Laboratories (of CEGB) Computer-based Education Research Laboratory (University of Illinois (USA))
C E R T	Centre d'Etudes et de Recherches de Toulouse (France) (Aerospace Research Centre) Council for Education, Recruitment and Training for the Hotel Industry (Eire)
C E R T I C O	Committee on Certification (of ISO)
C E R T S M	Centre d'Etudes et de Recherches Techniques Sous-Marines (France) (Underwater Techniques Studies and Research Centre)
C E R V A	Consortium Europeen de Realisation et de Vente d'Avions

C E S	Cleveland Engineering Society (USA)
	Committee of European Shipowners
	Conference of European Statisticians (of UN)
	prefix to numbered series of reports issued by Department of Civil Engineering, West Virginia University (USA)
C E S A	Central Ecuatoriana de Servicios Agricolas (Ecuador) (Centre for Agricultural Services)
C E S E	Council for Environmental Science and Engineering (of CEI and CSTI)
C E S E M I	Computer Evaluation of Scanning Electron Microscope Images
C E S I	Centre for Economic and Social Information (of ECOSOC (UN))
C E S L	Civil Engineering Systems Laboratory (University of Illinois (USA))
C E S M	Continuous Electro-Slag Melting
C E S M E	Centro de Servicios Metalurgicos (Chile) (Central Metallurgical Industrial and Domestic Equipment Testing Centre)
C E S P	Centrais Electricas de Sao Paulo SA (Brazil) (State Electric Power Enterprise)
	Correlation Echo Sound Processor
C E S S E	Council of Engineering and Scientific Society Executives (USA)
C E S S S	Council of Engineering and Scientific Society Secretaries (Canada and USA)
C E S T	Compacted Earth Sodium Treated
C E S T I	Centre d'Etudes des Sciences et Techniques de l'Information (Dakar) (Mass Communication Institute)
C E T	Critical Emulsification Temperature
C E T A	Corrosion Evaluation and Test Area (a project of NASA (USA))
C E T A M A	Commission d'Establissement des Methodes d'Analyse (France)
C E T E P A	Centre Interprofessionnel Technique d'Etudes de la Pollution Atmospherique (France)
C E T H E D E C	Centre d'Etudes Theorique da la Detection et des Communications (France) (Detection and Communication Theory Research Centre)
C E T I A	International Control, Electronics, Telecommunications, Instruments, Automation Exhibition

C E T T	Centro de Entreamiento para Tecnicos en Tele-comunicaciones (Venezuela) (Training Centre for Telecommunications Technicians)
C E U S A	Committee for Exports to the United States of America (of BOTB)
C E V	Carbon Equivalent Value
C E Z U S	Compagnie Europeenne du Zirconium Ugine-Sandvik (France)
C F	Characteristic Frequencies
	Complement Fixation
	Cortico-Fugal
C F A	Comunaute Financiere Africaine (African Financial Community)
	Component Flow Analysis
C F A N S	Canadian Forces Air Navigation School (Canada)
C F C	Carbon Fibre Cement Composite
	Cranfield (Institute of Technology) Fluidics Conference
C F C F	Central Flow Control Facility (of FAA (USA))
C F E	Controlled Flash Evaporation
C F I	Commonwealth Forestry Institute (Oxford University)
	Corporacion de Fomento Industrial (Dominican Republic) (Industrial Development Corporation)
	Council of the Forest Industries of British Columbia (Canada)
C F I E M	Canadian Armed Forces Institute of Environmental Medicine (Canada)
C F L P	Central Fire Liaison Panel (of British Insurance Association, Fire Protection Association, Confederation of British Industry and Chief Fire Officers Association)
C F M	Cerebral Function Monitor
	Collision-Force Method
C F M U	Compagnie Francaise des Minerais d'Uranium (France)
C F O	Consolidated Functions Ordinary
C F P A	Conference of Fire Protection Associations
C F P G	Context-Free Programmed Grammar
C F R	Caile Ferate Romane (Romania) (State Railways)
	Center for Future Research (University of California (USA))
	Commercial Fast Reactor

C F S	Central Frequency Sounding
	Combined File Search
C F S P L	Canadian Forces Special Projects Laboratory (of DREV (Canada))
C F S T	Context-Free Syntactical Translator
C F S T I	Clearinghouse for Federal Scientific and Technical Information (now NTIS (Department of Commerce (USA))
C F T R I	Central Food Technological Research Institute (India)
C F T S	Computerized Flight Test System
C F F T	Critical Flicker Fusion Threshold
C F 2	Central Flow Control Facility (of FAA (USA))
C G	Coast Guard (of DOT (USA))
C G A	Canadian Gas Association (Canada)
C G C R I	Central Glass and Ceramic Research Institute (India)
C G L	Corrected Geomagnetic Latitude
C G L O	Commonwealth Geological Liaison Office
C G M P	Cyclic Guanosine Monophosphate
C G M W	Commission for the Geological Map of the World
C G P L	Conversational Graphical Programming Language
C G S	Canadian Geotechnical Society (Canada)
	Cyclic Group Signal
C G T	Compagnie Generale Transatlantique (France)
	Corrected Geomagnetic Time
C H A	Concentric Hemispherical Analyser
	Coupled-Hard-Axis
C H A M P	*Cranfield (Institute of Technology)* Hybrid Automatic Maintenance Programme
C H A M P U S	Civilian Health And Medical Program of the Uniformed Services (USA)
C H A P	Computer Charring Ablation Programme
	Controlled Helium Atmosphere Plant
C H A R M	Checking, Accounting and Reporting for Member-firms (of the London Stock Exchange)
C H D	Coronary Heart Disease
C H D B	Compatible High Density Bipolar
C H E	Cholinesterase
C H E C	Commonwealth Human Ecology Council
C H E M T R E C	Chemical Transportation Emergency Center (of Manufacturing Chemists Association (USA))
C H E S S	Chemical Engineering Simulation System

CHETA	Chemical Thermodynamics and Energy Hazard Appraisal
CHIA	Canadian Hovercraft Industries Association (Canada)
CHINA	Chronic Infectious Neuropathic Agents
CHR	Coherent Heterodyne Receiver
CHRAC	Construction and Housing Research Advisory Council
CHS	Collimated Holes Structure
CI	Chemical Inspectorate (MOD) (later Quality Assurance Directorate (Materials), now Materials Quality Assurance Directorate)
	Current-awareness Information
CIA	Catering Institute of Australia (Australia)
	Compagnia Industriale Aerospaziale (Italy) (an industrial consortium)
	Computer Industry Association (USA)
CIAME	Commission Interministerielle pour les Appareils de Mesures Electriques et Electroniques (France)
CIANS	Collegium Internationale Activitas Nervosae Superioris (International Colloquy of Higher Nervous Functions) (of the World Psychiatric Association)
CIAP	Centre d'Information de l'Aviation Privee (France)
	Climatic Impact Assessment Program (of Department of Transportation (USA))
CIATO	Centre International d'Alcoologie/Toxicomanies (International Centre of Alcohol/Drug Addiction)
CIB	Classification Internationale des Brevets (International Classification of Patents)
	Conseil International du Batiment pour la recherche, l'etude et la documentation (International Council for Building Research, Studies and Documentation) (Netherlands)
	Convective Instability Base
CIBE	Confederation Internationale des Betteraviers Europeens (International Confederation of European Sugar Beet Growers)
CIC	Cloud In Cell
	Custom Integrated Circuit

C I C	Committee on Institutional Cooperation (of a number of Universities in the USA)
C I C A R	Co-operative Investigations of the Caribbean and Adjacent Regions (of IOC (UNESCO))
C I C C	Construction Industry Council of California (USA)
C I C L	Centre for Industrial Consultancy and Liaison (Edinburgh University)
C I C R I S	Co-operative Industrial and Commercial Reference and Information Service
C I C S	Customer Information Control System
C I C S A	Centro Informacion y Computo SA (Colombia)
C I D	Collision-Induced Dissociation
	Combined Immunodeficiency Disease
C I D A	Canadian International Development Agency (Canada)
C I D A D E C	Confederation Internationale des Associations d'Experts et de Conseils (International Confederation of Associations of Experts and Consultants)
C I D E C	Conseil International pour le Developpement du Cuivre (International Council for the Development of Copper) (Switzerland)
C I D H E C	Centre Intergouvernemental de Documentation sur l'Habitat et l'Environnement (Intergovernmental Centre for Documentation on Dwellings and the Environment)
C I E	Computer Interrupt Equipment
C I E C	Centre International des Engrais Chimiques (International Centre for Chemical Fertilizers)
C I E S	Consejo Interamericana Economico y Social (Inter-American Economic and Social Council)
C I E S M	Commission Internationale pour l'Exploration Scientifique de la Mediterranee (International Commission for the Scientific Exploration of the Mediterranean Sea) (Monaco)
C I F A S	Consortium Industriel Franco-Allemand pour le satellite *Symphonie*
C I F C	Centre for Inter-Firm Comparison
C I F R I	Central Inland Fisheries Research Institute (India)
C I F T	Central Institute of Fisheries Technology (India)
C I G	Coordinate Indexing Group (of Aslib)
C I G F E T	Complementary Insulated - Gate Field - Effect Transistor

C I G R E	Conference Internationale des Grands Reseaux Electriques (International Conference on High Tension Electric Systems)
C I I	Chartered Insurance Institute
C I L G	CIRIA Information Liaison Group
C I M	Canadian Institute of Mining and Metallurgy (Canada)
	Commission on Industry and Manpower (disbanded 1970)
	Computer-Input Microfilm
	Convention Internationale sur le Transport de Marchandises par Chemins de Fer (International Convention Concerning the Carriage of Goods by Rail)
C I M A F	Centro de Cooperacao dos Industriais de Maquinas-Ferramentas (Portugal) (Cooperative Centre for Machine Tool Manufacturers)
C I M E	Centro de Investigacion de Metodos y Tecnicas para Pequenas y Medianas Empresas (Argentina) (Centre for Investigating the Organisation and Methods of Small and Medium-Sized Businesses)
C I M E C	Comite des Industries de la Mesure Electrique et Electronique de la Communaute (Committee for the Electrical and Electronic Instrument Engineering Industries of the EEC)
C I M G	Construction Industry Marketing Group
C I M L	Comite International de Metrologie Legale (of OIML) (International Committee of Legal Metrology)
C I M O	Commission for Instruments and Methods of Observation (of WMO (UN))
C I M P L E	Card Image Manipulator for Large Entities
C I M P O	Central Indian Medicinal Plants Organization (India)
C I M S	Computer Installation Management System
C I N A P	*Cincinnati* Numerical Automatic Programming
C I N D A	*Chrysler* Improved Numerical Differencing Analyzer
	Computer Index of Neutron Data
C I N E C A	Co-operative Investigations of the northern part of the Eastern Central Atlantic (of IOC (UNESCO))

C I N F	Commission Intersyndicale de l'Instrumentation et de le Mesure Nucleaire Francaise (France) (French Nuclear Instrumentation and Measurement Group)
C I N T E L	Computer Interface to Television
C I O S T A	Comite International d'Organisation Scientifique du Travail en Agriculture (International Committee for Scientific Management in Agricultural Work)
C I O T	Centro Internacional de Operacion Telegrafica (Argentine) (International Operations Centre for Telegraphy)
C I P	Cataloguing In Publication
	Council of Iron Producers (dissolved 1972)
C I P A	Chartered Institute of Patent Agents
C I P E	Comitato Inter-ministeriale per la Programmazione Economica (Italy) (Inter-Departmental Committee for Economic Planning)
C I P E C	Conseil Intergovernmental des Pays Exportateurs du Cuivre (France) (Intergovernmental Council of Copper Exporting Countries)
C I R	Commission on Industrial Relations
C I R A 1965	COSPAR International Reference Atmosphere of 1965
C I R C	Circulation Input Recording Centre system
C I R C A	Computerized Information Retrieval and Current Awareness
C I R E D	International Conference on Electricity Distribution
C I R F S	Comite International de la Rayonne et des Fibres Synthetiques (France) (International Rayon and Synthetic Fibres Committee)
C I R I S	Completely Integrated Reference Instrumentation System
C I R K	*Computing Technology Center (Union Carbide Corporation* (USA)) Information Retrieval from Keywords
C I R M	Celestial Infra-Red Mapper
C I R P	College International pour l'etude Scientifique des Techniques de Production Mechanique (France) (International Institution for Production Engineering Research)
C I R S E A	Compagnia Italiana Ricerche Sviluppo Equipaggiamenti Aerospaziali (Italy)

C I R T	Conference on Industrial Robot Technology
C I S	Canadian Institute of Surveying (Canada)
	Cataloguing In Source
	Chartered Institute of Secretaries (now Institute of Chartered Secretaries and Administrators)
	Coal Industry Society
	Custom Integrated System
C I S A	Canadian Industrial Safety Association (Canada)
C I S A V I A	Civil Service Aviation Association
C I S C	Canadian Institute of Steel Construction (Canada)
	Construction Industry Stabilization Committee (USA)
C I S E	Centro Informazioni Studi Esperienze (of ENEL (Italy))
	Council of the Institution of Structural Engineers
C I S I C	California (USA) Information Systems Implementation Committee
C I S I R	Ceylon Institute of Scientific and Industrial Research (Ceylon is now Sri Lanka)
C I S L	Confederation Internationale des Syndicats Libres (International Confederation of Free Trade Unions)
C I T	Central Institute of Technology (New Zealand)
	Chartered Institute of Transport
	Convective Instability Top
	Crack Initiation Temperature
C I T C E	Comite International de Thermodynamique et de Cinetique Electro-Chimiques (International Committee of Electro-Chemical Thermodynamics and Kinetics) (now known as International Society of Electrochemistry (Switzerland))
C I T E L	Conferencia Interamericana de Telecomunicaciones (Inter-American Telecommunications Conference (of OAS))
C I T E N	Comite International de la Teinture et du Nettoyage (International Committee for Dyeing and Cleaning)
C I T E S	Current Intelligence Traffic Exploitation System
C I T R A	Compagnie Industrielle de Travaux (France)
C I T R A C	Central Integrated Traffic Control
C I T S - Mux	Central Integrated Test System Multiplex

C I T T A	Confederation Internationale des Fabricants de Tapis et de Tissus pour Ameublement (International Confederation of Manufacturers of Cloth and Woven Material for Furnishings)
C I V	Corona Inception Voltage
	Convention Internationale sur le Transport des Voyageurs et des Bagages par Chemins de Fer (International Convention concerning the Carriage of Passengers and Luggage by Rail)
C I V D	Cold-Induced Vasodilatation
C I V M	Collision-Imparted Velocity Method
C I V V	Commission Internationale Vol a Voile (International Commission for Gliding)
C J I S	California (USA) Criminal Justice Information System
C L	Chemiluminescence
C L A	Cargo Landing Adaptability
	Catholic Library Association (USA)
	Commonwealth Library Association (Jamaica)
	Country Landowners Association
C L A F	Centro Latinoamericano de Fisica (Brazil) (Latin American Centre for Physics)
C L A F I C	Class Featuring Information Compression
C L A M P	Computer Listing and Analysis of Maintenance Programmes
C L A Q	Centro Latinoamericano de Quimica (Latin American Centre for Chemistry)
C L A S B	Citizens League Against the Sonic Boom (USA)
C L A S P	Computer Laboratory Systems Project (of the Royal School of Mines)
	Cylindrical Laser Plasma
C L A S S	Capacity Loading and Scheduling System
	Carrier Landing Aid Stabilization System
	Close Air Support System
C L B	Continuous Line Bucket
C L C	Cost of Living Council (USA)
C L C D	Clearinghouse and Laboratory for Census Data (of Center for Research Libraries (USA))
C L D	Coincidence - Ledge - Dislocation
	Compression Load Deflection
C L D A T A	Cutter Location Data
C L E A	Conference on Laser Engineering and Applications (of OSA and IEEE (USA))

C L E A R	County Law Enforcement Applied Regionally (Hamilton County, USA)
C L E M	Closed Loop Ex-vessel Machine
C L E P A	Comite de Liaison de la Construction d'Equipements et de Pieces d'Automobiles (of EEC) (Liaison Committee of the Manufacture of Automobile Fittings and Parts)
C L E T S	California (USA) Law Enforcement Telecommunications System
C L G P	Cannon-Launched Laser-Guided Projectile
C L I A	Collective Linear Ion Accelerator
C L I M	Cellular Logic-In-Memory
C L I P E R	Climatology and Persistence
C L I P R	Computer Laboratory for Instruction in Psychological Research (University of Colorado (USA))
C L I R A	Closed Loop In-Reactor Assembly
C L M - P D N	prefix to numbered/dated series of Program (adp) Documentation Notes issued by Culham Laboratory (UKAEA)
C L O O G E	Continuous Log of On Going Events
C L O R	Centraine Laboratorium Ochrony Radiologicznej (Poland)
C L O S	Command to Line Of Sight
	Controlled Line Of Sight
C L P	Contact Lens Practitioners
C L R	Combined Line and Recording
	Constant Load Rupture
C L R I	Central Leather Research Institute (India)
C L S	Country Library Service (New Zealand)
C L S A	California Land Surveyors Association (USA)
C L U S A N	Cluster Analysis
C L U S T E R	Central London Land Use System and Employment Register
C L W	College of Librarianship, Wales
C L Y D E	Computer-graphics Language for Your Design Equations
C M	Central Meridian
C M A	Compania Mexicana de Aviacion (Mexico)
	Composite Medium Amplifier
	Contractors Mutual Association (USA)
	Cylindrical Mirror Analyser
C M A E	Contingency Movement After-Effect
C M B	Corrective Maintenance Burden

87

C M B E S	Canadian Medical and Biological Engineering Society (Canada)
C M C	California (USA) Advisory Commission on Marine and Coastal Resources
	Carboxymethyl Cellulose
	Critical Micelle Concentration
C M C S A	Canadian Manufacturers of Chemical Specialties Association (Canada)
C M E S	Center for Marine and Environmental Studies (Lehigh University (USA))
C M F	Cast Metal Federation
	Cement Makers Federation
	Coherent Memory Filter
	Common Mode Failure
	Cytoplasmic Metabolic Factor
C M F R I	Central Marine Fisheries Research Institute (India)
C M G	Commission on Marine Geology (of IUGS)
C M I	Cell-Mediated Immunity
	Comite Maritime International (Belgium) (International Maritime Committee)
	Computer-Managed Instruction
	Cornell Medical Index Questionnaire
C M I S	Common Manufacturing Information System
	Computer-oriented Management Information System
C M M	Coordinate Measuring Machine
C M M A	Crane Manufacturers Association of America (USA)
C M M E	Chloromethyl Methyl Ether
C M O S	Complementary-symmetry Metal Oxide Semiconductor
C M P	Canadian Mineral Processors (Canada)
	Concrete Mixing and Placing
C M R	Center for Materials Research (Stanford University (USA))
	Code Matrix Reader
C M R S	Central Mining Research Station (India)
C M S	Cement-Modified Soil
	Chemical Metallizing System
	College of Marine Studies (Delaware University (USA))
	Compiler Monitor System
	Construction Management System

CMS	Conversational Monitor System
CMSCI	Council of Mechanical, Speciality Contracting Industries (USA)
CMSR	Central Management Staff Record
CMT	Cadmium Mercury Telluride
	California Mastitis Test
	Committee on Marine Technology (replaced by MTRB in 1972)
	Computer-Managed Training
CMTI	Central Machine Tool Institute (India)
CMTOS	Cassette Magnetic Tape Operating System
CMTP	Canadian Manpower Training Programme (of DMI (Canada))
CMTT	Commission Mixte CCIR/CCITT pour les Transmissions Televisuelles et Sonores
CMV	Cytomegalovirus
CN	Cholesteryl Nonanoate
	Chromosome Number
CNA	Committee for Nautical Archaeology
CNAM	Conservatoire National des Arts et Metiers de Paris (France)
CNC	Computerized Numerical Control
CNCT	Consejo Nacional de Ciencia y Tecnologia (Mexico) (National Council of Science and Technology)
CNDF	Complex-valued Non-linear Discriminant Function
CNE	Combined Neutral and Earth
CNEC	Comision Nacional de Energia Nuclear (Chile) (National Atomic Energy Commission)
CNEL	Community Noise Exposure Level
CNEN	Comision Nacional de Energia Nuclear (Mexico) (National Atomic Energy Commission)
	Comissao Nacional de Energia Nuclear (Brazil) (National Atomic Energy Commission)
	Conseil National de l'Energie Nucleaire (Luxembourg) (National Council for Atomic Energy)
CNEP	Cable Network Engineering Programme
CNFRA	Centre National Francais de la Recherches Antarctiques (France) (French National Centre for Antarctic Research)
CNG	Compressed Natural Gas
CNI	Composite Noise Index

89

C N I	Commissariat National a l'Informatique (Algeria) (National Agency for Data Processing)
C N I P A	Committee of National Institutes of Patents Agents (Netherlands)
C N K	Common Noun Keywords
C N P	Card Network Planning
C N P F	Conseil National du Patronat Francais (France) (French National Council of Employers)
C N R	Carboxy Nitroso Rubber Composite Noise Rating
C N R C	Centro Nacional de Radiacion Cosmica (Argentine) (National Cosmic Radiation Centre)
C N S E E	Convention of National Societies of Electrical Engineers of Western Europe
C N V	Contingent Negative Variation
C O A D S	Command and Administrative Data System (USDOD)
C O A L	Committee on Arid Lands (of AAAS (USA))
C O A M P	Computer Analysis of Maintenance Policies
C O A P	California (USA) Comprehensive Ocean Area Plan Combat Optimization and Analysis Programme
C O A X	COBOL Abbreviation Expander
C O B	Commission des Operations de Bourse (France)
C O B A E	Comissao Brasiliera de Atividades Espaciais (Brazil) (Brazilian Commission for Space Activities)
C O B E L P A	Association des Fabricants de Pates, Papiers et Cartons de Belgique (Belgium) (Belgian Association of Pulp, Paper and Carton Manufacturers)
C O B I	Council on Biological Information
C O B I L I T Y	COBOL Utility
C O B L O S	Computer Based Loans System (of AERE)
C O B R A	Computer Oriented Bearing Response Analysis Curved Orthotropic Bridge Analysis
C O B S I	Council on Biological Sciences Information (of FASEB (USA))
C O C	Cholesteryl Oleyl Carbonate
C O C A A H O S	Committee on Classical Articles and History of Statistics (USA)
C O C B	Crossed Olivocochlear Bundle
C O C E A N	Compagnie d'Etudes et d'Exploitation des Techniques Oceans (France)

C O C E M A	Comite des Constructeurs Europeens de Material Alimentaire (Committee of European Manufacturers of Foodstuffs)
C O C E S N A	Corporacion Centroamericana de Servicios de Navegacion Aerea (of CACM) (Honduras) Central American Air Navigation Service Corporation)
C O C O M	Coordinating Committee (of NATO)
C O D	Carrier-Onboard Delivery aircraft
	Constrained Optimal Design
C O D A	Crack Opening Displacement Application
C O D E C	Coder-Decoder
	Coding-Decoder Device
C O D E M	Coded Modulator-Demodulator
C O D I F A C	Comite de Developpement d'Industrie de la Chaussure et des Articles Chaussants (France) (Committee for the Development of the Footwear Industry)
C O D I L	Context Dependent Information Language
C O D I L S	Commodity Oriented Digital Input Label System
C O D M	Committee on Dynamic Measurement (of American Petroleum Institute (USA))
C O D O T	Classification of Occupations and Directory of Occupational Titles (of Department of Employment)
C O E	prefix to numbered series of reports issued by the Coastal and Ocean Engineering Division, Texas A and M University (USA)
C O E D	Composition and Editing Display
C O E E S	Central Office Equipment Estimation System
CO En CO	Committee for Environmental Conservation
C O F F T I	Contracting Operator Fast Fourier Transform Identification
C O F I	Council of Forest Industries of British Columbia (Canada)
C O F I R S	COBOL from *International Business Machines* RPG Specifications
C O F P A E S	Committee on Federal Procurement of Architect-Engineer Services (USA)
C O G A P	Computer Graphics Arrangement Programme
C O G D	Circular Outlet Gas Duct
C O G L A D	*Coast Guard* (USA) LORAN Assistance Device
C O G M	Committee on Natural Gas Fluids Measurement (of American Petroleum Institute (USA))
C O H A R T	Costs of Hard Rock Tunnelling

C O Hb	Carboxyhaemoglobin
C O H O	Coherent Oscillator
CO I D	Council of Industrial Design (became the Design Council in 1972)
C O I L	COMPAS (Computer Acquisition System) On-line Interactive Language
C O I N	COBOL Indexing and Maintenance Package
C O I N S	Committee on Improvement of National Statistics (of IASI)
C O L	Computerized Office Layout
C O L T	Council on Library Technology (USA)
C O L T S	Contrast Optical Laser Tracking System
C O M	Computer Output Microfilm
	Computer Output Microfilmer
	Computer Output Microfilming
C O M A D	Computer Methods for Automatic Diagnosis
C O M A P	Conversational Macro Package
COMARAIRMED	Commander Maritime Air Forces Mediterranean (of NATO)
C O M B O	Computation of Miss Between Orbits
C O M D A C	Component Design Augmented by Computer
C O M E P A	Comite Europeen de Liaison du Commerce de Gros des Papiers et Cartons (European Liaison Committee of Wholesalers of Paper and Cardboard)
C O M E S A	Committee on Meteorological Effect of Stratospherical Aircraft
C O M E T	Committee for Middle East Trade (of BOTB)
C O M E X	Compagnie Maritime d'Expertises (France)
C O M F O R	International Computer Forum and Exposition
C O M I T	Computing system *Massachusetts Institute of Technology* (USA)
C O M L A	Commonwealth Library Association
C O M L O	Compass Locator
C O M L O S A	Committee of Liner Operators - South America
C O M M A N D S	Computer Operated Marketing, Mailing and News Distribution System (of Building Research Establishment (DOE))
C O M M O D O R E	Command Modular Operation Room Equipment
COMNAVSOUTH	Commander, Allied Naval Forces Southern Europe (of NATO)
C O M P	Computer-Oriented Microwaves Practices

COMPAC	Commonwealth Pacific Cable (submarine telephone cable connecting Canada, Hawaii, Fiji, New Zealand, and Australia)
COMPACE	Control of Material Planning Activities
COMPACT	Computer Oriented Modular Planning and Control
	Computer Predicting and Automatic Course Tracking
COMPARE	Computer Oriented Method of Programme Analysis, Review and Evaluation
COMPAS	Committee on Physics and Society (of American Institute of Physics (USA))
COMPASS	Computer Optimal Media Planning And Selection System
	Computer Oriented Method of Patterns Analysis for Switching Systems
COMP CON	IEEE (USA) Computer Society Annual Conference
COMPEC	Computer Peripherals Exhibition and Conference
COMPENDEX	Computerized Engineering Index
COMPSY	Computer Support in Military Psychiatry (US Army)
COMSAP	Computerized Static Automatic Restoring Equipment for Power System
COMSAT	Committee on the Survey of Materials Science and Engineering (of National Academy of Sciences (USA))
COMSEC	Telecommunications Security
COMSEQIN	Component Sequencing and Insertion
COMSER	Commission on Marine Science and Engineering Research (of UN)
COMSL	Communication System Simulation Language
COMSUP	Communications Supervisor
COMT	Catechol-O-Methyltransferase
COMTECH	Computer Micrographics Technology
COMTEL	Comision Nacional de Telecommunications (Chile) (National Telecommunications Commission)
COMTELCA	Comision Tecnica de las Telecomunicaciones de Centroamericana (of CEMA) (Nicaragua) (Technical Commission for Telecommunications in Central America)
COMURHEX	Societe pour la Conversion de l'Uranium en Metal et en Hexafluorure (France)

93

C O N A C Y T	Consejo Nacional de Ciencia y Tecnologia (Mexico) (National Council for Science and Technology)
C O N A D	Continental Air Defense Command (USDOD)
C O N A D E	Consejo Nacional de Desarrollo (Argentina) (National Development Council)
C O N A R T	Consejo Nacional de Radiodifusion y Television (Argentina) (National Radio Broadcasting and Television Council)
C O N A S T I L	Compania Colombiana de Astilleros Ltda. (Colombia)
C O N A S U P O	Compania Nacional de Subsistencias Populares (Mexico) (State Grain Purchasing and Sales Agency)
C O N C A N A C O	Confederacion de Camaras Nacionales de Comercio (Mexico) (Confederation of National Chambers of Commerce)
C O N C A T	Conventional Catamaran
C O N C A W E	Conservation of Clean Air and Water (a Western European Study Group set up by some oil companies)
C O N C E X	Conselho Nacional de Comercio Exterior (Brazil) (National Council for External Trade)
C O N C O R D	Conference Coordinator (a computer programme)
C O N E S C A L	Centro Regional Construcciones Escolares para America Latina (Mexico) (Regional Centre for School Building in Latin America)
C O N E X	Container Express
C O N F I C S	*Cobra* (Huey Cobra Helicopter) Night Fire Control System
C O N F O R M	Constrained Force Model
	Conversational Form Format Generator
C O N I C Y T	Comision Nacional de Investigacion Cientifica y Tecnologica (Chile) (National Commission for Scientific and Technical Research)
C O N I E	Comision Nacional de Investigacion del Espacio (Spain) (National Commission for Space Research)
C O N P A S P	Construction Project Alternative Selection Programme
C O N R E D S	Contingency Readiness System
C O N R E P	Connected Replenishment
C O N S A L	Conference of South-east Asian Librarians
C O N S A S	Conference of South African Surveyors

C O N S T R A D O	Constructional Steel Research and Development Organization (of the British Steel Corporation)
C O N S U E L	Comite National pour la Securite des Usagers de l'Electricite (France) (National Committee for the Safety of Users of Electricity)
C O N T E L	Conselho Nacional de Telecomunicacoes (Brazil) (National Telecommunications Council)
C O P A	Comite des Organisations Professionnelles Agricoles de la CEE (Committee of the Agricultural Industry Associations of the European Economic Community)
	Compania Panemena de Aviacion (Panama)
C O P A C	Committee on Pollution Abatement and Control (National Research Council (USA))
C O P E B R A S	Companhia Petroquimica Brasileira (Brazil)
C O P E P	Commission Permanente de l'Electronique au Commissariat general du Plan (France)
C O P I C S	Communications Oriented Production Information and Control System
C O P M	Committee on Petroleum Measurement (of the American Petroleum Institute (USA))
C O P O L	Council of Polytechnic Librarians
C O P R	Centre for Overseas Pest Research (of ODA (Foreign and Commonwealth Office))
C O P R A I	Comissao de Produtividade da Associaco Industrial Portuguesa (Portugal) (Productivity Committee of the Portuguese Industrial Association)
C O P S	Computerized Optimization Procedure for Stabilators
	Computer-Oriented Police System (New York State (USA))
	Conversational Problem Solver
C O P S S	Committee of Presidents of Statistical Societies (USA)
C O R	Curiosity-Orientated Research
C O R A	Code for One-dimensional Reactor Analysis
C O R A P R O	Controle-Radioprotection (Belgium)
C O R A T	Christian Organisations Research and Advisory Trust
C O R C	Co-operative Octane Requirement Committee
C O R D	Computer Reinforced Design
	Coordination (computer programme)
C O R D A	Computerised Reservations System *Royal Dutch Airlines*

C O R D E	Corporacion Dominicana Empresas Estatalas (Dominican Republic) (State Aerospace Corporation)
C O R E N	Combustibili per Reattori Nucleari (Italy)
C O R F O	Corporacion de Fomento de la Produccion (Chile) (Production Development Corporation)
C O R P O R A L	Corporate Resource and Allocation
C O R P O S A N A	Corporacion de Obras Sanitarias (Paraguay) (Water and Sewage Service Corporation)
C O R T E X	Communications Orientated Real-Time Executive
C O S	Carbonyl Sulphide
	Clinical Orthopedic Society (USA)
	Communications Oriented System
C O S / M O S	Complementary Symmetry Metal Oxide Semiconductor
C O S A	Council of Sections and Affiliates (of Land Survey Division, ACSM (USA))
C O S A M	Co-Site Analysis Model
C O S E M C O	Comite des Semences du Marche Commun (Seed Committee of the Common Market (European Economic Community))
C O S I N E	Computer Sciences in Electrical Engineering (committee of the Commission on Education of the National Academy of Engineering (USA))
C O S M	Committee on Static Measurement (of the American Petroleum Institute (USA))
C O S M A T	Committee on the Survey of Materials Science and Engineering (of the National Academy of Sciences (USA))
C O S M O	Communications Simulation Model
C O S M O S	Centralization of Supply Management Operations System (US Army)
	Coastal Survey Marine Observation System
	Commercial Systems using Modular Software
	Complementary Symmetry Metal Oxide Semiconductor
C O S P A R	Committee on Space Research (France) (of the International Council of Scientific Unions)
C O S T	Committee on Science and Technology (India)
	Cooperation Europeenne dans le domaine de la recherche Scientifique et Technique (Foundation to Sponsor European Cooperation in Science and Technology)

C O S T A R	Conversational On-line Storage And Retrieval
C O S T I	Centre for Scientific and Technological Information (of NCRD (Israel))
C O T	Computer-Output-Typesetting
	Cyclo-octatetraene
C O T A W S	Collision, Obstacle, Terrain and Warning Systems
C O T I	Central Officials Training Institute (Korea)
C O T M S	Computer-Operated Transmission Measuring Set
C O T T I	Commission du Traitement et de la Transmission de l'Information (France) (Commission for Data Handling and Transmission)
C O U R T	Cost Optimization Utilizing Reference Techniques
C O V O S	Groupe d'etudes sur les Consequences des Vols Stratospheriques (France) (Study Group on the Effects of Stratospheric Flight)
C P	Circuit-to-Pin ratio
	Contractile Pulse
	Constant Potential
	Creatine Phosphate
C P A	Canadian Petroleum Association (Canada)
	Chesapeake Physics Association (USA)
	Chipboard Promotion Association
	Coherent Potential Approximation
	Commonwealth Pharmaceutical Association
	Concrete Pipe Association of Great Britain
	Consumer Protection Agency (USA)
	Contractors Plant Association
C P A A	Current Physics Advance Abstracts (of American Institute of Physics (USA))
C P A B	Computer Programmer Aptitude Battery
C P A F	Cost-plus-Award Fee
C P A I	Canvas Products Association International (USA)
C P B	Corporation for Public Broadcasting (USA)
	Current Physics Bibliographies (of American Institute of Physics (USA))
C P C	Ceramic Printed Circuit
C P D	Citrate-Phosphate-Dextrose
	Contact Potential Difference
C P D M	Chebychev Polynomial Discriminant Method
C P D S	Carboxypyridine Disulphide
C P E	Chlorinated Polyethylene
	Council on Physics in Education (USA)

C P E	Cytopathic Effect
C P E A	Colorado Professional Electronic Association (USA)
C P E H S	Consumer Protection and Environmental Health Service (of Public Health Service (HEW) (USA))
C P F R C	Central Pacific Fisheries Research Center (of NMFS (USA))
C P G	Clock-Pulse Generator
	Controlled-Pore Glass
C P H A	Canadian Public Health Association (Canada)
C P H E R I	Central Public Health Engineering Research Institute ((India)
C P I	Closed Pore Insulation
	Computing Power Index
	Coronary Prognostic Index
	Corrugated Plate Interceptor
C P I A	Chemical Propulsion Information Agency (USA)
C P I C	Canadian Police Information Centre (Canada)
	Coastal Patrol and Interdiction Craft
C P I C C	Consumer Product Information Coordinating Center (of General Services Administration (USA))
C P I L S	Correlation Protected Instrument Landing System
C P K	Creatinine Phosphokinase
C P L	Commonwealth Parliamentary Library (Australia)
	Computer Programme Library (of NEA (OECD))
C P L E E	Charged Particle Lunar Environmental Experiment
C P M	Computer Performance Monitor
	Continuous Processing Machine
	Current Physics Microform (of American Institute of Physics (USA))
C P M A	Computer Peripheral Manufacturers Association (USA) (now ACDPI)
C P M S	Computer Plotting Matrix System
C P P	Concrete Paver Project
	Current Purchasing Power
C P R	Cost Performance Report
C P R I	Cold Pressor Recovery Index
C P R S	Central Policy Review Staff (of the Cabinet Office)

C P S	CERN Proton Synchroton
	Contingency Planning System
	Contour Plotting System
	Conversational Programming System
	Cooley Programming System (Cooley Electronics Laboratory, Michigan University (USA))
C P S A	Current Physics Selected Articles (of American Institute of Physics (USA))
C P S C	Consumer Product Safety Commission (USA)
C P S R	*Cossor* Precision Secondary Radar
C P S T	Capacitive Position Sensing Transducer
C P T	Center for Particle Theory (University of Texas (USA))
	Cockpit Procedures Trainer
	Contralateral Pyramidal Tract
	Current Physical Titles (of the American Institute of Physics (USA))
C P U C	California Public Utilities Commission (USA)
C P V	Concrete Pressure Vehicle
C P V C	Chlorinated Polyvinyl Chloride
C P W D	Central Public Works Department (India)
C P W M	Clock Pulse Width Modulation
C P X	Charged Pigment Xerography
C Q A	Computer-aided Question Answering
C R	Consultant Report
	Convertible Rotor
C R A C	Construction Research Advisory Council (now Construction and Housing Research Advisory Council)
C R A M	Critical Resource Allocation Method
C R A M D	Cosmic Ray Anti-Matter Detector
C R A M M	Coupon Reading And Marking Machine
C R C	Cancer Research Campaign
	Center for Naval Analyses Research Contribution (USN)
	Clinical Research Centre (of MRC)
	Communications Research Centre (Department of Communications (Canada))
	Co-ordinating Research Council (sponsored by SAE and American Petroleum Institute (USA))
	Cotton Research Corporation
C R C - A P R A C	Coordinating Research Council - Air Pollution Research Advisory Committee (USA)
C R D F	Cathode Ray Direction Finder

C R E	Commercial Relations and Exports Division (of DTI)
C R E A T E	Computational Resources for Engineering and Simulation, Training and Education
C R E A T I O N	Crew Allocation
C R E D I T	Cost Reduction Early Decision Information Techniques
C R E S	Center for Research in Engineering Science (University of Kansas (USA))
	Constant Ratio Elasticity of Substitution
C R E S A	Cuarzo Radioelectrico Espanol SA (Spain)
	Combat Reporting System (USAF)
C R E S T	Committee on Reactor Safety Technology (of NEA (OECD))
C R F	Corticotrophin Releasing Factor
C R F I	Custom Roll Forming Institute (USA)
C R F S	Crash-Resistant Fuel System
C R G	Catalytic-Rich Gas
C R H L	Collaborative Radiological Health Laboratory (USA)
C R I	Caribbean Research Institute (University of the Virgin Islands)
	Cement Research Institute of India (India)
	Coconut Research Institute (Sri Lanka)
	Comite de Recherche en Informatique (France) (Research Committee on Data Processing)
	Crops Research Institute (Ghana)
C R I M P	Computer Report on Importance
C R I N	Cocoa Research Institute of Nigeria (Nigeria)
C R I S	Comprehensive Research Injury Scale
C R I S T A L	Contracts Regarding an Interim Supplement to Tanker Liability for Oil Pollution
C R L	Center for Research Libraries (USA)
	Council on Library Resources (USA)
C R M	Computer Resources Management
C R M S	Close Range Missile System
C R O M	Capacitive Read Only Memory
	Control and Ready-Only Memory
C R O S	Computerized Reliability Optimization System
C R O S S B O W	Computerised Retrieval of Organic Structures Based On Wiswesser
C R P	Components Reliability Programme
	Counter-Rotating Platform

C R P L	Central Radio Propagation Laboratory (USA) (now Institute for Telecommunication Sciences and Aeronomy (of NOAA (USA))
C R R	Carrier Removal Rate
C R R I	Central Road Research Institute (India)
C R S C	Center for Research in Scientific Communication (Johns Hopkins University (USA))
C R S E	prefix to numbered/lettered series of monographs on Cold Regions Science and Engineering issued by CRREL (US Army)
C R S S	Critical Resolved Shear Stress
C R S S A	Centre de Recherches du Service de Sante des Armees (France) (Army Medical Service Research Centre)
C R T	Cathode Ray Tube
	Choice Reaction Time
	Combat Readiness Training
C R T C	Canadian Radio and Television Commission (Canada)
C R T F	Create Test Files
C R T P B	Canadian Radio Technical Planning Board (Canada)
C R U	Control and Reporting Unit
C R U Z E I R O	Servicos Aereos Cruzeiro do Sul SA (Brazil)
C R W R	Center for Research in Water Resources (Texas University (USA))
C S	Center for Cybernetic Studies (University of Texas (USA))
	The Chemical Society
	prefix to numbered series of Recommended Practices for Cast Steel Shot issued by SAE (USA)
	prefix to numbered series of reports issued by the Department of Computer Science, Stanford University (USA)
	Conditioned Stimulus
	Ortho-chlorobenzliden-malonitrile (a gas named after its inventors - Dr. B. B. Carson and Dr. R. W. Stoughton)
C S A	Cryogenic Society of America (USA)
C S A C	Consumer Standards Advisory Committee (of BSI)
C S B	Carrier and Side Band
C S C	Computer Science Center (University of Maryland (USA))

C S C E	Canadian Society for Chemical Engineering (Canada)
	Canadian Society for Civil Engineering (Canada)
	Conference on Security and Cooperation in Europe
C S C F E	Civil Service Council for Further Education
C S C R	Center for Surface and Coatings Research (Lehigh University (USA))
C S D	Computerized Standard Data
	Control Surveys Division (of ACSM (USA))
	Construction Systems Division (of CERL (US Army))
	Crack Surface Displacement
C S E	Central Studies Establishment (of Australian Defence Scientific Service)
C S E A	California State (USA) Electronics Association
C S E L T	Centro Studi e Laboratori Telecomunicazioni (Italy) (Telecommunications Research Centre and Laboratory)
C S E R B	Computers, Systems and Electronics Requirements Board (of DTI)
C S F	Cerebrospinal Fluid
	Configuration State Function
C S F B	Channel State Feedback
C S G	Context-Sensitive Grammar
	Council of State Governments (USA)
C S H	Conventional Spin Hamiltonian
C S I	Construction Surveyors Institute
C S I I	Centre for the Study of Industrial Innovation
C S I O	Cavity-Stabilized IMPATT Oscillator
	Central Scientific Instruments Organisation (India)
C S I R	Council for Scientific and Industrial Research (Ghana)
C S I T	Committee on Social Implications of Technology (of IEEE (USA))
C S K	Co-operative Study of the Kuroshio and adjacent region (of IOC (UNESCO))
C S L	Computer Systems Laboratory (of NIH (HEW) (USA))
	Context-Sensitive Language
C S L P	Center for Short-Lived Phenomena (of Smithsonian Institution (USA))
C S M	Camborne School of Mines

C S M	Cement-Sand-Molasses
	Centro Sperimentale Metallurgico (Italy) (Metallurgy Research Centre)
	Chopped Strand Mat
	Commission for Synoptic Meteorology (of WMO (UN))
	Computer System Manual
	Corn-Soya Milk
C S M A	Chemical Specialties Manufacturers Association (USA)
	Communications Systems Management Association (USA)
C S M C R I	Central Salt and Marine Chemicals Research Institute (India)
C S M E	Canadian Society for Mechanical Engineers (Canada)
C S M R S	Central Soil Mechanics Research Station (India)
C S M S	Computerized Specification Management System
C S N D T	Canadian Society for Non-Destructive Testing (Canada)
C S O	Central Seismological Observatory (India)
	Central Statistical Office (Ethiopia)
C S O C R	Code Sort Optical Character Recognition
C S O D	Crack Surface Opening Displacement
C S P	Chartered Society of Physiotherapy
	Chlorosulphonated Polyethylene
	Coherent Signal Processor
	Commercial Sub-routine Package
	Continuous Seismic Profiling
	Council for Scientific Policy (disbanded 1972) (replaced by Advisory Board of the Research Councils)
	Count Strength Product
C S P I	Center for Science in the Public Interest (USA)
C S P P	Committee on Science and Public Policy (of AAAS (USA))
C S P R T	Compound Sequential Probability Ratio Test
C S Q	Central Site Queueing
C S Q C	Ceylon Society for Quality Control (Ceylon is now called Sri Lanka)
C S R	Chemically Stimulated Rubber
C S R L	Computer Science Research Laboratory (University of Arizona (USA))
C S R S	Central Sericulture Research Station (India)

C S S	Cordless Switchboard System
	Council for Science and Society
	Cryogenics Storage System
C S S A	Crop Science Society of America (USA)
C S S E	Conference of State Sanitary Engineers (USA)
	Control Systems Science and Engineering Department (University of Washington (USA))
C S S M	Central Site Simulation Model
C S S P	Continuous System Simulation Programme
C S 3	Combat Service Support System (US Army)
C S T	Consolidated Schedule Technique
	Critical Solution Temperature
C S T P	Committee for Scientific and Technical Personnel (of OECD) (disbanded 1970)
C S U	Colorado State University (USA)
C S U - A T S P	Colorado State University, Department of Atmospheric Science (USA)
C S U K	Chamber of Shipping of the United Kingdom
C S W	Cleveland School of Welding (USA)
	Concentrated Sea Water
C S W S	Crew-Served Weapon Night Vision Sight
C T	Compact Tension
C T A	Cement-Treated Aggregate
	Chain Testers Association of Great Britain
	Centro Tecnico Aeroespacial (Brazil) (Aerospace Technical Centre)
	Collision Threat Assessment
C T A F	Comite des Transporteurs Aeriens Francais (France) (French Air Transport Association)
C T A P	Cleveland (Ohio (USA)) Transport Action Program
C T B	Cement-Treated Base
	Companhia Telefonica Brasileira (Brazil)
C T C	Canadian Transport Commission (Canada)
	Central Training Council (of Department of Employment)
	Charge Transfer Complex
	Chlortetracycline
	Compact Transpiration Cooling
	Continuously Transposed Conductor
C T C C	Central Transport Consultative Committee
C T C S	Component Time Control System
C T D	Charge-Transfer Device

C T E	Charge-Transfer Efficiency
	Coefficient of Thermal Expansion
	Computer Telex Exchange
C T E E	Chlorotrifluor Ethylene
C T F A	Cosmetic, Toiletry and Fragrance Association (USA)
C T F O I C	Cabinet Task Force on Oil Import Control (USA)
C 3 E M	Curriculum Committee for Computer Education for Management (of ACM (USA))
C T I	Calculo y Tratamiento de la Informacion (Spain)
	Cooling Tower Institute (USA)
C T I O	Cerro Tolo Interamerican Observatory
C T L	Compiler Target Language
C T M	Composite-Tape-Memory
C T N	Cellulose Trinitrate
C T N E	Compania Telefonica Nacional de Espana (Spain) (National Telephone Company of Spain)
C T P	Ctyidine Triphosphate
C T P I B	Carboxy-Terminated Polyisobutylene
C T P V	Coal Tar Pitch Volatiles
C T R	Controlled Thermonuclear Reactor
C T R L	Cotton Technological Research Laboratory (India)
C T S	Center for Theoretical Studies (Miami University (USA))
C T V	Cable Television
C U - C S D	Cornell University, Department of Computer Science (USA)
C U B A N A	Empresa Consolidada Cubana de Aviacion (Cuba) (State Air Line)
C U C S	Computation-Universal Cellular Space
C U D A S	Computer Ultrasonic Data Analysis System
C U D N	Common User Data Network
C U E	Chemical Underwater Explosive
	Component Utilization Effectiveness
C U E R L	Columbia University Electronics Research Laboratories (USA)
C U J T	Complimentary Uni-Junction Transistor
C U L D A T A	Comprehensive Unified Land Data
C U L P R I T	Cull and Print
C U M L A U D E	Computerized Understanding of Morphology - Language Acquisition Under Development in Education
C U M A R C	Cumulated Machine-Readable Cataloguing

4*

C U P I D	Create, Update, Interrogate and Display
C U R S	Centre Universitaire de la Recherche Scientifique (Morocco) (University Centre for Scientific Research)
C U S I P	Committee on Uniform Security Identification Procedures (of the American Bankers Association (USA))
C V	Constant Viscosity
	Constant Voltage
	Continuous Vulcanization
C V A	Calendar Variations Analysis
C V C	Current-Voltage Characteristic
C V C C	Compound, Vortex and Controlled Combustion
C V D	Carbon Vacuum Deoxidized
	Constancy of Visual Direction
	Co-ordination of Valve Development (MOD)
C V D T	Constant Volume Drop Time
C V L	Centruum voor Lastechniek (Netherlands) (now part of NIL)
C V N	Charpy V-notch
C V R	Current-Viewing Resistor
C V S	Computer-controlled Vehicle System (for traffic control)
	Constant Volume Sampling
C V S D	Continuous Variable Slope Delta
C V S F	Conduction Velocity of Slower Fibres
C V T	Concept Verification Testing
C V T R	Charcoal Viral Transport
C W	Clockwise
	Cold Welding
	Constant Weight
C W A	Cooling Water Association
C W A C	Central Water Advisory Committee
C W C	Cloud Water Content
C W D	Clerical Work Data
C W I T	Colour-Word Interference Test
C W M	Clerical Work Measurement
C W P R S	Central Water and Power and Power Research Station (India)
C W R A	Canadian Water Resources Association (Canada)
C W S	Collision Warning System
	Control Wheel Steering
C W S A	Contract Work Study Association

C W W P S	Cornish Water Wheels Preservation Society (now merged into the Trevithick Society)
C Y T A	Cyprus Telecommunications Authority (Cyprus)

D

D Mat	prefix to series of reports issued by MOD(PE) Directorate of Materials
D A	Dopamine
D A A D	Deutscher Akademischer Austauschdienst (Germany) (German Academic Exchange Service) Deutscher Akademischer Austauschmienst (German Academic Exchange System)
D A B S	Discrete Address Beacon System
D A C	Development Assistance Committee (of OECD) Didode-Assisted Commutation
D A C C	Data and Computation Center (University of Wisconsin (USA))
D A C E	Data Acquisition and Control Executive
D A C O M	Double Average Comparison
D A C S	Directorate of Aerospace Combat Systems (of Canadian Armed Forces)
D A D	Dial-a-Design (computer based design service of Ferranti & Systemshare Ltd.)
D A D C	Digital Air Data Computer
D A D E C	Design And Demonstration Electronic Computer
D A D I O S	Direct Analogue to Digital Input-Output System
D A D P	Dialkyl Dithiophosphate
D A D P T C	Defence ADP Training Centre (MOD)
D A D S	Data Acquisition and Display System
D A F	Delayed Auditory Feedback Dynamic Axial Fatigue
D A F S	Department of Agriculture and Fisheries for Scotland
D A I	Direct Access Information Doubly Auto-Ionizing
D A I R I	Dissertation Abstracts International Retrospective Index
D A I S	Digital Avionics Information System Direct Access Intelligence Systems
D A I S Y	Domestic Appliances Information System
D A K	Dansk Atomreaktor Konsortium (Denmark)
D A L	Downed Aircraft Locator
D A L R	Dry-Adiabatic Lapse Rate
D A L S	Diver Auditory Localization System

D A M A	Demand Assignment Multiple Access
D A M E	Director Area Mechanical Estimating
D A M I D	Discounting Analysis Model for Investment Decisions
D A M N	Dynamic Analysis of Mechanical Networks
D A M U S C	Direct Access, Multi-User, Synchrocyclotron Computer
D A M U T	Ducted Air Medium Underground Transmission
D A N	Diaminonaphthalene
D A N A T O M	Selskabet for Atomenergiens Industrielle Udnyttelse (Denmark) (Association for the Industrial Development of Atomic Energy)
D A O	Directory of Amateur Observers
D A P P	Data Acquisition and Processing Program (of USAF)
D A P R	Digital Automatic Pattern Recognition
D A R A	Deutsche Arbeitsgemeinschaft fur Rechenanlagen (Germany) (German Computer Association)
D A R C	Deutscher Amateur-Radio-Club (Germany)
D A R E	Differential Analyzer Replacement
	UNESCO Computerized Data Retrieval System for the Social and Human Sciences
D A R M E	Directorate of Armament Engineering (of Canadian Armed Forces)
D A R P A	Defense Advanced Research Projects Agency (USDOD)
D A R S	Digital Attitude Reference System
D A R T	*DatagraphiX* Automated Retrieval Techniques
	Demand Actuated Road Transit
	Directional Automatic Realignment of Trajectory
	Disappearing Automatic Retaliatory Target
D A S A	Defense Atomic Support Agency (USDOD) formerly Armed Forces Special Weapons Project now Defense Nuclear Agency)
D A S D	Direct Access Storage Device
D A S S	Demand Assignment Signalling and Switching
D A S T	Division of Applied Science and Technology (of FWPCA (USA))
D A S Y S	Data System Environment Simulator
D A T	Data Abstract Tape
	Desk-top Analysis Tool
D A T A R	Delegation General a l'Amenagement du Territoire et a l'Action Regional (France) (Government Regional Planning Agency)

D A T A S	Data in Associative Storage
D A T E	Dial Access Technical Education (telephone information service of IEEE (USA))
D A T E C	Differential and Alignment Unit and Total Error Corrector
D A T E L	Data Telecommunication
D A T G E N	Data Generator Utility Routines
D A W N S	Design of Aircraft Wing Structures
d B	Decibel
D B	Deutsche Bundesbahn (Germany) (German Federal Railway)
D B A S	Delmarva Business Advisory Service (University of Delaware (USA))
D B B O L	Digital Building Block Oriented Language
D B B T Z	Dibutylaminomethyl Benzotriazole
D B C S	Deterministic Bounded Cellular Space
D B D L	Data Base Definition Language
D B E	Design Basis Earthquake
D B H	Developmental Big Hydrofoil
D B L	Data Base Language
D B M S	Data Based Management System
D B N	Dibutylnitrosamine
D B O S	Disc-Based Operating System
D B P	Dibutylphthalate
D B R	Deutscher Bildungsrat (Germany) (German Education Council)
D B S	Dibenzylsulphide
	Division of Biologics Standards (of FDA (USA)) (now Bureau of Biologics)
	Dominion Bureau of Statistics (Canada)
D B S O	Dibenzylsulphoxide
D B S T	Double Bituminous Surface Treatment
D B T D L	Dibutylin Dilaurate
D B T G	Data Base Task Group (of CODASYL)
D C	prefix - preceded by date/number - of Draft Standards available for Public Comment issued by BSI
D C A	Dichloroacetylene
D C A A	Defense Contract Audit Agency (USDOD)
D C B	Double Cantilever Beam
D C C	Dicyclohexyl-carbodiimide
D C E O	Defense Communications Engineering Office (of Defense Communications Agency (USDOD))
D C F P	Dynamic Cross-Field Photomultiplier

D C G F F	Diode-Coupled Gated Flip-Flop
D C I C	Defense Ceramic Information Center (Batelle Memorial Institute (USA)) (now part of Metals and Ceramics Information Center)
D C I E M	Defence and Civil Institute of Environmental Medicine (of DRB (Canada))
D C L A	District of Columbia (USA) Library Association
D C M	Dichloromethane
D C O A	Direct Current Operational Amplifier
D C O L	Direct Control Oriented Language
D C P	Defense Concept Plan (USDOD)
	Digestible Crude Protein
	Digital Cursor Positioner
D C P A	Defense Civil Preparedness Agency (USDOD)
D C P D	Dicyclopentadiene
D C P L	Distributed Control Programming Language
D C P S K	Differentially-Coherent Phase-Shift-Keyed
D C R F	Die Casting Research Foundation (of the American Die Casting Institute (USA))
D C R P	Direct Current Reverse Polarity
D C R T	Division of Computer Research and Technology (of NIH (HEW) (USA))
D C S	Damage Control Suit
	prefix to numbered series of technical reports isued by Department of Computer Science, Rutgers - the State University, New Brunswick (USA)
	Directa Centrala je Statistics (Romania) (Central Statistics Office)
	Distributed Computer System
D C S M	Deterministic Complete Sequential Machine
D C S P	Defense Communications Satellite Program (USDOD) (formerly IDCSP)
	Direct Current, Straight Polarity
D C T M	Directional Control Test Missile
D C V D	Directorate Co-ordinated Valve Development (MOD)
D D	prefix to numbered series of Drafts for Development issued by BSI
D D A	Diemaking and Diecutting Association (USA)
D D B	Double-Declining Balance
D D C	Defense Documentation Center (of DSA (USDOD))
D D D	Detailed Data Display

D D D I C	Department of Defense Disease and Injury Code (USDOD)
D D F	Data Description Facility
D D L	Data Description Language
	Differential Distribution Laws
D D L C	Data Description Languages Committee (of CODASYL)
D D R	Decision-Directed Receiver
	Double-Drift-Region
D D S	Development Documentation System
	Discrete Depth Sampler
D D T A	Derivative Differential Thermal Analysis
D E	Department of Employment
	Deterministic Equivalent
D E A	Dairy Engineers Association (merged with PPA)
D E C M	Deception Electronic Counter-Measures
D E C O N S U L T	Deutsche Eisenbahn Consulting (Germany)
D E E	Diethyl Ether
	Digited Evaluation Equipment
D E E P	Data Exception Error Protection
	Describe Each Element in the Procedure
D E E P S E A T	Deep-Sea System for Evaluating Acoustic Transducers
D E E S	Dynamic Electronic Environment Simulator
D E F	Diethyl Fumarate
D E F (A U S T)	prefix to numbered series of Australian Defence Specifications and Standards issued by Defence (Industrial) Committee, Dept. of Defence (Australia)
D E F U N C T	Desirability Function
D E G S	Diethylene Glycol Succinate
D E L D I S	Delay Equalizer Selection
D E L F I C	Department of Defense Land Fallout Interpretive Code (USDOD)
D E L I M I T E R	Definitive Limit Evaluator
D E L T I C	Delay Line Time Compressor
D E M	Dynode Electron Multiplier
D E M A T E L	Decision-Making and Trial Evaluation Laboratory (Battelle (Geneva))
D E M O N	Diminishing Error Method for Optimization of Networks
D E M O S	Dendenkosha Multi-access On-line System
D E M P	Diethylmethylphosphate
D E M P T	Diethylmethylphosphorothionate

D E M S	Defensively Equipped Merchant Ship
D E N	Diethylnitrosamine
D E N T E L	Departmento Nacional de Telecomunicacoes (Brazil) (National Department of Telecommunications)
D E P	Department of Employment and Productivity (formerly Ministry of Labour) (now Department of Employment)
	Di-isopropyl Ethylphosphate
D E P I C T	Defense Electronics Products Integrated Control Technique
D E P L O C	Depot-Location
D E Q M A R	Determining Economic Quantities of Maintenance Resources
D E R	Division of Environmental Radiation (Bureau of Radiological Health (USA))
D E S	Design and Evaluation System
	Diethylstilboestrol
	Dynamic Environment Simulator
D E S C	Defense Electronics Supply Center (DSA (USDOD))
D E S I D O C	Defence Scientific Information and Documentation Centre (India)
D E S U	Delhi Electric Supply Undertaking (India)
D E T A	Diethylenetriamine
D E T C	Defence Engineering Terminology Committee (MOD)
D E U A	Diesel Engineers and Users Association
D E V	Duck Embryo Vaccine
D E V I L	Direct Evaluation of Index Language
D F	Dissipation Factor
D F A	Desferrioxamine
D F C	Dairy Farmers of Canada (Canada)
D F D R	Digital Flight Data Recorder
D F E T	Drift Field Effect Transistor
D F G	Deutsche Forschungsgemeinschaft (German Research Association)
D F H	Developmental Fast Hydrofoil
D F I S A	Dairy and Food Industries Supply Association (USA)
D F L D	Distribution Free Logic Design
D F O A	Desferrioxamine
D F R	Delayed Free Recall
D F S	Direct Function Search
D F S M	Deterministic Finite-State Machine

D F T	Discrete Fourier Transform
D F T I	Distance From Threshold Indicator
D F V L R	Deutsche Forschungs- und Versuchsanstalt fur Luft- und Raumfahrt (Germany) (German Aerospace Research and Testing Institute)
D F W	Diffusion Welding
D G	Diesel Generator
D G A	Dense Grade Aggregate
D Ga O	Deutsche Gesellschaft fur angewandte Optik (Germany) (German Society for Applied Optics)
D G B	Deutsche Gewerkschaftsbund (Germany) (German Trade Union Confederation)
D G C M A	Defense and Government Contracts Management Association (USA)
D G D	Deutsche Gesellschaft fur Dokumentation (Germany) (German Society for Documentation)
D G E B A	Diglycidyl Ether of Bisphenol A
D G O R	Deutschen Gesellschaft fur Operations Research (Germany) (German Society for Operational Research)
D G R S T	Delegation Generale a la Recherche Scientifique et Technique (France) (Government Scientific and Technical Research Agency)
D G S O	Director-General of Safety (Operations) (of CAA)
D G T D	Directorate General of Technical Development (India)
D G V S	Doppler Ground Velocity System
D G Zf P	Deutsche Gesellschaft fur Zerstorungsfreie Pruvfverfahren (Germany) (German Society for Non-destructive Testing)
D H A	District Heating Association
D H I A	Dairy Herd Improvement Associations (USA)
D H O	Dihydrogen Oxide
D H S	Data Handling System
	Dual Hardness Steel
D H S S	Department of Health and Social Security
D H T	Discrete Hilbert Transform
D H X	Dump Heat Exchanger
D I	Delegation a l'Informatique (France) (Central Office for Data Processing)
	Desert Institute (Egypt)
D I A L	Databank Inquiry Answering Link
D I A L A T O R	Diagnostic Logic Simulator

D I A L S	Dendenkosha Immediate Arithmetic and Library Calculation System
D I C	Digital Integrating Computer
	Disseminated Intravascular Coagulation
D I C A P	Digital Circuit Analysis Programme
D I C A S S	Directional Command Activated Sonobuoy System
D I C U P	Dicumyl Peroxide
D I D D F	Dual Input Discrete Describing Function
D I D F	Dual Input Describing Function
D I D O	Device Independent Disk Open
D I E C A S T	Display Interaction Enhancing Computer Aided Shape Technique
D I E N	Diethyltriamine
D I F F T R A P	Digital Fast Fourier Transform Processor
D I G	Doppler-Inertial Gyrocompass
D I G S	Digital Inertial Guidance System
D I L	Digital Integrated Logic
D I L S	Doppler Instrument Landing System
D I M A	Direct Imaging Mass Analysis
D I M E	Disc Management Environment
D I M E L E C	Direction des Industries Mecaniques, Electriques et Electroniques (France)
D I M E S	Defense Integrated Management Engineering System (us Army)
	Digital Image Manipulation and Enhancement System
D I M P	Diisopropyl Methyl Phosphonate
D I N A	Direct Noise Amplification
D I N P	Diisononyl Phthalate
D I P	Defence Industry Productivity Programme (of Department of Industry, Trade and Commerce) (Canada)
	Ductile Iron Pipe
	Dynamic Inclined Plane
D I P E	Diisopropyl Ether
D I P S	Dendenkosha Information Processing System
	Digital Information Processing System
D I Q A P	Defence Industries Quality Assurance Panel (of MOD and Industry)
D I R	Defect Introduction Rate
	Defence Industrial Research Programme (of Defence Research Board (Canada))
D I R A C	Direct Access

D I S	prefix to numbered series of Draft International Standards (issued by ISO)
D I S A	Diffraction Size Frequency Analyser
D I S C L O S E	*Dunchurch Industrial Staff Training College* Learn Ourselves Exercise
D I S C O I D	Direct Scan Operating with Integrating Delays
D I S C O L A	Digital Integrated Solid-state Controller for Low-cost Automation
D I S C O P	Digital Simulation of Continuous Processes
D I S C U S	Disposal and Collection User Simulation
	Data-Line Concentration System
D I S F P	Disc Indexed Sequential File Management Package
D I S S P L A	Display Integrated Software System and Plotting Language
D I T	Dual Input Transponder
D I T A	Design-In Test Points and Alarms
D I T C	Department of Industry, Trade and Commerce (Canada)
D I V E M A	Divinyl Ethermaleic Anhydride
D K S	Dansk Kartografisk Selskab (Denmark) (Cartographic Society of Denmark)
D L A	Distributed Lumped Active
D L C	Data Link Control
D L C B	Drifting Limited *or* Low Capability Buoy
D L C O - E A	Desert Locust Control Organization for Eastern Africa (Ethiopia)
D L C S	Data-Line Concentration System
D L F E T	Depletion-mode Load Field Effect Transistor
D L G	Dynamic Lead Guidance
D L L	Dial Long Line
D L M	Depolarized Light Mixing
D L M A	Decorative Lighting Manufacturers and Distributors Association
D L O G S	Division Logistics System (US Army)
D L P	Division of Library Programs (USOE)
	Dynamic Limit Programming
D L S	Data Librarian System
	Dital Logic Simulator
D M A	Defense Mapping Agency (USDOD)
	Dimethylamine
	Direct Memory Access
	Division of Military Application (of USAEC)

D M A A	Dimethylacetamide
	Direct Mail Advertising Association (USA)
D M A A C	Defense Mapping Agency Aerospace Center (of DMA (USDOD))
D M A B	Dimethylamine Borane
D M A C	Direct Memory Access Channel
D M A C S	Descriptive Macro Code Generation System
D M A H C	Defense Mapping Agency Hydrographic Center (of DMA (USDOD))
D M A P P	Dimethylallyl Pyrophosphate
D Mat	prefix to numbered series of reports issued by Director of Research-Materials (MOD)
D M A T C	Defense Mapping Agency Topographic Center (of DMA (USDOD))
D M B	Double Mouldboard ploughing
D M B A	Dimethylbenzanthracene
D M D	Double Meridian Distance
D M D E L	Dimethyldiethyl Lead
D M E	Dynamic-Mission Equivalent
D M F A	Dimethylformamide
D M I	Department of Manpower and Immigration (Canada)
	Division of Manpower Intelligence (of Health Manpower Education Bureau (HEW) (USA))
D M I C	Defense Metals Information Center (Battelle Memorial Institute (USA) (now part of Metals and Ceramics Information Center)
D M L	Database Manipulation Language
	Data Macro Language
	Data Manipulation Language
D M N	Dimethylnitrosamine
D M O S	Double-diffused Metal Oxide Semiconductor
D M O S T	Double-diffused Metal Oxide Semiconductor Technology
D M P	Diisopropyl Methylphosphate
D M R C	Defence Maintenance and Repair Committee (MOD)
D M R L	Defence Metallurgical Research Laboratory (India)
D M S	Defense Mapping School (of DMA (USDOD))
	Dense Media Separation
	Digital Measuring System
	Dual Manoeuvring Simulator

D M S C	Defence Materiel Standardization Committee (of MOD)
D M S D S	Direct Mail Shelter Development System
D M S O	Dimethyl Sulphoxide
D M T	Deep Mobile Target
D M T G	Data Manipulation Task Group (of CODASYL)
D M T I	Digital Moving Target Indicator
D M T S	Dynamic Multi-Tasking System
D M V	Dual-Mode Vehicle
D M V S	Dynamic Manned Vehicle Simulator
D N A	Defense Nuclear Agency (USDOD)
	Direccion Nacional del Antartico (Argentina) (National Administration for the Antarctic)
	Direction de la Navigation Aerienne (France) (Civil Aviation Administration)
D N A C	Division of Numerical Analysis and Computing (of the National Physical Laboratory)
D N A M	Division of Numerical and Applied Mathematics (of the National Physical Laboratory)
D N C	Direct Numerical Control
D N E F	Departamento Nacional de Estradas de Ferro (Brazil) (National Department of Railways)
D N E R	Departamento Nacional de Estradas de Rodagem (Brazil) (National Department of Highways)
D N F	Disjunctive Normal Form
D N P	Deoxyribonucleoprotein
	Dinitrophenyl
D N P L	Daresbury Nuclear Physics Laboratory (of Science Research Council) (now the Daresbury Laboratory)
D N P M	Departamento Nacional de Producao Mineral (Brazil) (National Department for Mineral Production)
D N R	Department of National Revenue (Canada)
D N S	Department for National Savings
D N S S	Defence Navigation Satellite System
	Doppler Navigation Satellite System
D n V	Det norske Veritas (Norwegian Ship Classification Society)
D O	Dissolved Oxygen
D O A	Dominant Obstacle Allowance
D O A M S	Distant Object Attitude Measurement System
D O B	Depth of Burst

D O B E T A	Domestic Oil Burning Equipment Testing Association
D O C	Delay Opening Chaff
	Deoxycholate
	Dissolved Organic Carbon
D O C S	Distribution Operation Control System
D O C T O R	Dictionary Operation and Control for Thesaurus Organisation
D O D A C	Department of Defense (USA) Ammunition Code
D O E	Department of the Environment
D O L	Department of Labor (USA)
D O L A N	Design Office Language
D O M	Design-Out Maintenance
	Dissolved Organic Matter
	Dissolved Oxygen Monitor
D O M E X	Display Oriented Macro Expander
D O N A	Dynamic Organizational Network Analysis
D O O M	Deep Ocean Optical Measurement
D O R De C	Domestic Refrigeration Development Committee
D O R I S	Designer's On-line Real-time Interactive Secretary
D O R L S	Directors of Ontario Regional Library Systems (Canada)
D O S	Di-Octyl Sebacate
D O S P	Deep Ocean Sediment Probe
D O T	Displacement Oriented Transducer
	Domain Tip
D O T - H S	prefix to numbered series of Multidisciplinary Accident Investigations issued by Department of Transportation National Highway Traffic Safety Administration (USA)
D O T - T S C	Department of Transportation, Transportation Systems Center (USA)
D O T G	Di-o-tolyl-guanidine
D O T R A M	Domain Tip Random Access Memory
D O V	Data-over-Voice
D O V A C K	Differential, Oral, Visual, Aural, Computerised Kinaesthetic
D P A	Diphenylamine
	Direction de Piles Atomiques (of CEN (France)) (Directorate of Atomic Piles)
D P D	Dicyclopentadiene Dioxide
D P D S	Defense Property Disposal Service (of DSA (USDOD))

D P E T	Diretoria de Pesquisas e Ensino Tecnico (Brazil) (Directorate of Research and Technical Education of the Brazilian Army)
D P F	Dense Plasma Focus
D P G	Diphosphoglycerate
D P M	Digital Panel Meter
D P N	Dipropylnitrosamine
D P O	Diphenyl Oxide
D P P	Diphenylol Propane
D P P H	Diphenylpicrylhydrazyl
D P R	Dial Pulse Receiver
	Direct Particle Rolling
D P S	Descent Propulsion System
	Design Problem Solver
	Deterministic Pattern Search
	Dial Pulse Sender
	Differential Phase Shift
	Disc Programming System
	Distributed-Parameter System
D Q A B	Defence Quality Assurance Board (MOD)
D R	Danmarks Radio (Denmark)
	prefix to numbered series of reports issued by the Defence Research Board (Canada)
	prefix to numbered series of reports issued by Atmospheric Sciences Laboratory of ECOM (US Army)
D R A E	Defence Research Analysis Establishment (Department of National Defence (Canada))
D R B C	Delaware River Basin Commission (USA)
D R C	Disaster Research Center (Ohio State University (USA))
D R C M	Differential Reinforced Clostridial Medium
D R E S S	Dendenkosha Real-time Sales and Inventory Management System
D R I	Direct Read-out Infra-red
	Dynamic Response Index
D R I - U P	Decent Respectable Individuals - United for Progress (USA) (a society)
D R I C	Defence Research Information Centre (MOD (PE))
D R I F T	Diagnostic Retrievable Information For Teachers
D R I P	Digital Ray and Intensity Projector
D R I R	Direct Read-out Infra-Red
D R L	Data Retrieval Language
D R L (M)	Defence Research Laboratory (Materials) (India)

D R L M S	Digital Radar Land Mass Simulator
D R M E	Direction des Recherches et Moyens d'Essais (France) (Defence Agency for the Coordination of Research and Testing)
D R M P	Division of Regional Medical Programs (of NIH (USA))
D R O	Disablement Resettlement Officer
D R P G	Detroit (USA) Rubber and Plastics Group
D R R	Division of Research Resources (of NIH (USA))
D R S	Data Relay Satellite
D R U G R	Drug Registry programme
D S	Decomposition Sintering
D S A	Defense Supply Association (USA) (now American Logistics Association)
	Dielectric Stimulated Arcing
	Dimensionally Stable Anode
	Door and Shutter Association
	Down Sensor Assembly
D S A A	Defense Security Assistance Agency (USDOD)
D S A C	Defence Scientific Advisory Council (MOD)
	Defense Security Assistance Council (USDOD)
D S A R C	Defense Systems Acquisition Review Council (USDOD)
D S B	Danske Statsbaner (Denmark) (Danish State Railways)
D S B S C	Double Sideband Suppressed Carrier
D S C	Differential Scanning Calorimetry
	Dynamically Self-Checked
D S Cl	Durable Sprayed Cladding
D S D	Data-Scanner Distributor
D S D T	Deformographic Storage Display Tube
	Discrete-Space Discrete-Time
D S F	Dansk Skibsteknisk Forkningsinstitut (Denmark) (Danish Ship Research Institute)
D S F C	Direct Side Force Control
D S F T	Detection Scheme with Fixed Thresholds
D S G	Digital Signal Generator
D S I	Dairy Science International (USA)
D S I D	Disposable Seismic Intrusion Detector
D S I S	Defence Scientific Information Service (of DRB (Canada))
D S I S I	Double-Sided Inter-Symbol Interference
D S L	Defence Science Laboratory (India)
	Digital Simulation Language

D S L I M	Double-Sided Linear Induction Motor
D S L T	Detection Scheme with Learning of Thresholds
D S M	Dynamic Scattering Mode
D S M S	Defense Systems Management School (USDOD)
D S N S	Division of Space Nuclear Systems (USAEC)
	Doppler Sonar Navigation System
D S O	Data Set Optimiser
D S P	Direct System Platemaker
D S S	Deep Seismic Sounding
	Distribution System Simulator
D S S M	Digital Signal Sinusoidal Modulation
D S T L	Digital-Summation Threshold-Logic
D S U C R	Doppler-Shifted Ultrasonic Cyclotron Resonance
D T	Delta Technique
	Deuterium-Tritium
D T A	Direccao de Exploracao dos Transportes Aereos (Mozambique)
	Dynamic Test Article
D T A S	Data Transmission And Switching System
D T A S I	Digital Time Assignment Speech Interpolation
D T B	Danmarks Tekniske Bibliotek (Denmark) (National Technical Library of Denmark)
D T C	Desk Top Computer
D T D	prefix to numbered series of Specifications issued by MINTECH, later by DTI and Ministry of Aviation Supply, and now by MOD(PE) (published by HMSO)
D T E	Dynamic Tear Energy
D T G	Derivative Thermogravimetry
D T I	Department of Trade and Industry (formed in 1970 by the amalgamation of the Board of Trade and part of the Ministry of Technology)
D T M	Digital Talk-out Module
D S T L	Digital Test Oriented Language
D T S	Diagnostic Test Sequence
D T S S	*Dartmouth (College)* (USA) Time-Sharing System
D T U L	Deflection Temperature Under Load
D U A L	Dynamic Universal Assembly Language
D U A Labs	National Data Use and Access Laboratories (USA)
D U C K	prefix to numbered series of reports issued by Drexel University Combustion Kinetics Laboratory (USA)
D U L	Design Ultimate Load

D U N M I R E	*Dundee University* Numerical Methods Information Retrieval Experiment
D U T	Device Under Test
D U V	Data-under-Voice
D U X	Data Utility Complex
D V A	Design Verification Article
D V B	Disability Veiling Brightness
	Divinylbenzene
D V C C S	Differential Voltage Controlled Current Source
D V G W	Deutscher Verein vor Gas-und Wasserfachmannern (Germany) (German Society of Gas and Water Experts)
D V P	Discounted Present Value
D W	Drop-Weight
D W M I	Diamond Wheel Manufacturers Institute (USA)
D W R	Divided Winding-Rotor
D Y D E	Dynamic Debugger
D Y N A M O	Dynamic Modeller
D Y N A M O - S	Dynamic Modeller-Simulator
D Y N A S A R	Dynamic Systems Analyzer
D Y N F E T	Dynamic Four Phase Non-overlapping Clock Field Effect Transistor
D Y N S Y S	Dynamics Systems Simulator
D Z W	Deutsche Dokumentations Zentrale Wasser (Germany) (German Water Documentation Office)

E

E A	Environmental Agency (Japan)
E A A	Electronics Association of Australia (Australia)
	Experimental Aircraft Association (USA)
E A A A	European Association of Advertising Agencies (Switzerland)
E A C	East African Community
	Effective Attenuation Coefficient
E A C R P	European-American Committee on Reactor Physics
E A D I	Extrapolated Alternating Direction Implicit
E A E	Experimental Autoimmune Encephalomyelitis
E A E M	European Airlines Electronics Meeting
E A E S P	Escola de Administracao de Empresas de Sao Paula (Brazil) (Sao Paula School of Business Administration)

E A E T	East African External Telecommunications Company
E A F F R O	East African Freshwater Fisheries Research Organisation (Uganda)
E A F I T	Escuela y Finanzas e Instituto Technologico (Colombia) (Management School)
E A G	Electro-Antennogram
E A H Y	European Architectural Heritage Year
E A I M R	East African Institute for Medical Research (Tanzania)
E A I R O	East African Industrial Research Organization (Kenya)
E A L A	East African Library Association (dissolved 1973)
E A L R C	East African Leprosy Research Centre (Uganda)
E A L S	East African Literature Service (Headquarters in East African Agriculture and Forestry Research Organization (Kenya))
E A M C	European Airlines Montparnasse Committee
E A M D	East African Meteorological Department (Kenya)
E A M F R O	East African Marine Fisheries Research Organization (Tanzania)
E A M R C	East African Medical Research Council (Tanzania)
E A M T C	European Association of Management Training Centres (now European Foundation for Management Development)
E A M V B D	East African Institute of Malaria and Vector-Borne Diseases (Tanzania)
E A P C O	East African Pesticides Control Organization
E A P M	European Association for Personnel Management
E A P T	East African Posts and Telecommunications Corporation
E A R	East African Railways
	Experimental Array Radar
E A R B	European Airlines Research Bureau (Belgium)
E A R L	Electronically Accessible Russian Lexicon
	Extended Algorithmic " R " Languages
E A R O M	Electrically Alterable Read-Only Memory
E A R S	Electro-Acoustic Rating System
	Epilepsy Abstracts Retrieval System
E A S	Electronique Aero-Spatiale (France)
	Equivalent Airspeed

E A S C O N	Electronics and Aerospace Systems Convention and Exposition (IEEE (USA))
E A S E	Escape And Survival Equipment
E A S P	prefix to numbered series of Edgewood Arsenal (US Army) Special Publications
E A T C	Electronic Automatic Temperature Controller
E A T I C	East African Tuberculosis Investigation Centre (Kenya)
E A T R O	East African Trypanosomiasis Research Organisation (Uganda)
E A V R I	East African Virus Research Institute (Uganda)
E A V R O	East African Veterinary Research Organization (Kenya)
E B	Estradiol Benzoate
E B A A	Eye Bank Association of America (USA)
E B C S	European Barge Carrier System
E B E S S A	Societe Reunis d'Energie du Bassin de l'Escaut SA (Belgium)
E B F	Externally Blown Flap
E B I	Electron Drift Instability
E B I C	Electron Beam Induced Current
E B I R	Electron Bombardment Induced Response
E B I R D	Electron Beam Ionization of Semiconductor Devices
E B M	Electron Beam Microanalysis
	English Beet Molasses
E B M L M	Electron Beam Membrane Light Modulator
E B P	Estradiol Binding Protein
E B Q	Economic Batch Quantity
E B R	Electron Beam Recorder
	Electron Beam Recording
	Electron Beam Reproducer
E B S	Electron Beam Semiconductor
	Electron Bombarded Semiconductor
	Electron Bombarded Silicon
	Emergency Broadcast System (USA)
E B S C	European Bird Strike Committee
E B W	Electron Beam Welding
E C	Electrical Conductivity
	Electrochromic
	Electronic Calculator
	European Communities (consisting of ECSC, EEC, EURATOM)
E C / L S S	Environmental Control/Life Support System

E C A	Electronic Control Amplifier
E C A C	European Civil Aviation Conference
E C A M	Extended Communications Access Method
E C B	Efferent Cochlear Bundle
	Electrically Controlled Bi-refringence
	Environmental Conservation Board (of the Graphic Communications Industries (USA))
E C C	Electrochemical Concentration Cell
	Equipment Configuration Control
E C C P	Engineering Concepts Curriculum Project (USA)
E C C S	Emergency Core Cooling System
E C F M G	Educational Council for Foreign Medical Graduates (USA)
E C F R P C	East Central Florida Regional Planning Council (USA)
E C G D	Export Credits Guarantee Department
E C H	Electron Cyclotron Heating
E C H O	Enteric Cytopathogenic Human Orphan
E C I L	Electronics Corporation of India Limited (India) (government owned)
E C I P	European Cooperation in Information Processing (an organisation)
E C L	Electrogenerated Chemiluminescence
E C L A	Economic Commission for Latin America (of UN)
E C L A T E L	Empresa Commercial Latinoamericana de Tele-comunicaciones (Latin America Commercial Telecommunications Enterprise)
E C L S S	Environmental Control and Life Support System
E C M	Equivalence Class Mask
	Extended Core Memory
E C M & M R	European College of Marketing and Marketing Research
E C M A	European Computer Manufacturers Association
E C M B	European Conference on Molecular Biology
E C M R A	European Chemical Marketing Research Association
E C M W F	European Centre for Medium-range Weather Forecasting
E C N L	Equivalent-Continuous Noise Level
E C O D U	European *Control Data* Users Association
E C O P E T R O L	Empressa Colombiana de Petroles (Colombia) (State oil company)
E C O R	Engineering Committee on Oceanic Resources (of CEI and the Royal Society)

E C O R	Engineering Committee on Ocean Resources (of IOC (UNESCO))
E C O S E C	European Cooperation Space Environment Committee
E C P	Electronic Channelling Pattern
	Exchange Control Programme
E C P E	External Combustion Piston Engine
E C P S	Effective-Candle-Power-Seconds
E C Q A C	Electronic Components Quality Assurance Committee
E C R	Electronic Cash Register
	Endogenous Circadian Rhythm
	Error Cause Removal
E C R H	Electron Cyclotron Resonance Heating
E C R I	Emergency Care Research Institute (USA)
E C S	Electrochemical Society (USA)
	European Communication Satellite
	Executive Compensation Service (of Management Centre Europe)
	Experimental Communications Satellite
E C S L	Extended Control and Simulation Language
E C S S	European Communication Satellite System
	Extendable Computer System Simulator
E C T C	East Coast Telecommunications Center (of STRATCOM)
E C U	Experimental Cartography Unit (of Natural Environment Research Council)
E C U T O R I A N A	Compania Ecuatoriana de Aviacion (Ecuador)
E D	Electrodeposition
	Electro-Dialysis
	prefix to numbered series of reports issued by Engineering Division, Army Engineer Reactors Group (US Army)
	numbered series of Exposure Drafts issued by Accounting Standards Steering Committee
E D A	Economic Development Administration (of Department of Commerce (USA))
	European Disposables Association
E D A - O E R	Economic Development Administration, Office of Economic Research (Department of Commerce (USA))
E D A X	Energy Dispersive Analysis X-ray
E D B	Export Data Branch (of DTI)
E D C	Electronic Digital Computer

E D C	Energy Distribution Curve
E D C L	Electric-Discharge Convection Laser
E D E	Electronic Defence Evaluator
E D F	Environmental Defense Fund (USA)
E D I N E T	Education Instruction Network
E D M F	Extended Data Management Facility
E D M L	Electric Discharge Mixing Laser
E D P	Experimental Data Processor
E D R	Experimenterende Danske Radiomatorer (Denmark) (Danish Amateur Radio Society)
E D R C	Economic and Development Review Committee (of OECD)
E D R S	ERIC Document Reproduction Service (USOE)
	Expanded Data Reporting System
E D S	Electronic Data Switching
	Energy Dispersive Spectrometer
	Environmental Data Service (formerly of ESSA now of NOAA (USA))
E D S A T	Educational Satellite
E D S T M	Environmental Data Service Technical Memoranda (formerly of ESSA now NOAA (USA))
E D T	Electrodeless Discharge Tube
E D X	Energy Dispersive X-ray analysis
E E	Exoelectron
E E A	Educational Equipment Association
	Essential Elements of Analysis
	Explosive Embedment Anchor
E E C	EUROCONTROL Experimental Centre (France)
E E C G S	Emergency Evaporative Coolant Garment System
E E E	Eastern Equine Encephalitis
	Electrical, Electronic and Electro-mechanical
	Exoelectron Emission
E E L	Emergency Exposure Limit
E E P	Engineering Experimental Phase buoy
E E P A C	Eastern Electronics Packaging Conference (USA)
E E P C	Engineering Export Promotion Council (India)
E E Q	Empresa Electrica Quito (Ecuador)
E E R	prefix to numbered series of reports issued by Ohio University, Department of Electrical Engineering (USA)
	Energy-Efficiency Ratio
E E R A	Electrical and Electronic Retailers Association
E E R C	Earthquake Engineering Research Center (California University (USA))

E E R L	Explosive Excavation Research Laboratory (US Army)
E E R O	Explosive Excavation Research Office (of AEWES (US Army))
E E S D	Electromechanical and Environmental Systems Division (of CERL (US Army))
E F A	Empresa Ferrocarriles Argentinos (Argentine) (Argentine State Railways)
E F A B	Establissement d'Etudes et de Fabrications d'Armaments de Bourges (of Groupement Industriel des Armements Terrestres (France))
E F C	Equivalent Full Charges
	Etched Flexible Circuitry
E F C E	European Federation of Chemical Engineers
E F C I S	Societe pour l'Etude et la Fabrication de Circuits Integres Speciaux (France)
E F C S	European Federation of Cytological Societies
E F D A R S	Expandable Flight Data Acquisition and Recording System
E F F F	Electrical Field-Flow Fractionation
E F I	Electronic Fuel Injection
	Enrico Fermi Institute (University of Chicago (USA))
E F I E	Electric Field Integral Equation
E F L	Emitter Function Logic
E F M D	European Foundation for Management Development
E F N M S	European Federation of National Maintenance Societies
E F O P	Economic Feasibility of Projects and Investments
E F P H	Effective Full Power Hours
E F P S	European Federation of Productivity Services
E F T	Embedded Figure Test
E F T A	European Flexographic Technical Association
E F V A	Educational Foundation for Visual Aids
E G A	Effluent Gas Analysis
E G A T	Electricity Generating Authority of Thailand (Thailand)
E G C	Economic Growth Center (Yale University (USA))
E G C M	European Group for Co-operation in Management
E G M E	Ethylene Glycol Monomethyl Ether
E G P	Ethno-, geo-, polycentric
E G P C	Egyptian General Petroleum Corporation (Egypt)

E G R	Exhaust Gas Re-circulation
	Exhaust Gas Re-cycle
E H A A	Epidemic Hepatitis Associated Antigen
E H D	Elastohydrodynamic
E H L	Elastohydrodynamic Lubrication
	Environmental Health Laboratory (USAF)
E H M O	Extended Huckel Molecular Orbital
E H S	Environmental Health Service (of PHS (USA))
E H S I	Electronic Horizontal Situation Indicator
E H T	Electrothermal Hydrazine Thruster
E H V	Extra High Voltage
E I	Electron Impact
E I A - J	Electronics Industry Association of Japan (Japan)
E I A C	Electronic Industries Association of Canada (Canada)
E I A J	Engineering Industries Association of Japan (Japan)
E I C O N	Electronic Index Console
E I D	Electron Impact Desorption
	Electron-induced Ion Desorption
E I E M A	Electrical Installation Equipment Manufacturers Association
E I L	Electrical Insulating Liquids
	Engineers India Limited (India) (government owned technical consultancy agency)
E I M M A	East India Metal Merchants Association (India)
E I P C	European Institute of Printed Circuits
E I R	Eidgenossisches Institut fur Reaktorforschung (Switzerland) (Federal Institute for Reactor Research)
E I R A	Ente Italiano Rilievi Aerofotogrammetrici (Italy) (National Authority for Survey by Aerial Photo-grammetry)
E I S	Electronic Inquiry System
	Environmental Impact Statement
	Export Intelligence Service (of DTI)
	Extended Instruction Set
E I W L S	Extended Iterative Weighted Least Squares
E I Z	Engineering Institute of Zambia (Zambia)
E J P	Excitatory Junctional Potential
E L A	Equipment Leasing Association
E L A B	Elektronikklaboratoriet (of NTH (Norway))
E L A M P	Exchange Line Multiplexer Analysis Programme
E L A S	Elasticity (a group of computer programmes)

E L B	Emergency Locator Beacon
E L C A	Electronic Linear Circuit Analysis programme
E L C B	Earth-Leakage Circuit Breaker
E L C U	Electrical Control Unit
E L D C	European Lead Development Committee
E L D O	European Space Vehicle Launcher Development Organization (to be merged into a new European Space Agency in 1974)
E L E C S Y S	Integrated Electronic Engineering System
Electro - R A M	Electro-mechanical Redundant Actuator Mechanism
E L E E D	Elastic Low Energy Electron Diffraction
E L I P S	Electron Image Projection System
E L M S	Experimental Library Management System
E L R	Environmental Report (a numbered series issued by many authorities in the USA—to identify the specific body originating the report it is often necessary to know also the EIS (Environmental Impact Statement) Number)
E L R A F T	Efficient Logic Reduction Analysis of Fault Trees
E L S A	Electronic Lobe Switching Antenna
	Experimental System for Simulation and Animation
E L S A G	Elettronica San Giorgio (Italy)
E L S B M	Exposed Location Single Buoy Mooring
E L S I	Extra Large Scale Integrated
E L S I E	Electronic Location of Status Indicating Equipment
	Emergency Life-Saving Instant Exit
E M A	Egyptian Medical Association (Egypt)
	Electron Microprobe Analysis
	Engine Manufacturers Association (USA)
E M A C	Educational Media Association of Canada (Canada)
E M A G	Electron Microscopy and Analysis Group (of the Institute of Physics)
E M A S	*Edinburgh (University)* Multi-Access System
	Employment Medical Advisory Service (of Department of Employment)
E M B R A T E L	Empresa Brasileira de Telecomunicacoes (Brazil) (State owned company for inter-state and international telecommunication services)
E M C D A S	Electro-Magnetic Compatibility Data Acquisition System

E M C O N	European Congress on Electron Microscopy
E M D	Eidgenossische Militar-department (Switzerland) (Federal Defence Department)
	Electronique Marcel Dassault (France)
E M E	Electromagnetic Effectiveness
	Electromagnetic Emission
E M F	European Meeting on Ferroelectrics
E M I S	Ecosytem of Machines Information System
	Effluent Management Information System
E M I T	Enzyme Multiplied Immunassay Technique
E M L	Earthquake Mechanisms Laboratory (of ESSA (USA)) (later of NOAA, then transferred in 1973 to USGS)
	Equal Matrix Languages
E M M	Earth, Moon and Mars
	Electron Mirror Microscope
E M M A	Electronic Mask Making Apparatus
	Electronic Mathematic Model-Analogue
	Electron Microscope-Microprobe Analyser
	Engineering Mock-up and Manufacturing Aid
	Equalized Maintenance, Maximum Availability
	Eye Movement Measuring Apparatus
E M O S	European Meteorological Satellite
E M P	Ethylmercury Phosphate
E M P A	Electron Microprobe Analysis
	European Maritime Pilots Association
E M P A S S	Electromagnetic Performance of Aircraft and Ships System (a project of the USN)
E M P H A S I S	Evaluation Management using Past History Analysis for Scientific Inventory Simulation
E M P R E M A R	Empresa Maritima del Estado (Chile)
E M P R E S S	Electromagnetic Pulse Radiation Environment Simulator for Ships
E M R	Electromagnetic Riveting
	Department of Energy, Mines and Resources (Canada)
E M R L	Engineering Materials Research Laboratory (Brown University (USA))
E M R O	Eastern Mediterranean Regional Office (of WHO (UN))
E M S	Electromagnetic Susceptibility
	Electromotive Surface
E M S A	Electron Microscopy Society of America (USA)
	Electron Microscope Surface Area

E M T	Electromechanical Transmission
E M U	Electronic Materials Unit (of RRE)
E M V	Expected Monetary Values
E N A	Ecole Nationale d'Administration (France) (National School of Management)
E N A C	Ecole Nationale de l'Aviation Civile (France) (National School of Civil Aviation)
E N A P	Empresa Nacional de Petroleo (Chile) (National Petroleum Authority)
	Escuela Nacional de Administracion Publica (El Salvador) (National School of Public Administration)
E N B	Ethylidenenorborene
E N C O E	British National Committee on Ocean Engineering
E N C O R E	Enlarged Compact by Respond
E N D	External Negative Differential
E N D C	Eighteen Nation Committee on Disarmament (later Conference of the Committee on Disarmament)
E N D E S A	Empresa Nacional de Electricidad SA (Chile) (National Electricity Authority)
E N D E X	Environmental Data Index
E N D F	Evaluated Nuclear Data File
E N E A	European Nuclear Energy Agency (of OECD) (now NEA)
E N E L	Ente Nazional per l'Energia Elettrica (Italy) (State Electricity Authority)
E N H E R	Empresa Nacional Hidroelectrica del Ribagorzana (Spain)
E N I	Ente Nazionale Idrocarburi (Italy) (National Hydrocarbons Authority)
E N M G	Electroneuromyographic
E N P I	Ente Nazionale per la Prevenzione degli Infortuni (Italy) (National Authority for Accident Prevention)
E N P O C O N	Environmental Pollution Control
E N P V	Expected Net Present Value
E N R	Emissora Nacional de Radiodifusao (Portugal)
E N S A E	Ecole Nationale Superieure de l'Aeronautique et de l'Espace (France) (National College for Aeronautics and Aerospace)
E N S A I S	Ecole Nationale Superieure des Arts et Industrie de Strasbourg (France)

E N S B	Ecole Nationale Superieure de Bibliothecaires (France) (National College of Librarianship)
E N S I D E S A	Empresa Nacional Siderurgica SA (Spain)
E N S T A	Ecole Nationale Superieure de Techniques Avancees (France) (National College of Advanced Techniques)
E N T	Empresa Nacional de Telecomunicaciones (Argentine) (National Telecommunications Authority)
E N T E L	Empresa Nacional de Telecomunicaciones (Bolivia) (National Telecommunications Authority)
	Empresa Nacional de Telecomunicaciones (Ecuador) (National Telecommunications Authority)
	Empresa Nacional de Telecomunicaciones (Peru) (National Telecommunications Authority)
	Empresa Nacional de Telecomunicaciones (Chile) (National Telecommunications Authority)
E N U S A	Empresa Nacional del Uranio SA (Spain)
E N V I T E C	International Exhibition for Environmental Protection and Environmental Technique
E O A R	European Office of Aerospace Research (USAF)
E O D	Explosive Ordnance Disposal
E O I	Electro-Optical Imaging
E O I S	Electro-Optical Imaging System
E O Q C	European Organisation for Quality Control (Netherlands)
E O S	Earth Observation Satellite
	Earth Observatory Spacecraft
	Earth to Orbit Shuttle
	Equation Of State
E O S S	Earth Orbital Space Station
	Engineering Operational Sequencing System
E P A	Economic Planning Agency (Japan)
	Electron Probe Analyzer
	Environmental Protection Agency (USA)
E P A B X	Electronic Private Automatic Branch Exchange
E P A S A	Electron Probe Analysis Society of America (USA)
E P C	Economic Policy Committee (of OECD)
	Edge Punched Card
	Educational Publishers Council
	Electrically Pulsed Chamber
	Engine-Performance Computer
	Experiment Pointing and Control
E P C A	European Petrochemical Association

E P E R A	Extractor Parachute Emergency Release Assembly
E P F	European Packaging Federation (Netherlands)
E P G A	Emergency Petroleum and Gas Administration (USA)
E P I C	Electronically Processed Inter-unit Cabling
	Electronic Properties Information Center (USAF) (now under Purdue University (USA))
	Engineers Public Information Council (USA)
	Epitaxial Passivated Integrated Circuit
	Evidence Photographers International Council (USA)
	Extended Programme for Individual Compensation
E P I D	Electrophoretic Image Display
E P I R B	Emergency Position-Indicating Radio Beacon
E P L	Economic Policy and Licensing (a branch of the Civil Aviation Authority)
E P L O	Electronic Plotting
E P M	Electrophoretic Mobility
E P M S	Engine Performance Monitoring System
E P O C	Earthquake Prediction Observation Centre (of ERI (Japan))
	Eastern Pacific Ocean Conference
E P P	Erythropoietic Protoporphyria
E P P M A	Expanded Polystyrene Product Manufacturers Association
E P P M P	European Power Press Manufacturers Panel
E P P S	Edwards Personal Preference Schedule
E P R	Exhaust Pressure Ratio
	Eye-Point-of-Regard
E P R I	Electric Power Research Institute (USA)
E P S	Electric Propulsion System
E P S E L	Electric Power Systems Engineering Laboratory (Massachusetts Institute of Technology (USA))
E P S O C	Earth Physics Satellite Observation Campaign (initiated by the Smithsonian Astrophysical Observatory)
E P S P	Excitatory Post-Synaptic Potential
E P S S	Experimental Packet Switched Service (of the British Post Office)
E P T	Electronic Perspective Transformation system
E P T I S A	Estudios y Proyectos Tecnicos Industriales SA (Spain)
E P Z	Electron Polar Zone

E Q D	Electrical Quality Assurance Directorate (of MINTECH (now of MOD (PE))
E Q Q	Electric Quadrupole-Quadrupole
E R	prefix to numbered series of Economic Regulations issued by the Civil Aeronautics Board (USA)
	Electro-reflectance
	Endoplasmic Reticulum
E R A	Earthquake Risk Analysis
	Electron Ring Accelerator
	European Rotogravure Association (Germany)
	Evaporative Rate Analysis
E R A P	Earth Resources Aircraft Program (USA)
	Exchange Feeder Route Analysis Programme
E R A S E	Electronic Radiation Source Eliminator
E R A U	Embry-Riddle Aeronautical University (USA)
E R B	Earth Radiation Budget
	Economic Requirement Batching
	Engineers Registration Board (of the Council of Engineering Institutions)
E R C	Engineering and Research Center (of Bureau of Reclamation (USA))
	Engineering Research Center (Arizona State University (USA))
	Environmental Resources Center (Georgia Institute of Technology (USA))
E R C P	Endoscopic Retrograde Cholangiopancreatography
E R D E	Explosives Research and Development Establishment (MINTECH) (now MOD (PE))
E R D L	Explosives Research and Development Laboratory (India)
E R E P	Earth Resources Experiment Package
E R F A	Conference on Economics of Route Air Navigation Facilities and Airports
E R I	Earthquake Research Institute (Tokyo University (Japan))
	Engineering Research Institute (Iowa State University (USA))
E R I A	Estudios y Realizaciones en Informatic a Aplicada (Spain)
E R I C / ch E S S	ERIC Clearinghouse for Social Studies (University of Colorado and Social Science Education Consortium (USA))

E R I C / C L I S	ERIC Clearinghouse on Library and Information Sciences (American Society for Information Science (USA))
E R I C / C R E S S	ERIC Clearinghouse on Rural Education and Small Schools (New Mexico State University (USA))
E R I R	Extended-Range Instrumentation Radar
E R I S T A R	Earth Resources Information Storage, Transformation, Analysis and Retrieval (of Auburn University (USA))
E R L	Emergency Reference Level
	ESSA Research Laboratories (USA) (now Environmental Research Laboratories (of NOAA (USA))
E R L T M	Environmental Research Laboratories Technical Memorandum (of NOAA (USA))
E R L U A	Environmental Research Laboratory, University of Arizona (USA)
E R M A C	Electromagnetic Radiation Management Advisory Council (USA)
E R M S	Electrical Resistivity Measuring System
E R N	Effective Radiation Node
E R N I E	Electronic Random Number Indicating Equipment
E R O P A	Eastern Regional Organization for Public Administration (Philippines)
E R O S	Earth Resources Observation Systems (a program of USGS (USA))
E R O W S	Expendable Remote-Operating Weather Station
E R R	Explosive Echo-Ranging
E R S P	Earth Resources Survey Program (USA)
E R U P T	Elementary Reliability Unit Parameter Technique
E R V	Expiratory Reserve Volume
	Extract-Release Volume
E S	Environmental Survey
E S A	Employment Standards Administration (of Department of Labor (USA))
	European Space Agency (to be formed in 1974 by merging ELDO and ESRO)
E S A A	Electricity Supply Association of Australia (Australia)
E S A C	Environmental Systems Applications Center (Indiana University (USA))
E S A R	Employment Service Automatic Reporting system

E S C	Electronic Systems Committee (of SAE (USA))
	Elongation-Sensitive Cell
	Erythropoietin-sensitive Stem Cells
	Evanescent Space Charge
E S C A W T	European Steering Committee for APT Workshop Technology
E S C E S	Experimental Satellite Communication Earth Station (of ISRO (India))
E S C I	European Society for Clinical Investigation
E S C O W	Engineering and Scientific Committee on Water (New Zealand)
E S D	Electronics Systems Division (of ISRO (India))
	Electron Simulated Desorption
	Export Services Division (of DTI)
E S D A C	European Space Data Centre (of ESRO) (now Department of Information Handling of ESOC (ESRO))
E S D E R C	European Semiconductor Device Research Conference
E S D L	*Electro Technical Laboratory* (Japan) System Description Language
E S F	European Social Fund
	Extended Spooling Facility
E S F I	Epitaxial Silicon Films on Insulators
E S G	Electronik-System-Gesellschaft (Germany)
	Electrosplanchnography
E S I C	Environmental Science Information Center (of EDS (NOAA) (USA))
E S I P	Engineering Societies International Publications Committee
E S L	Earth Sciences Laboratories (of ESSA (now NOAA) (USA))
	Earth Sciences Laboratory (of USAETL)
	Electroscience Laboratory (of Ohio State University (USA))
E S L A B	European Space (Research) Laboratory (of ESRO) (now Department of Space Science of ESTEC (ESRO))
E S M	Education Simulation Model (of UNESCO)
E S M A	Engraved Stationery Manufacturers Association (USA)
E S M A L U X	Societe d'Electricite de Sambre-et-Meuse, des Ardennes et du Luxembourg (Belgium)
E S M R	Electrically Scanning Microwave Radiometer

E S O	European Southern Observatory (Hamburg, Germany) (administered by six European States)
E S O C	European Space Operations Centre (of ESRO)
E S O M A R	European Society for Opinion and Market Research (Belgium)
E S O N E	European Standards of Nuclear Electronics (of EURATOM)
E S P	Echeloned Series Processor
	Electromagnetic Surface Profiler
	Electronic Systems Planning
	Electro-Static Precipitation
	Engineering Society of Pennsylvania (USA)
	Extended Segment Processing
E S P D	Export Services and Promotions Division (of DTI)
E S R	Electronic Slide-Rule
	Equivalent Series Resistance
	Erythrocyte Sedimentation Rate
E S R A N G E	European Space (Sounding-Rocket Launching) Range (of ESRO) (transferred to the control of Sweden in 1972 but retains name)
E S R M	Electroslag Remelting
E S R O	European Space Research Organization (to be merged into a European Space Agency in 1974)
E S S A D F	Electronic Switching System Arranged with Data Features
E S S A	Environmental Science Services Administration (Department of Commerce (USA)) (merged into NOAA in 1970)
	Environmental Survey Satellite
E S S D E R C	European Solid State Device Research Conference
E S T	Elastic Surface Transformation
E S T A	Earth Sciences Technologies Association (USA)
	Electronically-Scanned TACAN Antenna
E S T L	European Space Tribology Laboratory (of ESRO)
E S T P	Electronic Satellite Tracking Programme (of International Association of Geodesy)
E S T R A C K	European Space Satellite Tracking and Telemetry Network (of ESRO) (now Department of Satellite Data Acquisition of ESOC (ESRO))
E S V	Experimental Safety Vehicle
E T	Effective Temperature
	Ethanthiol

E T	Evapo-transpiration
ETA/MDUSAS	*Engineering Technology Analysts, Inc.* Mobile Drilling Unit Structural Analysis System
E T A / N A M E	*Engineering Technology Analyst, Inc.* Naval Architecture Marine Engineering computer programme
E T A S	Etablissement d'Experiences Techniques d'Angers (of DTAT (France))
E T B	Electronic Test Block
E T B S	Etablissement d'Experiences Techniques de Bourges (of DTAT (France))
E T C	Earth Terrain Camera
	Extendible Compiler
E T F A	European Technological Forecasting Association
E T H	Extra-Terrestrial Hypothesis
E T I C	English-Teaching Information Centre (of the British Council)
E T I P	Experimental Technology Incentives Program (of NSF and NBS (USA))
E T K	Epitesugyi Tajekoztatasi Kozpont (Hungary) (Information Centre for Building)
E T L	Electro Technical Laboratory (Japan) (now General Electronic Research Laboratory)
	Emergency Tolerance Limit
E T N A	Electrolevel-Theodolite Naval Alignment system
E T N S	Electronic Train Number System
E T P M	Societe Entrepose pour les Travaux Petroliers Maritimes (France)
E T R	Effective Thyroxine Ratio
E T R A C	Educational Television and Radio Association of Canada (Canada)
E T S	Educational Time-sharing System
	Electronic Translator System
	Engineering Test Satellite
	European Tetratology Society (Sweden)
E T S U	East Tennessee State University (USA)
E T U	Ethylene Thiourea
E T V	Elevating Transfer Vehicle
E U C L I D	Easily Used Computer Language for Illustrations and Drawings
E U D I S E D	European Documentation and Information System for Education (of the Council of Europe)

E U G R O P A	Union des Distributeurs de Papiers et Cartons de la CEE (Union of Distributors of Paper and Cardboard of the European Economic Community)
Eu I G	Europium Iron Garnet
E U M A B O I S	European Committee of Woodworking Machinery Manufacturers
E U M A P R I N T	European Committee of Associations of Printing and Paper Converting Machinery Manufacturers
E U R	prefix to numbered-lettered series of reports issued by EURATOM
E U R E M A I L	Conference de l'Industrie Europeenne Productrice d'Articles Emailles (Conference of the European Industry for the Production of Enamelled Goods)
E U R I M	European Conference on Research into the Management of Information Systems and Libraries
E U R O A V I A	Association of European Aeronautical and Astronautical Students
E U R O C A E	European Organisation for Civil Aviation Electronics (France)
E U R O C E A N	European Oceanographic Association
E U R O C H E M I C	European Organisation for the Chemical Processing of Irradiated Fuels (of OECD)
E U R O C O N	European Conference on Electrotechnics
E U R O C O T O N	Comite des Industries du Coton et des Fibres Connexes de la CEE (Committee of the Cotton Industries of the European Economic Community)
E U R O F E U	European Committee of the Manufacturers of Fire Engines and Apparatus
E U R O F U E L	Societe Europeenne de Fabrication de Combustibles a Base d'Uranium pour Reacteurs a Eau Legere (France)
E U R O P H O T	European Council of Professional Photographers (Belgium)
E U R O S A C	European Federation of Manufacturers of Multiwall Paper Sacks (France)
E U R O S T A T	Statistical Office of the European Communities
E U S A M A	European Shock Absorber Manufacturers Association
E U S E C	Conference of Engineering Societies of Western Europe and the USA (dissolved 1971)

E U S I D I C	European Association of Scientific Information Dissemination Centres
E U V	Energetic Ultra-Violet
	Expected Utility Value
E U V S H	Equivalent Ultra-Violet Solar Hours
E V	prefix to SAE (USA) numbered series of Austenitic Exhaust Valve Steels
E V A F	Europaische Vereinigung Industrieller Marksforscher (European Association for Industrial Marketing Research)
E V G	Electrically-supported Vacuum Gyro
E V M	Engine Vibration Monitoring
E V S	Electronic Voice Switching System
	Electro-optical Viewing System
	Electro-optical Visual Sensor
	Expected Value Saved
E W	Electroslag Welding
	Ether-Water
E W A C	Effluent and Water Advisory Committee (of the Water Research Association)
I W G A E	European Working Group on Acoustic Emission
E W P	Exploding Wire Phenomena
E W S F	European Work Study Federation (now European Federation of Productivity Services)
E X A C T	International Exchange of Authenticated Electronic Component Performance Tests Data
E X A F S	Extended X-ray Absorption Fine Structure
E X A P T	Extended subsets of APT (Automatically Programmed Tools)
E X C O	Executive Committee (of ISO (Switzerland))
E X F O R	International Neutron Data Exchange System
E X W	Explosion Welding

F

F	prefix to numbered series of Factory Forms issued by H.M. Factory Inspectorate, Dept. of Employment
	prefix to numbered : dated series of Fabric Standards issued by BSI (letter is sometimes preceded by a number)
F A	Ferrocarriles Argentinos (Argentina) (Argentina Railways)

F A	Formaldehyde
	Furfuryl Alcohol
F A A	Faculty of Accountants and Auditors
	Fuerza Aerea Argentina (Argentina) (Military Air Force)
F A A - A D S	Federal Aviation Administration Aircraft Development Service (of DOT (USA))
F A A - A M	Federal Aviation Administration, Office of Aviation Medicine (of DOT (USA))
F A A - A V	Federal Aviation Administration, Office of Aviation Policy and Plans (of DOT (USA)) ·
F A A - E M	Federal Aviation Administration, Office of Systems Engineering Management (of DOT (USA))
F A A - F S	Federal Aviation Administration, Flight Standards Service (of DOT (USA))
F A A - M S	Federal Aviation Administration, Office of Management Services (of DOT (FAA))
F A A - N A	Federal Aviation Administration, National Aviation Facilities Experimental Center (of DOT (USA))
F A A - N O	Federal Aviation Administration, Office of Noise Abatement (of DOT (USA))
F A A D S	Forward Area Air Defence System
	Forward Area Anti-aircraft Defence System
F A B	Forca Area Brasileira (Brazil) (Military Air Force)
FABRIMETAL	Federation des Entreprises de l'Industrie des Fabrications Metalliques (Belgium)
F A C / S C A R	Forward Air Control/Self-Contained Airborne Reconnaissance
F A C E L	Feature Analysis Comparison and Evaluation Library
F A C S	Feedback and Analysis of Control Statistics
F A C S S	Federation of Analytical Chemistry and Spectroscopy Societies (USA)
F A C T	Fully Automated Cataloguing Technique
F A C T - A I D	FACT (Flexible Automatic Circuit Tester) Automatic Interconnection Device
F A C T - L I F T	FACT (Flexible Automatic Circuit Tester) Low Insertion Force Technique
F A C T - Q U I C	FACT (Flexible Automatic Circuit Tester) Quick Universal Interface Connector
F A C T A N	Factor Analysis
F A C T S	Federation of Australian Commercial Television Stations (Australia)

F A D E S	Fuselage Automated Design
F A E	Figural After-Effect
	Fuel-Air Explosive
F Ae B	Force Aerienne Belge (Belgium) (Military Air Force)
F Ae C	Force Aerienne Congolaise (Congo) (Kinshasa) (Military Air Force)
F Ae G	Fuerza Area Guatemalteca (Guatemala) (Military Air Force)
F A F	Final Approach Fix
F A F R	Fatal Accident Frequency Rates
F A G	Flughafen Frankfurt AG (Germany)
F A I C	Federation of Australian Investment Clubs (Australia)
F A I R S	*Federal Aviation Administration* (USA) Information Retrieval System
F A M	Fast Auxiliary Memory
F A M O S	Floating-gate Avalanche-injection Metal Oxide Semiconductor
F A M O U S	French-American Mid-Ocean Undersea Study
F A M S	Forecasting And Modelling System
F A M S N U B	Frequencies And Mode Shapes of Non-Uniform Beams
F A O	Food and Agricultural Organization (of UN) (Italy)
F A O E	Federation of African Organisations of Engineers
F A P	Fuerza Aerea del Peru (Peru) (Military Air Force)
F A P E L	Fabrieken van Aktieve en Passieve Electronische Bouwelementen in Nederland (Netherlands)
F A P S	Financial Analysis and Planning System
	Committee on the Future of the American Physical Society (of the Society (USA))
F A R	Filament Atom Reservoir
	Fixed Acoustic Range
F A R A	Formula Air Racing Association
F A R S	Failure Analysis Report Summary
F A S	Fast Announcement Service (of NTIS (USA)) (now Trade Announcement Service)
	Foreign Area Studies (of The American University (USA))
	Foreign Agricultural Service (USDA)
F A S S T	Friends of Aerospace Supporting Science and Technology
F A S T	Fan and Supersonic Turbine
	Feed And Speed Technology

F A S T	Field Asymmetry Sensing Technique
	Freight Automated System (of USDOD)
	Fully Automated Switching Teletype
F A S T Net	Fully Automated Switched Telecommunications Network
F A T A L	Fit Anything To Anything you Like
F A T C A T	Frequency And Time Circuit Analysis Technique
F A T E	Formulating Analytical and Technical Estimate
F A T I P E C	Federation d'Associations de Techniciens des Industries des Peintures, Vernis, Emaux et Encres d'Imprimerie de l'Europe Continentale (European Federation of Paint and Printing Ink Technologists (France))
F A T M E	Fabbrica Apparecchiature Telefoniche e Materiale Elettrico (Italy)
F A T T	Forward Area Tactical Typewriter
	Fracture Appearance Transition Temperature
F A U L	Five Associated University Libraries (in Western New York (USA))
F A V	Fuerzas Aereas Venezolanas (Venezuela) (Military Air Force)
F A W A C	Farm Animals Welfare Advisory Committee
F B A	Freshwater Biological Association
F B B	Functional Building Block
F B F C	Franco-Belge de Fabrication de Combustible (Belgium)
F B R	Full Boiling-Range fuel
F B R F	Full Boiling-Range Fuel
F C A	Functional Configuration Audit
F C A W	Flux Cored Arc Welding
F C C	Flat Conductor Cable
	Fluid Cat Cracking
F C C I	Federal Clean Car Incentive program (USA)
F C C T S	Federal COBOL Compiler Testing Service (of NBS and DOD (USA))
F C C U	Fluid Cat Cracking Unit
F C E S	Flight Control Electronics System
F C I	Federated Chamber of Industries (South Africa)
	Fertiliser Corporation of India (India)
	Food Corporation of India (India)
F C I A	Foreign Credit Insurance Association (USA)
F C I C	Fiber and Composites Information Center (Battelle-Columbus Laboratories (USA))

F C M	prefix to dated-numbered series issued by Federal Coordinator for Meteorological Services and Supporting Research (of NOAA (USA))
F C P	Free Conducting Particle
F C S	Farmer Cooperative Service (USDA) (Gun) Fire Control System
F D A	Form-dimethylamide
F D A R	Federal Department of Agricultural Research (Nigeria)
F D A U	Flight Data Acquisition Unit
F D E P	Flight Data Entry and Print-out
F D E U	Field Drainage Experimental Unit
F D F R	Federal Department of Forestry Research (Nigeria)
F D M A	Frequency Division Multiple Access
F D P	Fast Digital Processor Fibrinogen Degradation Products
F D S	File Description System
F D T I	Food, Drink and Tobacco Industry Training Board
F D V R	Federal Department of Veterinary Research (Nigeria)
F D X	Full-Duplex
F E / P C	Ferroelectric/Photoconductive
F E A B L	Finite Element Analysis Basic Library
F E A N I	Federation Europeen d'Associations Nationales d'Ingenieurs (European Federation of National Associations of Engineers) (France)
F E A S I B L E	Finite Element Analysis Sensibly Implemented By Least Effort
F E B E L B O I S	Federation Belge des Industriels du Bois (Belgium) (Belgian Federation of the Timber Industry)
F E B E L T E X	Federation de l'Industrie Textile Belge (Belgium) (Federation of the Belgian Textile Industry)
F E C	Fall Electronics Conference (IEEE (USA)) Forward Error Control
F E C A	Facilities Engineering and Construction Agency (of HEW (USA))
F E C A I C A	Federacion de Camaras y Associaciones Industriales de Centroamerica (Honduras) (of CACM) (Federation of Industrial Chambers and Associations of Central America)

F E C H I M I E	Federation des Industries Chimiques de Belgique (Belgium) (Federation of the Belgian Chemical Industries)
F E C S	Federation of European Chemical Societies
F E C S A	Fuerzas Electricas de Cataluna SA (Spain)
F E D A S	Federation of European Delegation Associations of Scientific Equipment Manufacturers, Importers, and Dealers in the Laboratory, Industrial and Medical Fields
F E D I S	Front-End Design-Information System
F E E D B A C	Foreign Exchange, Eurodollar and Branch Accounting
F E F	Foundry Educational Foundation (USA)
F E F A N A	Federation Europeenne des Fabricants d'Adjuvants pour la Nutrition Animale (European Federation of Manufacturers of Additional Ingredients for Animal Foodstuff)
F E F C O	Federation Europeene des Fabricants de Carton Ondule (European Federation of Corrugated Container Manufacturers) (France)
F E F I	Flight Engineers Fault Isolation
F E F P	Fuel Element Failure Propagation
F E G	Flug-Elektronik-Gesellschaft (Germany)
F E G U A	Ferrocarriles de Guatemala (Guatemala) (State Railways)
F E I C	Federation Europeenne de l'Industrie du Contreplaque) (European Federation of the Plywood Industry)
F E L	Fritz Engineering Laboratory (of Lehigh University (USA))
F E L A B A N	Federacion Latinoamericana de Bancos (Colombia) (Latin-America Banking Federation)
F E L T	Fluid Encapsulated Launch Technique
F E M	Field-Effect Modified
F E M A	Fire Equipment Manufacturers Association (USA)
	Flavor and Extract Manufacturers Association (USA)
	Foundry Equipment Manufacturers Association (USA)
F E N O S A	Fuerzas Electricas del Noroeste SA (Spain)
F E O	Federal Energy Office (USA)
F E P	Film Epoxypolyamide
	Front-End Processor

F E P F	Federation Europeenne des Industries de Porcelain et de Faience de Table et d'Ornementation (European Federation of the Porcelain and Pottery Industries)
F E R	Federation of Engine Remanufacturers
F E R O P A	Federation Europeene des Syndicats de Panneaux de Fibres (European Federation of Manufacturers Associations of Fibre Panels)
F E S	Final Environmental Survey
	Fluidic Environmental Sensor
F E S S	Finite Element Solution System
F E T A	Fire Extinguishing Trades Association
F E T C	Field-Effect-Transistor-Capacitor
F E T E	FORTRAN Execution Time Estimator
F E V	Forced Expiratory Volume
F E V E	Ferrocarriles de Via Estrecha (Spain) (State Narrow Gauge Railway Organisation)
F E X T	Far-End Cross Talk
F F	Flash-Filament
F F A	Flug- und Fahrzeugwerke Altenrhein (Switzerland)
F F B	Frequency Feedback
F F C	Food Freezer Committee
F F F	Field-Flow Fractionation
F F H T	Fast Fourier-Hadamard Transform
F F I T P	Federation Francaise d'Instituts Techniques du Petrole (France) (French Federation of Petroleum Technical Institutes)
F F M E D	Fixed Format Message Entry Device
F F P	Ferromagnetic Fine Particles
4 F R	Four-Frequency Radar
F F T	Fixed Time Test
F F V V	Federation Francaise de Vol a Voile (France) (French Federation of Gliding)
F G A A	Federal Government Accountants Association (USA)
F G C	Flight Guidance and Control
F G G E	First GARP Global Experiment
F G O R C	Flower Gardens Ocean Research Center (of Marine Biomedical Institute (University of Texas) (USA))
F G R A A L	FORTRAN-extended Graph Algorithmic Language
F G V	Field-Gradient Voltage
F H	Frequency Hopping

F H A	Finance Houses Association
F H E	Fast Hydrofoil Escort
Fh F	Fraunhofer-Gesellschaft zur Forderung der angewandten Forschung (Germany) (Fraunhofer Society for the Advancement of Applied Research)
F H L B B	Federal Home Loan Bank Board (USA)
F H T	Fast Hadamard Transform
	Finite Hilbert Transform
F H W A	Federal Highway Administration (of Department of Transportation (USA))
F H W A - A K	FHWA—Alaska Division (USA)
F H W A - A L A	FHWA—Alabama Division (USA)
F H W A - A R K	FHWA—Arkansas Division (USA)
F H W A - A S	FHWA—American Samoa Division (USA)
F H W A - A Z	FHWA—Arizona Division (USA)
F H W A - C A	FHWA—California Division (USA)
F H W A - C O L O	FHWA—Colorado Division (USA)
F H W A - C O N N	FHWA—Connecticut Division (USA)
F H W A - D E	FHWA—Delaware Division (USA)
F H W A - G A	FHWA—Georgia Division (USA)
F H W A - H I	FHWA—Hawaii Division (USA)
F H W A - I A	FHWA—Iowa Division (USA)
F H W A - I D A	FHWA—Idaho Division (USA)
F H W A - I L L	FHWA—Illinois Division (USA)
F H W A - I N D	FHWA—Indiana Division (USA)
F H W A - K A N S	FHWA—Kansas Division (USA)
F H W A - K Y	FHWA—Kentucky Division (USA)
F H W A - L A	FHWA—Louisiana Division (USA)
F H W A - M D	FHWA—Maryland Division (USA)
F H W A - M I C H	FHWA—Michigan Division (USA)
F H W A - M N	FHWA—Minnesota Division (USA)
F H W A - M O	FHWA—Missouri Division (USA)
F H W A - M O N T	FHWA—Montana Division (USA)
F H W A - N C	FHWA—North Carolina Division (USA)
F H W A - N D	FHWA—North Dakota Division (USA)
F H W A - N E B	FHWA—Nebraska Division (USA)
F H W A - N H	FHWA—New Hampshire Division (USA)
F H W A - N J	FHWA—New Jersey Division (USA)
F H W A - N M	FHWA—New Mexico Division (USA)
F H W A - N Y S	FHWA—New York State Division (USA)
F H W A - O H I O	FHWA—Ohio Division (USA)
F H W A - O K	FHWA—Oklahoma Division (USA)
F H W A - O R	FHWA—Oregon District (USA)

F H W A - P A	FHWA—Pennsylvania Division (USA)
F H W A - R I	FHWA—Rhode Island Division (USA)
F H W A - S C	FHWA—South Carolina Division (USA)
F H W A - S D	FHWA—South Dakota Division (USA)
F H W A - T E X	FHWA—Texas Division (USA)
F H W A - T N	FHWA—Tennessee Division (USA)
F H W A - U T	FHWA—Utah Division (USA)
F H W A - V A	FHWA—Virginia Division (USA)
F H W A ·· V T	FHWA—Vermont Division (USA)
F H W A - W A	FHWA—Washington Division (USA)
F H W A - W I S	FHWA—Wisconsin Division (USA)
F H W A - W V	FHWA—West Virginia Division (USA)
F H W A - W Y O	FHWA—Wyoming Division (USA)
F I - M S	Field Ionization Mass Spectrometry
F I - X	Fighter-Interceptor-Experimental
F I A	Factory Insurance Association (USA)
	Fluorescent Indicator Adsorption
F I A N E	Fonds d'Intervention et l'Action pour la Nature et l'Environnement (France) (Action Fund for Nature and the Environment)
F I A P	Federation Internationale de l'Art Photographique (Switzerland) (International Federation of Photographic Art)
F I A T	Fonds d'Intervention d'Amenagement du Territoire (France) (Development Fund)
F I A T A	Federation Internationale des Associations de Transitaires et Assimiles (International Federation of Forwarding Agents Associations) (Switzerland)
F I C	Film Integrated Circuit
F I C C I	Federation of Indian Chambers of Commerce and Industry (India)
F I C O	Flight Information and Control of Operations
F I D	Floating Input Distortion
F I D - R R S	Federation International de la Documentation Research Referral Service
F I D E	Federation de l'Industrie Dentaire en Europe (France) (Federation of the Dental Industry in Europe)
F I D I C	Federation Internationale des Ingenieurs Conseil (International Federation of Consulting Engineers) (Netherlands)
F I D O	Fog Investigation and Dispersal Operation
F I E	Fluoride Ion Electrode

F I E L D	First Integrated Experiment for Lunar Development
F I E N	Forum Italiano dell Energia Nucleaire (Italy) (Italian Nuclear Forum)
F I E O	Federation of Indian Export Organisations (India)
F I E T	Facultad de Ingenieria Electronica y Telecommunicaciones (Colombia) (School of Electronic and Telecommunications Engineering)
F I F I	Flexible Ideal Format for Information
F I G	Federation Internationale des Geometres (International Federation of Surveyors) (Germany)
F I G A Z	Federation de l'Industrie du Gaz (Belgium) (Gas Industry Federation)
F I G E D	Federation Internationale des Grande Entreprises de Distribution (International Federation of Large Distribution Undertakings)
F I G O	Federation Internationale de Gynecologie et d'Obstetrique (Switzerland) (International Federation of Gynaecology and Obstetrics)
F I I G	Federal Item Identification Guide (of USDOD)
F I L A	Federation of Indian Library Associations (India)
F I L E S	FAMECE (US Army) Integrated Logistics Evaluation Simulator
F I M	Field Ion Microscopy
F I M L	Full-Information Maximum-Likelihood
F I M S	Functionally Identified Maintenance System
F I M T M	Federation des Industries Mecaniques et Transformatrices des Metaux (France) (Federation of Metal Processing Industries)
F I N D	prefix to numbered series of Fiche Index for Nuclear Dockets issued by USAEC
	Forecasting Institutional Needs for *Dartmouth* (Dartmouth College (USA))
F I N D E R	Fingerprint-Reader
F I P S - P U B	prefix to numbered series of publications issued by NBS (USA) Office of Information Processing Standards
F I R	Finite Duration Impulse Response
F I R L	Franklin Institute Research Laboratories (USA)
F I R S T	Federal Information Research Science and Technology network (of COSATI) (USA)
	Fire Information Retrieval System Techniques

F I S	Federation Internationale du Comerce des Semences (Netherlands) (International Federation of the Seed Trade)
F I S H R O D	Fiche Information Selectively Held and Retrieved On Demand
F I T	Flexible Interface Technique
	Floating Input Transistor
	Functional Industrial Training
F I T A C	Federacion Interamericano de Touring y Automovil Clubes (Argentina) (Inter-American Federation of Touring and Automobile Clubs)
	Film Industry Training and Apprenticeship Council
F I T C	Fluorescein Isothiocynate
F I T C E	Federation des Ingenieurs des Telecommunications de Communaute Europeenne (Belgium) (Federation of Telecommunications Engineers of the European Community)
F I V	Federation de l'Industrie du Verre (Belgium) (Federation of the Glass Industry)
F L	Fan Lift
	Fight Level
	Foot Lambert
F L A G	FORTRAN Load And Go
F L A M E S	Fabrication Labour and Material Estimating Service
F L A M R	Forward Looking Advanced Multimode Radar
F L A R E	Florida Aquanaut Research Expedition (of NOAA (USA))
F L A S H	Flash Lights And Send Help
F L C	Federal Library Committee (USA)
F L D	Flux Lattice Dislocation
	Fraunhofer Line Discriminator
F L E M	Flyby-Landing Excursion Mode
F L E X I M I S	Flexible Management Information System
F L I C	Film Library Information Council (USA)
F L I P	Floating Laboratory Instrument Platform
F L L	Frequency Locked Looped
F L O	First Lunar Observatory
F L O C O N	Floating Container
F L O P P	Floating Power Platform
F L R	Forward Looking Radar
F L S	Fundacion La Salle de Ciencias Naturales (Venezuela)

F L T	Flight Line Tester
F L T S A T C O M	Fleet Satellite Communication System (USN)
F L Y B A R	Flying By Auditory Reference
F M	Facilities Management
	File Maintenance
F M A	Fabricating Machinery Association (USA)
	Fabrica Militar de Aviones (Argentina) (Military Aircraft Factory) (State owned)
	Farm Management Association
	Ferrocenylmethyl Acrylate
	Fire Marshals Association of North America (USA)
	Food Machinery Association (now merged with TIPA)
	Fundamental Mode Asynchronous
F M A N A	Fire Marshals Association of North America (USA)
F M B	Federation of Master Builders
F M B T	Future Main Battle Tank
F M C	Forward Motion Compensation
F M C W	Frequency Modulated Intermittent /Continuous
F M F	Food Manufacturers Federation
F M F F	Frequency Modulation Feed Forward
F M G	Foundry Marketing Group
F M I C W	Frequency Modulated Intermittent/Continuous Wave
F M L P	Field Mirror Landing Practice
F M M A	Ferrocenylmethyl Methacrylate
F M R	Field Maintenance Reliability
F M S	Federation of Materials Societies (USA) (comprising ASNT, ASM, IEEE, ACS, SME, ACerS, NACE and AICheE)
	Frequency-Multiplexed Subcarrier
F M T	Field Modulation Technique
F M T M	Friction Materials Test Machine
F N	Fabrique Nationale Herstal (Belgium)
F N A P	FORTRAN Network-Analysis Programme
F N I C	Food and Nutrition Information and Educational Materials Centre (of National Agricultural Library (USA))
F N Ke	Fachnormenausschuss Kerntechnik (Germany) (Nuclear Technology Standards Committee)
F N R	Fachnormenausschuss Radiologie (Germany) (Radiology Standards Committee)
F N S	Food and Nutrition Service (of USDA)

F N S	Functional Neuromuscular Stimulation
F O A M S	Forecasting, Order Administration and Master Scheduling
F O B W	Frequencies of Occurrence of Binary Words
F O C	Fire Offices Committee (of some of the fire insurance companies in Great Britain)
F O C A L	Formula Calculator
	Formulating On-line Calculations in Algebraic Language
F O C A S	*Ford (Motor Company)* Operating Cost Analysis System
F O C C P A C	Fleet Operations Control Center, Pacific Fleet (USN)
F O C I A	Fibre Optics Coupled Image Amplifier
F O C O N	Fibre Cone Optics
F O C S	Freight Operation Control System
F O C U S	Forum of *Control Data* Users (USA)
F O E	Friends of the Earth (a society concerned with ecological and environmental problems)
F O E P	Frog Otolith Experiment Package
F O G R A	Forschungsgesellschaft fur Druck- und Repro-duktionstechnik (Germany) (Research Society for the Printing and Graphic Arts Industry)
F O O S	Fail-Operational-Fail-Operational-Fail-Safe
F O P	Forward Operating Pad
F O P E R P I C	Association for the Development of Further Pro-fessional Training in the Foundry and Related Industries (France)
F O P S	Falling Object Protective Structure
	File Oriented Programming System
	Forecast Operating System
F O P S A	Federation of Productivity Services Association
F O R A T O M	Forum Atomique Europeen (France) (European Atomic Forum)
F O R D S	Floating Ocean Research and Development Station
F O R E M	File Organization and Evaluation Modeling
F O R M A L	Formula Manipulation Language
F O R M S	File Organization Modelling System
F O R S C O M	Forces Command (US Army)
F O R T R A	Federation of Radio and Television Retailers Association
F O S I L	FOCAL (Formulating On-line Calculations in Algebraic Language) Simulator Language

F O V	Field Of View
F O W	Forge Welding
F P	Fluorescent Particle
F P A	Flight Path Accelerometer
	Flying Physicians Association (USA)
F P B	Fast Patrol Boat
F P C E A	Fibreboard Packaging Case Employers Association
F P I S	Fixed Price Incentive with Successive Targets
F P L	Forest Products Laboratory (of Forest Service (USDA))
F P M	prefix to numbered series of Federal Personnel Manuals issued by the Civil Service Commission (USA)
F P N	Fixed Pattern Noise
F P P	Fixed-Pitch Propeller
F P R	Flat Plate Radiometer
F P R I	Fire Protection Research International (USA)
	Forest Products Research Institute (Ghana)
F P R L	Forest Products Research Laboratory (now the Princes Risborough Laboratory (of the Building Research Establishment (DOE))
F P R S	Forest Products Research Society (USA)
F P S	Financial Planning Simulator
	Focus Projection and Scanning
F P V	Fowl Plague Virus
F Q R	Formal Qualification Review
F R	Faculty of Radiologists
	Final Report
F R - R S R	Fortele Aeriene ale Republicii Populare Romania (Romania) (Air Force of the Romanian People's Republic)
F R A C A S	Filter Response Analysis for Continuously Accelerating Spacecraft
F R A M	Failure Rate Assessment Machine
F R A M E	Fund for the Replacement of Animals in Medical Experiments
F R A T	Facilities Relative Allocation Technique
	Free Radical Assay Technique
F R B	Fisheries Research Board (of the Department of Fisheries and Forestry (Canada))
F R E D	Fast Reading Electronic Digitizer
F R E D D Y	Family Robot for Entertainment Discussion and Education, the Retrieval of Information and the Collation of Knowledge

F R E I	Forest Research and Education Institute (Sudan)
F R E L I S	Frequency Lists
F R I	Fulmer Research Institute (of Institute of Physics)
F R L	Free-Recall Learning
F R M E	Frequency Response Measuring Equipment
F R M V	Free Running Multivibrator
F R P	Fast Retinal Potential
F R S	Fire Research Station (merged into the Building Research Establishment, 1972 (of DOE))
F R T R A	Federation of Radio and Television Retailers Association
F R T V	Forward Repair and Test Vehicle
F R U C O M	Federation Europeene des Importateurs de Fruits Secs, Conserves, Epices et Miel (European Federation of Importers of Dried Fruits, Preserves, Spices and Honey)
F R U S A	Flexible Rolled-Up Solar Array
F R W	Friction Welding
F S	Fiber Society (USA)
F S A S	Fluidic Stability Augmentation System
F S C	Federal Science Council (USA)
F S C M	Federal Supply Code for Manufacturers (USA)
F S D	Fisher Significant Difference
F S D A	Frequency Spectral Density Analysis
F S I I	Fuel System Icing Inhibitor
F S M	Finite-State Machine
F S P E	Federation of Societies of Professional Engineers (South Africa)
F S P L S	Florida Society of Professional Land Surveyors (USA)
F S P S	Federation of Sailing and Powerboat Schools
F S P T	Federation of Societies for Paint Technology (USA)
F S R B	prefix to Forest Service Research Bulletins issued by the Forest Products Laboratory (USDA)
F S S	Flying Spot Scanner
	Fossil Stromgen Sphere
	Frequency-Selective Surface
F S S U	Federated Superannuation System for Universities
F S T S	Fire Service Training School (DTI)
F S U	Florida State University (USA)
F S V	Feline Sarcoma Virus
F T	Ferroresonant Transformer

F T / O P A S	Funds-In-Trust Operational Assistance Scheme (of ITU (UN))
F T A	Flexographic Technical Association (USA)
F T C	Fast Time Constant
	Float Trend Chart
F T D A S	Flight Test Data Acquisition System
F T H	Fourier Transform Hologram
F T I	Fixed Time Interval
F T I T B	Furniture and Timber Industry Training Board
F T L O	Fast Tuned Local Oscillator
F T M	Flight Test Manual
F T R	Filestore Transfer Routine
F T S	Flexible Test Station
F U F O	Full Fusing Option bomb
F U R S T	FORTRAN Unit Record Simulation Technique
F U S	Far Ultraviolet Spectrometer
	FORTRAN Utility System
F U S E	Federation for Unified Science Education (USA)
F V C	Forced Vital Capacity
F V R	Feline Viral Rhinotracheitis
F V R D E	Fighting Vehicles Research and Development Establishment (MOD) (merged into MVEE, 1970)
F V T	Flash Vacuum Thermolysis
F W	Flash Welding
	Fresh Water
F W C	Filament-Wound Cylinder
F W G P M	Federal Working Group on Pest Management (USA)
F W H M	Full-Wave Half Modulation
F W O	Federation of Wholesale Organisations
F W P C A	Federal Water Pollution Control Administration (Department of the Interior (USA)) (later FWQA)
F W Q A	Federal Water Quality Administration (now Water Quality Office (of EPA (USA)))
F W T	Fast Walsh Transform
F Z P	Fresnel Zone Plate

G

G	prefix to numbered:dated series of Electrical Equipment and Indicating Instruments standards issued by BSI (letter is sometimes preceded by a number)

G/MFCS	Gun/Missile Fire Control System
GA	Gemmological Association
	Group Atmosphere
GAAC	Graphic Arts Advertisers Council (USA)
GAADV	Graphic Arts Association of the Delaware Valley (USA)
GAAP	Generally Accepted Accounting Principles
GAAT	General Agreement on Tariffs and Trade (of UN)
GAATS	*Gander (Canada)* Automated Air Traffic System
GAEC	Greek Atomic Energy Commission (Greece)
GAESD	Graphic Arts Equipment and Supply Dealers (of Printing Industries of America (USA))
GAF	Gesellschaft fur Aeroslforschung (Germany) (Society for Aerosol Research)
	Government Aircraft Factories (of Department of Supply (Australia))
GAI	Guild of Architectural Iremongers
GAIA	Graphic Arts Industries Association (Canada)
GAIAL	Groupement pour l'Amenagement et l'Exploitation des Infrastructures Aeroportuaires Locales (France)
GAIF	General Assembly of Internation Federations (Switzerland)
GALAXY	General Automatic Luminosity And X-Y measuring engine
GALF	Groupement des Acousticiens de Langue Francaise (France)
GAMA	General Aviation Manufacturers Association (USA)
GAMAS	*Gulf (General Atomic Inc.)* Atomic Materials Assay System
GAMI	Groupement pour l'Avancement de la Mecanique Industrielle (France)
GAMIS	Graphic Arts Marketing Information Service (of Printing Industries of America (USA))
GAMMA	Graphically Aided Mathematical Machine
GAMP	Global Atmospheric Program (of NASA and NCAR (USA))
GAMS	Groupement pour l'Avancement des Methodes Physiques d'Analyse
GAN	Gyro-compass Automatic Navigation
GAP	Graphical Automatic Programming
GARC	Graphic Arts Research Center (Rochester Institute of Technology (USA))

G A R E X	Ground Aviation Radio Exchange
G A R S	Gyrocompassing Attitude Reference System
G A S	General Adaption Syndrome
G A S H	Guanidinium Aluminium Sulphate Hexahydrate
G A S P T	Generalized Axially Symmetrical Potential Theory
G A S T	Greenwich Apparent Sidereal Time
G A T B	General Aptitude Test Battery (of USES)
G A T C	Graphic Arts Technical Committee (of ASQC (USA))
G A T E	GARP Atlantic Tropical Experiment (of WMO and ICSU)
G A T T	Gate Assisted Turn-off Thyristor
G A T T I S	Georgia Institute of Technology (USA) Technical Information Service
G A V R S	Gyrocompassing Attitude and Velocity Reference System
G B H	Graphiste-Benzalkonium-Heparin
G B R A	Gas Breeder Reactor Association
G B R P	General Bending Response Programme
G B T	Generalized Burst Trapping
	Global Ballistic Transport
G B T C	Generalized Burst Trapping Codes
G C	Gas Chromatography
G C B	General Circuit Breaker
G C C A	Graphic Communications Computer Association (of PIA (USA))
G C D G	Gas Chromatography Discussion Group (of the Institute of Petroleum)
G C E P	Governing Council for Environmental Programmes (of the UN)
G C E S	Generalized Constant Elasticity of Substitution
G C F I	Gulf and Caribbean Fisheries Institute (USA)
G C F R C	Gulf Coastal Fisheries Research Center (of NMFS (USA))
G C M	Gaussian Cosine Modulation
G C N R	Gas Core Nuclear Rocket
G C O S	General Comprehensive Operating Supervisor
G C R	Galactic Cosmic Radiation
	Group Coded Recording
G C S C	Guidance Control and Sequencing Computer
G C S P C	Graphic Communications Specials Projects Section (of the Printing Industries of America (USA)

G C U G A	Grounded Current Unity-Gain Amplifier
G D A	Gas Distribution Administration (Iraq)
G D D	Growing Degree Day
G D F	Gaz de France (France)
G D L	Gas-Dynamic Laser
G D M S	Generalized Data Management Systems
G D P A	General Dental Practitioners Association
G D P S	Global Data Processing System (of WWW (WMO))
G D S	Graphical Display System
G E A	Garage Equipment Association
	Graph Extended ALGOL
G E A N S	Gimbaled ESG (Electrostatic Gyro) Aircraft Navigation System
G E C C M S E F	Group to Establish Criteria for Certifying Munitions Systems to Electro-magnetic Fields (of USAEC and USDOD)
G E D R T	Groupe Europeen d'Echange d'Experience sur la Direction de la Recherche Textile (European Group for the Exchange of Information on Textile Research)
G E E D A	Groundnut Extractions Export Development Association (India)
G E E I A	Ground Electronics Engineering Installation Agency (USAF) (merged into AFCS, 1971)
G E F A C S	Groupement des Fabricants d'Appareils Sanitaires en Ceramique de la CEE (Group of Manufacturers of Ceramic Sanitary Ware of the European Economic Community)
G E F A P	Groupement Europeen des Associations Nationales de Fabricants de Pesticides (European Group of National Associations of Manufacturers of Pesticides)
G E I S H A	Gun Electron Injection for Semiconductor Hybrid Amplification
G E L T S P A P	Group of Experts on Long-Term Scientific Policy and Planning (of IOC (UNESCO))
G E M	Graphite Electrode Contouring Machine
G E M C S	General Engineering and Management Computation System
G E M M	Generalized Electronic Maintenance Model
G E M S	Generalized Evaluation Model Simulator
	Global Environmental Monitoring System
G E N E S E S	General Network Service System
G E N E S Y S	Graduate Engineering Education System (USA)

G E N I R A S	General Information Retrieval and Application System
G E N T R A S	General Training System
G E O	Gas and Electric Operations
G E O S E C S	Geochemical Ocean Sections Study (a project of NSF (USA) for IDOE)
G E P I	Gestion e Partecipazioni Industriali (Italy) (a government holding company)
G E R C O S	Groupement d'Etudes et de Realizations des Compresseurs Speciaux (France)
G E R S	Groupe d'Etudes et de Recherches Sous-marines (France)
G E S A	Gas y Electricida SA (Spain)
G E S A M P	Joint Group of Experts on the Scientific Aspects of Marine Pollution (of UNESCO, FAO, IMCO, WMO, WHO, and IAEA)
G E S P L	Generalised Edit System Programming Language
G E T	Gross Error Test
G E W	Ground Effect Wing
G F A	Group Feed-back Analysis
G F A E	Government (USA) Furnished Avionics Equipment
G F C I	Ground Fault Circuit Interrupter
G F C S	Gun Fire Control System
G F D L	Geophysical Fluid Dynamics Laboratory (of NOAA (USA))
G F I	Groupement Francais d'Informatique (France)
G F M	Government (USA) Furnished Material
G F T	Generalized Fast Transform
	Graphical Firing Table
G f W	Gesellschaft fur Weltraumforschung (Germany) (Society for Space Research)
G G	Gravity Gradient
G G D	Generalized Gamma Distribution
G G G	Gadolinium Gallium Garnet
G G O	Glavnayo Geofizicheskaya Observatoriya (USSR) (Main Geophysical Observatory)
G G R A	Gelatine and Glue Research Association (now merged into BFMIRA)
G G S	Gravity Gradient Satellite
	Gyro Gunsight
G H R	Gross Heat Rate
G H R H	Growth Hormone Releasing Hormone

G H S P	Great High Schools Program (USA)
G H T	Gesellschaft fur Hochtemperatur-Reaktor-Technik (Germany)
G I A T	Groupement Industriel des Armements Terrestres (France)
G I D C	Gujarat Industrial Development Corporation (India)
G I I N	Groupe Intersyndicale de l'Industrie Nucleaire (France)
G I I P	Groupement Internationale de l'Industries Pharmaceutique des Pays de la CEE (International Group of the Pharmaceutical Industries of the European Economic Community)
G I M P A	Ghana Institute of Management and Public Administration (Ghana)
G I N A	Gas Industries Network Analyser
G I N O	Graphical Input Output
GINI F	GINO FORTRAN IV
G I P E C	Groupe d'Etudes International pour l'utilization de Profils Creux dans la Construction (Switzerland) (International Study Group on the Use of Hollow Sections in Construction)
G I P M E	Global Investigation of Pollution in the Marine Environment (a project of the IOC (UNESCO))
G I P S Y	General Information Processing System Geographic Incremental Plotting System
G I S P	General Information System for Planning
G I T I S	prefix to dated/numbered series of reports issued by Georgia Institute of Technology School of Information Sciences (USA)
G K V	Gesamtverband Kunststoffverarbeitende Industrie (Germany)
G K W W	Gesprachskrels Wissenschaft und Wirtschaft (Germany (Science and Industry Discussion Committee)
G L A A D S	Gun Low Altitude Air Defence System
G L A D S	Long-range Gun Low-altitude Air Defence System
G L B C	Great Lakes Basin Commission (USA)
G L D C	Great Lakes Data Center (of EDS (NOAA) (USA))
G L D S	Ground Laser Designator Station
G L F C	Great Lakes Fisheries Commission (USA)
G L I A S	Greater London Industrial Archaeology Society
G L I M	General Light Inter-reflection Model

G L O L	*Golay* Logic Language
G L O P R	*Golay* Logic Processor
G L O W	Gross Lift-Off Weight
G L P	Generalized Lattice-Point
	General Letter Package
G L S E	Generalized Least Squares Estimation
G L U L A M	Glued Laminated wood
G M A	Gas Metal-Arc
G M A W	Gas Metal-Arc Welding
G m b H	Gesellschaft mit beschrankter Haftung (Limited Company)
G M D	Gesellschaft fur Mathematik und Datenverarbeitung (Germany) (Research Corporation for Mathematics and Data Processing)
G M D H	Group Method of Data Handling
G M L S	Guided Missile Launching System
G M O	Gadolinium Molybdate
	Glyceryl Monooleate
G M S	General Maintenance System
	Geostationary Meteorological Satellite
	Glyceryl Monostearate
G M T O	Gas Meter Testing Office (of DTI)
G M TS	Gidrometeorologicheskyy Nauchno Issledovatel'-skiy Tsenter (USSR) (Scientific Research Center for Hydrometeorology)
G N A T S	Generalized Numerical Analysis of Thermal Systems
G N C	Global Navigation Chart
G N I	Grid Node Interface
G N M A	Government National Mortgage Association (USA)
G N R	Gaseous Nuclear Rocket
G n V	Gesellschaft fur Nukleare Verfahrenstechnik (Germany)
G O A L S	Geometrical Optical Analysis of Lens Systems
G O C	Grosseinkaufsgesellschaft Osterreichischer Cunsumvereine (Austria)
G O D	Guidance and Orbit Determination for Solar Electric Propulsion
G O G E G A	Comite Generale de la Cooperation Agricole de la CEE (General Committee of Agricultural Cooperation of the European Economic Community)

GOLD STAR	Generalized Organization of Large Data-bases; a Set-Theoretic Approach to Relations
GOS	Global Observing System (of WWW (WMO))
	Graphical Output Scheme
GOSS + D	GEORGE Operating System Support and Development
GOSSIP	Generalized Organizational System Summarizer and Information Processor
GOT	Glutamic Oxaloacetic Transaminase
GPAP	General Purpose Associative Processor
GPBTO	General Purpose Barbed Tape Obstacle
GPDL	Graphical Picture Drawing Language
GPES	Ground Proximity Extraction System
GPI	Glucosephospate Isomerase
	Ground Position Indicator
GPL	Geographic Position Locator
GPLA	General Price Level Accounting
GPLS	General Purpose Logic Simulator
GPMA	Grocery Products Manufacturers Association (Canada)
GPMG	General Purpose Machine Gun
GPMP	Group on Parts, Materials and Packaging (of IEEE) (USA)
GPP	Graphic Part Programmer
GPSDIC	General Purpose Scientific Document Image Code
GPSDW	General Purpose Scientific Document Writer
GPT	Glutamic-Pyruvic Transaminase
GPYS	General Purpose Yard Simulator
GQA	Grain Quality Analyzer
GRAFLAN	Graphic Language
GRAID	Graphical Aid
GRAN	Global Rescue Alarm Network
GRAPHIDI	Graphical Interpretive Display System
GRAPHSYS	Graphics Software System
GRASS	Gas Release and Swelling Subroutine
	Generalized Research Analysis Statistical System
GRC	Glass-fibre Reinforced Concrete
	Global Reference Code
GRCDA	Government Refuse Collection and Disposal Association (USA)
GRD	Gruppe fur Rustungsdienst (Switzerland) (Defence Procurement Agency of the Federal Defence Department)

G R D S R	Geographically Referenced Data Storage and Retrieval
G R E A T	Graphics Research with *Ellerbe Architects* (USA) Technology
G R F M	General Radio-Frequency Meter
G R G	Generalised Reduced Gradient
G R I	Gravure Research Institute (USA)
G R I D	Graphical Intermediate Data Format
G R I N	Graded-Index
G R I N D	Graphical Interpretive Display
G R I P S	Gaming, Random Interfacing and Problem Structuring
G R P	Group Repetition Period
G R P A	Groupe des Rapporteurs pour la Pollution de l'Air (of Economic Commission for Europe)
G R P P	Glass Reinforced Polypropylene
G R S	General Retrieval System
G R T	Gross Registered Ton
G R T P	Glass-fibre Reinforced Thermoplastics
G S / O P E R	prefix to numbered/dated/lettered series of reports issued by the General Steels Division of the British Steel Corporation
G S B C A	General Services Board of Contract Appeals (USA)
G S C	Geological Survey of Canada (of Department of Energy, Mines and Resources (Canada))
G S D	Geometric Standard Deviation
G S D T	Generalized Syntax Directed Translation
G S F	Gesellschaft fur Strahlen- und Umweltforschung (Germany) (Radiation and Environmental Research Corporation)
G S F C	Gujarat State Financial Corporation (India)
G S H	Generalized Spin Hamiltonian
G S I	Gesellschaft fur Schwerionenforschung (Germany) (Heavy Ion Research Corporation)
G S I C	Gujarat Small Industries Corporation (India)
G S L	Geophysical Sciences Laboratory (New York University (USA))
G S M / S M	prefix to dated-numbered series of reports issued by Air Force Institute of Technology (USAF)
G S R	Ground Surveillance Radar
G S S	Gonad-Stimulating Substance
G S S C	Georgia Schoolhouse Systems Council (USA)
G S S W	Gas-Shielded Stud Welding

G S T	Ground Sensor Terminal
G S V	*Grumman* Submersible Vehicle
G T A	Gravure Technical Association (USA)
G T A W	Gas Tungsten-Arc Welding
G T D	Geometrical Theory of Diffraction
G T G	Gold-Thioglucose
G T M T C	Galvothermomagnetic Transport Coefficient
G T O L	Graphic Take-Off Language
G T R E	Gas Turbine Research Establishment (India)
G T S	Geostationary Technology Satellite
	Global Telecommunication System (of WWW (WMO))
G U A T E L	Empresa Guatemalteca de Telecomunicaciones Internacionales (Guatemala) (International Tele-communications Authority)
G U B	Generalized Upper Boundary
G U E R A P	General Unwanted Energy Rejection Analysis Programme
G U G M S	Glavnoe Upravlenie Gidrometeorologicheskoi Sluzhby (USSR) (Administrative Agency of the Hydrometeorological Service)
G U T S	GERTS User's Terminal System
G V H	Graft Versus Host
G V M	Generating Volt Meter
G V U G A	Grounded Voltage Unity-Gain Amplifier
G W F	Gesellschaft fur Werkzeugmaschinenbau und Fertigungstechnik (Switzerland)
G W I	Grinding Wheel Institute (USA)
G W P S	prefix to publications issued by George Washington University (USA) on the Program of Policy Studies in Science and Technology
G Y F M	General Yielding Fracture Mechanics
G Y M P I	Gyromagnetic Polarizing Interferometer
G Z C	Gas-size Exclusion Chromatography

H

H A	Haemagglutinin
	Haemagglutination
	Hazard Analysis
H A A	Hepatitis Associated Antigen
	Height Above Airport
	Hospital Activity Analysis
	Human Asset Accounting

H A C	Herbicide Assessment Committee (of AAAS (USA))
	House Appropriations Committee (of United States Congress)
	Hydrogen-Assisted Cracking
H A D	Haemadsorption
H A D - N	Haemadsorption-Neutralization
H A D I O S	*Honeywell* Analogous-Digital Input-Output Subsystem
H A E C	High Altitude Economic Carrier
H A F O E	High Air Flow with Oxygen Enrichment
H A I	Haemagglutination Inhibition
	Hellenic Aerospace Industries (Greece)
H A I S A M	Hashed Index Sequential Access Method
H A L	Hindustan Aeronautics Limited (India) (Government owned)
H A L E	High Altitude Long Endurance
H A L O	High Altitude, Low Opening parachuting
H A M	Holandsche Aanneming Maatschappij (Netherlands)
H A N D S	High Altitude Nuclear Detection Studies
H A N E	Hereditary Angioneurotic Edema
H A P P I	Height And Plan Position Indicator
H A R L S	Horse Antiserum to Rabbit Lymphocytes
H A R M	High-speed Anti-Radar Missile
	High-velocity Anti-Radiation Missile
H A R P	Heater Above Reheat Point
H A R V E S T	Highly Active Residues Vitrification Engineering Study (a project of UKAEA)
H A S	Hospital Advisory Service for England and Wales
H A S J P L	H. Allen Smith Jet Propulsion Laboratory (California Institute of Technology (USA))
H A S L	Hertfordshire Association of Special Libraries
H A S P / R J E	Houston Automatic Spooling priority with Remote Job Entry
H A S T	High Altitude Supersonic Target
H A S T E	Have Auger Sensor Test and Evaluation
	Helicopter Ambulance Service To Emergencies
H A T	Height Above Touchdown
	High Altitude Temperature
	Hypoxanthine-aminopterin-thymidine
H A T O F F	Highest Astronomical Tide Of the Foreseeable Future
H A T O M	Highest Astronomical Tide Of the Month
H A T O Y	Highest Astronomical Tide Of the Year

H A T R	High-temperature Attenuated Total Reflectance
H A T R A C K	Hurricane and Typhoon Tracking
H A T S	Huntsville Association of Technical Societies (USA)
H B	symbol used to denote Brinell Hardness
H B Ab	Hepatitis B Antibody
H B Ag	Hepatitis B Antigen
H B D	Hydroxbutyric Dehydrogenase
H B F	House Builders Federation
H B T X	High Beta Toroidal Experiment
H C	Historical Cost
	Hydrocarbon
	prefix to numbered : dated series of Aerospace Standards issued by BSI
H C B	High Capability Buoy
H C D	Hollow Cathode Discharge
H C F	Hardened Compacted Fibres
	High Cycle Fatigue
H C G B	Helicopter Club of Great Britain
H C L	Hindustan Copper Limited (India) (Government owned)
H C P	Hexagonal Close Packed
	Hybrid Combustion Process
H C S	Human Chorionic Somatomammotropin
H C S S	Hospital Computer Sharing System
H C S T R	Homogeneous Continued Stirred Tank Reactor
H D A S	Hydrographic Data Acquisition System
H D B	High Density Bipolar
H D D	Head Down Display
H D F	Highly Dispersive Filter
H D L C	High Level Data Link Control Procedures (of ISO (Switzerland))
H D P	Hydrazine Diperchlorate
H D P E	High Density Polyethylene
H D R	Health Data Recorder
H D W	Hydrodynamic Welding
H D X	Half-Duplex
H E	High-Elongation
H E A L S	*Honeywell* Error Analysis and Logging System
H E A O	High Energy Astronomy Observatory
H E A P S	High Energy Alpha-Proton Spectrometer
H E A R T	Hawaii Environmental Area Rapid Transport system
H E B A H	Heat Engine/Battery Hybrid

H E C	Heavy Engineering Corporation (India) (Government owned)
H E C A D	Human Engineering Computer Aided Design
H E C B	Highways Engineering Computing Branch (of DOE)
H E E D	High Energy Electron Diffraction
H E I	Heat Exchange Institute (USA)
	Holographic Exposure Index
H E I - T	High Explosive Incendiary Tracer
H E I T	High Explosive Incendiary with Tracer
H E L	Hugoniot Elastic Limit
	Hydraulic Engineering Laboratory (California University (USA))
H E L A C	Helix Linear Accelerator
H E L A S T	*Human Engineering Laboratory* (US Army) Armor System Tests
H E L B A T	*Human Engineering Laboratory* (US Army) Battalion Artillery Tests
H E L H A T	*Human Engineering Laboratory* (US Army) Helicopter Armament Tests
H E L I S T	*Human Engineering Laboratory* (US Army) Infantry System Tests
H E L M S	Helicopter Multifunction System
H E L N A V S	Helicopter Navigation System
H E L O S	Highly Eccentric Lunar Occultation Satellite
H E L P	Heuristic Etching-pattern Layout Programme
	High Energy Landing Problem
	Highly Extendible Language Processor
	Hybrid Electronic Layout Programme
H E M	Hybrid Electro-Magnetic
H E M A C	Hybrid Electro-Magnetic Antenna Coupler
H E P L	High-Energy-Pulse Laser
H E P S	High-Energy Proton Spectrometer
H E R	Hydrogen Evolution Reaction
H E R P E S	High Energy Recovery Pressure and Enthalpy Sensor
H E T P	High Equivalent to a Theoretical Plate
H E W C	Highly Enriched Waste Concentrates
H F A K	Hollow Fibre Artificial Kidney
H F D	High Field Domain
H F D A	High Fidelity Dealers Association
H F I D	Hydrogen Flame Ionisation Detection
H F S	Hypothetical Future Samples

H F T	prefix to dated-numbered series of reports issued by the Human Factors in Technology Research Group, California University (USA)
H F W B	High Frequency Wire Broadcasting
H G A	Homogentisic Acid
H G C A	Home Grown Cereals Authority
H G E E A	Huntsville General Electric Engineers Association (USA)
H G H	Human Growth Hormone
H G M S	Helicopter Gravity Measuring System
H G P R T	Hypoxanthine - Guanine Phosphoribosyltransferase
H G S I T V C	Hot Gas Secondary Injection Thrust Vector Control
H I	Haemagglutinin Inhibition
H I A	Hompolar Inductor Alternator
H I A A	Hydroxyindoleacetic Acid
H I C	Hot-Isostatic-Compaction
H I C A T	High Altitude Clear Air Turbulence
H I C L A S S	Hierarchical Classification
H I C S S	Hawaii International Conference on System Sciences
H I D	High-Intensity Discharge
H I D E C S	Hierarchical Decomposition of Systems
H I E	Heat Input Equivalent
H I F A R	High Flux Australian Reactor (AAEC (Australia))
H I F R E N S A	Hispano-Francesa de Energia Nuclear SA (Spain)
H I L A B	Heavy Ion Laboratory
H I L A C	Heavy Ion Linear Accelerator
H I N D A L C O	Hindustan Aluminium Corporation (India)
H I O M T	Hydroxyindole-O-Methyl Transferase
H I P	Hot Isostatic Pressing *or* Pressure
	Hyperbolic Integer Programming
H I P A A S	High performance Advanced Attack System
H I P A C	Heavy Ion Plasma Accelerator
H I P E R F L I R	High-Performance Forward-Looking Infra-Red
H I P E X	Harmonic Identification Pitch Extraction
H I P H	High Institute of Public Health (Alexandria University (Egypt))
H I P S	High Integrity Protective Systems
H I R A D	*Hitachi* Re-Adhesion Device
H I R L	High Intensity Runway Lighting
H I R S	Holographic Information Retrieval System
H I R T	High Reynolds Number Tunnel (USAF)

6*

H I R U P	High Intensity Radiation Utilization Project (of BARC (India))
H I S	Hood Inflation System
	Hospital Information System
H I T I	High Integrity Trip Initiators
H I T P - S E A P	High-Ignition-Temperature Propellants, Self Extinguishing at Atmospheric Pressure
H I T S	Hydro-acoustic Impact Timing System
H I V E	High Integrity Voting Equipment
H I V I P	*Hitachi* Visual Image Processing Robot
H L B	Hydrophilic-lipophilic Balance
H L G	Hybrid Lens Guide
H L H / A T C	Heavy Lift Helicopter Advanced Technology Component
H L M	Habitations a Loyer Modere (France) (Moderate Rent Housing Organization)
H L S	Heavy Liquid Separation
	High Level Scheduler
H L S I	Hybrid Large Scale Integrated
H L V	Herpes-Like Virus
H M D	Helmet-Mounted Display
H M D A	Hexamethylene Diamine
H M I	Hahn-Meitner-Institute fur Kernforschung (Germany) (Hahn-Meitner Institute for Nuclear Research)
	Heavy Maintenance Interval
H M M E	Hydroquinone Monomethyl Ether
H M O S	Health Maintenance Organization Service (of HEW (USA))
H M P	Hexametaphosphate
H M S	Hexose Monophosphate Shunt
H M S A	Head-Mounted Sonic Aid
H M T	Hindustan Machine Tools Limited (India) (Government owned)
H M T A	Hexamethylenetetramine
H M T A - I	Hexamethylenetetramine Hydroiodide
H M W	High Molecular Weight
H M X	Cyclotetramethylenetetranitramine
H N R	Handwritten Numerical Recognition
H n R N A	Heterogenous Nuclear Ribonucleic Acid
H N V	prefix to numbered series of High Alloy Intake Valve Material issued by SAE (USA)
H O B O	Homing Bomb
H O B O S	Homing Bombing System

H O G S	Homing Optical Guidance System
H O P S	Highway Optimization Programme System
H O S	Human Operator Simulator
H O S S	Halo-Orbit Space Station
H O T - D A M	Higher Order Tree Dual Approximation Method
H P	Horizontal Polarization
H P A	Hexahydrophthallic Anhydride
H P B W	Half Power Beam-width
H P C	Hydroxpropylcellulose
H P D	High Performance Diesel
H P H W	High Pressure Hot Water
H P L C	High Performance Liquid Chromatography
H P L L	High Pressure Life Laboratory
H P M M	Horizontal Planar Motion Mechanism
H P N S	High Pressure Nervous Syndrome
H P P O	High Pressure Partial Oxidation
H P R	High Penetration Resistant
	Hot Particle Rolling
H P S	Hazardous Polluting Substances
	Head Position Sensing
	Health Physics Society (USA)
H R	prefix to numbered: dated series of Heat Resisting Wrought Alloys standards issued by BSI
	High Resilient
H R A	High-speed Research Aircraft
H R E	Hypersonic Ramjet Engine
H R G	Hydrocarbon Research Group (of the Institute of Petroleum)
H R I S	Highway Research Information Service (of US HRB and AASHO)
H R L E L	High-Radiation-Level Examination Laboratory (of ORNL (USAEC))
H R M R	Human Readable Machine Readable
H R M S	Human Resources Management System
H R P	Horse-radish Peroxidase
H R R L	High-Repetition-Rate Laser
H R S	Hydraulics Research Station (formerly of MINTECH subsequently transferred to DOE)
H R S C M R	High-Resolution Surface-Composition Mapping Radiometer
H R W	Hard Red Winter Wheat
H S	Holographic Stereogram

H S	prefix to numbered series of reports issued by School of Hygiene and Public Health (Johns Hopkins University (USA))
H S A	Hollandse Signaalapparaten (Netherlands)
H S A S	Hard Stability Augmentation System
H S B	Hochleistungs-schnellban Studiengesellschaft (Germany)
H S C	High Sulphur Content
	Hydrogen Stress Cracking
H S C L	Hindustan Steel Construction Limited (India) (Government owned)
H S D	Horizontal Situation Display
H S D D	Half Second Delay Detonator
H S D T	High Speed Diesel Train
H S E B	Haryana State Electricity Board (India)
H S F	Heat Stimulated Flow
H S F - A C T H	Hypothalmic Secretory Factor for Adreno-Corticotropic Hormone
H S F G	High Strength Friction Grip
H S G	High-Speed Grinding
H S I	Horizontal Situation Indicator
H S I / C D I	Horizontal Situation Indicator/Course Deviation Indicator
H S L	Hytran Simulation Language
H S M	Hard Structures Munition
	Harmonic Subcarrier Method
H S M H A	Health Services and Mental Health Administration (of PHS (USA))
H S R	High Speed Rail
H S R D	prefix to series of dated : numbered reports issued by National Center for Health Services Research and Development (of HEW (USA))
H S T	High Speed Train
H S U	Hartridge Smoke Units
H T A	Heterogeneity Arrangement
	Hypophysiotropic Area
H T C T	High Temperature Chemical Technology (a project of UKAEA)
H T I	High Temperature Isotropic
H T L	Hearing Threshold Level
	Heat Transfer Laboratory (of Minnesota University (USA))
	High Threshold Logic
H T L S	High-Torque, Low-Speed

H T O V L	Horizontal Take-Off Vertical Landing
H T P	High-Temperature Phase
H T P I B	Hydroxy Terminated Polyisobutylene
H T S	High Temperature Gas-cooled Reactor System
	Hyper-Thin Septum
H T S T	High-Temperature - Short Time
H T T	Heat Treatment Temperature
H U D - H P M C	Department of Housing and Urban Development, Assistant Secretary for Housing Production and Mortgage Credit (USA)
H U D W A S	Head-up Display Weapon Aiming System
H U F	Highway Users Federation for Safety and Mobility (USA)
Hum R R O	Human Resources Research Organization (USA)
H U R R A N	Hurricane Analogue
H U W	Harwell (*Atomic Energy Research Establishment*) User's Workshop
H V	Hochschulverband (Germany) (Association of University Teachers)
H V A	Homovanillic Acid
H V A C	High Voltage Alternating Current
H V C S	High-Vacuum Calibration System
H V D C	High-Voltage Direct Current
H V E M	High Voltage Electron Microscopy
H V H D	High-Voltage-Hold-Down
H W C	Hot Waste Concentrates
H W O	Hot Water Oxidizer
H W S	Hazardous Waste Service (of UKAEA)
Hy A	Hydro- og Aerodynamisk Laboratorium (Denmark) (Hydrodynamics and Aerodynamics Laboratory)
H Y D A S	Hydrographic Data Acquisition System
H Y P T V	Hypersonic Test Vehicle
H Y V E	Hydrogen Ventilated Enclosure
H Z L	Hindustan Zinc Limited (India) (Government owned)

I

I - C N I	Integrated Communications-Navigation-Identification
I - M L S	Interim Microwave Landing System
I A	Indian Airlines (India)

I A - E C O S O C	Inter-American Economic and Social Council (of OAS)
I A A	Institute of Automobile Assessors
	International Academy of Astronautics (of IAF)
I A A B	Inter-American Association of Broadcasters
I A A C	Inter-American Accounting Conference
	International Agricultural Aviation Centre (Netherlands)
I A A L D	International Association of Agriculture Librarians and Documentalists
I A A S	Institute of Advanced Architectural Studies (University of York)
I A B	ICSU Abstracting Board
I A B O	International Association of Biological Oceanography (Denmark) (of IUBS)
I A C	Industry Advisory Council (of USDOD and Industry)
	International Agricultural Centre (Netherlands)
	International Association for Cybernetics
I A C A	International Air Carrier Association
	International Air Charter Association (Switzerland)
I A C B	Inter-Agency Coordination Board (of the UN)
	International Association of Convention Bureaus
I A C I A	Incorporated Association of Cost and Industrial Accountants
I A C M E	International Association of Crafts and Small and Medium-sized Enterprises
I A C S	Indian Association for the Cultivation of Science (India)
	International Association of Classification Societies
I A D B	Inter-American Defense Board (of OAS)
I A D C	International Association of Drilling Contractors (USA)
I A E A	International Atomic Energy Agency (Austria) (of UN)
I A E C O S O C	Inter-American Economic and Social Council (of OAS)
I A E G	International Association of Engineering Geology
I A E I	International Association of Electrical Inspectors
I A E S	Interim Aquanaut Equipment System

I A F	Image Analysis Facility digital computer
	Indian Air Force (India)
	Initial Approach Fix
I A F C	International Association of Fire Chiefs
I A F F	International Association of Fire Fighters
I A G	International Administrative Data Processing Group (of IFIP)
I A G A	International Association of Geomagnetism and Aeronomy (USA)
I A G E B S	International Association of Gerontology (European Biological Section)
I A G O D	International Association for the Genesis of Ore Deposits
I A G P	International Antarctic Glaciological Project (of Australia, France, USA and USSR)
I Agr E	Institution of Agricultural Engineers
I A G S	Inter-American Geodetic Survey (Defense Mapping Agency (USDOD))
I A H S	International Association of Hydrological Sciences (Hungary)
I A I	Ion Acoustic Instability
	Israel Aircraft Industries (Israel)
I A I A S	Inter-American Institute of Agricultural Sciences (of OAS)
I A I E	Inter-American Institute of Ecology
I A I R	International Association of Industrial Radiation (France)
I A I S	Industrial Aerodynamics Information Service (of British Hydromechanics Research Association)
I A L	Indian Airlines (India)
	Investment Analysis Language
I A L L	International Association of Law Libraries
I A L P	International Association of Logopedics and Phoniatrics (Spain)
I A L S	International Association of Legal Science (Belgium)
I A M	Image Analyzing Microscope
	Institute of Administrative Management
	Institute of Advanced Motorists
	Interactive Algebraic Manipulation
I A M A	Institut za Altane Masine i Alate (Yugoslavia) (Institute for Machine Tools and Tooling)
I A M A M	International Association of Museums of Arms and Military History

I A M A P	International Association of Meteorology and Atmospheric Physics (Canada) (of IUGG)
I A M C R	International Association for Mass Communication Research (Switzerland)
I A M F E	International Association on Mechanization of Field Experiments
I A M F E S	International Association of Milk, Food and Environmental Sanitarians (USA)
I A M G	International Association for Mathematical Geology
I A M S	International Association of Microbiological Societies (Canada)
I A N E C	Inter-American Nuclear Energy Commission (USA) (of OAS)
I A O L	International Association of Orientalist Librarians (Hawaii)
I A P C	International Association for Pollution Control
I A P C O	International Association of Professional Congress Organizers (Belgium)
I A P I P	International Association for the Protection of Industrial Property
I A P P	International Association for Plant Phyiology (Switzerland)
I A Q	International Association for Quality (now International Academy for Quality)
I A R	Institute for Agricultural Research and Special Services (Ahmadu Bello University (Nigeria))
	Institut fur Angewandte Reaktorphysik (Germany) (Institute for Applied Reactor Physics)
I A R B	Italian Aviation Research Branch of Air-Britain
I A R C	International Agency for Research on Cancer (France) (of WHO (UN))
	International Amateur Radio Club
I Arm	Inspectorate of Armaments (MOD) (now QAD (Weapons))
I A R S	Institute of Agricultural Research Statistics (India)
I A S	Indicated Air Speed
	Integrated Antenna System
	Invariant-Azimuth States
	Isolated Antenna System
I A S A	Insurance Accounting and Statistical Association (USA)
I A S C	International Accounting Standards Committee (of ICCAP)

I A S E	Inter-American Association of Sanitary Engineering
I A S I	Inter-American Statistical Institute (of OAS)
I A S M	Istituto per l'Assistenza allo Sviluppo del Mezzogiorno (Italy) (Institute for Assistance in the Development of Southern Italy)
I A S P E I	International Association of Seismology and Physics of the Earth's Interior (USA)
I A S S	Incorporated Association of Architects and Surveyors
	Institute of Advanced Architectural Studies
	International Association of Survey Statisticians
	International Aviation Snow Symposium
I A S S M D	International Association for the Scientific Study of Mental Deficiency
I A T	International Atomic Time
	Iodine-Azide Test
I A T A E	International Accounting and Traffic Analysis Equipment
I A T P	International Airlines Technical Pool
I A T L I S	Indian Association of Teachers of Library Science (India)
I A T T C	Inter-American Tropical Tuna Commission
I A U	Interface Adaptor Unit
	International Association of Universities (France)
	International Astronomical Union (of ICSU)
I A V C E I	International Association of Volcanology and Chemistry of the Earth's Interior (Italy)
I A W A	International Association of Wood Anatomists (USA)
I A W P R	International Association on Water Pollution Research (South Africa)
I B	Isobutylene
I B A	Independent Broadcasting Authority
	Israel Broadcasting Authority (Israel)
I B A R	Interafrican Bureau for Animal Resources (of OAU)
I B C	Institute of Building Control
I B C C	International Bureau of Chambers of Commerce
	International Business Contact Club
I B C S	Integrated Battlefield Control System
I B C S / T R I CAP	Integrated Battlefield Communication Systems/ Triple Capability - Armoured, Infantry and Air Cavalry

I B E	International Bureau for Epilepsy
	International Bureau of Education (of UNESCO)
I B E R L A N T	Iberian Atlantic Command (of NATO)
I B F	Internally Blown Flap
I B F D	International Bureau of Fiscal Documentation
I B F I	International Business Forms Industries (of Printing Industries of America (USA))
I B G	Institute of British Geographers
I B I	Inter-governmental Bureau for Information (of UNESCO)
I B I - I C C	IBI-International Computation Centre (of UNESCO)
I B I S	Infrared Background-limiting Imaging Seeker
	Intranet Business Information System
I B M	Indian Bureau of Mines (India)
I B N R	Incurred But Not Reported
I B R D	International Bank for Reconstruction and Development (USA) (of UN)
I B R O	International Brain Research Organisation (France)
I B S	Ionospheric Beacon Satellite
I B S A T	Indexing By Statistical Analysis Techniques
I B T	Incompatible Blood Transfusion
I B T E	Imperial Board of Telecommunications of Ethiopia (Ethiopia)
I B W	Impulse Bandwith
I B W C	International Boundary and Water Commission (USA)
I B W C - P R B	International Boundary and Water Commission, Planning and Reports Branch (USA)
I C	Information Circular
	Inspiratory Capacity
I C A	Institute of Chartered Accountants in England and Wales
	Inter-Governmental Council for Automatic Data Processing
	International Communications Association
	International Cooperative Alliance
I C A A	International Civil Airports Association (France)
I C A D S	*Interdata* Computer Aided Drafting System
I C A F	International Committee on Aeronautical Fatigue
I C A M	Institute of Corn and Agricultural Merchants
	Integrated Communications Access Method
I C A M C	International Conference on Automation of Mines and Collieries

I C A O	International Civil Aviation Organisation (Canada) (of UN)
I C A P	Instituto Centroamericano de Administracion Publica (Costa Rica) (Central American Institute of Public Administration)
I C A P	International Committee of Architectural Photogrammetry (of ICOMOS and ISP)
I C A P R	Inter-departmental Committee on Air Pollution Research
I C A S	International Council of the Aeronautical Sciences
I C A T	International Convention of Amateurs in Television
I C B O	International Conference of Building Officials (USA) (now part of CABO)
I C C	International Chamber of Commerce (France)
	International Computation Centre (Italy)
	International Conference on Communications
	International Coordinating Committee for the Presentation of Science and the Development of Out-of-School Scientific Activities (Belgium)
	Inverted Common Collector
I C C A I A	International Coordinating Council of Aerospace Industries Associations
I C C A P	International Coordinating Committee for the Accountancy Profession
I C C A T	International Commission for the Conservation of Atlantic Tunas
I C C C	International Conference on Computer Communication
	International Congress on Construction Communications
I C C C S	International Committee of Contamination Control Societies
I C C E	International Council for Correspondence Education
I C C L A	International Centre for Coordination of Legal Assistance (Switzerland)
I C C P	Impressed Current Cathodic Protection
	Institute for Certification of Computer Professionals (USA)
I C D	Immune Complex Disease
	Interface Control Document
	Isocitric Dehydrogenase

I C D A	International Classification of Diseases Adapted for Use in the United States
I C D C	Indian Cotton Development Council (India)
I C E	In-Car Entertainment
	Institute of Consumer Ergonomics
	Instituto Costarricense de Electricidad (Costa Rica) (Institute of Electricity)
	Internal Combustion Engine
	Inventory Control Effectiveness (US Army)
I C E D	Interprofessional Council on Environmental Design
I C E L	Instituto Colombiano de Energia Electrica (Colombia) (an agency of the Ministry of Public Works)
I C E L A	International Computer Exposition for Latin America
I C E M	International Council for Educational Media
	Intergovernmental Committee for European Migration (Switzerland)
I C E P	Intra-Corporate Entrepreneurial Programme
I C E T K	International Committee of Electrochemical Thermodynamics and Kinetics (now International Society of Electrochemistry)
I C F E T	Inhomogeneous Channel Field-Effect Transistor
I C F G	International Cold Forging Group
I C F S	International Conference on Fluid Sealing
I C F T U	International Confederation of Free Trade Unions
I C G	Inter-Union Commission on Geodynamics (France) (of ICSU)
I C H	Institute of Child Health
I C H T S P	International Conference on the Hydraulic Transport of Solids in Pipes
I C I A S F	International Congress on Instrumentation in Aerospace Simulation Facilities
I C I C	Inertagency Committee on Intermodal Gargo (of DOT, CAB, FMC, and ICC (USA))
	International Copyright Information Centre (of UNESCO)
I C I C I	Industrial Credit and Investment Corporation of India (India)
I C L G	International and Comparative Librarianship Group (of the Library Association)
I C L M	Induced Course Load Matrix

I C M	Institute for Composite Materials (USA)
	Institute of Credit Management
I C M A	Institute of Cost and Management Accountants
I C M B E	International Conference on Medical and Biological Engineering
I C M C S T	International Conference on Microelectronics, Circuits and System Theory
I C M E E	Institution of Certificated Mechanical and Electrical Engineers (South Africa)
I C M I	International Commission of Mathematical Instruction (of UNESCO)
I C M M	Incomplete Correlation Matrix Memory
I C M P	International Conference on Medical Physics
I C M P H	International Centre of Medical and Psychological Hypnosis (Italy)
I C M R	Indian Council of Medical Research (India)
I C M S	Integrated Circuit and Message Switch
	Interdepartmental Committee for Meteorological Services (USA)
I C M S E	Interagency Committee on Marine Science and Engineering (USA)
I C N	International Council of Nurses (Switzerland)
I C N B	International Committee of Nomenclature of Bacteria (now International Committee on Systematic Bacteriology (of IAMS))
I C N N D	Interdepartmental Committee of Nutrition for National Defense (USA)
I C O	International Congress of Orientalists
I C O G R A D A	Internation Council of Graphic Design Associations (Netherlands)
I C O M O S	International Council of Monuments and Sites (France)
I C O N S	Information Center on Nuclear Standards (of ANS (USA))
I C O R	Interagency Commission on Ocean Resources (USA)
I C O T	Institute of Coastal Oceanography and Tides
I C P	Industry Cooperation Programme (of FAO (UN))
	Intra-Cranial Pressure
I C P E A C	International Conference on the Physics of Electronic and Atomic Collisions
I C P L	International Committee of Passenger Lines
I C P M	International Commission on Polar Meteorology

I C P M	International Congress of Physical Medicine
I C P O	International Criminal Police Organization (also known as INTERPOL)
I C P R	Inter-university Consortium for Political Research (USA)
I C R	Institute for Computer Research (Chicago University (USA))
	Ion Cyclotron Resonance
I C R C	International Committee of the Red Cross (Switzerland)
I C R F	Imperial Cancer Research Fund
I C R L	Injury Control Research Laboratory (of Community Environmental Management Bureau (HEW (USA)))
I C R M S	Integrated Computer-Reactor Monitoring System
I C R O	International Cell Research Organization
I C R U	International Commission on Radiological Units (now International Commission on Radiation Units and Measurements) (USA)
I C R U M	International Commission on Radiation Units and Measurements (USA)
I C S	Integrated Composite Spinning
	International Computing Symposium
	Intracranial Self-stimulation
	Ionization Current Source
I C S A	Institute of Chartered Secretaries and Administrators
I C S B	International Committee on Systematic Bacteriology (of IAMS)
I C S H	Interstitial Cell Stimulating Hormone
I C S H B	International Committee for Standardization in Human Biology (Belgium)
I C S I D	International Centre for Settlement of Investment Disputes (USA)
	International Council of Societies of Industrial Design (Belgium)
I C S L	Interactive Continuous Simulation Language
I C S P R O	Inter-Secretariat Committee on Scientific Programmes Related to Oceanography (of IOC (UNESCO))
I C S S D	International Committee for Social Sciences Documentation
I C S S R	Indian Council for Social Science Research (India)

I C S U	International Council of Scientific Unions (Italy)
I C S U / A B	ICSU Abstracting Board
I C T	Institution of Corrosion Technology
	Insulating Core Transformer
I C T A	International Conference on Thermal Analysis
I C T U	Irish Congress of Trade Unions (Eire)
I C U	Interface Control Unit
I C U M S A	International Commission for Uniform Methods of Sugar Analysis
I C V A N	International Committee on Veterinary Anatomical Nomenclature
I C W A	Institute of Cost and Works Accountants (now Institute of Cost and Management Accountants)
I C W A I	Institute of Cost and Works Accountants of India (India)
I C W P	Interstate Conference on Water Problems (USA)
I D A	Industrial Development Authority (Eire)
	Integrated Digital Avionics
	Intermediate Dialect of ATLAS (Abbreviated Test Language for Avionics Systems)
	International Development Association (USA) (of UN)
I D A A N	Instituto de Acueductos y Alcantarillados Nacionales (Panama) (Institute of National Aqueducts and Underground Sewers)
I D A C	Istituto di Acustica (of CNR (Italy)) (Institute of Acoustics)
I D A D S	Information Displays Automatic Drafting System
I D A P S	Image Data Processing System
I D B I	Industrial Development Bank of India (India)
I D B R A	International Drivers Behaviour Research Association
I D C	Industrial Development Certificate
	International Documentation in Chemistry
	Iterated Deferred Corrections
I D C H E C	Intergovernmental Documentation Centre on Housing and Environment (France)
I D C M A	Independent Data Communications Manufacturers Association (USA)
I D D D	International Direct Distance Dialing
I D E	Industrial Development Executive (of DTI)

I D E	Instituto para Directores de Empresa (Mexico) (Institute for Business Managers)
I D E A	Information Display Evolution and Advances
	Instituto para el Desarrollo de Ejecutives en la Argentina (Argentina) (Institute for the Development of Managers)
I D E C S	Image Discrimination, Enhancement, Combination, Sampling
I D H E C	Institut Des Hautes Etudes Cinematographiques (France) (Institute for Advanced Studies in Cinematography)
I D I	Institut de Developpement Industriel (France) (Industrial Development Institute)
I D I I O M	*Information Displays Incorporated* Input-Output Machine
I D I S	Intrusion Detection and Identification System
I D M H	Input Destination Message Handler
I D P L	Indian Drugs and Pharmaceuticals Limited (India) (Government owned)
I D R C	International Development Research Centre (Canada)
I D R O	Industrial Development and Renovation Organization (Iran)
I D S	Interim Decay Storage
I D S C	International Demographic Statistics Center (of Population Division, Census Bureau, Department of Commerce (USA))
I D S S	Integral Direct Station Selection
I D T S	Improved Doppler Tracking System
I D V M	Integrating Digital Voltmeter
I D W	Institut fur Dokumentationwesen (Germany) (Institute for Documentation Projects)
I E (I)	Institution of Engineers (India)
I E A	Indian Engineering Association (India)
I E A B	Internacia Esperanto-Asocio de Bibliotekistoj (International Association for Esperanto Speaking Librarians)
I E Aust	Institution of Engineers, Australia
I E B M	Interplay of Engineering with Biology and Medicine (a committee of the National Academy of Engineering (USA))
I E C	Israel Electric Corporation (Israel) (Government controlled)

I E C C A	Inter-Establishment Committee for Computer Applications (of MOD (PE))
I E C I C	International Engineering and Construction Industries Council (USA)
I E D S	Integrated Engineering Design Service
I E E E	Institute of Electrical and Electronics Engineers (USA)
I E E E - P E S	IEEE (USA) Power Engineering Society
I E F	Integral Equation Formulation
I E G	Internal Engine Generator
I E I	Institution of Engineering Inspection (now Institute of Quality Assurance)
I E M	Ion-Exchange Membranes
I E M A	Indian Electrical Manufacturers Association (USA)
I E M G I	Imperial Ethiopian Mapping and Geography Institute (Ethiopia)
I E M P	Internal Electromagnetic Pulse
I E N	Institut d'Etudes Nucleaires (Algeria) (Institute of Nuclear Studies)
	Istituto Elettrotecnico Nazionale (Italy) (National Electrotechnical Institute)
I E N S	Indian and Eastern Newspaper Society (India)
I E P	Isoelectric Point
I E R F	Industrial Educational and Research Foundation
I E S	Illuminating Engineering Society (USA)
	Invariant-Ellipticity States
I E S A	Illuminating Engineering Society of Australia (Australia)
	Indiana Electronic Service Association (USA)
	Instituto de Estudios Superiores de Administracion (Venezuela) (Institute for Advanced Management Studies)
I E S C	International Executive Service Corps (USA)
I E S E	Instituto de Estudios Superiores de la Empresa (Spain) (Institute for Advanced Management Studies)
I E V D	Integrated Electronic Vertical Display
I E X	Institute of Export
I F A	Indirect Fluorescent Antibody
	Integrated File Adaptor
	Interface Adapter
	International Fighter Aircraft

I F A	International Fiscal Association
	Inverse-Function Amplifier
	Israel Futurologist Association (Israel)
	Istituto di Fisica dell Atmosfera (Italy) (Institute of Atmospheric Physics)
I F A M	Information Systems for Associative Memories
I F A P	Istituto Formazione Addestramento Professionale (of IRA (Italy) (Administration Training Institute)
I F A P T	Compagnie Internationale d'Informatique APT (Automatically Programmed Tools)
I F A T C C	International Federation of Associations of Textile Chemists and Colourists (Switzerland)
I F A T E	International Federation of Airworthiness Technology and Engineering
I F C	Industrial Finance Corporation (India)
	Instrument Flight Center (USAF)
	International Finance Corporation (USA) (of UN)
	International Foundry Congress
I F C I	Industrial Finance Corporation of India (India)
I F C S	Integrated Fire Control System
I F E	Instituto de Fomento Economico (Panama) (Institute for Economic Development)
I F F	Institute of Freight Forwarders
I F F C O	Indian Farmers Fertilizer Cooperative (India)
I F H E	International Federation of Hospital Engineering
I F I P	International Federation for Information Processing (Switzerland)
I F L	Integer Function Language
I F L A	International Federation of Landscape Architects
I F M I S	Integrated Facilities Management Information System (US Army)
I F P	Institut Francaise du Petrole (France) (French Institute of Petroleum)
I F P M A	International Federation of Pharmaceutical Manufacturers Association (Switzerland)
I F P S	International Fluid Power Symposium
I F P W A	International Federation of Public Warehousing Associations
I F R	Immediate Free Recall
I F R C	International Futures Research Conference
I F R I	Inland Fisheries Research Institute (Sudan)

I F S	prefix to numbered series of Instrument Fact Sheets issued by NOIC (of NOAA (USA))
	Internal Focus Sensor
I F S C C	International Federation of Societies of Cosmetic Chemists
I F T	Indirect Fluorescent Antibody Test
	Interfacial Tension
I F T C	International Film and Television Council (Italy)
I F T F	International Fur Traders Federation
I F V M E	Inspectorate of Fighting Vehicles and Mechanical Equipment (MOD) (now QAD(FVE))
I F Y G L	International Field Year of the Great Lakes (a joint USA and Canada project, 1972)
I G	Iris Guide
I G A	Insulation Glazing Association
	International Grenfell Association
I G A E A	International Graphic Arts Education Association (USA)
I G A T	Iranian Gas Trunkline (of National Iranian Oil Company) (Iran)
I G L D	International Great Lakes Datum
Ig M	Immunoglobulin M
I G M	Istituto Geografico Militare (Italy) (Military Geography Institute)
I G N	Instituto Geografico Nacional (Guatemala) (National Geographic Institute)
I G S	Institute of Geological Sciences
	Intercapillary Glomerulosclerosis
I G S N	International Gravity Standardisation Net
I G T	Institute of Gas Technology (USA)
I G T S	Interactive Graphic Transit Simulator
I G U	International Geographical Union (USA) (of ICSU)
I G W E S	Inert Gas Wire Enamel Stripper
I H B	International Hydrographic Bureau (of IHO (Monaco))
I H B T D	Incompatible Haemolytic Blood Transfusion Disease
I H D	International Hydrological Decade (of UNESCO)
I H E A	International Health Evaluation Association
I H F	Industrial Hygiene Foundation of America (USA)
I H O	International Hydrographic Organisation (Monaco)
I HOSP E	Institute of Hospital Engineering

I H R	Infra-red Heterodyne Radiometer
I H S	Integrated Heat Sink
I H S R	Improved High Speed Rail
I H T S	Integrated Hybrid Transistor Switch
I H U	Instantaneous Unit Hydrograph
I I	Image Intensification
I I A	Information Industries Association (USA)
	Institute of Internal Auditors
I I A S	Inter-American Institute of Agricultural Sciences
I I A S A	International Institute for Applied Systems Analysis (Austria)
I I C	Indian Investment Centre (India)
	International Institute for Cotton
	Isotopes Information Center (ORNL (USAEC))
I I E C	Inter-Industry Emission Control program (USA)
I I E M	Indian Institute of Experimental Medicine (India)
I I E Q	Illinois Institute for Environmental Quality (USA)
I I I E	Indian Institute of Industrial Engineers (India)
I I M A	Indian Institute of Management (India)
I I M T	International Institute for the Management of Technology (Italy)
I I P	Institute of Incorporated Photographers
I I P A C S	Integrated Information Presentation and Control System
I I P F	International Institute of Public Finance
I I R	Isobutylene-isoprene Rubber
	Infinite Duration Impulse Response
I I R A	International Industrial Relations Association
I I R B	Institut International de Recherches Betteravieres (Belgium) (International Institute for Sugar Beet Research)
I I S	Integral Information System
I I S C O	Indian Iron and Steel Company (India) (Government owned)
I I S I	International Iron and Steel Institute (Belgium)
I I S L	International Institute of Space Law (France)
I I S S	International Institute for Strategic Studies
I I S W M	Institute of Iron and Steel Wire Manufacturers
I I T	Indian Institute of Technology (India)
I I T A	International Institute of Tropical Agriculture (Nigeria)
I I T C	Insurance Industry Training Council

I J I R A	Indian Jute Industry's Research Association (India)
I J M A	Indian Jute Mills Association (India)
I J S - R	prefix to numbered series of reports issued by Nuklearni Institut Jozef Stefan (Yugoslavia)
I Kh F	Institut Khimicheskoi Fiziki (USSR) (Institute of Chemical Physics)
I K V	Institut fuer Kunststoffverarbeitung (Germany) (Institute for Plastics Manufacture)
I L A	International Law Association
I L A C S	Integrated Library Administration and Cataloguing System
I L A F	Identical Location of Accelerometer and Force
I L A M S	Infra-red Laser Atmospheric Monitoring System
I L D	Indentation Load Deflection
I L E E D	Inelastic Low Energy Electron Diffraction
Illum E S	Illuminating Engineering Society
I L M	Independent Landing Monitor
I L O	Injection Locked Oscillator
	International Labour Organziation (Switzerland) (of UN)
I L R	Institute of Library Research (University of California (USA))
I L R V	Integral Launch and Re-entry Vehicle
I L S	Industrial Liaison Scheme (of MINTECH and later DTI) (disbanded 1973)
	International Latitude Service
I L S S	Inter-Laminar Shear Strength
I L T M S	International Leased Telegraph Message Switching (of the British Post Office)
I L Z R O	International Lead Zinc Research Organisation (USA)
I M	Institute of Marketing and Sales Management
	Institutet for Metalforskning (Sweden) (Institute for Metals Research)
	Instrument Myopia
	Inter-Modulation
I M A	Indian Medical Association (India)
	International Management Association
	Ion Microprobe Analyzer
I M A C	Illinois State Library (USA) Microfilm Automated Catalog
	International Management Advisory Council (of the British Institute of Management)

I M A C E	Association des Industries Margarinieres des pays de la CEE (Association of Margarine Manufacturing Industries of the Countries of the European Economic Community)
I M A G E	Intruder Monitoring And Guidance Equipment
I M A M	Instituto Mexicano de Administracion (Mexico) (Mexican Institute of Management)
I M A T	Intermodal Automated Transfer
I M B I	Institute of Medical and Biological Illustration
I M B L M S	Integrated Medical and Behavioural Laboratory Measurement System
I M B M	Institute of Municipal Building Management
I M C A S	Interactive Man/Computer Augmentation Systems
I M C O	Improved Combustion
	Intergovernmental Maritime Consultative Organization (of UN)
I M D	Independent Module Development
	Indian Meteorological Department (India)
I M E	Institution of Military Engineers (India)
	Institution of Municipal Engineers
	International Magnetospheric Explorer
I M E D E	Institut pour l'Etude des Methodes de Direction de l'Entreprise (Switzerland) (Institute for the Study of Business Management)
I M E P	Indicated Mean Effective Pressure
I M F	International Monetary Fund (USA) (of UN)
I M G	International Modular Group
I M I	Interim Manned Interceptor
	Israel Military Industries (of Ministry of Defence (Israel))
I M I C	Interval Modulation Information Coding
I M I S	Institute of Medical Illustrators in Scotland
	International Marketing Information Service (of Bureau of International Commerce (USA))
I M L	Intermediate Machine Language
I M M A C	Inventory Management and Material Control
I M M S	Ion Microprobe Mass Spectrometer
I M P	*ICL* Micromation Pack
	Integrated Macro Package
	Interactive Machine-language Programming
	Inventory Management Package

I M P A	International Maritime Pilots Association
	International Master Printers Association
I M P A C	Information for Management Planning Analysis and Coordination
I M P A C T	Improved Management of Procurement and Contracting Techniques (US Army)
	Integrated Management Planning and Control Techniques
I M P A T T	Impact Ionization Avalanche Transit Time
I M P A V	Inter-urban Microwave-Powered Air-cushion Vehicle
I M P C	International Municipal Parking Congress
	Istituto di Arte Mineraria (Italy) (Institute of Mining Engineering)
I M P I C S	Integrated Manufacturing Programme Information and Control System
I M R	Institute of Marine Resources (California University (USA))
I M R A	Industrial Marketing Research Association
I M R S	International Mutual Response System
I M R U	Industrial Materials Research Unit (London University)
I M S	Information Management System
	Division of Inorganic and Metallic Structure (of the National Physical Laboratory)
	Institute of Manpower Studies
	Institute of Mathematical Statistics (Michigan State University (USA))
	Institute on Man and Science (USA)
I M S C O	Initial Maritime Satellite Consortium (six United States and two British oil companies and tanker operators)
I M S E	Integrated Mean Square Error
I M S O	Institute of Municipal Safety Officers
I M S S O C	*Institute of Manpower Studies* System of Occupational Classification
I M T A	Institute of Municipal Treasurers and Accountants (now Chartered Institute of Public Finance and Accountancy)
I M T M A	Indian Machine Tool Manufacturers Association (India)
I M T R A N	Implicit Transport
I M U	International Mathematical Union (of ICSU)

I M W I C	International Maize and Wheat Improvement Centre (Mexico)
I N A	Industrija Nafte (Yugoslavia) (State Oil Agency)
I N A C A P	Instituto Nacional de Capacitacion Profesional (Chile) (National Institute of Professional Training)
I N A D	Instituto Nacional de Administracion para el Desarrollo (Guatemala)
I N A P	Inverse Nyquist Analysis Programme
I N A P A	Instituto Nacional de Aquas Potables y Alcantarillados (Dominica) (National Institute of Public Water Supply and Sewage)
I N A R	Institute of Northern Agricultural Research (USA)
I N C	Instituto Nacional de Canalizaciones (Venezuela) (National Institute of Dredging)
I N C A	Innovation through Creative Analysis
I N C A E	Instituto Centroamericano de Administracion de Empresas (Nicaragua) (Central American Institute of Business Management)
I N C A P	Instituto de Nutricion de Centroamerica y Panama (Guatemala) (Institute of Nutrition of Central America and Panama)
I N C A S	Integrated Navigation and Collision Avoidance System
I N C O L D A	Instituto Colombiano de Administracion (Colombia) (Colombian Institute of Management)
I N C O R A	Instituto Colombiano de la Reforma Agraria (Colombia) (Colombian Institute of Agrarian Reform)
I N C O S	Integrated Control System
I N C R A	International Copper Research Association
I N C R A P L A N	Integrated Crew and Aircraft Planning
I N D A	Instituto Nacional de Desenvolvimento Agrario (Brazil) (National Institute of Agrarian Development)
I N D A L	Indian Aluminium Company Limited (India)
I N D O C	Information-Documentation and Communication
I N D O R	Internuclear Double Resonance
I N E A	International Electronics Association (Germany)
I N E R H I	Instituto Ecuatoriano de Recursos Hidraulicos (Ecuador) (Institute of Water Resources)
I N F I R S	Inverted File Information Retrieval System (of UKCIS)
I N F L O	Integrated Flight Optimization system

I N F N	Istituto Nazionale di Fisica Nucleare (Italy) (National Institute of Nuclear Physics)
I N F O R	Information Network and File Organization
I N F O R M	Information for Minnesota (a service provided by a consortium of five libraries in Minnesota (USA))
	International Reference Organization in Forensic Medicine and Sciences (USA)
I N F O R M A C	Immediate Information For Merchant And Customer
I N F O R M A P	Information Necessary for Optimum Resource Management and Protection
I N F O T E R M	International Information Centre for Terminology (Austrian Standards Institute (Austria))
I N G A	Interactive Graphic Analysis
I N I	Istituto Nazionale dell'Informazione (Italy) (National Institute of Information)
I N I E X	Institut National des Industries Extractives (Belgium)
I N L P	Integer Non-Linear Programming
I N M A S	Institute of Nuclear Medicine and Allied Sciences (India)
I N M M	Institute of Nuclear Materials Management (USA)
I N P C	Irish National Productivity Committee (Eire)
I N P E	Instituto de Pesquisas Espaciais (Brazil) (Institute of Space Research)
I N P L A Y	Random Access Microfilm Information Retrieval Display System
I N Q U A	International Union for Quaternary Research
I N R A	Instituto Nacional de la Reforma Agraria (Cuba) (National Institute for Agrarian Reform)
I N R A T	Institut National de la Recherche Agronomique de Tunisie (Tunisia) (National Research Institute of Agronomy)
I N R F	Institut National de Recherches Forestieres (Tunisia) (National Institute of Forestry Research)
I N R S	Institut National de Recherche Scientifique (Rwanda) (National Institute of Scientific Research)
I N S	Institute for Nuclear Study (Tokyo University (Japan))
	Institute of Naval Studies (of Center for Naval Analyses (USN))

I N S	Institute of Nuclear Sciences (of DSIR (New Zealand))
I N S A T	Indian National Satellite
I N S E A N	Instituto per Studi ed Esperenze di Architettura Navale (Italy) (National Institute for Naval Architecture Research and Testing)
I N S F O P A L	Instituto Nacional de Fomento Municipal (Colombia)
I N S I G H T	Instructional Systems Investigation Graphic Tool
I N S O R A	Instituto de Organizacion y Administracion (Chile)
I N S P E C	Information Service in Physics, Electrical and Electronics Engineering, Computer and Control Engineering (of IEE and IEEE (USA))
I N S P E C T	Integrated Nationwide System for Processing Entries from Customs Terminals (Australia)
Inst M P	Institute of Management in Printing
I N S T O P	Institut National Scientifique et Technique d'Oceanographie et de Peche (Tunisia) (National Scientific and Technical Institute of Oceanography and Fisheries)
Inst Phys	Institute of Physics
I N S U R V	Board of Inspection and Survey (USN)
I N T	Instituto Nacional de Tecnologia (Brazil) (National Institute of Technology) Isaac Newton Telescope
I N T A A S	Integrated Aircraft Armament System
I N T A L	Instituto para la Integracion de America Latina (Argentina) (Institute for Latin America Integration)
I N T A S S	*Intel* Assembler
I N T E C H	Instituto Technologica (Chile) (Technical Institute)
I N T E C O L	International Association for Ecology
I N T E C O M	International Council for Technical Communication
I N T E R B R A N T	Union Intercommunale des Centrales Electriques du Brabant (Belgium)
I N T E R C O	International Code of Signals
I N T E R C O M	Societe Intercommunale Belge de Gaz et Electricite (Belgium)
I N T E R C O M S A	Intercontinental de Communicaciones por Satellite SA (Panama)

INTERCON	International Convention and Exposition (of IEEE (USA))
INTERKAMA	International Congress and Exhibition for Instrumentation and Automation
INTERMAG	International Magnetics Conference (of IEEE (USA))
INTERNET	Interactive Network Analysis
INTERPOL	*see* ICPO
INTERSPACE	Interactive System for Pattern Analysis, Classification, and Enhancement
INTESCA	Internacional de Ingenieria y Estudios Tecnicos SA (Spain)
INTI	Instituto Nacional de Tecnologia Industrial (Argentina) (National Institute of Industrial Technology)
INTIME	Interactive Textual Information Management Experiment
INTIPS	Intelligence Information Processing System
INTP	Institut National des Telecommunications et des Postes (Madagascar) (National Institute of Telecommunications and Posts)
IN2P3	Institut National de Physique Nucléaire et de Physique des Particules (France) (National Institute of Nuclear and Particle Physics)
INTLOC	Interdiction of Lines of Communication
INTOSAI	International Organization of Supreme Audit Institutions
INVL	Invariant Magnetic Latitude
IO	Image Orthicon
IOA	Indian Optometric Association (India)
IOAHPR	International Organisation for the Advancement of High Pressure Research (now International Association for the Advancement of High Pressure Research and Development)
IOBC	International Organization for Biological Control of Noxious Animals and Plants
IOC	Indian Oil Corporation (India)
	Initial Operational Capacity
IOCU	International Organisations of Consumers Unions (Netherlands)
IOE	International Organisation of Employers (Switzerland)
IOFC	Indian Ocean Fisheries Commission

I O H C	Institute for Occupational Hazard Control (of New York University and AIIE (USA))
I O I C	Integrated Operational Intelligence Center (USN)
I O M	Institute of Metals (to be merged into the Metals Society in 1974)
	Institute of Office Management (now the Institute of Administrative Management)
I O M A	International Oxygen Manufacturers Association (USA)
I O M T R	International Organisation for Motor Trades and Repairs (Netherlands)
I O N	Isthmo-Optic Nucleus
I O P	Input/Output Processor
	Institute of Physics
I O P E C	Iranian Oil Exploration and Production Company (Iran)
I O P L	Internal Optical Path Length
I O P O	Internal Optical Parametric Oscillator
I O R	Institute of Operational Research
I O R S	Inflatable Occupant Restraint Systems
I O S	Institute of Oceanographic Sciences (of Natural Environment Research Council)
I O S N	Indian Ocean Standard Net
I O T A	Institute of Theoretical Astronomy
I O T T	Institute of Operating Theatre Technicians
I O T T S G	International Oil Tanker Terminal Safety Group
I P	Index of Preprogramming
	Induced Polarization
	Information Processor
	Instrumentation Paper
	Ionization Potential
	Ionized Particle
I P A	Institute of Public Affairs (Australia)
I P A A	Independent Petroleum Association of America
I P A C S	Interactive Pattern Analysis and Classification System
I P A D	Integrated Programmes for Aerospace-vehicle Design
I P A D E	Instituto Panamericano de Alta Direccion de Empresa (Mexico) (Panamerican Institute for Business Management)
I P A E	Instituto Peruano de Administracion de Empresas (Peru) (Peruvian Institute of Business Management)

I P A R S	International Programmed Airlines Reservation System
I P A R T	Institute of Photographic Apparatus Repair Technicians
I P B	Inventions Promotion Board (India)
I P B A	India, Pakistan, and Bangladesh Association
I P C	Impurity Photoconductivity
	Institute of Paper Chemistry (USA)
	Instituto de Plasticos y Caucho (Spain) (Institute of Plastics and Rubber)
I P C L	Indian Petro-Chemicals Corporation (India)
I P C R	Institute of Physical and Chemical Research (Japan)
I P C S	Integrated Propulsion Control System
I P D F	Intensity Probability Density Function
I P E	Asociacion de Investigacion Tecnica de la Industria Papelera Espanola (Spain) (Technical Research Association of the Spanish Paper Industry)
	Instituto Portugues da Embalagen (Portugal) (Portuguese Institute of Packaging)
I P E N	Pan-American Naval Engineering Institute
I P F	Institut Francaise du Petrole, des Carburants et Lubrifiants (France) (French Institute of Petrol, Motor Fuels and Lubricants)
I P F E O	Institut des Producteurs de Ferro-alliages d'Europe Occidentale (Institute of Producers of Iron Alloys of Western Europe)
I P G	Independent Publishers Guild
I P I	Industrial Production Index
	Infinite Position Indicator
	International Petroleum Institute
	International Press Institute (Switzerland)
I P I A	Induced Psycho-Intellectual Activity
I P I R A	Indian Plywood Industries Research Association (India)
I P I S	Instrument Pilot Instructor School (USAF)
I P L	Image Processing Laboratory (California Institute of Technology (USA))
	Improved Position Locator
I Plant E	Institution of Plant Engineers
I P L O	Institute of Professional Librarians of Ontario (Canada)
I P M	Institut de Physique Meteorologique (Senegal) (Institute of Physical Meteorology)

I P M	Institute Pasteur du Maroc (Morocco) (Pasteur Institute of Morocco)
	Integrated Manufacturing Planning
I P M A	In-plant Printing Management Association (USA)
I P N	Inter-penetrating Polymeric Network
I P P	Imaging Photopolarimeter
	Institut fur Plasmaphysik (Germany) (Institute for Plasma Physics)
	Isopentenyl Pyrophosphate
I P P A	Irish Professional Photographers Association (Eire)
I P P M A	In-Plant Printing Management Association (USA)
I P P R	Intermittent Positive Pressure Respiration
I P P S	Institute of Physics and the Physical Society (now the Institute of Physics)
I P S	Improved Plow Steel
	Interactive Planning System
	Interactive Programming System
	International Pyrheliometric Scale
I P S J	Information Processing Society of Japan (Japan)
I P S O	Initiating Production by Sales Order
I P S P	Inhibitory Post-Synaptic Potential
I P T	Individual Perception Threshold
I P T C	International Press Telecommunication Committee
I P T H	Immunoreactive Parathyroid Hormone
I Q A	Institute of Quality Assurance
I Q E C	International Quantum Electronics Conference
I Q I	Image Quality Indicator
I Q M H	Input Queue Message Handler
I R	Inland Revenue
	Interagency Report
	Institut fur Raumfahrttecknik (Institute for Space Technology) (of Technical University, Berlin (Germany))
	Insulation Resistance
	Israel Railways (Israel)
I R - N D T	Infra-Red Non-Destructive Testing
I R A	Inertial Reference Assembly
	Intermediate Range Aircraft
	Investment-Return Assumption
I R A D	Independent Research And Development
I R A D E S	Istituto Ricerche Applicate Documentazione e Studi (Italy)

I R A N D O C	Iranian Documentation Centre (Iran)
I R A P	Industrial Research Assistance Programme (of NRC (Canada))
I R A S	Interdiction Reconnaissance Attack System
I R A T E	Inertial Range Atmospheric Turbulence Entrainment
I R B	Industry Reference Black
I R C	Industrial Reorganisation Corporation (disbanded 1970)
	Institute of Naval Studies Research Contribution (of CNA (USN))
I R C C S	Intrusion-Resistant Communications Cable System
I R D C	Industrial Research and Development Center (Virginia University (USA))
I R D E	Instruments Research and Development Establishment (India)
I R D I A	Industrial Research and Development Incentives Act (administered by Department of Industry, Trade and Commerce (Canada))
I R E	Indian Rare Earths Limited (of Department of Atomic Energy (India))
I R E D A	International Radio and Electrical Distributors Association
I R E E	Institution of Radio and Electronics Engineers (Australia)
I R F	Instrument Reliability Factors
	Interrogation Repetition Frequency
I R G A	Infra-Red Gas-Analyser
I R G O M	International Research Group on Management (headquarters in the University of Rochester (USA))
I R H E	Instituto de Recursos Hydraulicos y Electrification (Panama)
I R I	Immunoreactive Insulin
	Interuniversitair Reactor Instituut (Netherlands)
I R I A	Institute Recherche d'Information et d'Automatique (France) (Research Institute of Data Processing and Automation)
	Indian Rubber Industries Association (India)
I R I E	Infra-Red Interference Envelope
I R I S	International Radiation Investigation Satellite
I R I S H	Infra-Red Image Seeker Head

I R L	Index Retrieval Language
	Interactive Root Locus
	Ionosphere Research Laboratory (Pennsylvania State University (USA))
I R L A	Independent Research Library Association (USA)
I R L C S	International Red Locust Control Service (Zambia)
I R L S	Infra-Red Line Scanner
	Infra-Red Linescan System
I R M	Interim Research Memorandum
I R M A	Infra-Red Milk Analyser
	Interactive Real-time Music Assembler
I R N D T	Infra-Red Non-Destructive Testing
I R O S	Increased Reliability of Operational Systems
I R P	Image Retaining Panel
	International Reference Preparation (medical preparations approved by WHO Expert Committee on Biological Standardization)
I R R	Israel Research Reactor
I R R P	Improved Rearming Rates Project (USN)
I R R P O S	Interdisciplinary Research Relevant to the Problems of Our Society (a project of NSF (USA))
I R R U	Industrial Relations Research Unit (University of Warwick)
I R S	Institut fur Reaktorsicherheit (Germany) (Institute for Reactor Safety)
	Internal Revenue Service (of Treasury Dept) (USA)
I R S A	Industrial Radiographic Service Association (USA)
I R S E	Institution of Railway Signal Engineers
I R S L L	Image Recording System, Low Light
I R T	Infra-Red Temperature
	Institute for Rapid Transit (USA)
	Institut fur Rundfunktechnik (Germany) (Institute for Radio Engineering)
	Inter-Response Time
	Isotope Ratio Tracer
I R T D A	Indian Roads and Transport Development Association (India)
I R T S	Infra-Red Temperature Sounder
	Irish Radio Transmitters Society (Eire)
I R T T D	Infra-Red Transmission Through the Diffusion
I R U S	Infantry Rifle Unit Study (US Army)

IS(PE)MA

I S (P E) M A	Industrial Safety (Protective Equipment) Manufacturers Association
I S A	International Safety Academy (USA)
	International Sociological Association
	International Standard Atmosphere
I S A A	Institute of South African Architects (South Africa)
I S A E	Indian Society of Agricultural Engineers (India)
I S A F	Intermediate Super-Abrasion Furnace
I S A G E X	International Satellite Geodesy Experiments (sponsored by COSPAR)
I S A R	Inter-Seamount Acoustic Range
I S A S	Illinois State Academy of Science (USA)
	Institute of Space and Aeronautical Science (India)
	Institute of Space and Aeronautical Science (Tokyo University) (Japan)
	Isotopic Source Assay System
I S B	Independent Sideband
I S B D	International Standard Bibliographic Description
I S C	International Seismological Centre
I S C A	International Standards Steering Committee for Consumer Affairs (of ISO (Switzerland))
I S C C	Iron and Steel Consumer Council
I S C O L	International Systems Corporation of Lancaster (University of Lancaster)
I S C T R	International Scientific Committee for Trypanosomiasis Research
I S D G	Information Science Discussion Group
I S D O S	Information System Design and Optimization System
I S D P	Ice Shelf Drilling Projects
I S D S	Instruction Set Design System
	International Serials Data System (of the UNISIST programme)
I S E	Institution of Sales Engineers
	Integral of the Squared Error
	International Society of Electrochemistry
	International Society of Endocrinology (USA)
I S E C	International Solvent Extraction Conference
I S E F	International Science and Engineering Fair
I S E P S	International Sun-Earth Physics Satellite
I S E S	International Ship Electric Service Association
	International Society of Explosives Specialists

I S E S	International Solar Energy Society (Australia)
I S F	International Shipping Federation
	Intersection of the Shifted Fringes
I S F A	International Scientific Film Association
I S F C	Indicated Specific Fuel Consumption
I S F M S	Index Sequential File Management System
I S G	Inland Shipping Group (of the Inland Waterways Association)
	Interfacial Surface Generator
I S G P	International Society of General Practice (Germany)
I S G S H	International Study Group for Steroid Hormones
I S H C	Intersociety Safety and Health Committee (of the foundry industry) (USA))
I S I	In-Service Inspection
	Instrument Systems Installation
	International Statistical Institute (Netherlands)
	Inter-Symbol Interference
	Iron and Steel Institute (to be merged into The Metals Society in 1974)
I S I C	International Standard Industrial Classification of all Economic Activities (of UN)
I S I J U	Indian Statistical Institute and Jadaipur University (a computer developed by the two institutions)
I S I M E P	International Symposium on Identification and Measurement of Environmental Pollutants
I S I O	Institute for the Study of International Organisation (University of Sussex)
I S I S	Integral Spar Inspection System
	Integrated Set of Information Systems
	Integrated Scientific Information Service (of the International Labour Office) (Switzerland)
I S J C T	International Symposium on Jet Cutting Technology
I S L	Interactive Simulation Language
I S M	Independent Subcarrier Method
	Interactive Siting Method
	Interim Surface Missile
I S M A	Indian Sugar Mills Association (India)
I S M A P	Instrumentation System Margin Analysis Programme
I S M E	Institute of Sheet Metal Engineering

I S M E C	Information Service in Mechanical Engineering (of IMechE and IEE)
I S M G	International Scientific Management Group (of GARP Atlantic Tropical Experiment)
I S M H	Input Source Message Handler
I S O	Information-Structure-Oriented
	International Organization for Standardization (Switzerland)
I S O C A R P	International Society of City and Regional Planners
I S O D A T A	Iterative Self Organizing Data Analysis Technique A
I S O R I D	International Information System on Research in Documentation (a project of UNESCO)
I S P	Image Storage Panel
	Instruction Set Processor
I S P A	International Society for the Protection of Animals
	International Software Products Association (France)
I S P C C	International Ship Painting and Corrosion Conference
I S P E	Institutul de Studii si Proiectari Energetice (Romania) (Insitute for Power Studies and Designs)
I S P E C	Interagency Scientific Products Evaluation Committee (administered by GSA (USA))
I S P E M A	Industrial Safety (Protective Equipment) Manufacturers Association
I S P F	Integral Skinned Polyurethane Foam
I S P I C E	Interactive Simulated Programme Integrated Circuit Emphasis
I S P L	Incremental System Programming Language
I S P L S	Indiana Society of Professional Land Surveyors (USA)
I S P P	Illinois State Physics Project (USA)
I S P P M	Institut Scientifique et Technique des Peches Maritimes (France) (Sea Fishing Scientific and Technical Institute)
I S R	Institute of Surgical Research (US Army)
I S R A I N	Institut Superieur de Recherche Appliquee pour les Industries Nucleaires (Belgium) (Advanced Institute of Applied Research for the Nuclear Industries)

I S R C D V S	International Society for Research on Civilisation Diseases and Vital Substances
I S R O	Indian Space Research Organisation (India)
I S R O - M I T (I N S A T)	Indian Space Research Organisation and Massachusetts Institute of Technology (USA) Studies on the Indian National Satellite project
I S R R T	International Society of Radiographers and Radiological Technicians
I S S	Inertial Sensor System
	Intra-list Stimulus Similarity
	Ionosphere Sounding Satellite
	Ion Scattering Spectrometry
	Ion Source Spectrometry
	Istituto Superiore di Sanita (Italy) (Advanced Institute of Health)
I S S C C	International Solid-State Circuits Conference (IEEE (USA))
I S S M	Interim Surface-to-Surface Missile
I S S M I S	Integrated Support Services Management Information System (US Army)
I S S N	International Standard Serial Number (devised by ISO (Switzerland))
I S S P	Irish Society for Surveying and Photogrammetry (Eire)
I S T	Institute for Science and Technology (University of Michigan (USA))
	Integrated Switching and Transmission
	Interim STOL Transport
I S T A	Industrial Science and Technology Agency (of MITI (Japan))
	International Society for Technology Assessment
I S T A M	Israel Society for Theoretical and Applied Mechanics (Israel)
I S T C	Indo-Swiss Training Centre (India)
	Institute of Scientific and Technical Communicators
I S T C L	International Scientific and Technical Committee on Laundering
I S T R A N / P L	IHI (*Ishikawajima-Harima Heavy Industries Company*) (Japan) Structure Analysis/Plate Structure, Linear Analysis
I S U	Inertial Sensing Unit
	Iowa State University (USA)

I S U / C C L	Iowa State University, Cyclone Computer Laboratory (USA)
I S U - E R I	Iowa State University, Engineering Research Institute (USA)
I S V E S T A	Individual Survival Vest for Aircrew
I S W M	Institute of Solid Waste Management
I S W R R I	Iowa State Water Resources Research Institute (USA)
I S W S	Illinois State Water Survey (USA)
I T	The Industrial Tribunal
I T A	Independent Television Authority (now Independent Broadcasting Authority)
	Industrial Transport Association (now merged with the Chartered Institute of Transport)
	Institut du Transport Aerien (Institute of Air Transport) (France)
	International Thermographers Association (of Printing Industries Association of America (USA)
I T A C S	Integrated Tactical Air Control System
I T A E	Integral of Time Absolute Value of Error
I T A I	Institution of Technical Authors and Illustrators (now part of ISTC)
I T A L	Instituut voor Toepassing van Atoomenergie in de Landbouw (Netherlands) (Institute for the Application of Nuclear Energy to Agriculture)
I T A L S I E L	Societa Italiana Sistemi Informativ Elettronica (Italy)
I T C	International Teletraffic Congress
	International Training Centre for Aerial Survey (now International Institute for Aerial Survey and Earth Sciences (Netherlands))
I T C A	Independent Television Companies Association
I T C F	Institut Technique des Cereales et des Fourrages (of ACTA (France)) (Technical Institute for Cereals and Fodder)
I T C Z	Inter-Tropical Convergence Zone
I T D G	Intermediate Technology Development Group (Reading University)
I T E	Intercity Transport Effectiveness
I T E B	Institut Technique d'Elevage Bovin (of ACTA (France)) (Technical Institute for Cattle Rearing)

I T E C	Instituto Tecnologico de Electronica y Communi-caciones (Colombia) (Technical Institute of Electronics and Communications)
I T E F	Institut Teoreticheskoy i Eksperimental'noy Fiziki (USSR) (Institute of Theoretical and Experimental Physics)
I T E M	Integrated Test and Maintenance
I T E S C	International Tanker Equipment Standing Committee
I T F	Interactive Terminal Facility
I T F S	Instructional Television Fixed Service
I T G A	Isothermogravimetric Analysis
I T I	Indian Telephone Industries (India)
	Inter-Trial Interval
I T I C	International Tsunami Information Centre (Honolulu)
I T I R C	IBM (*International Business Machines*) Technical Information Retrieval Center
I T L C	Instant Thin Layer Chromatography
I T M	Institute of Tropical Meteorology (India)
I T M C	International Transmission Maintenance Centre
I T M I S	Integrated Transportation Management Information System (US Army)
I T O	Institute of Training Officers
I T P	Institute of Theoretical Physics (Stanford University (USA))
I T P A	Independent Telephone Pioneer Association (USA)
I T P P	Institute of Technical Publicity and Publications (now part of ISTC)
I T P R	Infrared Temperature Profile Radiometer
I T P R L	Individual Training and Performance Research Laboratory (of ARI (US Army))
I T P S	Income Tax Payers Society
	Internal Tele-Processing System
I T R C	Industrial Toxicology Research Centre (India)
I T R D C	Inland Transport Research and Development Council (now the Planning and Transport Research Advisory Council)
I T S	Industrial Training Service (sponsored by the Department of Employment and the CTC)
	Institute for Telecommunication Service (of Office of Telecommunications (USA))
	Insertion *or* Interval Test Signal

I T S C	International Telephone Service Centres
	International Tyre Specialists Congress
I T S E	Integral of Time Squared Error
I T T	Institute of Textile Technology (USA)
	Inter-stage Turbine Temperature
I T T E	Institute of Transportation and Traffic Engineering (University of California (USA))
I T U	International Telecommunication Union (Switzerland) (of UN)
I T X	Information Transfer Exchange
I U A I	International Union of Aviation Insurers
I U A T	International Union Against Tuberculosis
I U B T P	Inter-University Biology Teaching Project
I U C N	International Union for the Conservation of Nature and Natural Resources (Switzerland)
I U Cr	International Union of Crystallography (of ICSU)
I U C S	Inter-Union Commission on Spectroscopy (of ICSU)
I U G G	International Union of Geodesy and Geophysics (of ICSU)
I U H P S	International Union for the History and Philosophy of Science (of ICSU)
I U M P	International Upper Mantle Project (project concluded December, 1970)
I U N S	International Union of Nutritional Sciences (of ICSU)
I U O T O	International Union of Official Travel Organizations
I U P A B	International Union of Pure and Applied Biophysics (of ICSU)
I U P A C	International Union of Pure and Applied Chemistry (of ICSU)
I U P A P	International Union of Pure and Applied Physics (of ICSU)
I U S S P	International Union for the Scientific Study of Population
I U T A M	International Union of Theoretical and Applied Mechanics (of ICSU)
I V	Intravenous
I V A	Ingenjors Vetenskaps Akademeins (Sweden) (Academy of Engineering Societies)
I V B S	Industriele Vereniging tot Bevordering van de Stralingsveiligheid (Netherlands) (Industrial Association to promote Security from Radiation)

I V C S	Interior Voice Communications System
I V D	Inductive Voltage Divider
I V F	Instutet for Verkstadsteknisk Forskning (Sweden) (Institute for Production Engineering Research)
I V H M	In-Vessel Handling Machine
I V L	Institutet for Vatten -och Luftvards-forskning (Sweden) (Institute for Water and Air Research)
I V P	Instituto Venezolano de Petroquimica (Venezuela) (State Petrochemical enterprise)
	Intravenous Pyelogram
I V T	Infinitely Variable Transmission
	Internationale Vereinigung der Textileinkaufsverbande (Germany) (International Association of Textile Purchasing Societies)
I W	Induction Welding
I W A	Inland Waterways Association
I W C S	Integrated Wideband Communications System
I W E	Institution of Water Engineers
I W G N S R D	International Working Group on Nuclear Structure and Reaction Data
I W L S	Iterative Weighted Least Squares
I W P	Inverse Wulff Plot
I W R	Institute for Water Resources (US Army)
I W R A	International Water Resources Association (USA)
I W S	International Wool Secretariat
I W S O E	International Weddell Sea Oceanographic Expedition
I W T S	Integrated, Worldwide, Topographic System
I Y R U	International Yacht Racing Union

J

J A	Journal Article
J A C C	Joint Automatic Control Conference (USA)
J A C L A P	Joint Advisory Committee on Local Authority Purchasing
J A F N A	Joint USAF/NASA
J A M A	Japan Automobile Manufacturers Association (Japan)
J A M C	Japan Aircraft Manufacturing Corporation (Japan)
J A M I N T E L	Jamaica International Telecommunications Limited (Jamaica)

JAMSTEC	Japan Marine Science and Technology Centre (Japan)
JANNAF	Joint Army-Navy-NASA-Air Force (USA)
JAPIA	Japan Auto Parts Industries Association (Japan)
JAR	Job Appraisal Review
JARL	Japan Amateur Radio League (Japan)
JARTS	Japan Railway Technical Service (Japan)
JAS	Junior Astronomical Society
JASIN	Joint Air-Sea Interaction (a project sponsored by the Royal Society)
JAST	Jamaican Association of Sugar Technologists (Jamaica)
JAT	Jugoslovenski Aerotransport (Yugoslavia)
JBESA	Joint British Committee for Stress Analysis
JCAE	Joint Committee on Atomic Energy (of United States Congress)
JCAP	Joint Committee on Aviation Pathology
JCHST	Joint Committee on Higher Surgical Training (of Royal College of Surgeons and Association of Surgeons)
JCIA	Japan Camera Industry Association (Japan)
JCIT	Jerusalem (Israel) Conference on Information Technology
JCL	Job Control Language
JCPI	Japan Cotton Promotion Institute (Japan)
JCUDI	Japan Computer Usage Development Institute (Japan)
JCVS	JOVIAL Compiler Validation System
JDW	Jacket Decladding Waste solutions
JE	Japanese Encephalitis
JEC	Joint European Committee of Paper Exporters
JECC	Japan Electronic Computer Corporation (Japan)
JECMA	Japan Export Clothing Makers Association (Japan)
JEMIMA	Japan Electric Measuring Instruments Manufacturers Association (Japan)
JEPI	Junior Eysenck Personality Inventory
JERC	Japan Economic Research Centre (Japan)
JES	Japan Electroplating Society (Japan)
JET	Joint European Tokamak
JETDS	Joint Electronic Type Designation System (of NATO)
JETS	Job Executive and Transput Satellite
Joint Enroute Terminal System

J E V	Japanese Encephalitis Virus
J F E T T	Junction Field-Effect Transistor Tetrode
J F R O	Joint Fire Research Organisation
J F T O T	Jet Fuel Thermal Oxidation Test
J G S D F	Japan Ground Self Defence Force
J H R P	Joint Highway Research Project (of Purdue University, Indiana State Highway Commission and the FHWA (USA))
J H U - C R S C	Johns Hopkins University - Centre for Research in Scientific Communication (USA)
J I B A	Japan Institute of Business Administration (Japan)
J I C	Jet Induced Circulation
	Joint Iron Council (dissolved 1972)
J I D A	Japan Industrial Designers Association (Japan)
J I D C	Jamaica Industrial Development Corporation (Jamaica)
J I L A - I C	Joint Institute for Laboratory Astrophysics - Information Center (University of Colorado (USA))
J M C	Japan Monopoly Corporation (Japan)
J M I A	Japan Mining Industry Asssociation (Japan)
J M I F	Japan Motor Industrial Federation (Japan)
J M M A	Japan Microscope Manufacturers Association (Japan)
J M M I I	Japan Machinery and Metals Inspection Institute (Japan)
J M S D F	Japan Maritime Self Defence Force (Japan)
J M S P O	Joint Meteorological Satellite Program Office (USA)
J M T R	Japan Material Testing Reactor (of JAERI)
J N S	Japan Nuclear Society (Japan)
J N U L	Jewish National and University Library (Israel)
J O I D E S	Joint Oceanographic Institutions for Deep Earth Sampling
J O N S D A P	Joint North Sea Data Acquisition Programme (of Belgium, Netherlands and United Kingdom)
J O S S	Joint Ocean Surface Study (sponsored by Naval Oceanographic Office (USN))
J P A	Japan Petroleum Association (Japan)
J P C	Japan Productivity Centre (Japan)
J P D C	Japan Petroleum Development Corporation (Japan)
J P L	Jet Propulsion Laboratory (California Institute of Technology (USA)) (now H. Allen Smith Jet Propulsion Laboratory)

J P L - S T A R	Jet Propulsion Laboratory (California Institute of Technology) Self Testing And Repairing computer
J P P S C	Joint Petroleum Products Sub-Committee (of DMSC (MOD))
J P R S	Joint Publications Research Service (of NTIS (USA))
J R B A C	Joint Review Board Advisory Committee (of some trade associations and the CBI)
J R C	Joint Research Centre (of EURATOM)
J R S M A	Japan Rolling Stock Manufacturers Association (Japan)
J R T	Jugoslovenska Radiotelevizija (Yugoslavia)
J R V	Jugoslovensko Ratno Vazduhoplovstvo (Yugoslavia) (Military Air Force)
J S A E	Society of Automotive Engineers of Japan (Japan)
J S A P	Japan Society of Applied Physics (Japan)
J S C E R D G G	Joint-Service Civil Engineering Research and Development Coordinating Group (USDOD)
J S E A	Japan Ship Exporters Association (Japan)
J S E A C	Joint Societies Employment Advisory Committee (USA) (of IEEE, AIChE, AIAA, ASME, NSPE, AIME, ASCE) (now Coordinating Committee of Society Presidents)
J S E P	Joint Services Electronics Program (USA)
J S M E A	Japan Ship Machinery Export Association (Japan)
J S P A	Japan Screen Printing Association (Japan)
J S P S	Japan Society for the Promotion of Science (Japan)
J S Q C	Japan Society for Quality Control (Japan)
J S S	Jet Strip System
	Job Shop Simulation
J S T	Jet STOL Transport
J S U N	Jupiter, Saturn, Uranus and Neptune
J T E S	Japan Techno-Economics Society (Japan)
J T R A	Job Task Requirements Analysis
J T R U	Joint-services Tropical Research Unit (Australia) (administered by (MOD (PE)) and Australian Department of Supply)
J T S A	Joint Technical Support Activity (of Defense Communications Agency (USDOD))
J T U	Jackson Turbidity Units
J U S K	Jugoslovenski Savez Organizacija za Unapredenje Kvaliteta i Pouzdanosti (Yugoslavia) (Yugoslavian Organisation for Quality Control)

J U S S I M	Justice System Interactive Model
J W C A	Japan Watch and Clock Association (Japan)
J W D S	Japan Work Design Society (Japan)

K

K A C	Kuwait Airways Corporation (Kuwait)
K A N D I D A T S	*Kansas (University)* Digital Image Data System
K A R	Knot Area Ratio
K A R L D A P	Karlsruhe Data Processing and Display System (of EUROCONTROL)
K A S C	Knowledge Availability Systems Center (University of Pittsburgh (USA))
K A S P	Kehr Activated Sludge Process
K A T	Key-to-Address Transformation
K C C T	Kaolin Cephalin Clotting Time
K C L	Kirchhoff's Current Law
	Knitting Cylinder Lubrication
K C R T	Keyboard Cathode Ray Tube
K E A	Kansas Electronics Association (USA)
K E C O	Korea Electric Company (Korea)
K E T	Krypton Exposure Technique
K E T A	Kentucky Electronics Technicians Association (USA)
K F C	Kerala Finance Corporation (India)
K F K	Kernforschungszentrum, Karlsruhe (Germany) (Nuclear Research Centre, Karlsruhe)
K G O	Kiruna Geophysical Observatory (Sweden)
K H D	Klockner-Humboldt-Deutsch (Germany)
K H I	Kelvin-Helmholtz Instability
K I	Korrosionsinstitutets (Sweden) (Corrosion Institute)
K I A S	Knots Indicated Air Speed
K I T C O	Kerala Industry and Technical Consultancy Organisation (India)
K L I C	Key-Letter-In-Context
K M K	Standige Konferenz der Kultusminister der Lander in der Bundesrepublik Deutschland (Germany) (Standing Conference of Ministers of Education and Cultural Affairs of the Lander in the Federal Republic of Germany)
K N C V	Koninklijke Nederlandse Chemische Vereniging (Netherlands) (Royal Netherlands Chemical Society)

K N S M	Koninklijke Nederlandsche Stoomboot Maatschappij (Netherlands)
K N T C	Kenya National Trading Corporation (Kenya)
K O M R M L	Kentucky, Ohio, Michigan Regional Medical Library (USA)
K O S	*Kent (University)* On-line System
K O W A C O	Korea Water Resources Development Corporation (Korea)
K R E E P	Potassium (chemical symbol K), Rare Earth Elements, and Phosphorus
K S I D C	Kerala State Industrial Development Corporation (India)
K T A	Kerntechnischer Ausschuss (Germany) (Nuclear Technology Committee)
K T G	Kerntecnische Gesellschaft (Germany) (Nuclear Society)
K T H	Kungliga Tekniska Hogskolan (Sweden) (Royal Technical University)
K U	Kentucky University (USA)
K V L	Kirchhoff's Voltage Law
K W A C	Keyword Augmented in Context
K W I P	Keyword Word in Permutation

L

L	prefix to numbered: dated series of Aluminium and Light Alloy standards issued by BSI (letter is sometimes preceded by a number)
L A A	Leucocyte Ascorbic Acid
L A A D	Latin American Agribusiness Development Corporation
L A A S	Laboratoire d'Automatique et de ses Applications Spatiales (of CNRS (France)) (Laboratory for the the application of Automation to Space Research)
	London Amateur Aviation Society
L A B	Lead-Acid Battery
	Low Altitude Blanking
L A B E N	Laboratori Elettronici e Nucleari (Italy) (Electronic and Nuclear Laboratories)
L A B O R E L E C	Laboratoire Belge de l'Industrie Electrique (Belgium) (Joint Laboratory of the Belgian Electricity Industry)

L A B O R I A	Laboratoire de Recherche en Informatique et en Automatique (France) (Research Laboratory for Data Processing and Automation)
L A B P	Lethal Aid for Bomber Penetration
L A B S	Laser Active Boresight System
L A C	Linear Amplitude-Continuous
	Lunar Aeronautical Chart
L A C D	Limited-Amplitude, Controlled-Decay
L A C E	Liquid Air Cycle Engine
	Lunar Atmosphere Composition Experiment
L A D	Library Administration Division (of the American Library Association)
	Logarithmic Analogue-to-Digital
	Lunar Atmosphere Detector
L A D A R	Laser Detection And Ranging
L A D E	Lineas Aereas del Estado (Argentina) (State Air Lines including the Military Air Force)
L A D E C O	Linea Aerea del Cobre (Chile)
L A E D	Low Angle Electron Diffraction
L A G E	Lineas Aereas Guinea Ecuatorial (Republic of Equatorial Guinea) (National Air Line)
L A G E O S	Laser Geodetic Satellite
L A H	Lithium Aluminium Hydride
L A H A	Linear Array Hybrid Assembly
L A I C A	Lineas Aereas Interiores de Catalina (Colombia)
L A I R	Letterman Army Institute of Research (US Army)
L A L	Local Adjunct Language
L A M A	Locomotive and Allied Manufacturers Association (now Railway Industry Association of Great Britain)
L A M B D A	Language for Manufacturing Business and Distribution Activities
L A M I S	Local Authority Management Information System
L A M S	London Association of Master Stonemasons
L A N	Linea Aerea Nacional (Chile) (National Air Line)
L A P	Leucine Aminopeptidase
	Leucocyte Alkaline Phosphatase
	Lineas Aerias Paraguayas (Paraguay) (National Air Line)
L A P P E S	Large Power Plant Effluent Study
L A P S	Lovelace (Foundation for Medical Education and Research (USA)) Aerosol Particle Separator
L A P S S	Laser Airborne Photographic Scanning System
L A R	Light Artillery Rocket

L A R	Liquid Argon
L A R C	Library Automation Research and Consulting Association (USA)
	Lighter Amphibious Resupply Craft
	Low Altitude Ride Control
L A R P	Launch and Recovery Platform
L A R S	Laboratory for Application of Remote Sensing (Purdue University (USA))
	Laser Aerial Rocket System
L A R S I S	Library Association Reference and Special Information Section
L A S	Lower Airspace
L A S A R	Logic Automated Stimulus And Response
L A S C R	Light Activated Silicone Controlled Rectifier
L A S E R	London and South Eastern Library Region
L A S S	Lanthanum Polystyrene Sulphonate
	Lockheed Airline System Stimulation
	Logistics Analysis Simulation System
L A S T	Low Altitude Supersonic Target
L A T	Latex Agglutination Test
	Lowest Astronomical Tide
L A T G	Laboratory Automation Trials Group (of DHSS)
L A T I S	Lightweight Airborne Thermal Imaging System
L A T O F F	Lowest Astronomical Tide of the Foreseeable Future
L A T O M	Lowest Astronomical Tide of the Month
L A T O Y	Lowest Astronomical Tide of the Year
L A T R I X	Light Accessible Transistor Matrix
L A T S	*Litton (Systems (Canada) Ltd))* Automated Test Set
L A U	Linear Accelerometer Unit
L A V	Linea Aeropostal Venezolana (Venezuela)
L A W S	Light Aviation Warning Service (of the Meteorological Office)
L A X R A Y	Large X-ray Survey Experiment
L B A	Linear-Bounded Automation
	Luftfahrt Bundesamt (Germany) (West German Civil Aviation Authority)
L B C M	Locator at Back Course Marker
L B I	Long-Baseline Interferometer *or* Interferometry
L B J C C	London Boroughs Joint Computer Committee
L B L	Lawrence Berkeley Laboratory (University of California (USA))
L B L G	Large Blast Load Generator

L B M S U	London Boroughs Management Service Unit
L B O	Line Build-Out
L B P	Length Between Perpendiculars
L B W	Laser Beam Welding
L C	Liquid Chromatography
L C A	Laboratoire Centrale de l'Armament (of DTAT (France))
L C A O - M O - S C F	Linear Combination of Atomic Orbitals in Molecular Orbital, Self-Consistent Field
L C A O S C F	Linear Combination of Atomic Orbitals Self-Consistent Field
L C A R	Low-Coverage Acquisition Radar
L C B	Limited Capability Buoy
L C C M	Life Cycle Cost Model
L C C P	Life Cycle Computer Programme
L C D	Liquid Crystal Display
L C D O S E M	Local Civil Defence Operating Systems Evaluation Model
L C E	Lightweight Load Carrying Equipment
L C F	Launch Control Facility
	Liquid Complex Fertilizer
	Low Cycle Fatigue
L C G	Liquid Cooled Garment
L C I	Learner Centred Instruction
	Liquid Crystal Institute (Kent State University (USA))
L C L	Landing Craft Logistic
L C L U	Landing Control and Logic Units
L C M	Large Capacity Core Memory
	Liquid Curing Method
	Lymphocytic Choriomeningitis
L C O M	Logistics Composite Model
L C R	Logarithmic Correlators Ratiometer
L C R U	Lunar Communications Relay Unit
L C S	Linked Cross Sectional
L C S E	Laser Communication Satellite Experiment
L C T	Laboratoire Central de Telecommunications (France)
L D A	Landing Distance Available
	Local Density Approximation
	Localizer-type Directional Aid
L D A M	Local Damage Assessment Model
L D E	Long-Delayed Echoes

L D G O	Lamont Doherty Geological Observatory (Columbia University (USA))
L D I N	Lead-in Lighting System
L D L	Language Description Language
L D M	Linear Delta Modulation
L D O S	Long Duration Orbital Simulator
L D R	Linear Decision Rules
L D S R A	Logistics Doctrine, Systems and Readiness Agency (US Army) (now Logistics Evaluation Agency)
L D S S	Laser Designator Seeker Systems
L D V	Laser Doppler Velocimeter *or* Velocimetry
L E - V G F	Liquid Encapsulation-Vertical Gradient Freeze
L E A	Laboratorio de Engenharia de Angola (Angola) (Engineering Laboratory of Angola)
	Linear Embedding Algorithm
	Logistics Evaluation Agency (US Army)
L E A A	Law Enforcement Assistance Administration (Department of Justice (USA))
L E A D	Laboratoire d'Electronique et d'Automatique Dauphinois (France)
L E A D E R	*Lehigh (University)* (USA) Automatic Device for Efficient Retrieval
L E A D E R M A R	*Lehigh (University* (USA)) Answer to Demand for Efficient Retrieval - Mart Library
L E A F	LISP Extended Algebraic Facility
L E A F A C	Local Employment Acts Financial Advisory Committee (of Department of Trade and Industry) (dissolved 1973)
L E A M	Lunar Ejecta and Meteorites Experiment
L E A N S	*Lehigh (University)* (USA) Analog Simulator
L E A P	Laboratory Evaluation and Accreditation Program (of NBS (USA))
	Lambda (Corporation) Efficiency Analysis Programme
L E A P S	Law Enforcement Agencies Processing System (Massachusetts (USA))
	Local Exchange Area Planning Simulation
L E C	Liquid Encapsulation-Czochralski
L E D	Light Emitting Device
L E D C	Low Energy Detonating Chord
L E D U	Local Enterprise Development Unit (of Ministry of Commerce (Northern Ireland))

L E E P	Library Education Experimental Project (of Syracuse University (USA))
L E F	Light-Emitting Film
L E F M	Linear Elastic Fracture Mechanics
L E M	Laser Emission Microprobe
L E M A G	Laboratory Equipment and Methods Advisory Group (of DHSS)
L E M R A S	Law Enforcement Manpower Resource Allocation System
L E O	Littoral Environment Observation
L E O K	Laboratorium voor Elektronische Ontwikkelingen voor de Krijsmacht (Netherlands) (Electronic Development Laboratory for the Armed Forces)
L E P	Laboratoires d'Electronique et de Physique Appliquee (France)
L E P O R	Long-term Expanded Programme of Oceanic Exploration and Research (of IOC (UNESCO))
L E R M I S T O R	Learning Materials Information Store
L E R S C	Locomotion Evaluation Recognition and Statistical Comparison
L E S	*Lincoln* (Lincoln Laboratory, Massachusetts Institute of Technology) Experimental Satellite
L E S A - A - A	Least Squares Adjust-And-Analysis Programme
L E S L	Law Enforcement Standards Laboratory (of NBS (USA))
L E T	*Lincoln* (Lincoln Laboratory, Massachusetts Institute of Technology) Experimental Terminal
L E T I	Laboratoire d'Electronique et de Technologie de l'Informatique (France)
L F C	Load Frequency Control
L F E	Laminar Flow Element
L F L	Lower Flammable Limit
L F M	Limited-area Fine-mesh Model
	Linearly Modulated Frequency
L F R A P	Long Feeder Route Analysis Programme
L F T	Latext Fixation Test
	Lensless Fourier Transformation
L F T E G	Liquid Fuelled Thermo-Electric Generator
L F V	Lunar Exploration Flying Vehicle
L G B	Lateral Geniculate Body
L G C	Laboratory of the Government Chemist (DTI)
L G D M	Laser-Guided Dispenser Munition
L G E C	Lunar Geological Exploration Camera
L G I	Linear Gas-discharge Indicator

L G N	Lateral Geniculate Nucleus
L G O R U	Local Government Operational Research Unit (of Royal Institute of Public Administration)
L G R	Letter of General Representation
	Localised Gain Region
L G S	Landing-Guidance System
L H	Lateral Hypothalamus
	Lateral Hypothalmic
L H - R H	Luteinizing Hormone Releasing Hormone
L H C	London Housing Consortium
L H G	Local Haemolysis in Gel
L I A	Linear Induction Accelerator
L I B E C	Light Behind Camera
L I B E R	Ligue des Bibliotheques Europeennes de Recherche (League of European Research Libraries)
L I B G I S	Library General Information Survey (of National Center for Educational Statistics (USOE) (USA))
L I D	Liquid Interface Diffusion
	Lunar Ionosphere Detector
L I D I A	Learning In Dialog
L I E D	Large Industrial Engineering Development (a project of the Japanese Government)
L I F	Lighting Industry Federation
L I L	Large Ionic Lithophile
	Law of the Iterated Logarithm
	Local Interaction Language
	Lunar International Laboratory (of International Academy of Astronautics) (now MARECEBO)
L I M R V	Linear Induction Motor Research Vehicle
L I N C	*Lincoln Laboratory* (Massachusetts Institute of Technology) Instrument Computer
L I N C O	Linear Composition
L I N C O T T	Liaison, Interface, Coupling, Technology Transfer
L I N C S	Language Information Network and Clearinghouse System (Center for Applied Linguistics (USA)
L I N K	Lambeth Information Network
L I P S	Laboratory Information Processing System
	Laser Image Processing Scanner
L I R	Laser Image Recorder
L I R T A	Laboratoire d'Infrarouge Technique et Appliquee (France)

L I S	Laboratory Implementation System
	Lanthanide Induced Shift
L I S E	Librarians of Institutes and Schools of Education
L I S P	List Processing
L I S T A R	*Lincoln* (Lincoln Laboratory, Massachusetts Institute of Technology) Information Storage and Associative Retrieval system
L I T E	Industria Libraria Tipografica Editrice (Italy)
	Legal Information Through Electronics (of USDOD)
L I T E S	Ladies In Technical Electronic Servicing (USA)
L I T S	Light Interface Technology System
L I U	Laboratories Investigation Unit (of Department of Education and Science)
L I V	Linear, Invariant
L I W	Light-weight Individual Weapon
L I X	Liquid Ion Exchange
L J C	London Joint Committee of Graduate and Student Engineers
L L A	Louisiana Library Association (USA)
L L C	Liquid-Liquid Chromatography
L L F E T	Linear Load Field Effect Transistor
L L F M	Low Level Flux Monitor
L L G	Lighting Liaison Group (Electricity Council, Lighting Industry Federation, ECA, APLE, DLMA, and IES)
L L L	Low Level Logic
	Low-Light-Level
L L R	Log-Likelihood Ratio
L L S A	Louisiana Land Surveyors Association (USA)
L L T V	Low-light Level Television
L M	Liquid Mercury
L M - M H D	Liquid Metal Magnetohydrodynamics
L M C	Large Magellanic Cloud
L M C S S	Letter Mail Code Sorting System
L M F	Liquid Methane Fuel
	Linear Multistep Formulae
L M G	Light Machine Gun
	London Medical Group
L M I	Logistics Management Information
L M I C S	Logistics Management Information and Control System
L M I S	Logistics Management Information System
L M S	Least Mean Square

L M S A	Labor-Management Services Administration (of Department of Labor (USA))
	Large Metoscale Area
L M V E	Linear, Minimum Variance Estimation
L N E C	Laboratorio Nacional de Engenharia Civil (Portugal) (National Civil Engineering Laboratory)
L N F	Laboratori Nazional di Frascati (Italy)
L N P	Leg Negative Pressure
L N P F	Lymph Node Permeability Factor
L N R S	Limited Night Recovery System
L N T P B	Laboratoire National des Travaux Publics et du Batiment (Algeria) (National Laboratory of Public Works and Building)
L O A	Length Overall
L O B S T E R	Long Term Ocean Bottom Settlement Test for Engineering Research
L O C	Large Optical Cavity
L O C A	Loss-of-Coolant Accident
L O C A T E	Library of Congress (USA) Automation Techniques Exchange
L O C O S	Local Oxidation Of Silicon
L O F A A D S	Low-altitude Forward Area Air Defence System
L O F E R	Laundau Orbital Ferromagnetism
L O F T	Low-Frequency Radio Telescope
L O G A I R	Logistics Command Contract Airlift System (USAF)
L O G C O S T	Logistics Cost Model
L O G I C	Laser Optical Guidance Integration Concept
L O G I M P	Local Government Implementation
L O G M A P	Logistics System Master Plan (US Army)
L O G M I S	Logistics Management Information Systems (US Army)
L O G O	Limit Of Government Obligation
L O G P L A N	Logistics Plan (USDOD)
L O I	Limiting Oxygen Index
L O L A	London On-line Local Authorities
L O L I T A	Library On-Line Information and Text Access (Oregon State University Library (USA)
L O M	Locator at the Outer Marker
L O P A C	Load Optimisation and Passenger Acceptance Control
L O P A I R	Long Path Infra-Red

L O R	Level Of Repair
L O R A	Lecturer Oriented Response Analysis
L O R A E	Long Range Attitude and Events
L O R A M	Level of Repair for Aeronautical Material
L O R A S	Linear Omnidirectional Airspeed System
L O R C O	Long Range Planning Group (of ISO (Switzer-land))
L O R C S	League of Red Cross Societies
L O R O	Lobe-On-Receive-Only
L O S	Limit Order Switching system
L O S S	Lunar-Orbit Space Station
L O T	Load-on-Top (a method of marine tanker cleaning)
	Polskie Linie Lotnicze (Poland) (National Air Line)
L O T A W S	Laser Obstacle Terrain Avoidance Warning System
L O V E R	Lunar Orbiting Vehicle for Emergency Rescue
L P	Lumbar Puncture
L P A S A	Linear Pulse-height Analyzer Spectrum Analysis
L P C	Low Pressure Compressor
L P D	Landing Ship Personnel and Dock
	Lateral Photoelectric Detector
L P D A	Log-Periodic Dipole Array
L P E	Liquid-Phase Epitaxial *or* Epitaxy
L P F	Large Particle Furnace
L P G	Liquified Propane Gas
L P G I T A	Liquid Petroleum Gas Industry Technical Association
L P I	Logistics Performance Indicator
L P L	Lunar and Planetary Laboratory (University of Arizona (USA))
L P L A	Log-Periodic Loop Antenna
L P M	Lunar Portable Magnetometer
L P O	Lunar Parking Orbit
L P P M	Low Pressure Permanent Mould
L P R M	Local Power Range Monitor
L P S	Laboratory of Plasma Studies (Cornell University (USA))
	Laboratory Peripheral System
	Lipopolysaccharide
L P S / P I A	Lithographic Platemakers Section of Printing Industries of America (USA)
L P S F	Lens-Pinhole Spatial Filter

L P U U	Linear Programming Under Uncertainty
L Q I V	Linear, Quasi Invariant
L R	Liaison Report
L R A	Lace Research Association (now merged with HATRA)
L R A L S	Long-Range Approach and Landing System
L R B A	Laboratoire de Recherches Balistiques et Aerodynamics (France) (Ballistics and Aerodynamics Research Laboratory) (now SEP)
L R C	Linear Responsibility Charting
L R C D	Linear Rule of Cumulative Damage
L R C U	Lunar Communications Relay Unit (mounted on LRV)
L R D C	Learning Research and Development Center (University of Pittsburg (USA))
L R F	Low Rigid Frame
	Luteinizing Releasing Factor
L R G B	Long-Range Glide Bomb
L R I E	Limb Radiance Inversion Experiment
L R I R	Limb Radiance Inversion Radiometer
L R L	Lawrence Radiation Laboratory (University of California (USA)) (now Lawrence Berkeley Laboratory)
L R M T S	Laser Ranger and Marked Target Seeker
L R P A	Long-Range Patrol Aircraft
L R P D S	Long-Range Position Determining System
L R S M	Laboratory for Research on the Structure of Matter (University of Pennsylvania (USA))
L R T	Laser Ray Tube
	Launch, Recovery and Transport
L R 3	Laser Ranging Retroreflector
L S	prefix to numbered series issued by Labor Standards Bureau (of Department of Labor (USA))
	Lecture Series
L S A	Light Strike Aircraft
L S A B	London Society of Air-Britain
L S A W	Laser-Supported Absorption-Waves
L S B	Lower Sideband
L S C	Laser-Supported Combustion
	Linear Sequential Circuit
	Liquid-Solid Chromatography
L S D	Land Surveys Division (of ACSM (USA))
	Laser-Supported Detonation
	Least Significant Difference

L S E	London School of Economics and Political Science
L S F	Line Spread Function
L S F S	Lateral Separation Focus Sensor
L S G	Lunar Surface Gravimeter
L S H S	Low Sulphur Heavy Stock
L S H T M	London School of Hygiene and Tropical Medicine
L S I	Leadless Sealed Device
L S I G	Line Scan Image Generator
L S I T V	Liquid Secondary Injection Thrust Vector Control
L S M	Lunar Surface Magnetometer
L S N L I S	Lunar Science Natural Language Information System
L S P	Levitated Spherator
	Logical Signal Processor
L S P C	Logistics Systems Policy Committee (USDOD)
L S R	Lanthanide Shift Reagent
	Loop Signalling Repeater
L S S	Logistic Self-Support
L S S A	Laboratory Supply Support System (of OAR (USAF))
L S T	Large Space Telescope
	Large Stellar Telescope
	Light STOL Transport
	Lunar Space Tug
L S V	Linear Shift-Varying
L T	Laser Trimming
L T E	Laplace's Tidal Equations
	Local Thermodynamic Equilibrium
	London Transport Executive (of the Greater London Council)
L T F C S	Laser Tank Fire Control System
L T F V	Less Than Fair Value
L T G	Lufttransportgeschwader (Germany) (Transport Element of the German Military Airforce)
L T I	Low Temperature Isotropic
L T M	Long-Term Memory
L T M T	Low Temperature Thermomechanical Treatment
L T P	Low-Temperature Phase
L T S	Laser Time Sharing
	Laser-Triggered Switching
	Lincoln Training System (of Lincoln Laboratory, Massachusetts Institute of Technology (USA))
L T S G	Laser-Triggered Spark Gap

L T T A	Long Tank Thrust-Augmented
L T T A D	Long Tank Thrust-Augmented *Delta*
L T T A S	Light Tactical Transport Aircraft System
L T T A T	Long-Tank Thrust Augmented *Thor* (now called THORAD)
L T U	Lateral Thrust Unit
L U A	Lens Users Association (a service of the Sira Institute)
L U C I D	*Loughborough University* Computerised Information and Drawings
L U C S	London University Computing Services
L U F T H A N S A	Deutsche Lufthansa AG (Germany)
L U S T	List Update Sort and Total
L U T	Loughborough University of Technology
L U X A I R	Societe Anonyme Luxemborgeoise de Navigation Aerienne (Luxembourg) (National Airline)
L U X A T O M	Syndicat Luxembourgeois pour l'Industrie Nucleaire (Luxembourg)
L V	Low Viscosity
L V C P	Low Valence Chromium Plating
L V D T	Linear Voltage Differential Transducer
L V H	Left Ventricular Hypertrophy
L V H A Z	Low Velocity - High Attenuation Zone
L V L	Low Velocity Layer
L V N	Limiting Viscosity Number
L V R	Line Voltage Regulator
L V R C N	Lehigh Valley (USA) Regional Computing Network
L W B	Long Wheelbase
L W F	Light-weight Fighter
L W L	Land Warfare Laboratory (US Army)
	Limited War Laboratory (US Army) (now Land Warfare Laboratory)
L W P	Low-Waterplane
L W S S	Letter Writing Support System
L X C	Liquid-ion Exchange Chromatography
L Z C	Liquid-size Exclusion Chromatography
L Z M	Lysozyme

M

M	prefix to numbered : dated series of Miscellaneous Aerospace Standards issued by BSI

M	prefix to numbered series of Business Monitor - Miscellaneous Series issued by DTI
M & F C S	Management and Financial Control System
M - I L S	Microwave Instrument Landing System
M A	prefix to numbered series of Marine Engineering standards issued by BSI
M A A	Minimum Audible Angles
M A A C L	Multiple Affect Adjective Check List
M A B F	Mobile Assault Bridge/Ferry
M A B U S	Multi-Access Broadcast Unit System
M A C	Maintenance Analysis Center (of FAA (USA))
	Marker-and-Cell
	Ministerio de Agricultura y Cria (Venezuela) (Ministry of Agriculture and Animal Breeding)
M A C C S	Marine Corps Air Command Control System (US Marine Corps)
M A C D A C	Man Communication and Display for an Automatic Computer
M A C E	Magnetic Aid to Compatibility Engineering
	Master Control Executive
M A C M A	Mid-Atlantic Construction Management Association (USA)
M A C O M	Maintenance Assembly and Check-Out Model
M A C R I T	Manpower Authorization Criteria
M A C R O	Methodology for Allocating Corporate Resources to Objectives
M A C S	Merchant Airship Cargo Satellite
M A D	Magnetic Anti-submarine Detector
M A D A R S	Malfunction Detection, Analysis, and Recording Subsystem
M A D G E	Microwave Aircraft Digital Guidance Equipment
M A D S	Meteorological Airborne Data System
M A E	Department of Mechanical and Aerospace Engineering (Rutgers - The State University, New Brunswick (USA))
	Movement After-Effect
M A F F S	Modular Airborne Fire Fighting System
M A F I	Mafi-Fahrzeugwerke International (Germany)
M A F I S	Management Farm Information Service
M A F L I R	Modified Advanced Forward Look Infra-Red
M A G E N	Matrix Generating and Reporting System
M A G F E T	Magnetic Metal - Oxide - Semiconductor Field - Effect Transistor

M A G I C	Modern Analytical Generator of Improved Circuits
	Motorola Automatically Generated Integrated Circuits
M A G L E V	Magnetic Levitation
M A G P I E	Markov Game Planar Intercept-Evasion
M A I	Machine-Aided Indexing
M A I L S	Multiple-Antenna Instrument Landing System
M A I N S	Marine Aided Inertial Navigation System
M A L R	Mortar/Artillery Locating Radars
M A L U	Mode Annunciator and Logic Unit
M A M C	Methylammonium Methyldithlocarbamate
	Mining and Allied Machinery Corporation (India) (government owned)
M A M S	Memory And Memory Sequencer
M A M T F	Mobile Automated Microwave Test Facility
M A N	Magnetic Automatic Navigation
	Manual
M A N A V	Shipborne Integrated Manoeuvring and Navigation project
M A N Z	Medical Association of New Zealand (New Zealand)
M A O	Mechanization of Algebraic Operations
M A P	Machine Analyzer Package
	Maintenance Assessment Panel
	Management Analysis and Projection
	Maximum *a posteriori* Probability
	Method of Approximation Programming
	Missed Approach Point
	Modular Accounting Plan
M A P L E	Marketing and Product Line Evaluation
M A P O R D	Methodological Approach to Planning and Programming USAF Operational Requirements, Research and Development
M A P P	Madras Atomic Power Project (India)
M A P S	Management Aids Programme Suite
	Management Analysis and Planning System
	Manpower Analysis and Performance Standards
	Microprogramable Arithmetic Processor System
	Migratory Animal Pathological Survey
	Modec (Mitsui Ocean Development and Engineering Company (Japan)) Anchor Piling System

M A P T O E	Management Practices in Tables of Organization and Equipment Units (a programme of the US Army)
M A Q	Measures for Air Quality (a programme of NBS (USA))
M A R	Magneto-Acoustic Resonance
	Medium-Range Artillery Rocket
	Mid Atlantic Ridge
M A R A I R M E D	Maritime Air Forces Mediterranean (of NATO)
M A R B A	Mid-America Regional Bargaining Association (USA)
M A R C	Multiple Access Remote Computing
M A R C O G A Z	Union des Industries Gazieres des Pays du Marche Commun (Union of the Gas Industries of the Common Market)
M A R C S	Marine Structures Computer System
M A R D	Military Aeronautical Research and Development
M A R D I	Malaysian Agricultural Research and Development Institute (Malaysia)
M A R D S	Medium Artillery Delivered Sensors
M A R I S	Material Readiness Index System
M A R L A B	Mobile Air Research Laboratory
M A R L S	Missouri Association of Registered Land Surveyors (USA)
M A R M A P	Marine Resources Monitoring, Assessment, and Prediction Program (of NMFS (NOAA) (USA))
M A R S	Mid-Air Recovery System
	Military Affiliate Radio System
	Monitoring, Accounting, Reporting and Statistical
	Motorola Automatic Routing System
	Multiple Access Retrieval System
M A R S A T	Maritime Satellite System
M A R S Y A S	*Marshall (Space Flight Center* (NASA) (USA)) System for Aerospace Systems Simulation
M A R T	Mobile Automatic Radiating Tester
M A R V	Manoeuvrable Re-entry Vehicle
M A S	Malaysian Airline System (Malaysia)
	Manufacture nationale d'Armes de Saint Etienne (of Groupement Industriel des Armaments Terrestres (France))
	Medical Advisory Service (of the Civil Service Department)
	Medical Audit Statistics

M A S	Metal-Alumina-Semiconductor
	Minnesota Academy of Science (USA)
M A S A	Medical Association of South Africa (South Africa)
	Multiple Anodic Stripping Analyser
M A S A L	Michigan Academy of Science, Arts and Letters (USA)
M A S A R	Management Assurance of Safety, Adequacy and Reliability
M A S C	Management Systems Concept
M A S C O T	Multi-Access Systems Control Terminal
	Management Advisory System using Computerized Optimization Techniques
M A S E G	Microwave Antenna Systems Engineering Group (of ISRO (India))
M A S H	Micro-Analytic Simulation of Households
M A S P A C	Microfilm Advisory Service of the Public Archives of Canada
M A S S	Manual Analysis Scan System
	MARC (Machine-Readable Cataloguing) Automated Serials System
	Maritime Anti-stranding Sonar System
M A S S O P	Multi-Automatic System for Simulation and Operational Planning
M A S S T	Major Ship Satellite Terminal
M A S S T E R	Modern Army Selected Systems Test Evaluation and Review (US Army)
M A S T	Magnetic Annular Shock Tube
	Military Assistance for Safety in Traffic (a joint programme of DOD and DOT (USA))
	Model Assembly Sterilizer for Testing
M A S T A C S	Manoeuvrability Augmentation System for Tactical Air Combat Simulation
M A S T I F F	Modular Automated System To Identify Friend from Foe
M A T	Manufacture nationale d'Armes de Tulle (of Groupement Industriel des Armements Terrestres (France))
	Modular Allocation Technique
	Moving Annual Trend
M A T A D O R	Mobile And Three-dimensional Air Defence Operations Radar
M A T C	Maximum Acceptable Toxicant Concentration

M A T C H	Manned Attack Torpedo Carrying Helicopter
	Materials and Activities for Teachers and Children
	Meteorological Analog Test and Evaluation
M A T E	Machine-Aided Translation Editing
	Modular Automatic Test Equipment
	Multiband Automatic Test Equipment
M A T E L O	Maritime Air-radio Telegraph Organization (a high-frequency communications network of the Royal Air Force)
M A T L A B	Materials Laboratory (of Naval Ship Research and Development Center (USN))
M A T O	Military Air Traffic Operations
M A T P S	Machine Aided Technical Processing System
M A T S	Midcourse Airborne Target Signatures
	Mission Analysis and Trajectory Simulation programme
M A T S U	Marine Technology Support Unit (of UKAEA)
M A T T S	Multiple Airborne Target Trajectory System
M A T Z	Military Airport Traffic Zones
M A V	Magyar Allamvasutak (Hungary) (State Railways)
M A V I S	Master Vision Screener
M A W L O G S	Models of Army Worldwide Logistics Systems (US Army)
M A W A	Missile Attack Warning and Assessment
M B	Methylene Blue
M B A	Malta Broadcasting Authority (Malta)
	Mortgage Bankers Association (USA)
M B A S I C	advanced version of BASIC programming language
M B B	Messerschmitt-Bolkow-Blohm (Germany)
M B C	Multiple Burst Correction
M B D A	Metal Building Dealers Association
M B E	Molecular Beam Epitaxy
M B F R	Mutual and Balanced (Armed) Force Reductions
M B L	Marine Biological Laboratory (of CEGB)
M B P O	Military Blood Program Office (USDOD)
M B P R E	Multi-type Branching Process in a Random Environment
M B R	Mineracoes Brasilieras Reunidas (Brazil)
M B S	Manchester Business School (University of Manchester)
M B S A	Methylated Bovine Serum Albumin
M B T	Mechanical Bathythermograph
	Mercaptobenzothiazole

M B Z	Magnesia-Buffered Zinc Oxide
M C	Metrology Centre (of National Physical Laboratory)
M C & G	Mapping, Charting and Geodesy Directorate of the Defense Intelligence Agency (USDOD)
M C A	Multi-Channel Analyser
	Multiple Classification Analysis
M C A A	Mason Contractors Association of America (USA)
	Mechanical Contractors Association of America (USA)
M C A C S	Marine Centralized Automatic Control System
M C A P	Medical Commission on Accident Prevention
	Microwave Circuit Analysis Package
M C C	Mechanical Chemical Code
M C C A	Manufacturers Council on Color and Appearance (USA)
M C D	Magnetic Circular Dichroism
	Months for Cyclical Dominance
M C E	Management Centre Europe (Belgium) (of the International Management Association)
M C F	Measurement Compensation Factor
	Mission-Critical Function
	Mutual Coherence Function
M C F C	Multi-Configuration Frozen Core
M C H	Methylcyclohexane
M C H F R	Minimum Critical Heat Flux Ratio
M C H R	Medical Committee for Human Rights (USA)
M C I C	Metals and Ceramics Information Center (USDOD)
M C I S	Materials Control Information System
M C L	Microcomputer Compiler Language
M C L O S	Manual Command to Line Of Sight
M C L W G	Major Calibre Light Weight Gun
M C M	Mine Counter-Measures
	Multilayer Ceramic Module
M C M V	Mine Counter-Measures Vessel
M C P	Management-Control Programme
	Micro-Channel Plate
M C P A	Michigan Concrete Paving Association (USA)
M C P L	Members of *Congress* for Peace through Law (USA)
	Multiple-Cue Probability Learning
M C R L	Mapping and Charting Research Laboratory (Ohio State University (USA))
M C R S	Micrographic Catalogue Retrieval System

M C S	Maximal Compatible Set
	Method of Constant Stimuli
	Monochlorostyrene
M C S I B	Management Consulting Services Information Bureau (of BIM)
M C T	Memory Cycle Time
M C T A S	Military/Commercial Transport Aircraft Simulation
M C T S S A	Marine Corps Tactical Systems Support Activity (US Marine Corps)
M C U	Microprogrammed Control Unit
M D A	Malfunction Detector Analyzer
	Metal Deactivator
	Minimum Descent Altitude
	Modified Diffusion Approximation
M D C	Malta Development Corporation (Malta)
	Miniature Detonation Chord
M D C C	Monaural Detection with Contralateral Cue
M D D T	Master Digital Data Tape
M D I S	Ministere du Developpement Industriel et Scientifique (France) (Ministry of Industrial and Scientific Development)
M D M	Modified Davidon Method
M D N A	Machinery Dealers National Association (USA)
M D P	Meteorological Datum Plane
M D P I	Management Development and Productivity Institute (Ghana)
M D P N E	Ministere de la Protection de la Nature et de l'Environnement (France) (Ministry for the Protection of Nature and the Environment)
M D R	Metal Distribution Ratio
M D S	Management Decision System
	Management Display System
	Mathematics Diagnostic System
	Medical Data System
	Metal-Dielectric Semiconductor
	Multi-dimensional Scaling
M D S I C	Metal-Dielectric-Semiconductor Integrated Circuit
M D T S	Modular Data Transaction System
	Modular Data Transfer System
M E	Magneto-Electronic
	Multiple Effect distillation

M E / A E R O S P A C E	Department of Mechanical and Aerospace Engineering (Syracuse University Research Institute (USA))
M E A	Metropolitan Electricity Authority (Thailand)
	Minimum Enroute Altitude
M E A D	Microbial Evaluation Analysis Device
M E A M	Department of Mechanical Engineering and Applied Mechanics (University of Pennsylvania (USA))
M E A PS	Maintenance Engineering Analysis Procedures
M E C A	Multivalued Electronic Circuit Analysis
M E C C A	Minnesota (USA) Environmental Control Citizens Association
M E C H T R A M	Mechanization of Selected Transportation Movement Reports (US Army)
M E D	Multiformat Electroluminescent Displays
M E D A L S	Modular Engineering Draughting and Library System (of the Computer-Aided Design Centre of DTI)
M E D C A T	Medium Altitude Clear Air Turbulence
M E D C O M	Mediterranean Communications System
M E D H O C	Macro-Economic Databank *House of Commons*
M E D I H C	Military Experience Directed Into Health Careers (joint project of DOD and HEW (USA))
M E D I S	International Symposium on Medical Information Systems
M E D I S T A R S	Medical Information Storage and Retrieval System (of USN)
M E D L I N E	MEDLARS On-Line (of NLM (USA))
M E E D	Microbial Ecology Evaluation Device
M E F	Multi-purpose Electric Furnace
M E F R	Maximal Expiratory Flow Rate
M E G	Magnetoencephalogram
	Magnetoencephalography
	Multipactor Electron Gun
M E L	Magnetic-suspension, Evacuated-tube, Linear-motor-propulsion
	Ministere de l'Equipement et du Logement (France) (Ministry of Equipment and Housing)
M E L A	Middle East Librarians Association (USA)
M E L E T A	Mechanical Endurance Load on Environment Test Apparatus
M E M	Magnetic Electron Multiplier
	Maximum Entropy Method
	Mirror Electron Microscope

M E M A	Motor and Equipment Manufacturers Association (USA)
M E M B E R S	Microprogrammed Experimental Machine with a Basic Executive for Real-time Systems
M E M B R A I N	Micro-electronic Memories and Brains
M E M M	Multi-Echelon Markov Model
M E M O	Model for Evaluating Missile Observation information
M E N	Multiple Earthed Neutral
M E N D A P	Melbourne (Australia) Network Dimensioning and Analysis Programmes
M E N T O R	Mobile Electrical Network Testing, Observation and Recording
M E O	Mass in Earth Orbit
M E O S	Microsomal Ethanol-Oxidizing System
M E P	Maximum Entropy Principle
M E P A	Masters Electro-Plating Association (USA)
M E P P	Marine Electric Power Plant
M E R	Magneto-Elastic Resonance
M E R C	Minimum Electrical Resistance Condition
M E R D C	Mobility Equipment Research and Development Center (US Army)
M E R I T	Mechanical Engineers Reading Improvement Techniques
	Michigan (USA) Educational Research Information Triad (joint educational computing network between Michigan State University, Wayne State University, and University of Michigan)
M E R L	prefix to dated-numbered series of reports issued by the Department of Mechanical Engineering, McGill University (Canada)
M E R S A R	Merchant Ship Search and Rescue
M E R T S	Micropound Extended Range Thrust Stand
M E S A	Marine Eco-Systems Analysis
	Mechanical Equipment Stowage Area (in the *Apollo* lunar module base)
	Miniature Electrostatically Suspended Accelerometer
	Modular Electrical Stimulation Apparatus
M E S B I C	A Minority Enterprise Small Business Investment Company
M E S F E T	Metal-Semiconductor Field-Effect Transistor
M E S G	Micro-Electrostatic Gyro
M E S L	Membrane Encapsulated Soil Layer

M E S O N E T	Meso-meteorological Network
M E S S	Multiple Enclosure Simplification Shield
M E S U C O R A	International Exhibition of Measurement, Control, Regulation and Automation
M E T	Methemoglobin
	Modularised *or* Mobile Equipment
M E T A	Maryland Electronics Technicians Association (USA)
M E T E R	Machine Examination Teaching, Evaluation, and Re-education
M E T R A	Multiple Event Time Recording Apparatus
M E T R O	Metering and Traffic Recording with Off-line processing
M E T R R A	Metal Re-radiation Radar
M E U	Microcellular Elastomeric Urethanes
Me V E Ms J	Mercury, Venus, Earth, Mars, Jupiter
M E W S	Microwave Electronic Warfare System
M E W T	Matrix Electrostatic Writing Technique
M E X E	Military Engineering Experimental Establishment (MOD) (merged into MVEE, 1970)
M E X I C A N A	Compania Mexicana de Aviacion (Mexico)
M F	prefix to numbered series of reports issued by Magneto-Fluid Dynamics Division, New York University (USA)
	Matched-Filter
M F A	Metal Fixing Association for Ceiling Systems
	Motor Factors Association
M F B	Medial Forebrain Bundle
M F C	Multi-Frequency Code
M F C S	Medical Function Control System
	Missile Fire Control System
M F E	Moire Fringe Effects
M F F	Metal Finishers Foundation (USA)
M F H B F	Mean Flying Hours Between Failure
M F I	Metal Fabricating Institute (USA)
M F L	Maintenance-Free Lifetime
M F R	Multi-Frequency Responser
M F R T	Modulated Frequency Radio Telephony
M F S K	Multiple Frequency-Shift Keying
M F U W	Magnetic Force Upset Welding
M G / C C D	prefix to numbered series of reports issued by BISRA
M G D	Million Gallons per Day
M G G B	Modular Guided Glide Bomb

M G O S	Metal-Glass-Oxide-Silicon
M G R L	MIND Grammar-Rule Language
M H	Multiple Halide
M H D L	Magnetohydrodynamic Laser
M H I	Material Handling Institute (USA)
M H L G	Ministry of Housing and Local Government (absorbed into the Department of the Environment, 1970)
M H M A	Mobile Home Manufacturers Association (USA)
M H T C	Multiphasic Health Testing Centre
M H V	Miniature Homing Vehicle
M H W	Multi-Hundred Watt
M I A S	Management Information and Accounting System
M I A T C O	Mid-America International Agri-Trade Council (USA)
M I C	Magnesium Industry Council
	Mechanized Information Center (of Ohio State University Libraries (USA))
	Microwave Integrated Circuit
	Minimal Inhibitory Concentration
M I C H U - S G	prefix to dated-numbered series of reports issued by Michigan University, Sea Grant Program (USA)
M I C O S	Modular Industrial Control Oriented Systems
M I C O T	Minimum Completion Time
M I C R O N	Micro-Navigator
M I D A	Major Items Data Agency (US Army)
M I D A S	Management Information Decision and Accounting Simulator
	Maritime Industrial Development Area Schemes
	Micro-Image Data Addition System
	Mixed Data Structures
	Multiple Input Data Acquisition System
	Myriad Interactive Data Analysis System
M I D F	Multiple Input Describing Functions
Mi D O C	Mildew Defacement of Organic Coatings
M I D R	Mandatory Incident and Defect Reporting
M I D S	Management Information and Decision System
M I D U	Malfunction Insertion and Display Unit
M I E C C	Motor Industry Education Consultative Committee
M I F	Manual Intervention Facility
	Migration Inhibitory Factor
M I G	Miniature Integrating Gyro

M I L O C	Military Oceanography
M I L P	Mixed Integer Linear Programming
M I L V A N	Military Van
M I N C I S	*Minnesota* (USA) Crime Information System
M I N D	Management of Information through Natural Discourse
M I N D E C O	Mining Development Corporation (Zambia) (State owned)
M I N D E N	Mechanized Interconnection Design
M I N E R V A	Minimization of Earthworks Vertical Alignment
	Multiple Input Network for Evaluating Reactions, Votes, and Attitudes
M I N I	Miniscope
M I N I C S	Minimal Input Cataloguing System
M I N I T	Minimum Idle Time
M I N P O S T E L	Ministry of Posts and Telecommunications
M I N Q U E	Minimum Norm Quadratic Unbiased Estimation
M I N T E C H	Ministry of Technology (disbanded 1970)
M I N T E X	*Minnesota (University)* (USA) Interlibrary Teletype Experiment
M I N T S	Mutual Institutions National Transfer System (of NAMSB (USA))
M I O R	Memorial Institute for Ophthalmology Research (USA)
M I P	Mixed Integer Programming
M I P A S	Management Information Planning and Accountancy Service
M I P S	Million Instructions per Second
M I P V C F	Multiple-Input Phase-Variable Canonical Form
M I R A	Miniature Infra-Red Alarm
M I R S	Micro Interactive Retrieval System
M I R S I M	Mineral Resource Simulation Model
M I R T	Meteorological Institute for Research and Training (Egypt)
M I R U	Myocardial Infarction Research Unit (University of Alabama (USA)
M I S	Maturation-Inducing Substance
	Medical Information System
M I S A R	Miniature Information Storage And Retrieval system
M I S E R	Mean Integral Square Error
M I S L	Mysore Iron and Steel Works Limited (India)
M I S L I C	Mid and South Staffordshire Libraries in Co-operation

M I S T	Minor Isotope Safeguards Technique
M I S T R E S S	Mini-STRESS (a version of the STRESS computer programme)
M I T S G	prefix to series of dated-numbered series of reports issued by Massachusetts Institute of Technology (USA) Sea Grant Project Office
M I U S	Modular Integrated Utility System
M I Z	Materialinformations-zentrum der Marine (Germany)
M J D	Management Job Description
M L	Maximum Likelihood
	prefix to numbered series of reports issued by Microwave Laboratory (Stanford University (USA))
M L A	Malta Library Association (Malta)
	Marine Librarians Association
	Michigan Library Association (USA)
M L A B	Modeling Laboratory
M L B	Motor Life Boat
	Multi-layer Board
M L C	Magnetic Ledger Card
	Mainlobe Clutter
	Manoeuvre Load Control
	Mixed Leukocyte Culture
	Mixed Lymphocyte Culture
	Multi-layer Laminated Ceramic
M L C B	Moored Limited or Low Capability Buoy
M L C S	Multi-levelling Component System
M L D	Marineluchtvaartdienst (Netherlands) (Naval Air Force)
	Masking Level Difference
	Maximum-Likelihood Decoding
	Metachromatic Leukodystrophy
M L D D	Mooring Leg Deployment Device
M L E	Measured Logistics Effects
M L H	Minimum List Heading (of the Standard Industrial Classification)
M L I S	Metal-Liquid-Insulator Semiconductor
M L L W	Mean Lower Low Water
M L M	Maximum Likelihood Method
	Membrane Light Modulator
M L M I S	Minnesota (USA) Land Management Information System
M L O	Mechanized Letter Office

M L P	Multiparametric Linear Programming
M L P D	Modified Log Periodic Dipole
M L R V	Manned Lunar Roving Vehicle
M L S	Microwave Landing System
M L S A	Minnesota Land Surveyors Association (USA)
M L T	Magnetic Local Time
M L V	Moloney Leukaemia Virus
M L V S S	Mixed Liquor Volatile Suspended Solids
M L W	Medium-Level Waste
M M A	Multifunction Microwave Aperture
M M E A	Metallic Mineral Exploration Agency (of MITI (Japan))
M M F	Maximum Mid-expiratory Flow
	Micromation Microfilm
M M F A N E	Master Metal Finishers Association of New England (USA)
M M I C	Millimetre-wave Integrated Circuit
M M I P S	Multiple Mode Integrated Propulsion System
M M I S	Maintenance Management Information System
M M P I	Minnesota Multiphasic Personality Inventory
M M R	Massed Miniature Radiography
M M S	Minimum Mean Square
M M T C	Marine Minerals Technology Center (of ERL (NOAA) (USA))
	Minerals and Metals Trading Corporation (India) (Government owned)
M M T V	Mouse Mammary Tumour Virus
M N C	Multi-National Corporation
M N F	Modulated Normal Function
M N G	Modulated Noise Generator
M N O S	Metal-Nitride-Oxide Semi-conductor
M O	Microwave Oven
M O A S	Ministry of Aviation Supply (formed 1970, disbanded 1971)
M O A T	Methods of Appraisal and Test
M O B	Mouse Olfactory Bulb
M O B S	Mobile Ocean Basing System
M O B S S L - U A F	*M. J. Merritt* and *D. S. Miller's* Own Block Structured Simulation Language — Unpronounceable Acronym For
M O C	Method of Characteristics
M O C - L A M P	Method of Characteristics Laser and Mixing Programme
M O C A	Minimum Obstruction Clearance Altitude

M O C S	Multi-channel Ocean Colour Sensor
M O D (P E)	Ministry of Defence (Procurement Executive)
M O D A P S	Modal Data Acquisition and Processing System
M O D C O N	Man Machine System for the Optimum Design and Construction of Buildings
M O D R	Microwave Optical Double Resonance
M O D S	Manpower Operation Data System
M O E	Maximum Output Entropy
M O F A C S	Multi-Order Feedback And Compensation Synthesis
M O G A	International Conference on Microwave and Optical Generation and Amplification
M O G A S	Motor Gasoline
M O L A R	Mortar/Artillery Locating Radar
M O L E	Market Odd-Lot Execution system
M O M	Metal-metal Oxide-Metal
	Metal-Oxide-Metal
M O M S	*Michigan's* (Michigan University (USA)) Own Mathematical System
M O N	Motor Octane Number
M O N A	Modular Area Navigation
M O N A L	Mobile Nondestructive Assay Laboratory
M O T E C	Multi-Occupational Training and Education Centre (of RTITS)
M O P P	Mechanization of Planning Processes
M O P S	Mechanized Outside Plant Scheduling System
M O R	Modulus of Ruture
M O R D	Magneto-Optic Rotary Dispersion
M O S A I C S	Melcom Optional Software Applications for Integrated Commercial Systems
M O S A S R	Metal Oxide Semiconductor Analogue Shift Register
M O S E S	Manned Ocean Sea Experimentation Station
	Molecular Orbital Self-consistent Energy System
M O S T	*Micromation* Output Software Translator
M O T	Ministry of Transport (merged into the Department of the Environment, 1970)
	Ministry of Transport (Canada)
M O T E C	Multi-Occupational Training and Education Centre (of RTITB)
M O T N E G	Meteorological Operational Telecommunication Network in Europe, Regional Planning Group (of ICAO)
M O V	Metal Oxide Varistors

M O W	Ministry of Works (New Zealand)
M P	Magnetic Permeability
	Multiphase
	Multipulse
M P A	Master Printers of America (USA)
	Magazine Publishers Association (USA)
	Man-Powered Aircraft
	Master Photographers Association of Great Britain
M P B W	Ministry of Public Building and Works (absorbed into Department of the Environment, 1970)
M P C	Maximum Permissible Concentration
	Metal Properties Council (USA)
M P Ca	Maximum Permissible Concentration in Air
M P C A	Minnesota Pollution Control Agency (USA)
M P C F	Millions of Particles per Cubic Foot
M P D R	Mono-Pulse Doppler Radar
M P D S	Market Price Display Service (of the London Stock Exchange)
M P E	Maximum Permissible Exposure
	Maximum Permitted Error
M P H P	Multiple-Pass Heuristic Procedure
M P I	Mannosephosphate Isomerase
	Maudsley Personality Inventory
	Maximum Precipitation Intensity
M P I F	Metal Powders Industries Federation (USA)
M P I S	Manpower and Personnel Information Systems (of FAA (USA))
M P L	Mathematical Programming Language
M P M	Metra Potential Method
	Multi-Purpose Missile
M P M S	Missile Performance Monitoring System
M P N	Most Probable Number
M P P	Marine Power Plant
	Minimum-Perimeter Polygon
M P S	series of Minimum Performance Specifications issued by EUROCAE
	Minimum Property Standards (of FHA (USA))
	Mixed Potential Systems
M P S / M M S	Multi-Purpose/Multi-Mission Ships
M P S X	Mathematical Programming System Extended
M P T	Ministry of Posts and Telecommunications
	Multiple Pure Tone
M P X	Multi-Programming Executive

M Q A D	Materials Quality Assurance Directorate (of MOD)
M R A	Matrix Reducibility Algorithm
	Multiple Regression Analysis
M R A A L S	*Marine* (United States Marine Corps) Remote Area Approach and Landing System
M R A M	Multi-mission Redeye Air-launched Missile
M R C	Materials Research Center (Lehigh University (USA))
M R C D	Memory Raster Colour Display
M R C S	Multiple RPV (Remotely Piloted Vehicle) Control System
M R D E	Mining Research and Development Establishment
M R D F	Marine Resource Development Foundation (Puerto Rico)
M R F	Meteorological Research Flight (of the Meteorological Office)
	Midbrain Reticular Formation
	Modular Rigid Frame
M R G	Marine Radioactivity Group (Scripps Institution of Oceanography (USA))
	Methane Rich Gas
M R I	Magnetic Rubber Inspection
	Microwave Research Institute (of PIB (USA))
M R I F	MSH (Melanphore Stimulating Hormone) Release Inhibiting Factor
M R I S	Maritime Research Information Service (of Highway Research Board and Maritime Administration (USA))
M R L	Maximised Relative Likelihood
M R M S	Metabolic Rate Measuring System
M R P P S	*Maryland* (*University*) (USA) Refutation Proof Procedure System
M R R	Monomer Reactivity Ratios
M R S M	Maintenance and Reliability Simulation Model
M R U	Manpower Research Unit (of the Department of Employment)
M R V	Mars Roving Vehicle
M S	prefix to numbered-dated-lettered series of reports issued by Department of Materials Science, Virginia University (USA)
	Meeting Speech
	Metal Semiconductor
	G. Mie Scattering
M S A	Matrix Scheme for Algorithms

M S A	Medical Service Administration (of HEW (USA))
	Minimum Sector Altitude
M S C	Magnitude Square of the Complex Coherence
	Manned Spacecraft Center (of NASA (USA)) (now called the Lyndon B. Johnson Space Center)
	Message Switching Concentration
	Military Sealift Command (USN)
	Multipotential Stem Cells
M S C D R	Mohawk Synchronous Communication Data Recorder
M S C P	Mean Spherical Candle Power
M S D B P	Mean Squared Distance Between Pairs
M S D D	Milli-Second Delay Detonator
M S D F	Maritime Self-Defence Force (Japan)
M S E	Mean Square Error
M S E P	Mean Square Error of Prediction
M S G	Monosodium Glutamate
M S H	Melanphore Stimulating Hormone
M S I R I	Mauritius Sugar Industry Research Insitute (Mauritius)
M S I S	Mask Shop Information System
M S I V	Main Steam Isolation Valve
M S K	Mitsubishi Shoje Kaisha (Japan)
M S L	Mapping Sciences Laboratory (of NASA (USA))
M S M	Metal-Semiconductor-Metal
M S M E A	Multiwall Sack Manufacturers Employers Association
M S N D	Mercury Substitution and Nucleonic Detection
M S P F E	Multi-Sensor Programmable Feature Extractor
M S R	Metal Sheet Rolling
M S R C E	Multi-carrier Station Remote Control Equipment
M S R F	Microwave Space Research Facility (of NRL (USN))
M S S	Magnetic Spark Spectrometer
	Manufacturers Standardization Society of the Valve and Fittings Industry (USA)
	Measurement-Standard Sensitive
	Moored Surveillance System
	Multi-Spectral Scanner
M S S L	*Mullard* Space Science Laboratory (University of London)
M S S W	Magnetostatic Surface Wave
M S T	Medium STOL Transport
	Minimum Spanning Tree

M S T L	Materials Science Toxicology Laboratories (University of Tennessee (USA))
M S T M	Mafatlal Scientific and Technological Museum (India)
M S T S	Military Sea Transportation Service (USN) (now Military Sealift Command)
M S T T E	Mobile Systems Target Tracking Emitters
M S V	Moloney Sarcoma Virus
M S W	Magnetostatic Waves
M T	Megaton
	Ministere des Transports (France) (Ministry of Transport)
M T B	Motor Torpedo Boat
M T B R	Mean Time Between Removals
M T B D R	Mean Time Between Depot Repair
M T B S F	Mean Time Between Significant Failures
M T B U M	Mean Time Between Unscheduled Maintenance
M T C	Mobile Tactical Computer
M T E	Maximum Temperature Engine
M T E L	Methyltriethyl Lead
M T F	Materialteknisk Forening (Norway) (Association for Testing of Materials)
	Metastable Time-of-Flight
M T F A	Modulation Transfer Function Area
M T G U	Main Turbine/Gearing Unit
M T H	Medium Transport Helicopter
M T H I	Methyltetrahydroindene
M T I A	Metal Trades Industry Association (Australia)
M T I S	Multiplex Transmitter Input Signals
M T L	Motivation and Training Laboratory (US Army) (now part of ARI (US Army))
M T L C	Mass Transfer Limiting Current
M T M - G P D	Methods Time Measurement and General Purpose Data
M S M T	Mutiple Terminal Monitor Task
M T P	prefix to numbered series of reports on Material Test Procedures issued by USATECOM
M T R	Meteor Trail Tracking Radar
M T R B	Marine Technology Requirements Board (of DTI)
M T S	Magnetotelluric Sounding
	Module Testing System
M T T	Mechanico-Thermal Treatment
M T T F S F	Mean Time To First System Failure

M T T F S R	Mean Time To First System Repair
M T T S A	Metropolitan Toronto Television Service Association (Canada)
M T T S F	Mean Time To System Failure
M T U	Motoren- und Turbinen-Union (Germany)
M T U R	Mean Time to Unscheduled Replacement
M T W	Management Teamwork
M U C R O M A F	Multiple Critical Root Maximally Flat
M U F	Material Unaccounted For
M U L T I P A C	Multiple Pool Processor And Computer
M U M	Mass Unbalance Modulation
M U M P S	*Massachusetts General Hospital* (Boston, USA) Utility Multiprogramming System
M U M S	Multiple Use MARC (Machine Readable Cataloguing) System
M U N	Memorial University of Newfoundland
M U P	Metalworking Under Pressure
M U R R	*Missouri University* (USA) Research Reactor
M U R S	Machine Utilisation Reporting System
M U S	Manned Underwater Station
M U S & T	Manned Undersea Science and Technology (a programme of NOAA (USA))
M U S E	Model to Understand Simple English
M U S T	Manned Undersea Science and Technology *see also* MUS&T
M U T	Modular Universal Terminal
M U X	Multiple User Experiment
M V	Mercury and Venus
	Mesenteric Vein
	Muzzle Velocity
M V A	Management of Variable Activity
	Measurement of Variable Activity
	Mevalonic Acid
M V B F	Motor Vehicle Brake Fluid
M V C	Microvoid Coalescence
M V E E	Military Vehicles and Engineering Establishment (MOD)
M V F	Moisture Volume Fraction
M V L U E	Minimum Variance, Linear Unbiased Estimator
M V M A	Motor Vehicles Manufacturers Association (USA)
M V P C C S	Motor Vehicle Post Crash Communications System
M V S	Modularized Vehicle Simulation

M V S S	prefix to numbered series of Motor Vehicle Safety Standards issued by NHTSA (USA)
M V T	Multiprogramming with a Variable number of Tasks
M V U	Minimum Variance Unbiased
M V U E	Minimum Variance Unbiased Estimator
M W (Th)	Megawatt (Thermal)
M W A E	Minimum-Weighted-Absolute-Error
M W E	Manned Working Enclosure
M W F C S	Multi-Weapon Fire Control System
M W H G L	Multiple-Wheel Heavy Gear Load or Loading
M W R	Method of Weighted Residuals
M Wt	Megawatt Thermal
M Z P	Modulated Zone Plate

N

N	prefix to numbered : dated series of Oxygen Equipment Standards issued by BSI
N A A	Neutron Activation Analysis
N A A A	National Aerial Applicators Association (USA)
N A A D	National Association of Aluminum Distributors (USA)
N A A G	North American Advisory Group (of BOTB)
N A A M M	National Association of Architectural Metal Manufacturers (USA)
N A A P	National Association of Advertising Publishers (USA)
N A A S	National Agriculture Advisory Service (now part of ADAS)
N A B E	National Association of Business Economists (USA)
N A B T	National Association of Biology Teachers (USA)
N A C	National Airways Corporation (South Africa) (a subsidiary of NAFCO)
	National Aviation Club (USA)
	prefix to numbered series of reports issued by Division of Numerical Analysis and Computing (of the NPL)
N A C A E	National Advisory Council on Art Education
N A C D	National Association of Chemical Distributors (USA)

N A C E	Neutral Atmospheric Composition Experiment
	Nomenclature Generale des Activites Econom-ique dans les Commautes Europeennes
N A C F	National Agricultural Co-operative Federation (Korea)
N A C F R C	North Atlantic Coastal Fisheries Research Center (of NMFS (USA))
N A C O A	National Advisory Committee on the Oceans and Atmosphere (USA)
N A C T A C	Navy Antenna Computer Tracking And Command system (USN)
N A D C - A E	Naval Air Development Center, Aero-Electronic Technology Department (USN)
N A D C - A M	Naval Air Development Center, Mechanics Department (USN)
N A D C - L S	Naval Air Development Center, Life Sciences and Bio-Equipment Group (USN)
N A D C - M R	Naval Air Development Center, Aerospace Medical Research Department (USN)
N A D M E	Noise Amplitude Distribution Measuring Equipment
N A D P H	Nicotinamide-Adenine Dinucleotide Phosphate
N A E C - E N G	Naval Air Engineering Center, Engineering Department (USN)
N A E E	National Association for Environmental Education
N A E M B	National Academy of Engineering Marine Board (USA)
N A E S T	National Archive for Electrical Science and Technology (of IEE)
N A F	Nederlands Atoomforum (Netherlands) (Netherlands Atom Forum)
N A F C O	National Airways and Finance Corporation (South Africa)
N A F R C	North Atlantic Fisheries Research Center (of NFMS (USA))
N A F T A	New Zealand/Australia Free Trade Agreement
N A G	National Association of Goldsmiths
N A I C	National Astronomy and Ionospheric Center (Arecibo Observatory (Puerto Rico) (administered by Cornell University (USA))
N A L	National Agricultural Library (of USDA)
N A M A	North American Mycological Assocation (USA)

N A M S B	National Association of Mutual Savings Banks (USA)
N A M C	National Association of Minority Contractors (USA)
N A M C W	National Association for Maternal and Child Welfare
N A M H	National Association for Mental Health
N A M L	Naval Aircraft Materials Laboratory (MOD)
N A M R L	Naval Aerospace Medical Research Laboratory (USN)
N A M S O	NATO Maintenance and Supply Organisation
N A P A L M	derived from its ingredients Aluminium Naphthenate and Palmitate
N A P A N	National Association for Prevention of Addiction to Narcotics (USA)
N A P C A	National Air Pollution Control Administration (of HEW (USA)) (now Air Pollution Control Office (of EPA (USA))
N A P H C C	National Association of Plumbing, Heating, and Cooling Contractors (USA)
N A P L	National Air Photo Library (of Directorate of Topographical Surveys (Canada))
N A P M	Nebraska Association of Purchasing Managers (USA)
N A P T C - A E D	Naval Air Propulsion Test Center, Aeronautical Engine Department (USN)
N A R B A	North American Regional Broadcasting Agreement
N A R D I C	Navy Research and Development Information Center (USN)
N A R F	Naval Air Rework Facility (USN)
N A R P	National Association of Railroad Passengers (USA)
N A R S C	National Association of Reinforcing Steel Contractors (USA)
N A R U C	National Association of Regulatory Utility Commissioners (USA)
N A S	National Airspace System (of FAA (USA)) Noise Abatement Society
N A S / N A E - E S B	National Academy of Sciences - National Academy of Engineering, Environmental Studies Board (USA)
N A S A D	National Association of Sport Aircraft Designers (USA)

N A S B O S A	National Academy of Sciences Board on Ocean Science Affairs (USA)
N A S C	National Association of Scaffolding Contractors
N A S C M V E	National Academy of Sciences Committee on Motor Vehicle Emissions (USA)
N A S D	National Association of Securities Dealers (USA)
N A S D A	National Space Development Agency (Japan)
N A S D A Q	*National Association of Securities Dealers* (USA) Automated Quotations
N A S I S	National Association for State Information Systems (of CSG (USA))
N A S M	National Air and Space Museum (of the Smithsonian Institute (USA))
N A S M I	National Association of Secondary Materials Industries (USA)
N A S N	National Air Sampling Network (of EPA (USA))
N A S S	Navigation Satellite System
N A S S A	National Aerospace Services Association (USA)
N A S T A	National Association of State Textbook Administrators (USA)
N A S T R A N	NASA (USA) Structural Analysis Programme
N A S U L G C	National Association of State Universities and Land-Grant Colleges (USA)
N A T A	North American Telephone Association (USA)
N A T C A P I T	Group of Experts on North Atlantic Capacity and Inclusive Tours (of the European Civil Aviation Conference)
N A T C S	National Air Traffic Control Service (of BOT) (now NATS (of CAA and MOD))
N A T E S A	National Alliance of Television and Electronics Service Associations (USA)
N A T S	National Air Traffic Service (of CAA and MOD)
N A U I	National Association of Underwater Instructors (USA)
N A V E L E C - S Y C O M	Naval Electronics Systems Command (USN)
N A V E O - R E C O V F A C	Naval Aerospace Recovery Facility (USN)
N A V M I R O	Naval Material Industrial Resources Office (USN)
N A V S H I P S	prefix to numbered series of publications issued by NSSC (USN)
N A V S P A S U R	Naval Space Surveillance system (USN)
N A V T R A	Naval Training Command (USN)

NAVTRA-EQUIPC	Naval Training Equipment Center (USN)
NAVWAS	Navigation and Weapon-Aiming Systems
NAVWASS	Navigation and Weapon-Aiming Sub-system
NAW	National Association of Wholesalers (USA)
NAWDC	National Association of Waste Disposal Contractors
NBA	National Braillie Association (USA)
NBAPA	National Benzole and Allied Products Association
NBC	Nigerian Broadcasting Corporation (Nigeria)
NBCCA	National Business Council for Consumer Affairs
NBDC	National Bomb Data Center (of United States Army and the Federal Bureau of Investigation)
NBES	Narrow-Beam Echo Sounder
NBFA	National Business Forms Association (USA)
NBFAA	National Burglar and Fire Alarm Association (USA)
NBG	National Botanic Gardens (India)
NBGRN	Narrow Band Gaussian Randon Noise
NBL	New Brunswick Laboratory (of USAEC)
NBM	Non-Book Materials
NBME	National Board of Medical Examiners (USA)
NBPC	National Branch Policy Committee (of British Institute of Management)
NBR	Nitrile Based Rubbers
NBS-BSS	prefix to numbered Building Science Series of publications issued by National Bureau of Standards (USA)
NBSIR	prefix to dated-numbered series of reports issued by National Bureau of Standards Institute of Basic Standards (USA)
NBSR	*National Bureau of Standards* (USA) Reactor
NBT	Nitro Blue Tetrazolium
NCA	National Constructors Association (USA)
NCADS	Numerical Control Advisory and Demonstration Service (of MINTECH and PERA) (terminated December, 1970)
NCAER	National Council of Applied Economics Research (India)
NCAR	National Center for Atmospheric Research (of National Science Foundation (USA))
NCATE	National Council for Accreditation of Teacher Education (USA)
NCB	Nickel-Cadmium Battery

N C B F A A	National Customs Brokers and Forwarders Association of America (USA)
N C C	National Climatic Center (of EDS (NOAA) (USA))
N C C D P C	NATO Command, Control and Information Systems and Automated Data Processing Committee
N C C M T	National Committee for Careers in Medical Technology (USA)
N C C S	National Council of Corrosion Societies
N C D A D	National Council for Diplomas in Art and Design
N C D C	National Coal Development Corporation (India)
	National Communicable Disease Center (now Center for Disease Control (HEW (USA))
N C D S	National Co-operative Development Corporation (India)
N C E	Newark College of Engineering (USA)
N C E C	National Center for Educational Communication (of USOE)
N C E C S	*North Carolina* (USA) Educational Computing System
N C E R	National Center for Earthquake Research (of USGS)
N C E T	National Center for Educational Travel (USA)
	National Council for Educational Technology (now Council for Educational Technology for the United Kingdom)
N C F S K	Non-Coherent Frequency-Shift-Keyed
N C G	Nuclear Cratering Group (US Army) (now EERO)
N C G E	National Council for Geographic Education (USA)
N chem L	National Chemical Laboratory (amalgamated with the National Physical Laboratory, 1965)
N C H E M S	National Centre for Higher Education Management Systems (at WICHE (USA))
N C H R P	National Cooperative Highways Research Program (administered by Highway Research Board (USA))
N C H S R D	National Center for Health Services Research and Development (of HEW (USA))
N C I C	National Crime Information Center (of Federal Bureau of Information (USA))
N C I T D	National Committee on International Trade Documentation (USA)
N C L	National Central Library (became part of the British Library Lending Division, 1973)

N C L	National Chemical Laboratory (India)
N C L E A	National Conference on Laboratory Evaluation and Accreditation (USA)
N C L I S	National Commission on Libraries and Information Science (USA)
N C L S	National Council of Land Surveyors (USA)
N C L T	Night Carrier Landing Trainer
N C M A	National Concrete Masonry Association (USA)
N C M H I	National Clearinghouse for Mental Health Information (of NIMH (USA))
N C M L	Naval Chemical and Metallurgical Laboratory (India)
N C M P	National Commission on Materials Policy (USA)
N C M R E D	National Council on Marine Resources and Engineering Development (USA) (disbanded 1971)
N C P	Network Control Programme
N C P I	National Computer Program Index (of the National Computing Centre)
N C R L	National Chemical Research Laboratory (South Africa)
N C R P M	National Committee on Radiation Protection and Measurement (USA)
N C S	Non-Collimated Sources
	Non-Crystalline Solid
	Numerical Control Society (USA)
N C S B C S	National Conference of States on Building Codes and Standards (USA)
N C S L	Naval Coastal Systems Laboratory (USN)
N C S R	National Council for Scientific Research (Zambia)
N C S T	National Committee on Science and Technology (India)
	Nigerian Council for Science and Technology (Nigeria)
N C S T R C	North Carolina Science and Technology Center Research Center (USA) (based on Duke University, University of North Carolina and North Carolina State University)
N C T	National Centre of Tribology (of AERE) (to become ESTL (ESRO))
	National Chamber of Trade
N C T A	National Cable Television Association (USA)
N C T C O G	North Central Texas Council of Governments (USA)
N C T J	National Council for the Training of Journalists

N C T M	National Council of Teachers of Mathematics (USA)
N C T R U	Navy Clothing and Textile Research Unit (USN)
N C U A	National Credit Union Administration (USA)
N D	Navy Distillate fuel
N D A	Non-Destructive Assay
N D A T	Non-Destructive Assay Techniques
N D B	Non-Directional Beacon
N D B C	National Data Buoy Center (of NOAA (USA))
N D B D P	National Data Buoy Development Project (of USGC (USA)) (now NDBC (NOAA))
N D B P O	National Data Buoy Project Office (of NOAA (USA))
N D C	National Development Council (New Zealand)
	Negative Differential Conductivity
N D C C	Non-Directional Cross Country
N D E	Non-Destructive Evaluation
N D M	Negative Differential Mobility
N D M S	Non-Directional Mud-and-Snow
N D P F	NASA (USA) Data Processing Facility
N D R	Negative Differential Resistance
N D R I	National Dairy Research Institute (India)
N D S	Naval Dental School (USN)
N D S U	North Dakota State University (USA)
N D T S	Non-Destructive Testing Society of Great Britain
N D V	Newcastle Disease Virus
N E A	National Electronics Association (USA)
	National Erectors Association (USA)
	Negative Electron Affinity
	Nuclear Energy Agency (of OECD)
N E A F C O	North-East Atlantic Fisheries Commission
N E B	National Energy Board (Canada)
N E C	National Energy Commission (Thailand)
N E C A	National Electrical Contractors Association (USA)
N E C A F	National Electromagnetic Compatibility Analysis Facility (of Department of Commerce (USA))
N E C A R	National Engineers Commission on Air Resources (of EJC (USA))
N E C I	Noise Exposure Computer Integrator
N E C T P	North-East Corridor Transportation Project (of Department of Transportation (USA))
N E D U	Navy Experimental Diving Unit (USN)
N E E D S	Neighbourhood Environmental Evaluation and Decision System

N E F	Norsk Elektroteknisk Forening (Norway) (Norwegian Electrical Engineers Association)
N E F B R A C S	Nearfield Bearing and Range Accuracy Calibration System
N E F D	Noise Equivalent Flux Density
N E H	National Endowment for the Humanities (USA)
N E H A	National Environmental Health Association (USA)
N E I	National Eye Institute (of NIH (HEW) (USA)) Noise-Equivalent Irradiance
N E I L C	New England (USA) Interstate Library Compact
N E I S S	National Electronic Injury Surveillance System (USA)
N E L	National Engineering Laboratory (DTI)
N E L A P T	*National Engineering Laboratory* Automatically Programmed Tools
N E M I	North European Management Institute (Norway)
N E M K O	Norges Elektriske Materiellkontrol (Norway) (Norwegian Board for Testing of Electrical Equipment)
N E M O	Naval Experimental Manned Observatory (USN) Non-Empirical Molecular Orbit
N E M S	*Nimbus-E* Microwave Spectrometer
N E P	Noise Equivalent Power
N E R	Nuclear Electric Resonance
N E R A C	New England Research Applications Center (University of Connecticut (USA))
N E R A M	Network Reliability Assessment Model
N E R B C	New England River Basins Commission (USA)
N E R C	National Environment Research Center (of EPA (USA))
N E R E M	Northeast Electronic Research and Engineering Meeting of IEEE (USA))
N E R H L	North Eastern Radiological Health Laboratory (of Bureau of Radiological Health (USA))
N E R O C	Northeast Radio Observatory Corporation (of 13 Universities (USA))
N E S A	Nebraska Electronic Service Association (USA)
N E S C	National Environmental Satellite Center (of ESSA) (now of NOAA (USA)) Naval Electronic Systems Command (USN)
N E S C T M	prefix to numbered series of Technical Memoranda issued by National Environmental Satellite Center (of ESSA later NOAA (USA))
N E S D A	North East Scotland Development Authority

N E S S	National Environmental Satellite Service (of NOAA (USA))
N E T A	National Electrical Testing Association (USA)
N E T R	NATO Electronic Technical Recommendation
N E T R E M	Net Requirements Estimation Model
N E T R S	NATO Electronic Technical Recommendations
N E U S	New Extensions for Utilizing Scientists (USA) (a non-profit corporation)
N E X T	Near-End Cross-Talk
N F A	National Foundry Association (USA)
N F A C	National Federation of Aerial Contractors
N F C A	Near-Field Calibration Array
N F D C	National Federation of Demolition Contractors
N F F C	National Film Finance Corporation
N F I B	National Federation of Independent Business
N F L D S	National Fire Loss Data System
N F M R	Non-linear Ferromagnetic Resonance
N F P C	National Federation of Plastering Contractors
N F R	Statens Naturvetenskapliga Forskningsrad (Sweden) (Swedish Natural Science Research Council)
N G	Natural Gas
N G A	National Geographical Association
N G A P D C	North Georgia Area Planning and Development Commission (USA)
N G B	National Guard Bureau (USDOD)
N G C	New General Catalogue of Nebulae and Clusters of Stars (compiled by J. L. E. Dreyer)
N G D C	National Geophysical Data Center (of the Environmental Data Service (NOAA) (USA))
N G E F	New Government Electric Factory (India)
N G F	Nerve Growth Factor
N G P	Nearest Grid Point
N G P A	Natural Gas Processors Association (USA)
N G S P	National Geodetic Satellite Program (of NASA (USA))
N H B	prefix to numbered series of Handbooks issued by NASA (USA)
N H B R C	National House Builders Registration Council (now National House-Building Council)
N H C	National Hurricane Center (of NOAA (USA))
N H L I	National Heart and Lung Institute (of NIH (USA))
N H R L	National Hurricane Research Laboratory (of ESSA) (now of NOAA (USA))

N H S B	National Highway Safety Bureau (of Federal Highway Administration (USA) (now NHTSA)
N H T S A	National Highway Traffic Safety Administration (of Department of Transportation (USA))
N H W	Department of National Health and Welfare (Canada)
N I	Neutraminidase Inhibition
N I A	National Interconnect Association (USA)
	National Irrigation Administration (Philippines)
N I A A A	National Institute on Alcohol Abuse and Alcoholism (USA)
N I A M D D	National Institute of Arthritis, Metabolism and Digestive Diseases (USA)
N I A S A	National Insurance Actuarial and Statistical Association (USA)
N I B	National Irrigation Board (Kenya)
N I B S	National Institute of Building Sciences (of NAS and NAE (USA))
N I B S C	National Institute for Biological Standards and Control
N I C	Naval Intelligence Command (USN)
	Newsprint Information Committee (USA)
N I C A T E L - S A T	Compania Nicaraguense de Telecomunicaciones por Satelite (Nicaragua)
N I C H D	National Institute of Child Health and Human Development (of NIH (USA))
N I C O L	*Nineteen Hundred* (computer) Commercial Language)
N I C P	National Inventory Control Points (US Army)
N I C S	NATO Integrated Communications System
N I C S M A	NATO Integrated Communications System Management Agency
N I C S O	NATO Integrated Communications Systems Organization
N I D A	National Institute of Development Administration (Thailand)
N I D C	National Industrial Development Corporation (India) (State owned)
	Nepal Industrial Development Corporation (Nepal)
N I D E R	Nederlands Institut voor Informatie, Documentatie en Registratuur (Netherlands) (Netherlands Institute for Information, Documentation and Filing) (now NOBIN)

N I E	National Institute of Education (of HEW (USA))
N I E H S	National Institute of Environmental Health Sciences (of NIH (USA))
N I F	Nordiska Institutet for Fargforskning (Denmark) (Scandinavian Institute for Paint and Printing Ink Research)
N I F F T	National Institute of Foundry and Forge Technology (India)
N I F O R	Nigerian Institute for Oil Palm Research (Nigeria)
N I H E	Northern Ireland Housing Executive
N I L	Nederlands Instituut voor Lastechniek (Netherlands) (Netherlands Welding Institute)
N I L S	Nuclear Instrumentation Landing System
N I M	National Institute for Metallurgy (South Africa)
	Nigerian Institute of Management (Nigeria)
	Nuclear Instrumentation Modular
N I M E X	Nomenclature for Imports and Exports (of EEC)
N I M H	National Institute of Mental Health (of PHS (USA)) (no longer in NIH but in Alcohol, Drug Abuse and Mental Health Administration)
N I M M S	*Nineteen-hundred* (Computer) Integrated Modular Management System
N I M R	National Institute for Medical Research (of the MRC)
N I M R A	National Industrial Materials Recovery Association
N I M R O D	*Nineteen-hundred* (Computer) Management and Recovery of Documentation
N I N A	Neutron Instruments for Nuclear Analysis
N I N D S	National Institute of Neurological Diseases and Stroke (of NIH (USA))
N I O	National Institute of Oceanography (India)
	National Institute of Oceanography (of Natural Environment Research Council) (now Institute of Oceanographic Sciences)
N I O C	National Iranian Oil Company (Iran)
N I O S H	National Institute for Occupational Safety and Health (of PHS (USA))
N I P	Non-Impact-Printer
N I P A L S	Nonlinear Iterative Partial Least Squares
N I P C C	National Industrial Pollution Control Council (USA)
N I P S	National Military Command System Information Processing System (USDOD)

N I R	Near Infra-Red
	Negative Impedance Repeater
N I R C	National Industrial Relations Court
	National Information Retrieval Colloquium (USA)
N I R M	prefix to numbered series of Interim Research Memoranda issued by Naval Warfare Analysis Group (of CNA (USN))
N I R R A	Northern Ireland Radio Retailers Association
N I S	National Institute for Standards (Egypt)
	Nordiska Ingenjorssamfundet (Sweden) (Scandinavian Engineers Association) (disbanded 1971)
N I S C	Naval Intelligence Support Center (USN)
N I S E E	National Information Service for Earthquake Engineering (of University of California and California Institute of Technology (USA))
N I S M	Non-deterministic Incomplete Sequential Machine
N I S P	National Information System for Psychology (of the American Psychological Association (USA))
N I S P A	National Information System for Physics and Astronomy (of the American Institute of Physics (USA))
N I S U S	Neutron Intermediate Standard Uranium Source
N I T	Negative Income Tax
N I T I E	National Institute for Training in Industrial Engineering (India)
N I T R	Nigerian Institute for Trypanosomiasis Research (Nigeria)
N I V R A	Nederlands Instituut van Registeraccountants (Netherlands) (Netherlands Institution of Chartered Accountants)
N K A	National Khmer Aviation (Cambodia) (Military Air Force)
N K F	Norsk Korrosjonsteknisk Forening (Norway) (Norwegian Corrosion Association)
N K T F	Norges Kvalitetstekniske Forening (Norway) (Norwegian Society for Quality Control)
N L C	Noctilucent Clouds
N L E T S	National Law Enforcement Teletype System (USA)
N L I	National Limestone Institute (USA)

N L L	National Lending Library for Science and Technology (became part of the British Library Lending Division of the British Library in 1973)
N L L S T	*see* NLL above
N L M	National Library of Medicine (of NIH (HEW) (USA))
N L M - B C N	National Library of Medicine (USA) Biomedical Communications Network
N L P	Non-Linear Programming
N L R	Nationaal Lucht- en Ruimtevaartlaboratorium (Netherlands) (National Aerospace Laboratory) Net Liquidity Ratio
N M A	National Management Association (USA) National Medical Association (USA)
N M A B	National Materials Advisory Board (of National Academy of Engineering and National Academy of Sciences (USA))
N M A C	Near Mid-Air Collision
N M A C T	Nuclear Material Accounting Control Team (of UKAEA)
N M A S	National Map Accuracy Standards (USA)
N M C	National Meteorological Center (of Weather Bureau (NOAA) (USA)) Naval Material Command (USN)
N M C S S C	National Military Command System Support Center (of NMCS (USDOD))
N M D C	National Mineral Development Corporation (India) (now part of SAIL (India))
N M D R	Nuclear Magnetic Double Resonance
N M F S	National Marine Fisheries Service (of NOAA (USA))
N M F S - C I R C	prefix to series of Circulars issued by NMFS (of NOAA (USA))
N M F S - S S R F	prefix to series of Special Scientific Reports on Fisheries issued by NMFS (of NOAA (USA))
N M G	Numerical Master Geometry
N M I T	New Material Introduction Team (of USAMERDC)
N M L	National Metallurgical Laboratory (India) Nuclear Magnetism Log
N M N H	National Museum of Natural History (USA)
N M P - T C N Q	N-methylphenazinium - Tetracyanoquinodimethane
N M P A	National Marine Paint Association (now part of PMAGB)

N M P S	prefix to dated/numbered series of Nuclear Marine Propulsion Summaries issued by AEEW (UKAEA)
N M R	N-Modular Redundancy
N M S	Nigerian Meteorological Service (Nigeria)
	Non-metric Multidimensional Scaling
N M V S A C	National Motor Vehicle Safety Advisory Council (of DOT (USA))
N N A	National Newspaper Association (USA)
N N A G	NATO Naval Armament Group
N N C	National Nuclear Corporation (partially government owned)
N N C S C	National Neutron Cross Section Center (of USAEC)
N N D T U	National Non-Destructive Testing Unit (of CEGB)
N N E	Noise and Number Exposure
N N M C	National Naval Medical Center (USN)
N N P	Net National Product
N N R	Nearest Neighbour Rule
N O A	National Oceanographic Association (USA) (now National Ocean Industries Association (USA))
N O A A	National Oceanic and Atmospheric Administration (of Department of Commerce (USA))
N O A A - F C M	prefix to dated-numbered series of reports issued by the Federal Coordinator for Meteorological Services and Supporting Research of NOAA (USA)
N O A A - T R - N M F S - C I R C	NOAA (USA) - Technical Report - National Marine Fisheries Service - Circular
N O A A - T R - N M F S - S S R F	NOAA (USA) - Technical Report - National Marine Fisheries Service - Special Scientific Report Fisheries
N O A C T	Navy Overseas Air Cargo Terminal (USN)
N O A H	Narrow-band Optimiziation of the Alignment of Highways
N O B S	Naval Observatory (USN)
N O D C	National Oceanographic Data Center (USA) (now merged with the Environmental Data Service (of NOAA (USA))
N O D L R	Night Observation Device - Long Range
N O E	Nap Of Earth
N O F	Nitrosyl Fluoride
N O I A	National Ocean Industries Association (USA)

N O I C	National Oceanographic Instrumentation Center (of NOAA (USA))
N O I S E	National Organization to Insure a Sound-controlled Environment (USA)
	Noise Information Service (Illinois Institute of Technology (USA))
N O L A P	Non-Linear Analysis Programme
N O L T R	prefix to numbered series of Technical Reports issued by the Naval Ordnance Laboratory (USN)
N O M E S	New England (USA) Offshore Mining Environmental Study (involving private industry, government and several universities)
N O M S S	National Operational Meteorological Satellite System (of NOAA (USA))
N O P M S	Network-Oriented Project Management Systems (a group of ANSI (USA))
N O R M	Not Operationally Ready due to Maintenance
N O R P A X	North Pacific Experiment
N O R R A	National Off-Road Racing Association (USA)
N O R S	Not Operationally Ready due to Supply
N O R S A R	Norwegian Large Aperture Seismic Array
N O R T H A G	Northern Army Group (of AFCENT (NATO))
N O S	National Ocean Survey (of NOAA (USA))
	Nederlandse Omroep Stichting (Netherlands)
N O S - I H T R	prefix to numbered series of reports issued by Naval Ordnance Station, Indian Head, Maryland (USN)
N O S F E R	Nouveau Systeme Fondamental pour la determination de l'Equivalent de Reference (of CCITT) (New Master System for determining Reference Equivalents)
N O S M	Noise Diotic, Signal Monaural
N O S O	Noise Diotic, Signal Diotic
N O T B A	National Ophthalmic Treatment Board Association
N O T S	Nuclear Orbit Transfer Stage
N P A	National Personnel Authority (Japan)
	Newspaper Publishers Association
N P A A S	National Passenger Accounting and Analysis Scheme (of British Rail)
N P A B	Nuclear Power Advisory Board
N P C	National Productivity Council (India)
	Naval Photographic Center (USN)
N P C A	National Paint and Coatings Association (USA)

N P D	Non-Planar Dipole antenna
N P D S	Nuclear Particle Detection System
N P E	Non-Polluting Engine
N P E A	National Printing Equipment Association (USA)
N P F M	Neural Pulse Frequency Modulation
N P F R C	North Pacific Fisheries Research Center (of NMFS (USA))
N P F S C	North Pacific Fur Seal Commission
N P I	Norsk Produktivitetsinstitutt (Norway) (Norwegian Productivity Institute)
N P L	National Physical Laboratory (DTI) National Physical Laboratory (India)
N P L - C H E M	prefix to numbered series of reports issued by the National Physical Laboratory, Division of Chemical Standards
N P L - I M S	prefix to numbered series of reports issued by the National Physical Laboratory, Division of Inorganic and Metallic Structure
N P L - M A	prefix to numbered series of reports issued by the National Physical Laboratory, Division of Numerical and Applied Mathematics
N P L - R P U	National Physical Laboratory (India), Radio Propagation Unit
N P M H O	Non-Profit Making Housing Organisation
N P N	Non-Protein Nitrogen
N P P T S	Nuclear Power Plant Training Simulator
N P R A	National Petroleum Refiners Association (USA) Naval Personnel Research Activity (USN) (now Naval Personnel and Training Research Laboratory)
N P S H A	Net Positive Suction Head Available
N P S H R	Net Positive Suction Head Requirements
N P S M	Non-Productive Standard Minute
N P T	Treaty for the Non-Proliferation of Nuclear Weapons (1970)
N P T A	National Paper Trade Association (USA)
N P T R L	Naval Personnel and Training Research Laboratory (USN)
N P U	National Pharmaceutical Union
N P V H	Net Present Value at the Horizon
N P V L A	National Paint, Varnish and Lacquer Association (USA)
N Py	Nitrosopyrrolidine
N R	Neutron Radiography

N R A	National Rifle Association of America (USA)
N R C	prefix to series of Research Contributions issued by the Naval Warfare Analysis Group (of CNA (USN))
N R C C	National Research Council of Canada, Division of Applied Chemistry
N R C D P	National Research Centre for Disaster Prevention (Japan)
N R C P	National Research Council of the Philippines (Philippines)
N R C S	Normalized Radar Cross Section
N R D C	National Research Development Corporation (of CSIR (India))
	Natural Resources Defense Council (USA)
N R D F	Non-Recursive Digital Filter
N R D P	National Research and Development Programme (of MITI (Japan))
N R D R	Non-Resetting Data Reconstruction
N R D R - C F	Non-Resetting Data Reconstruction with Continuous Feedback
N R D R - D F	Non-Resetting Data Reconstruction with Discrete Feedback
N R E A	Natural Resources and Energy Agency (of MITI (Japan))
N R I E S	National-Regional Impact Evaluation System
N R I S	Natural Resource Information System
N R J	Non-Reciprocal Junction
N R L	National Radiation Laboratory (New Zealand)
	National Reference Library of Science and Invention (in 1973 became Science Reference Library of the British Library)
	Naval Research Laboratory (of the Naval Research Office (USN))
N R L S I	National Reference Library of Science and Invention (in 1973 became Science Reference Library of the British Library)
N R M A	National Roads and Motorists Association (Australia)
N R P B	National Radiological Protection Board
N R R P D C	Neuse River Regional Planning and Development Council, North Carolina (USA)
N R S	Normal Rabbit Serum
	Normal Rake System
N R S A	Northern Radio Societies Association

N S A	National Slag Association (USA)
N S B	National Science Board (of National Science Foundation (USA))
	National Shipping Board (India)
	Norges Statsbaner (Norway) (Norwegian State Railways)
N S C	National Safety Council (India)
	National Science Council (Eire)
	National Supervisory Council for the Alarm Industry
N S C M	National Science Curriculum Materials project (Australia)
N S C W A	Nigerian Society of Cost and Works Accountants (Nigeria)
N S D B	National Science Development Board (Philippines)
N S F M	National Symposium on Fracture Mechanics (of ASTM (USA))
N S F O	Navy Special Fuel Oil
N S F O R T	Non-Standard FORTRAN
N S G	Nuclear Science Group (of IEEE (USA))
N S M B	Netherlands Ship Model Basin (Netherlands)
N S M R L	Naval Submarine Medical Research Laboratory (USN)
N S M R S E	National Study of Mathematics Requirements for Scientists and Engineers (USA)
N S M S E S	Naval Ship Missile Systems Engineering Station
N S P B	National Society for the Prevention of Blindness (USA)
N S P R I	Nigerian Stored Products Research Institute (Nigeria)
N S R	Neutrino Synchroton Radiation
N S R D L	Naval Ship Research and Development Laboratory (USN)
N S R D L / P C	Naval Ship Research and Development Laboratory, Panama City (USN)
N S R I	National Sea Rescue Institute (South Africa)
N S S	Neutral Speed Stability
	Nuclear Science Symposium
N S S A	National Suggestion Schemes Association
N S S F C	National Severe Storm Forecast Center (of NOAA (USA))
N S S L	National Severe Storms Laboratory (of ESSA) (now of NOAA (USA))

N S S P	Neutralisation Self-Solidification Process
N S S S	Nuclear Steam Supply System
N S T	Noise, Spikes and Transients
	Numerical Surveying Technique
N S T I C	Naval Scientific and Technical Information Centre (absorbed into DRIC in 1971) (MOD)
N S T P	National Space Technology Programme (administered by DTI with MOD technical assistance)
N S V	Noise, Shock and Vibration
N S W M A	National Solid Wastes Management Association (USA)
N T A	Near Terminal Area
	Nitrilotriacetate
	Nitrilotriacetate Acid
N T C	National Telemetering Conference (of IEEE (USA))
	National Textile Corporation (India) (state owned)
	National Translations Center (John Crerar Library, Chicago (USA))
N T C A	North Texas Contractors Association (USA)
N T D A	National Tyre Distributors Association
N T D P M A	National Tool, Die and Precision Machining Association (USA)
N T I D	National Technical Institute for the Deaf (Rochester Institute of Technology (USA))
N T I S	National Technical Information Service (Department of Commerce (USA))
N T I S - P K	NTIS Information Package - a numbered series issued by NTIS (USA)
N T I Search	NTIS (USA) on-line bibliographic search system
N T M L	National Tillage Machinery Laboratory (USA)
N T R D A	National Tuberculosis and Respiratory Disease Association (USA)
N T S	Nucleus Tractus Solitarius
N T S B	National Transportation Board (of DOT (USA))
N T S B - A A M	prefix to series of dated-numbered reports issued by Bureau of Aviation Safety, National Transportation Safety Board (of DOT (USA))
N T S B - A A R	National Transportation Safety Board (of DOT (USA)) - Aircraft Accident Report
N T S B - H A R	prefix to dated-numbered series of Highway Accident Reports issued by National Transportation Safety Board (of DOT (USA))

9*

N T S B - P A R	prefix to dated-numbered series of Pipeline Accident Reports issued by National Transportation Safety Board (of DOT (USA))
N T S B - R A R	prefix to dated-numbered series of Railroad Accident Reports issued by National Transportation Safety Board (of DOT (USA))
N T S B - R H R	prefix to dated-numbered series of Railroad/Highway Accident Reports issued by National Transportation Safety Board (of DOT (USA))
N T T P C	Nippon Telegraph and Telephone Public Corporation (Japan)
N T T R L	National Tissue Typing Reference Laboratory
N T T S	National Tower Testing Station (of CEGB)
N T W	Non-pressure Thermit Welding
N U C	Naval Undersea Research and Development Center (USN) (now Naval Undersea Center)
N U C L E N O R	Centrales Nucleares del Norte (Spain)
N U C O L	Numerical Control Language
N U L S	Net Unit-Load Size
N U M E P S	Numeric Meta Language Processing System
N U R A T	*Newcastle University* Root Analogue Tunneller
N U S C	Naval Underwater Systems Center (USN)
N U S C / N L	Naval Undersea System Center, New London Laboratory (USN)
N U S L	Navy Underwater Sound Laboratory (USN)
N U S L I P	*Nottingham University* Line Sequency Programme
N U T M A Q	Nuclear Techniques in Mining and Quarrying (a unit at AERE (UKAEA))
N U T S	*Newcastle University* Teaching System
N V	Naamloge Vennootschap (Limited Company)
	prefix to SAE (USA) numbered series of Low Alloy Constructional Steels
N V A E S	Novo-Voronezhskaya Atomnaya Energeticheskaya Stantisiya (USSR) (Novo-Voronezhskaya Atomic Power Station)
N V E	Nederslandse Vereniging voor Ergonomie (Netherlands) (Netherlands Ergonomics Society)
N V L	Nederlandse Vereniging voor Lastechniek (Nethlands Welding Society) (now part of NIL)
	Night Vision Laboratory (US Army)
N V R S	National Vegetable Research Station
N W A G	Naval Warfare Analysis Group (of Center for Naval Analyses (USN))

N W C	National Water Commission (USA) National Water Council
N W H	*Noren* Weld Hardening
N W H L	Naval Weapons Handling Laboratory (USN)
N W I D A	North West Industrial Development Association
N W P A	National Wooden Pallet and Container Association (USA)
N W S	National Weather Service (of NOAA (USA)) prefix to numbered series of publications issued by the Naval Warfare Analysis Group (of CNA (USN)) Noise Wiener Spectrum
N W S - C R	National Weather Service - Central Region (of NOAA (USA))
N W S - E R	National Weather Service - Eastern Region (of NOAA (USA))
N W S - S R	National Weather Service - Southern Region (of NOAA (USA))
N W S Y	Naval Weapons Station, Yorktown (USN)
N X S R	Non-Extraction Steam Rate
N Y C H A	New York Clearing House Association (USA)
N Y H A	New York Heart Association (USA)
N Y L A	New York Library Association (USA)
N Y M A C	National Young Managers Committee (of the BIM)
N Y M S	New York Microscopical Society (USA)
N Y S A A	New York State Association of Architects (USA)
N Y S A P L S	New York State Association of Professional Land Surveyors (USA)
N Y S I I S	*New York State* (USA) Identification and Intelligence System
N Y S P I N	*New York State* (USA) Police Intelligence Network
N Y U - A A	New York University, Department of Aeronautics and Astronautics (USA)
N Z A E C	New Zealand Atomic Energy Committee (New Zealand)
N Z A R T	New Zealand Association of Radio Transmitters (New Zealand)
N Z B C	New Zealand Broadcasting Corporation (New Zealand)
N Z B T O	New Zealand Book Trade Organization (New Zealand)

N Z E D	New Zealand Electricity Department (New Zealand)
N Z I A	New Zealand Institute of Architects (New Zealand)
N Z I C	New Zealand Institute of Chemistry (New Zealand)
N Z I E	New Zealand Institution of Engineers (New Zealand)
N Z I E R	New Zealand Institute of Economic Research (New Zealand)
N Z I M P	New Zealand Institute of Medical Photography (New Zealand)
N Z N A C	New Zealand National Airways Corporation (New Zealand)
N Z S	prefix to numbered series of Standards issued by SANZ (New Zealand)
N Z S A	New Zealand Society of Accountants (New Zealand)

O

O	prefix to numbered series of reports issued by AWRE (of UKAEA) (transferred to MOD, 1973)
O - T A W C S	Okinawa Tactical Air Weapons Control System
O A	Operational Analysis Code Package
	Optical Absorption
O A A	Obstetric Anaesthetists Association
	Orient Airlines Association
O A C P	Operational Analysis Code Package
O A M	Office of Aviation Medicine (of FAA (USA))
O A M S	Orbit Attitude and Manoeuvre System
O A N A	Organization of Asian News Agencies
O A O R	Oxygen Adsorption, Out-gassing, and Chemical Reduction
O A P E C	Organization of Arab Petroleum Exporting Countries
O A R	prefix to numbered series of Operations Analysis Reports issued by USAF Logistics Command Operations Analysis Office
O A R B	Orient Airlines Research Bureau
O A R T	Office of Advanced Research and Technology (of (NASA (USA)) (now office of Aeronautics and Space Technology)

O A S	Ohio Academy of Science (USA)
O A S I S	Oceanic and Atmospheric Scientific Information System (of NOAA (USA))
	Optimized Air-to-Surface Infra-red Seeker
O A T	Operational Acceptance Test
O A T M	Operations Analysis Technical Memorandum (numbered series issued by AFLC (USAF))
O A U	Organization of African Unity (Ethiopia)
O A W	Oxy-Acetylene Welding
O B A R	Ohio Bar Automated Research (Ohio State Bar Association (USA))
O B B	Oesterreichische Bundesbahnen (Austria) (Austrian Federal Railways)
O B E	Office of Business Economics (of Department of Commerce (USA)) (now part of the Social and Economic Statistics Administration)
O B E - S B C	prefix to dated-numbered series of Surveys of Current Business issued by Office of Business Economics (USA)
O B N	Office of Biochemical Nomenclature (of NAS/NRC (USA))
O B O	Ore/Bulk/Oil
O B P	Onboard Processor
O B R	Overseas Business Report (series issued by Bureau of International Commerce (USA))
O B S	Ocean Bottom Seismographic Station
	Omni Bearing Selector
O C	Obstacle Clearance (a panel of ICAO)
	Optic Chiasm
O C A M	Organisation Commune Africaine, Malgache et Mauricienne (Cameroon)
O C A S	On-line Cryptanalytic System
O C C G E	Organisation de Cooperation et de Coordination de la Lutte contre des Grandes Endemies
	Organisation de Cooperation et de Coordination in the Fight against Endemic Diseases)
O C C I	Optical Coincidence Co-ordinate Indexing
O C D	Office for Child Development (of HEW (USA))
O C E A C	Organisation de Coordination pour la Lutte Contre des Endemies en Afrique Centrale (Organisation for Coordination in the Fight against Endemic Diseases in Central Africa)
O C L C	Ohio College Library Center (USA)

O C M	On Condition Maintenance
	Optical Counter-Measures
O C M A	Oil Companies Materials Association
O C O M	Oficina Central de Organizacion y Metodos (Chile) (Central Office of Organisation and Methods)
O C P	Obstacle Clearance Panel (of ICAO)
	Open Circuit Potential
O C R U A	Optical Character Recognition Users Association (USA)
O C S	Office Computing System
	Office of Criteria and Standards (Bureau of Radiological Health (USA))
	Operations Control System
	Outer Continental Shelf
	Overseas Communication Service (India)
O C T I	Office Central des Transports Internationaux par Chemins de Fer (Switzerland) (Central Office for International Railway Transport)
O C U	Oscillator-Clock Unit
O D	Organizational Development
	Overburden Drill
O D A	Overseas Development Administration (of the Foreign and Commonwealth Office)
O D C	Oxyhaemoglobin Dissociation Curve
O D E C A	Organizacion de Estados Centro Americanos (Organization of Central American States) (Headquarters in El Salvador)
O D I	Overseas Development Institute
O D I N	Optimal Design Integration
O D M	Ministry of Overseas Development (disbanded in 1970 and replaced by ODA)
O D N	Ordnance Datum Newlyn
O D P C S	Oceanographic Data Processing and Control Systems
O D T W	Oppositely Directed Travelling Waves
O E D R C	Optico-Electronic Device for Registering Coincidences
O E G	Operations Evaluation Group (of CNA (USN))
O E I M C	Oklahoma Environmental Information and Media Center (East Central State College (USA))
O E O	Office of Economic Opportunity (of the Executive Office of the President (USA))
	Operational Equipment Objective

O E P	Office of Emergency Preparedness (of the Executive Office of the President (USA) (previously Office of Emergency Planning)
O E R	Office of Economic Research (of Economic Development Agency (USA))
	Office of Engineering Reference (Bureau of Reclamation, Dept. of the Interior (USA))
	prefix to numbered series of Operations Evaluation Reports issued by Operations Evaluation Group (of CNA (USN))
	Oxygen Evolution Reaction
O E R S	Organisation des Etats Riverains du Senegal (Senegal) (Organisation of Senegal River States)
O E S	prefix to numbered series of Operations Evaluation Studies issued by Operations Evaluation Group (of CNA (USN))
O E S B R	Oil Extended Styrene Butadiene Rubber
O E S R	Oil Extended Synthetic Rubber
O E T	Optico-Electronic Transducer
O F BW	Ozeanographische Forchungsanstalt der Bundeswehr (Germany) (Armed Forces Oceanographic Research Establishment)
O F C C	Office of Federal Contract Compliance (of Dept. of Labor (USA))
O F D S	Optimal Financial Decision Strategy
O F E M A	Office Francais d'Exportation de Materiel Aeronautique (France)
O F F S E T	Offshore Engineering Team (of NEL (DTI))
O F O	Orbiting Frog Otolith (an experiment carried out by NASA (USA))
O F R	On Frequency Repeater
	Open File Report
O G E	Out of Ground Effect
O G F T	Oesterreichische Gesellschaft fur Weltraumforschung und Flugkorpertechnik (Austria) (Austrian Society for Space Exploration and Rocket Technology)
O G V	Outlet Guide Vane
O H	prefix to numbered series of publications issued by NIOSH (HEW (USA))
O H D M S	Operational Hydromet Data Management System
O H E S	Office of Health and Environmental Science (of TVA (USA))

O H M	prefix to dated/numbered series on Oil and Hazardous Material issued by Water Programs Office (of EPA (USA))
O H M S E T T	Oil and Hazardous Materials Systems Environmental Test Tank (of EPA (USA))
O H P	Overhead Projector
O H R	Over-the-Horizon Radar
O H W	Oxy-Hydrogen Welding
O I A G	Oesterreichische Industrieverwaltungs Aktiengesellschaft (Austria) (Austrian Agency for the Reorganization of State Enterprises)
O I B F	Oesterreichische Institut fur Bibliotheksforschung, Dokumentations-und Informationswesen (Austria) (Austrian Institute for Library Research, Documentation, and Information Science)
O I P	Societe Belge d'Optique et d'Instruments de Precision (Belgium) (Belgian Society of Optics and Precision Instruments)
O I P E E C	Organisation Internationale pour l'Etude de l'Endurance des Cables (International Organisation for the study of the Endurance of Wire Ropes)
O I T	Organization Iberoamericaine de Television (Television Organization of Countries speaking Spanish or Portuguese)
O I T A F	Organizzazione Internazionale Transporti A Fune (Italy) (International Association for Transport by Rope)
O I V	Office International de la Vigne et du Vin (France) (Vine and Wine International Office)
O I W	Oceanographic Institute of Washington (USA)
O J E	On-the-Job Education
O Kh N	Otdelenie Khimischeskikh Nauk (Department of Chemical Sciences (of the Academy of Sciences) (USSR))
O K I	Organo Kemijska Industrija (Yugoslavia)
	Oesterreichisches Kunstoffinstitut (Austria) (Austrian Plastics Institute)
O K S U - R F	Oklahoma State University - Research Foundation (USA)
O L	Original Learning
O L D A P	On-Line Data Processor
O L E P	Osculating Lunar Elements Programme
O L F O	Open-Loop Feedback Optimal

O L P A R S	On-Line Pattern Analysis and Recognition System
O L S	Ordinary Least Squares
O L S A S S	On-Line System Availability and Service Simulation
O M A	Overseas Mining Association
O M B	Office of Management and Budget (USA)
O M B E	Office of Minority Business Enterprise (Dept. of Commerce (USA))
O M E	Office of Manpower Economics
O M F S	Optimum Metric Fastener System (of Industrial Fasteners Institute *and* ANSI (USA))
O M G E	Organization Mondiale de Gastro-Enterologie (World Organisation of Gastroenterology)
O M I	Ottico Meccanica Italiana (Italy)
O M L R S	Operations, Maintenance and Logistics Resources Simulation
O M P	Organisation and Monitor Programme
O M R	Optical Mark Reader
O M R S	On-site Management Records System (of CERL (US Army))
O M S	Orbital Manoeuvring System
O N A C	Office of Noise Abatement and Control (of Environmental Protection Agency (USA))
O N C F	Office National des Chemins de Fer (Morocco) (National Office of Railways)
O N G C	Oil and Natural Gas Commission (India)
O N P	Oficina Nacional de Pesca (Venezuela) (National Fisheries Office)
O N R A P	Oficina Nacional de Racionalizacion y Capacitacion de la Administracion Publica (Peru)
O N R L	Office of Naval Research, London (England) (USN)
O N S	Omega Navigation System
O N S E R	Organisme National de Securite Routiere (France) (National Road Safety Organisation)
O O G	Office of Oil and Gas (Department of the Interior (USA))
O O K D K	Orszagos Orvostudomanyi Konyvtar es Dokumentacios (Hungary) (National Medical Library and Centre for Documentation)
O O M	Original On-line Module
O O S	Orbit-to-Orbit Shuttle
O P	Occasional Paper
O P C	Ordinary Portland Cement

O P C S	Office of Population Censuses and Surveys
O P E	One-Particle-Exchange
O P E R U N	Operation Planning and Execution system for Railway Unified Network
O P I C	Overseas Private Investment Corporation (a Federal Agency in the USA)
O P I N S	*Oakland* (California (USA)) Planning Information System
O P K	Optokinetic
O P M	Optically Projected Map
O P M C	One Player Median Competitive
O P O	Optical Parametric Oscillator
O P S	Office of Pipeline Safety (USA)
	Omnidirectional Point Source
O P S A	Optimal Pneumatic Systems Analysis
O P S E T	Optional Set of Parameters
O P T A	Offshore Petroleum Training Association
O P T A G	Optical Aimpoint Guidance
O P T N E T	Optimum Private Trunk Network Embodying Tandems
O P V	Optical Path-length Variation
O Q A	Optical Quantum Amplifier
O R	prefix to numbered/dated reports issued by the Operational Research Department of BISRA
	Orientating Response
O R / H F	prefix to numbered/dated series of reports issued by BISRA
O R A	Office of Research Analyses (of OAR (USAF))
O R A C L E	Operational Research And Critical Link Evaluation
	Operations Research And Critical Link Evaluator
	Optimum Record Automation for Court and Law Enforcement (Los Angeles County (USA))
	Optional Reception of Announcements by Coded Line Electronics
O R A U	Oak Ridge Associated Universities (USA)
O R B E	Open Reciprocating Brayton Engine
O R B I S C A L	Orbiting Radio Beacon Ionosphere Satellite for Calibration
O R B I T	On-Line Reduced Bandwidth Information Transfer
O R C	Optimal Replacement Chart
	Organic Rankine Cycle
O R C H I S	*Oak Ridge* (*National Laboratory* (USAEC)) Computerized Hierarchical Information System

O R D E A L	*Oak Ridge (National Laboratory* (USAEC)) Data Evaluation and Analysis Language
	Orbital Rate Drive Electronics for *Apollo*
O R E	Operational Research Executive (of the National Coal Board)
	Optimum Resource Extraction
O R E L A	*Oak Ridge (National Laboratory* (USAEC)) Electron Linear Accelerator
O R F	Oesterreichischer Rundfunk (Austria) (Austrian Broadcasting Corporation)
O R G A L I M E	Organisme de Liaison des Industries Metalliques (Belgium) (European Association for Co-operation of the Metals Industry)
O R G D P	*Oak Ridge (National Laboratory* (USAEC)) Gaseous Diffusion Plant
O R I	Occurrence of Reinforcing Information
	Octane Requirement Increase
O R I C	*Oak Ridge (National Laboratory* (USAEC)) Isochronous Cyclotron
O R L A	Optimum Repair Level Analysis
O R M	Optimal Replacement Method
O R O	Office for Regional Operations (Bureau of Radiological Health (USA))
O R O S	Optical Read-Only Storage
O R O S S	Operational Readiness Oriented Supply System (US Army)
O R P	Office of Radiation Programs (of EPA (USA))
O R P / S I P	prefix to dated-numbered series of reports issued by ORP (of EPA (USA))
O R R	*Oak Ridge (National Laboratory* (USAEC)) Reactor
O R S	Operational Research Society
O R S A	Operations Research Systems Analysis
O R Socy	Operational Research Society
O R T F	Office de Radiodiffusion-Television Francaise (France)
O R T S	Operational Readiness Test System
O R V I D	On-line X-ray Evaluation over Video-Display including Documentation
O S	Orthogonal System
O S / M V T	Operating System, Allowing Multiprogramming with a Variable number of Tasks
O S A	Offshore Supply Association
O S A H R C	*see* OSHRC
O S A T	Optical Sensor And Tracker

O S C	Okanagan Study Committee (of CBCC (Canada))
O S C A R	Oscillogram Scan And Recorder system
O S C A S	Office of Statistical Co-ordination and Standards (Philippines)
O S C P	Ocean Sediment Coring Program (of NSF (USA))
O S D O C	Offshore Discharge of Container Ships
O S E A S	Ocean Sampling and Environmental Analysis System
O S E E	Optically Stimulated Exoelectron Emission
O S E M	Office of Systems Engineering and Management (of FAA (USA))
O S H A	Occupational Safety and Health Administration (of Dept. of Labor (USA))
O S H R C	Occupational Safety and Health Review Commission (USA)
O S I	Optimum Scale Integration
O S M	Omni Spectra Miniature
O S N C	Optical Society of Northern California (USA)
O S O	Offshore Supplies Office
O S P	Oceanographic Survey Recorder
O S R	Optical Scanner Reader
O S R L	Organizations and Systems Research Laboratory (of ARI (US Army))
O S S	Operations Support System
O S S L	Operating System Simulation Language
O S T	Office of Science and Technology (of PSAC (USA)) (disbanded 1973)
	Office of the Secretary of Transportation (USA)
O S T D	Office of Supersonic Transport Development (Dept. of Transportation (USA))
O S T I	Office for Scientific and Technical Information (of DES) (to become part of the British Library in 1974)
O S T I V	Organisation Scientifique et Technique International du Vol a Voile (International Scientific and Technical Organisation for Gliders and Sailplanes)
O S U	Ohio State University (USA)
	Oklahoma State University (USA)
O S U - C I S R C	Ohio State University Computer and Information Science Research Center (USA)
O S V	Ocean Station Vessel
O S W	Office of Saline Water (Dept. of the Interior (USA))

O T	Office of Telecommunications (Dept. of Commerce (USA))
O T / I T S R R	Office of Telecommunications Institute for Telecommunications Sciences Research Report (USA))
O T & E	Operational Test and Evaluation
O T A	Office of Technology Assessment (of Congress (USA))
	Organisation Mondiale du Tourism et de l'Automobile (United Kingdom) (World Touring and Automobile Organisation)
O T C	Office of Technical Cooperation (of UN)
	Offshore Technology Conference
	Overseas Telecommunications Commission (Australia)
O T C (A)	Overseas Telecommunications Commission (Australia)
O T D A	Office of Tracking and Data Acquisition (of NASA (USA))
O T E	Officine Toscane Elettromeccaniche (Italy)
O T F	Optical Transfer Function
O T H B	Over-The-Horizon Backscatter
O T I S	Occupational Training Information System
	Offset Target Indicator System
O T I U	Overseas Technical Information Unit (of DTI)
O T M	Office of Telecommunications Management (USA) (now Office of Telecommunications Policy)
	Organo-Transition-Metal
O T P	Office of Telecommunications Policy (USA)
O T P I	On Top Position Indicator
O T S	Orbital Test Satellite
O T S / E C S	Orbital Test Satellite/European Communications Satellite
O T S A	Oregon Television Service Association (USA)
O T S G	Once-Through Steam Generator
O T T O	Once Through Then Out
	Optical-to-Optical interface device
O T T S	Organisation of Teachers of Transport Studies
O T T W	Optical Telescope Technology Workshop (conference organised by NASA (USA))
O U R I	Oklahoma University Research Institute (USA)
O V A C	Organisation Value Analysis Chart
O V F	Over-Voltage Factor

O V S R	Office of Vehicle Systems Research (of NBS (USA)) (now of Department of Transportation)
O V V	Optically Violently Variable
O W M	Office Work Measurement
O W P	Office of Water Programs (of EPA (USA))
O W P C B	Ohio Water Pollution Control Board (USA)
O W R B	Oklahoma Water Resources Board (USA)
O W R C	Ontario Water Resources Commission (Canada)
O W S	Orbital Workshop
O X I M	Oxide-Isolated Monolith
O Z R F	Opposed Zone Reheating Furnace

P

P	Plasma
	prefix to numbered series on Production issued by BOT until mid-1970 and then by DTI
P / E	Price Earnings Ratio
P / F	Powder Forging
P / M	Powder Metallurgy
P A	Paired Associates
	Peroxide-Alkaline
	Presidents Association (managed in Europe by Management Centre Europe)
P A A	Pharmaceutical Association of Australia (Australia)
	Plasma Amino Acid
	Population Association of America (USA)
	Print Advertising Association (USA)
P A A B	Public Accountants and Auditors Board (South Africa)
P A B A	Paraaminobenzoic Acid
P A B D	Precise Access Block Diagram
P A B L O S	Programme to Analyse the Block System
P A C	Packaging Association of Canada (Canada)
	Peripheral Autonomous Control
	Pesticide Analysis Advisory Committee
	Planned Availability Concept
	Project Analysis and Control
	Public Accounts Committee (of Parliament, India)
	Public Administration Committee of the Joint University Council for Social and Public Administration

P A C B I R	Pacific Coast Board of Intergovernmental Relations (USA)
P A C C S - A D A	Post Attack Command Control System - Airborne Data Automation (USAF)
P A C C T	Programme and Evaluation Review Technique (PERT) and Cost Correlation Technique
P A C E	Package for Architectural Computer Evaluation Product Assurance Confidence Evaluator
P A C E R	Portable Aircraft Condition Evaluation Recorder Programme Assisted Console Evaluation and Review
P A C E S	Political Action Committee for Engineers and Scientists (USA)
P A C M S	Psycho-Acoustical Measuring System
P A C R A D	Practical Absolute Cavity Radiometer
P A C T	*Plessey* Automated COBOL Testing package
P A C T S	Programmer Aptitude/Competence Test System
P A D	Programmable Algorithm for Drafting
P A D A T	*Psychological Abstracts* Direct Access Terminal (service provided by American Psychological Association (USA))
P A D D S	PERA Automatic Detail Drawing System
P A D E L	Pattern Description Language
P A D S	Performance Analysis and Design Synthesis
P A E	Photo-Anodic Engraving Phthalic Acid Ether Polyarylene-ethylene
P A E T	Planetary Atmosphere Experiments Test
P A F	Printed And Fired
P A F A M	Performance And Failure Assessment Monitor
P A F I E	Pacific Asian Federation of Industrial Engineering (India) (until 1973)
P A G	Protein Advisory Group (of UN)
P A G E	Polyacrylamide Gel Electrophoresis
P A G O S	Programme for the Analysis of General Optical Systems
P A H	Para-aminohippurate
P A H E F	Pan-American Health and Education Foundation
P A I D	Parked Aircraft Intrusion Detector Programmers Aid In Debugging
P A L	Precision Artwork Language
P A L C	Passenger Acceptance and Load Control
P A L S	Positioning And Locating System
P A M	Precision Angular Mover

P A M A	Pulse Address Multiple Access
P A M C	Provisional Acceptable Means of Compliance (series issued by ICAO)
P A M D	Parallel Access Multiple Distribution
P A M M	British Ceramic Plant and Machinery Manufacturers Association
	Precision Automatic Measuring Machine
P A N	Peroxyacetyl Nitrate
P A N C A P	Practical Annual Capacity
P A N D A	Performance And Demand Analyser
P A N E E S	Professional Association of Naval Electronic Engineers and Scientists (USA)
P A O O	Philippine Academy of Ophthalmology and Otolaryngology (Philippines)
P A P	Paramagnetic Analysis Programme
P A P E	Photo-Active Pigment Electrophotography
P A P I	Polymethylene Polyphenyl Isocyanate
P A P M	Pulse Amplitude and Phase Modulation
P A R	Participation - Achievement - Reward
	Peak-to-Average Rating *or* Ratio
P A R A D I S E	Phased Array Radars And Divers Integrated Semiconductor Elements
P A R A N	Perimeter Array Antenna
P A R C	Profile Analysis and Recording Control system
P A R C O R	Partial Correlatives
P A R D	Precision Annotated Retrieval Display
	Project Activities Relationship Diagram
P A R I S	Postal Address Reader Indexer System
P A R M	Persistent Anti-Radiation Missile
P A R S	Parachute Altitude Recognition System
	Pershing Audio Reproduction System
	Programmed Airlines Reservation System
P A R S E C S	Programme for Astronomical Research and Scientific Experiments Concerning Space (of the Boeing Company (USA))
P A R T	Production Allocation and Requirements Technique
P A R T A N	Parallel Tangents
P A R T A N S D	Parallel Tangents and Steepest Descent
P A S	prefix to numbered : dated series of Public Authority Standards published by BSI
P A S A R	*Psychological Abstracts* Search and Retrieval (of American Psychological Association (USA))
P A S C	Pacific Area Standards Congress

P A S N Y	Power Authority of the State of New York (USA)
P A S P	Price Adjusting Sampling Plan
P A S S	Parked Aircraft Security System
	Patrol Advanced Surveillance System
	Precision Angulation and Support System
	Price Adjusted Single Sampling
P A S S I O N	Programme for Algebraic Sequences, Specifically of Input-Output Nature
P A S T R A M	Passenger Traffic Management System (DOD (USA))
P A T	Palleted Automated Transport
	Phenylazotriphenylmethane
	Prediction Analysis Technique
P A T E L L	*Psychological Abstracts* Tape Edition Lease or Licensing (of American Psychological Association (USA))
P A T R I C	Pattern Recognition and Information Correlation (an information system for analysing crimes in conjunction with a criminal's methods)
P A T R O L	Programme for Administrative Traffic Reports On-Line
P A T S	Precision Aircraft Tracking System
P A T S Y	Pulse-Amplitude Transmission System
P A T T	Programmable Automatic Transistor Tester
P A T X	Private Automatic Telegraph Exchange
P A U	Programmes Analysis Unit (of DTI and UKAEA)
P A V M	Proximity Automatic Vehicle Monitoring
P A W	Plasma-Arc Welding
P B F	Power Burst Facility
P B I	Protein-Bound Iodine
P B I B	Partially Balanced Incomplete Block
P B L G	Polybenzyl-L-Glutamate
P B P B	Pyridinium Bromide Perbromide
P B R I S	Pampanga-Bongabon Rivers Irrigation System (Philippines)
P B S	Phosphate Buffered Saline
	Press-Button Signalling
	Public Building Service (of GSA (USA))
P B T	Piggyback Twistor
P C	Photoconductivity
	Phthalocyanine
	Propylene Carbonate
P C A	Physical Configuration Audit
	Polarizer-Compensator-Analyzer

P C A	Polycaproamide
P C C	Polarity Coincidence Correlator
	Portland Cement Concrete
	Premature Chromosome Condensation
P C D	Polycarbodiimide
	Production Common Digitizer
P C E	Pseudo Cholinesterase
P C E A	Pacific Coast Electrical Association (USA))
P C G	Power-Conditioning Group
P C I	Prothrombin Consumption Index
P C I C	Pittsburgh Chemical Information Center (University of Pittsburgh (USA))
P C L	Polytechnic of Central London
P C M	Protein-Calorie Malnutrition
P C M F	Personnels des Cadres Militaires Feminins (France)
P C M R	Patient Computer Medical Record
P C N B	Pentachloronitrobenzene
P C O S	Process Control Extensions to Operating System/360
P C P	Peripheral Circumflex Pressure
	Programmable Circuit Processor
P C P A	Parachlorophenylalanine
P C P V	Prestressed Concrete Pressure Vessel
P C R I	Papanicolaou Cancer Research Institute (USA)
P C S	Prime Compatible Set
	Process Control Specification
	Project Control System
P C S A	Power Crane and Shovel Association (USA)
P C S M	Polydimethyl Carboxylate Metallosiloxanes
P C T	Perfect Crystal device Technology
	Portable Conference Telephone
P C U E	Presidents' Committee for the Urban Environment
P C V	Precursor Vehicle
P D	Photodielectric
	Propodite-dactylopodite
P D A	Parenteral Drug Association (USA)
	Photographic Dealers Association
P D C	Productivity and Development Center (Philippines)
	Programmable Digital Controller
	Public Dividend Capital

P D C S	Power Distribution and Conditioning System
P D D L	Perpendicular Diffraction Delay Line
P D E	Preliminary Determination of Epicentres
P D F	Probability Distribution Function
P D I	Powered Descent Initiation
	Prevalence, Duration and Intensity
P D M	Precedence Diagram Method
P D N F	Prime Disjunctive Normal Form
P D Q	Photo Data Quantizer
P D S	Problem Descriptor System
	Pulse Doppler Search
P D S O R	Positive Definite Successive Over-Relaxation
P D S T T	Pulse Doppler Single Target Track
P D U	Pilot's Display Unit
P D V O R	Precision Doppler VHF Omni-Range
P D X	Processor-controlled Digital Exchange
P E	prefix to lettered/numbered/dated series of reports issued by Plant Engineering Department of BISRA
	Potential Evaporation
P E A	Palmitoylethanolamide
	Provincial Electricity Authority (Thailand)
P E A C E R	Petroleum Employers Advisory Council on Employee Relations
P E A R L	Parts Explosion And Retrieval Language
	Periodicals Automation *Rand* (*Corporation* (USA)) Library
P E A S	Production Engineering Advisory Service (of DTI and PERA) (ceased operation March, 1971)
P E A T M O S	Primitive Equation and Trajectory Model Output Statistics
P E C	Peritoneal Exudate Cells
	Pulsed Eddy Current
P E D	Photoelectron Energy Distribution
	Pipework Engineering Developments (a section of the British Steel Corporation)
P E D A N T	Preprogrammable Evaluations based on a Data Normalizing Technique
P E E	Photo-Electron Emission
P E E M	Photoemission-Electron Microscope
P E F	Peak Exploratory Flow
P E F R	Peak Exploratory Flow Rate
P E G A	Polyethylene Glycol Adipate

P E H L A	Prufung Elektrischer Hochleistungsapparate (Germany) (Joint Testing Laboratory for Electrical High-power Equipment)
P E I A	Poultry and Egg Institute of America (USA)
P E I L S	Association of Prince Edward Island Land Surveyors (Canada)
P E J C	Professional Engineers Joint Council (South Africa) (now FSPE)
P E K	Phase Exchange Keying
P E L	Permissible Exposure Level
	prefix to numbered series of reports issued by Atomic Energy Board, South Africa
P E L S	Precision Emitter Location System
P E M	Primitive Equation Model
	Processor Element Memory
P E N C A N	underwater telephone cable between the Canary Islands and Spain
P E N D O R	Photon Echo-Nuclear Double Resonance
P E O N	Production d'Electricite d'Origin Nucleaire (France) (a consultative commission)
P E P	Paperless Electronic Payments
	Phosphoenolpyruvate
	Prototype Electro-Pneumatic train
P E P E	Parallel Element Processing Ensemble
P E P P	Professional Engineers in Private Practice (a section of NSPE (USA))
P E P P E R	Photo-Electric Portable Probe Reader
P E P S	Psychological, Economic, Political and Sociological
P E P S Y	Precision Earth Pointing System
P E R	Professional and Executive Recruitment (a service of the Department of Employment)
	Protein Efficiency Ratio
P E R C Y	Photo Electronic Recognition Cybernetics
	Purposive System
P E R I	Platemakers Educational and Research Institute (USA)
P E R S I D	Personnel Seismic Intruder Detector
P E S	Photoelectron Spectroscopy
	Power Engineering Society (of IEEE (USA))
P E S A	Petroleum Equipment Suppliers Association (USA)
P E S I S	Photo-Electron Spectroscopy of Inner-Shell
P E S L	Petroleum Exploration Society of Libya

P E S O S	Photo-Electron Spectroscopy of Outer-Shell
P E S T	Project Engineer Scheduling Technique
P E T	Photoelectric Transducer
P E T A	Portable Electronic Traffic Analyzer
P E T N	Pentaerythritol Tetranitrate
P E T R O B R A S	Petroleo Brasileiro (Brazil) (State Petroleum Enterprise)
P E T R O M I N	General Petroleum and Mineral Organization (Saudi Arabia)
P E T R O N O R	Refineria de Petroleos del Norte (Spain)
P E T R O S U L	Sociedade Portuguesa de Refinacao de Petroleos SARL (Portugal)
P E W	Percussion Welding
P F	Patrol Frigate
P F A	Production Flow Analysis
P F B	Petroleum Films Bureau
P F C	Propellant Fuel Complex (of ISRO (India))
P F C S	Primary Flight Control System
P F F F	Polypropylene Fibrillated Film Fibre
P F F T	Parallel Fast Fourier Transform
P F K	Perfluorokerosene
P F N	Pulse Forming Network
P F P	Pensions for Professionals (non-profit corporation organized by the American Chemical Society (USA))
P F R	Precision Fathometer Recorder
P F R A	Prairie Farm Rehabilitation Administration (Canada)
P F U	Plaque-Forming Unit
P F Z	Precipitate-Free Zone
P G	Production Group (of UKAEA) (in 1971 became British Nuclear Fuels Ltd. (a public company))
	Prostaglandin
	Pyrolytic Graphite
P G C	Pyrolytic Gas Chromatography
P G M	Periaqueductal Grey Matter
	Phosphoglucomutase
P G M O T	Pollution Generation Multiplier from Output Table
P G N C S	Primary Guidance, Navigation and Control System
P G N S	Primary Guidance and Navigation System
P G S	Parser-Generating System
P G W	Pressure Gas Welding

285

PHAROS	Plan Handling and Radar Operating System
PHASE	Package for Hospital Appraisal, Simulation and Evaluation
PHI	Phosphohexose Isomerase
PHILCOM-SAT	Philippine Communications Satellite Corporation (Philippines)
PHILCON	*Philips (N. V. Philips' Gloeilampenfabrieken)* Cams in Original Notation
PHILSA	Philippine Standards Association (Philippines)
PHLS	Public Health Laboratory Service
PHM	Patrol Hydrofoil Missile
PHMP	Primordial Hot Mantle Plume
PHOCAS	Photo Optical Cable Controlled Submersible
PHS	Precision Hover Sensor
	Public Health Service (of HEW (USA))
PHYSBE	Physiological Simulation Benchmark Experiment
PI	Packaging Institute (USA)
	Pocket Incendiary
PI-FET	Piezoelectric Field-Effect Transistor
PIA	Personnel Inventory Analysis
	Photographic Importers Association
PIANC	Permanent International Association of Navigation Congresses (Belgium)
PIBEE	Polytechnic Institute of Brooklyn, Department of Electrical Engineering (USA)
PIBEP	Polytechnic Institute of Brooklyn, Department of Electrophysics (USA)
PIBTS	Polyisobutenyl Tetraethylene Pentamine Succinimides
PIC	Photographic Industry Council (USA)
PICASSO	Pen Input to Computer And Scanned Screen Output
PICC	Professional Institutions Council for Conservation
PICLS	*Purdue University* (USA) Instructional and Computational Learning System
PICS	Plug-in Inventory Control System
PID	Publications and Information Directorate (India)
PIDC	Pakistan Industrial Development Corporation (Pakistan)
PIECE	Petroleum Industry Environmental Preservation Executive (Australia)
PIECOST	Probability of Incurring Estimated Cost
PIER	Product Inventory Electronically Recorded

P I F A L	Programme Instruction Frequency Analyser
P I G A	Pendulous Integrating Gyroscopic Accelerometer
P I G M A	Pressurized Inert Gas Metal Arc
P I H F	Periodic Inhomogeneous Film
P I I A	Pakistan Institute of Industrial Accountants (Pakistan)
P I I M	Planned Inter-dependency Incentive Method
P I L A R	Petroleum Industry Local Authority Reporting
P I L O T	Panel on Instrumentation for Large Optical Telescopes (of the Science Research Council)
P I M I S S	Pennsylvania (USA) Interagency Management Information Support System
P I M N Y	Printing Industries of Metropolitan New York (USA)
P I N D	Particle Impact Noise Detection
P I N S T E C H	Pakistan Institute of Nuclear Science and Technology (Pakistan)
P I N T	Power Intelligence
P I N T E C	Plastics Institute National Technical Conference
P I P	Persistent Internal Polarization
	Pollution Information Project (of NSL (Canada))
P I P S	Pattern Information Processing System
P I R E P	Pilot Intensive Rural Employment Programme (India)
P I R P	Proposed International Reference Preparation
P I S	Penning Ionization Spectroscopy
P I S T L	Printing Industries of St. Louis (USA)
P I T A S	Petroleum Industry Training Association
P I T B	Production Inspection and Test Branch (of CEGB)
P I V	Positive Infinitely Variable
P K	Psychokinesis
	Pyruvate Kinase
P K A	Primary Knock-on Atoms
P K P	Polskie Koleje Panstwowe (Poland) (Polish State Railways)
P K U	Phenylketonuria
P L	Photoluminescence
	prefix to lettered: dated series of Plastics Standards issued by BSI (letters are sometimes prefixed by a number)
P L A	Programmable Logic Array
P L A C O	Technical Planning Committee (of ISO (Switzerland))
P L A D S	Pulsed Laser Airborne Depth Sounding System

P L A N E T	Planning Evaluation Technique
	Plant Layout Analysis and Evaluation Technique
	Private Line Analysis and Network Engineering Tools
P L A N S	Plastic Analysis of Nonlinear Structures
P L C	Peritoneal Lymphoid Cell
	Programming Language Committee (of CODASYL)
P L C C	Power Line Carrier Communication
P L L	Peripheral Light Loss
P L L R C	Public Land Law Review Commission (USA)
P L M	Pulse Length Monitor
P L N	Potassium Lithium Niobate
P L O T	Programme Logic Table
P L P	Product Liability Prevention Conference
P L R G	Public Libraries Research Group (of the Library Association)
P L S	Positive Locking System
P L U M	Programmes Library Update and Maintenance
P L U N A	Primeras Lineas Uruguayas de Navegacion Aerea (Uruguay) (State airline)
P L U T O	Parts-Listing/Used-On Technique
P L Z T	Lead, Lanthanum, Zirconium, Titanium (derived from the chemical symbols Pb, La, Zr, Ti)
P M	Phase-Modulated
	Polarization Modulation
	Powder Metallurgy
	prefix to numbered series of Business Monitors on Production issued Monthly by DTI
P M A	Phenylmercuric Acetate
	Pyridylmercuric Acetate
P M A / A R R	Probable Missed Approach per Arrival
P M A C S	Project Management and Control System
P M A G B	Paint Makers Association of Great Britain
P M C	Programmable Matrix Controller
P M D A	Pyromelletic Dianhydride
P M E L	Precision Measurement Equipment Laboratories (USAF)
P M I	Personnel Management Information system
P M I S	Project Management Information System
P M L	Precision Mecanique Labinal (France)
P M L M	Photosensitive Membrane Light Modulator
P M M A	Paper Machinery Makers Association (now British Paper Machinery Makers Association)

P M N	Pasteurized Milk Network (of Public Health Services (USA))
P M N P	Platform Mounted Nuclear Power Plant
P M O	Phenylmethyloxadiazole
P M P	Piecewise Markov Process
P M R	Proton Magnetic Resonance
P M R N	Particulate Mineral Reinforced Polyamide (Nylon)
P M S	Peripheral Monitor System
	Projected-Map System
	Project Management System
P M S F	Phenylmethylsulphonyl Fluoride
P M S R C	Pittsburgh Mining and Safety Research Center (of Bureau of Mines (USA))
P M T	Photomechanical Transfer
	Photomultiplier Transit
P M 3	Programming Mode Three
P M T V	Potato Mop-Top Virus
P N A	Polynuclear Aromatic Hydrocarbons
P N A C P	Pacific Northwest Association for College Physics (USA)
P N B C	Pacific Northwest Bibliographic Center (Washington University (USA))
P N C	Photo-Nitrosation of Cyclohexane
	Pulse Compression Network
P N E	Peaceful Nuclear Explosion
P N G S	Primary Navigation and Guidance System
P N K A	Perusahaan Negara Kereta Api (Indonesia) (State Railways)
P N M T	Phenylethanolamine-N-Methyl Transferase
P N P	Precision Navigation Processor
	Programmed Numerical Path-controller
P N P A	Pennsylvania Newspaper Publishers Association (USA)
P N U	Protein Nitrogen Units
P O A	Polarized Orbital Approximation
	Preoptic Area
P O C S	Proper Oriented Cut-Set
P O D A S	Portable Data Acquisition System
P O D M	Preliminary Orbit Determination Method
P O E	Probability of Error
P O E M	Procedure for Optimizing Elastomeric Mountings
P O E T	Portable Optic-Electronic Tracker
P O F	Powder-On-Foil

P O H W A R O	Pulsated Overheated Hot Water Rocket
P O I N T E R	Pre-university Orbital Information Tracker Equipment and Recorder
P O L	Pacific Oceanographic Laboratories (of ERL (NOAA) (USA))
P O L A C A P	Port of London Authority Combined Accident Procedure
P O L A R	Production Order Locating And Reports
P O L L S	Parliamentary On-Line Library Study
P O L O	Problem-Oriented Language Organizer
P O L S	Planned Ocean Logistic System
P O L S T A R	Plant for On Load Short-circuit Testing And Research
P O L Y P	Problem Oriented Language for System Software Programming
P O L Y P A G O S	Polychromic Programme for the Analysis of General Optical Systems
P O M	Polycyclic Organic Matter
	Printer Output Microfilm
P O M C U S	Prepositioned Material Configured to Unit Sets
P O M P	Pre-coded Originating Mail Processor
P O M R	Problem Oriented Medical Records
P O P	Particle-Oriented Paper
	Prefocused Objective-Pinhole
	Probability of Precipitation
P O P A I	Point-of-Purchase Advertising Institute (USA)
P O Q L	Probability Outgoing Quality Limit
P O T F	Polychromatic Optical Thickness Fringes
P O U N C	Post Office Users National Council
P O W E R	Priority Output Writers, Execution processors and input Readers system
	PERT (Programme and Evaluation Review Technique) Oriented Work-scheduling and Evaluation Routine
P P	Professional Paper
P P / Q	Plant Protection and Quarantine Programs (of APHIS (USDA))
P P A	Periodical Publishers Association
	Process Plant Association
	Publishers Publicity Association (USA)
P P A N I	Professional Photographers Association of Northern Ireland
P P B E S	Programme Planning-Budgeting-Evaluation System

P P C	Production Planning and Control
P P C A	Productivity Promotion Council of Australia (Australia)
P P D	Purified Protein Derivative
P P E	Pre-Production Evaluation
	Problem Programme Evaluator
P P G	Primary Pattern Generator
P P I	Parallel Plate Interceptor
	Pass Point Instrument (a component of RACOMS)
P P I P	Physics Post-doctoral Information Pool (of American Institute of Physics)
P P I T B	Printing and Publishing Industry Training Board
P P L	Plasma Physics Laboratory (Princeton University (USA))
	Polypropylene
P P M	Periodic Pulsed Magnet
P P S	Polyphenylene Sulphide
	Polyphenylenesulphone
P P T	Probabilistic Potential Theory
P P T S	Pre-Planned Training System
P P W B	Prairie Provinces Water Board (Canada)
P P Z	Proton Polar Zone
P Q	prefix to numbered series of Business Monitors on Production issued Quarterly by DTI
P R	Primary Reference fuel
P R A	Paint Research Association
	Petroleum Retailers Association
P R A D S	Parachute Retro-rocket Air Drop System
P R A I E N	Centre de Preparation Practique aux Applications Industrielles de l'Energie Nucleaire (France) (Centre for Practical Preparations for Industrial Applications of Nuclear Energy)
P R A N G	Projection-Angle
P R E	Proton Relaxation Rate
P R E C I S	Preserved Context Index System
P R E F R E	Power Reactor Fuel Reprocessing Plant Project (of BARC (India))
P R E P	Programmed Electronics Patterns
P R E S A G E	Programme to Realistically Evaluate Strategic Anti-Ballistic Missile Gaming Effectiveness
P R E S S	Project Review, Evaluation, and Scheduling System
P R E S T	EEC Working Party on Policy for Scientific and Technical Research

P R F	Primary Reference Fuels
P R F D	Pulse-Repetition-Frequency Distribution
P R I	Paleontological Research Institution (USA)
P R I D E	Profitable Information by Design through Phased Planning and Control
P R I H	Prolactin Release-Inhibiting Hormone
P R I N U L	Puerto Rico International Undersea Laboratory (Puerto Rico)
P R I S E	Pennsylvania's Regional Instructional System for Education (USA)
P R I S M	Personnel Record Information System for Management
P R L	Physical Research Laboratory (India)
	Pioneering Research Laboratory (of NLABS (US Army)
	Princes Risborough Laboratory (of BRE)
P R N C	Puerto Rico Nuclear Centre (Puerto Rico)
P R O C O	Programmed Combustion
P R O C O N	Professional Conservation Group
P R O D	Programme for Orbit Development
P R O F	Prediction and Optimization of Failure Rate
P R O F A C T S	Product Formulation, Accounting and Cost System
P R O F O	Produksjonsteknisk Forskningsinstitutt (Norway) (Production Engineering Research Institute)
P R O M	Programmable Read-Only Memory
P R O M A P	Program for Refinement of the Materiel Acquisition Process (US Army)
P R O M I S	Prosecutor's Management Information System (of Law Enforcement Assistance Administration (USA))
P R O M I S E	Programming Managers Information System
P R O N T O	Programme for Numerical Tool Operation
P R O S E C	Association pour Favoriser la Diffusion des Appareils et Produits de Detection, de Protection et de Decontamination (France) (Association for the Promotion of Clothing and Products for Detection, Protection and Decontamination)
P R O T E C N A	International Exhibition for the Protection of Nature and its Environment
P R O T E U S	Propulsion Research and Open-water Testing of Experimental Underwater Systems

P R O V O	Stichting Proefbedrijf Voedselbestraling (Netherlands) (Experimental Station for Food Irradiation)
P R P	Power-deployed Reserve Parachute
	Programmed Random Process
P R R F C	Planar Randomly Reinforced Fibre Composites
P R T	Personal Rapid Transit
	Pulse-Repetition-Time
P R T B	*Purdue University* (USA) Real-Time BASIC
P R U R D C O	Puerto Rico Undersea Research and Development Corporation (Puerto Rico)
P R X	Processor-control Reed Exchange
P S	Photoemission Scintillation
P S A	Pacific Science Association
	Photographic Society of America (USA)
	Property Services Agency (of DOE)
P S A D 5 6	Provisional South American Datum of 1956
P S A W V	Professional Surveyors Association of West Virginia (USA) (previously of 'Northern West Virginia')
P S C	Propagating Space Charge
P S C C	Polymer Supply and Characterisation Centre (of RAPRA)
P S C L C	Potentiostatic Stress Corrosion Life Curve
P S D	Phase-Sensitive Detector
	Pore Size Distribution
	Power Spectral Density
P S E	Packet Switching Exchange
	Passive Seismic Experiment
P S E F	Pennsylvania Science and Engineering Foundation (USA)
P S F	Point Spread Function
	Polystyrene Foam
P S G	Planning System Generator
P S H	Productive Standard Hour
P S I	Personalized-Proctorial System of Instruction
	Pressurized Sphere Injector
P S I D	Patrol Seismic Intrusion Detector
P S I L	Preferred-frequency Speech Interference Level
P S L	Physical Science Laboratory (New Mexico State University (USA))
P S M	Productive Standard Minute
P S M D	Photoselective Metal Deposition
P S N	Potassium Sodium Niobate
P S P R T	Partial Sequential Probability Ratio Test

P S R	Perfectly-Stirred Reactor
	Pulsar
P S R D	Plant Science Research Division (of ARS (USDA))
P S R P	Physical Sciences Research Papers (issued by Air Force Cambridge Research Laboratories (USAF))
P S R V	Pseudo-Relative Velocity
P S S C P	Partially Submerged Supercavitating Propeller
P S S H A K	Primary Support Structures and Housing Assembly Kit
P S S M	Parking Systems Simulation Model
P S S T	Public Sector Standardization Team
P S T	Post Stimulus-Time
	Propeller STOL Transport
P S T N	Public Switched Telephone Network
P S T V	Potato Spindle Tuber Virus
P S U	Pennsylvania State University (USA)
P S U - I R L	Pennsylvania State University - Ionosphere Research Laboratory (USA)
P S W	prefix to numbered series issued by Pacific Southwest Forest and Range Experiment Station (Forest Service (USDA))
P S W F	Prolate Spheroidal Wave Function
P T	Propanthiol
	Pseudoternary
P T A	Plasma Thromboplastin Enzyme
P T A B	Photographic Technical Advisory Board (of ANSI (USA))
P T B	Patellar Tendon Bearing
	Physikalisch Technische Bundesanstalt (Germany) (National Physical Laboratory)
P T C	Part-Through Crack
	prefix to numbered-dated series of Performance Test Codes issued by ASME (USA)
P T C R	Positive Temperature Coefficient Resistance
P T D L	Programmable Tapped Delay Line
P T E	Parathyroid Extract
	Pressure Tolerant Electronic technology
P T F C E	Polytrifluorochlorethylene
P T H	Parathyroid Hormone
P T I	Pocket Incendiary
	Presentation of Technical Information Group (now part of ISTC)
P T L	Process and Test Language
P T L S	Programme-controlled Train Leading System

P T M T	Polytetramethyleneterephthalate
P T N	Pyramidal Tract Neuron
P T R	Part Throttle Reheat
P T R A C	Planning and Transport Research Advisory Council
P T S A	Para-Toluene Sulphonic Acid
P T T	Partial Thromboplastin Times
P T T I	Postal, Telegraph and Telephone International
P T W	Pressure Thermit Welding
P T Z	Pentylenetetrazol
P U	Purdue University (USA)
P U D	Planned Urban Development
P U E	Pick-Up Electrode
P U F A	Polyunsaturated Fatty Acids
P U F F T	*Purdue University* (USA) Fast FORTRAN Translator
P U L S E	Programme of Universal Logic Simulation for Electronics
P U N D I T	Portable Ultrasonic Non-destructive Digital Indicating Tester
P U R D A X	Public Utility Revenue Data Acquisition System
P U R O	Puromycin
P U S W A	Public Utilities Street Works Act, 1950
P V	Prevailing Visibility
P V A	Procedure Value Analysis
P V C	Premature Ventricular Contractions
P V C F	Phase Variable Canonical Form
P V D	Para-Visual Director
P V I	Pre-Vulcanisation Inhibitor
P V N	Paraventricular Nuclei
P V R C	Pressure Vessel Research Committee (of Welding Research Council (USA))
P V S	Plan-View Sizes
P V T	Paroxysmal Ventricular Tachycardia
P W	Private Wire
P W C	Precipitation Water Content
	Printed Wiring Card
P W H T	Post-Weld Heat Treatment
P W I	Pilot Warning Indicator system
P W I P	Participative Work Improvement Programme
P W M	Pokeweed Mitogen
P W M I	Pulse Width Modulated Inverter
P W P	Plasticized White Phosphorus
P W P M A	Philippine Welding Products Manufacturers Association (Philippines)

P W S	Proximity Warning System
P W T	Propulsion Wind Tunnel
P Z E M	Provinciale Zeeuwse Energie-Maatschappij (Netherlands)
P Z I T B	Polski Zwiazek Inzynierow i Technikow Budownictwa (Poland) (Polish Union of Construction Engineers and Technicians)

Q

Q-FAN	Quiet Fan
Q-RTOL	Quiet Reduced Take-Off and Landing
Q-STOL	Quiet Short Take-Off and Landing
Q & T	Quenched and Tempered
QAD	Quality Assurance Directorate (MOD)
QAD(FVE)	Quality Assurance Directorate (Fighting Vehicles and Engineer Equipment (MOD))
QAD (Mats)	Quality Assurance Directorate (Materials) (MOD) (now MQAD (MOD))
QAD(SC)	Quality Assurance Directorate (Stores and Clothing) (MOD)
QAD(W)	Quality Assurance Directorate (Weapons) (MOD)
QAEO	Quality Assurance and Engineering Office (of NLABS (US Army))
QAM	Quadrature-Amplitude Modulation
QAP	Quadratic Assignment Problem
QBS	Quebec Bureau of Standards (Canada)
QBW	Quasi-Biennial Wave
QCD	Quarters for Cyclical Dominance
QCE	Quality Control Engineer
QCM	Quartz Crystal Microbalance
QCS	Quality Control Specification
QCSEE	Quiet, Clean STOL Experimental Engine
QDC	Quick-Disconnect
QDGS	Quick-Draw Graphics System
QE/C	prefix to dated-numbered series of reports issued by Quality Evaluation Department (NAD-CR (USN))
QED	Quantum Electro-Dynamics
QEEL	Quality Evaluation and Engineering Laboratory (USN)
QETR	prefix to numbered series of reports issued by Quality Evaluation of NAD-CR (USN)
QFE	Quartz Fibre Electrometer

Q F R I	Queensland Fisheries Research Institute (Australia)
Q I	Quality Improvement
Q I A C	Quantimet Image Analyzing Computer
Q L	Query Language
Q M	Quinacrine Mustard
Q M A C	Quarter-orbit Magnetic Altitude Control
Q M S	Quadruple Mass Spectrometer
Q N F	Quadrature N-path Filter
Q O M A C	Quarter-Orbit Magnetic Attitude Control
Q R G A	Quadruple Residual Gas Analyzer
Q R I	Quick-Reaction Interceptor
Q R P G	Quebec Rubber and Plastics Group (Canada)
Q S	Queueing System
Q S A M	Queued Sequential Access Method
Q S C	Quasi-Sensory Communication
Q S E	Qualified Scientists and Engineers)
	Quantum Size Effect
Q S H	Quiet Short-Haul
Q S T O L	Quiet Short Take-Off and Landing
Q T	Quenched and Tempered
Q T A M	Queued Telecommunications Access Method
Q U A L T I S	a subscription information service on NDT provided by the NDTC (AERE, Harwell)
Q U A R K	Question and Response Kit
Q U A S T	Quality Assurance Service Test
Q U E S T	Quantification of Uncertainty in Estimating Support Tradeoffs
	Query Statutes
Q U E S T O L	Quiet Experimental STOL
Q U I L T	Quantitative Intelligence Analysis Technique
Q U I P	Quick Inquiry Processor
Q U I P S	Quiescent Plasma Studies
	Quiescent Uniform Ionospheric Plasma Simulator
Q U I S	*Queens University* (Belfast) Information Systems
Q U I S T O R	Quadruple Ion Store
Q U O B I R D	*Queens University* (Belfast) On-line Bibliographic Information Retrieval and Dissemination system
Q U O D A M P	*Queens University* (Belfast) Databank on Atomic and Molecular Physics
Q W O T	Quarter Wave Optical Thickness
Q W S S U S	Quasi-Wide-Sense-Stationary Uncorrelated Scattering

R

R & Q A	Reliability and Quality Assurance
R / M / A	Reliability, Maintainability and Availability
R - Nav	Area Navigation
R A	Retrograde Amnesia
	Right Ascension
R A C	Reflective-Array Compressor
R A C E	Remote Automatic Computing Equipment
	Response Analysis for Call Evaluation
	Rochester (New York (USA)) Area Commuter Express
R A C I	Royal Australian Chemical Institute (Australia)
R A C M A P	*Research Analysis Corporation* (USA) Macro Assembly Programme
R A C O N	Radar Navigational Beacon
R A C P	Royal Australasian College of Physicians (Australia)
R A C S	Royal Australasian College of Surgeons (Australia)
R A C S S	Retail Apparel Chain Store System
R A D	Right Angle Drive
R A D D S	*Raytheon* Automated Digital Design System
R A D I R	Random Access Document Indexing and Retrieval
R A D L E	Responsive Automatic Dial-out and Line Transfer Equipment
R A D O P	Radar/Optical
R A D O T	Radar Operator Trainer
	Recording Automatic Digital Optical Tracker
R A E	Royal Aircraft Establishment (MOD)
R A F M	Repair-At-Failure Maintenance
R A F T	Receiving Ambient Function Test
	Resource Allocation For Transportation
R A G	Ring Airfoil Grenade
R A G S	Route Analysis, Generation and Simulation
R A I	Radiotelevisione Italiana (Italy)
	Registro Aeronautico Italiano (Italy) (Air Registration Board)
R A I A	Royal Australian Institute of Architects (Australia)
R A I D S	Rapid Availability of Information and Data for Safety

RAILS	Reference And Inter-Library Loan Service (of state-assisted Universities in Ohio (USA))
RAL	Radio Annoyance Level
	Regional Adjunct Language
RALACS	Radar Altimeter Low-Altitude Control System
RALU	Register and Arithmetic-Logic Unit
RAM	Radar-Absorbing Material
	Random-Access Memory
	Random Adaptive Module
	Random Angle Modulation
	Redeye Air Missile
	Research and Application Module
	Reliability, Availability and Maintainability
	Resource Allocation Model
RAMMIT	Reliability And Maintainability Management Improvement Techniques
RAMP	Radar Mapping of Panama
	Reliability Assurance Maintenance Programme
RAMPLAN	Rock Mechanics Applied to Mine Planning
RAMS	Random Access Measurement System
	Remote Automatic Multipurpose Station
RAMUS	Remote Access Multi-User System
RANN	Research Applied to National Needs (a project of NSF (USA))
RAO	Response Amplitude Operator
RAPE	Radar Arithmetic Processing Element
RAPID	Random Access Photographic Index and Display
	Resource Allocation and Piping Isometric Drawing
	Rotating Associative Processor for Information Dissemination
RAPS	Rajasthan Atomic Power Station (India)
RAR	Reflect-Array Radar
RAREPS	Radar Reports
RARS	Register Access Relay Set
RAS	Replenishment At Sea
RASB	Rapid Access to Sequential Blocks
RASCAL	Rudimentary Adaptive System for Computer-Aided Learning
RASMP	Radiotherapy Apparatus Safety Measures Panel
RASS	Radar-Acoustic Sounding System
RASSR	Reliable Advanced Solid State Radar
RAT	Routing Automation Technique
RATCC	Radar Air Traffic Control Centre
RATE	Rate-Aided Tracking Equipment

R A T E K S A	Radiobranchens Tekniske og Kommercielle Sammenslutning (Denmark) (Radio and Television Retailers Association)
R A T E N	Random Threshold-Element Network
R A T P	Regie Autonome Transports Parisiens (Paris, France) (Paris Transport Authority)
R A T T L E	Road Accident Tabulation Language
R A T T S	Radar Telephone Transmission System
R A X	Rural Automatic Exchange
R B	Riksbibliotekjenesten (Norway) (National Agency for Research and Special Libraries, and Documentation)
R B C	Red Blood Cell
R B E	Relative Biological Efficiency
R B G F	Resin-Bonded Glass-Fibre
R B I	Reserve Bank of India (India)
R B M	Real-time Batch Monitor
R B T	Remote Batch Terminal
R C	Resistor-Capacitator
R C A A	Rocket City Astronomical Association (USA)
R C C	Reinforced Carbon-Carbon
R C C O	Reduction Circuit for Checker Outputs
R C E	Rotary Combustion Engine
R C F R	Rotating Cylinder Flap Rudder
R C M S	Resonator-Controlled Microwave Source
R C N	Relay-Contact Network
R C N C	Royal Corps of Naval Constructors (MOD)
R C O H	Reliability Controlled Overhaul Programme
R C P	Registry of Comparative Pathology (of AFIP (USDOD) and UAREP)
R C P A	Royal College of Physicians of Australia
R C Path	Royal College of Pathologists
R C P Ed	Royal College of Physicians of Edinburgh
R C P G	Regional Cooperative Physics Group (of educational institutions in Ohio, Michigan, Illinois and Pennsylvania (USA))
R C P I	Royal College of Physics of Ireland
R C Psych	Royal College of Psychiatrists
R C R	Randle Cliff Radar
	Rotating Cylinder Rudder
R C S	Radar Cross-Section
	Ride Control System
	Rotable Control System
	Royal College of Surgeons of England

R C S (C)	Royal College of Surgeons (Canada)
R C S Ed	Royal College of Surgeons of Edinburgh
R C T	Reverse Conducting Thyristor
R D / B / N	prefix to numbered series of reports issued by Berkeley Nuclear Laboratories (of CEGB)
R D A T	Research and Development Acceptance Testing
R D A U	Remote Data Acquisition Unit
R D C	Regional Dissemination Centers (of NASA (USA))
R D C A	Rural Districts Councils Association
R D E	Receptor Destroying Enzyme
	Rotating Disk Electrode
R D F	Radial Distribution Function
	Relational Data File
R D O E I	Research and Development Organization for Electrical Industry (India)
R D R	Research and Development Report
R D S O	Research, Design and Standardization Organization (of Indian Railways (India))
R D V P	Radar Video Data Processor
R E	Rare Earth
R E A C T	Reliability Evaluation And Control Techniques
R E A L C O S T	Resource Allocation Cost System
R E A P	Rural Environmental Assistance Program (USA)
R E B	Rare Earth Boride
R E C - E R C	prefix to dated-numbered series of reports issued by Bureau of Reclamation, Engineering and Research Center (US Department of the Interior)
R E C - O C E	prefix to dated-numbered series of reports issued by the Bureau of Reclamation, Office of the Chief Engineer (US Department of the Interior)
R E C A T	Cumulative Regulatory Effects on the Cost of Automotive Transportation (a study by Office of Science and Technology (USA))
R E C E P	Relative Capacity Estimating Capacity
R E C O M P	Retrieval and Composition
R E C O N	Remote Console
	Retrospective Conversion pilot project (of Library of Congress (USA))
R E D	Reconnaissance Engineering Directorate (of System Command's Aeronautical Systems Division (USAF))
	Reflection-Electron Diffraction
R E E	Rare-Earth Elements

R E E D	Radio and Electrical Engineering Division (of NRC (Canada))
R E E P	Regression Estimation of Event Probabilities
R E F L E C S	Retrieval From the Literature on Electronics and Computer Sciences
R E I	Reusable External Insulation
R E I L	Runway End Identifier Lights
R E L	Rapidly Extensible Language
R E L C O M P	Reliability Computation
R E L K I N	Relativistic Kinematics
R E M	Research Evaluation Method
	Rocket Engine Module
R E M A P	Regional Environmental Management Allocation Process
R E M B A S S	Remotely Monitored Battlefield-Area Sensor System
R E M C A L C	Relative Motion Collision Avoidance Calculator
R E M C A N	Repairable Multilayer Circuit Assembly Method
R E M L	Risley Engineering and Materials Laboratory
R E P E E T	Reusable Engines, Partially External Expendable Tankage
R E Q P	Recursive Equality Quadratic Programming
R E S	Reticuloendothelial System
R E S I S T O R S	The Radically Emphatic Students Interested in Science, Technology and Other Research Studies (USA)
R E S P	Remote-batch Station Programme
R E T A I N	Remote Technical Assistance and Information Network
R E T S P L	Reference Equivalent Threshold Sound Pressure Level
R E V I M A	Societe pour la Revision et l'Entretien du Material Aeronautique (France)
R E X A	Radioisotope-Excited X-ray Analyzer
R E X S	Radio Exploration Satellite
R F	Rigid Frame
R F C	Rosette Forming Cells
R F D M A	Rigid Foam Ducting Manufacturers Association
R F F	Research Flight Facility (of Environmental Research Laboratories (NOAA (USA))
	Resources for the Future, Inc. (USA) (non-profit corporation)
	Rocket Fabrication Facility (of ISRO (India))
R F F P	Rescue and Fire Fighting Panel (of ICAO)

R F F S A	Rede Ferroviaria Federal SA (Brazil) (Federal Railway Corporation)
R F Q	Request For Quote
R G	prefix to dated-numbered series of reports issued by Guidance and Control Directorate, Redstone Arsenal (US Army)
R G A	Residual-Gas Analysis
R G C S P	Review of General Concept of Separation Panel (of ICAO)
R G F	Range Gated Filtering
R G F C	Remote Gas Filter Correlation
R G F C S	Radar Gunfire Control System
R G O	Royal Greenwich Observatory (of Science Research Council)
R G P O	Range Gate Pull-Off
R G R D E	Rotating Gold Ring-Disc Electrode
R G S	Royal Geographical Society
R H A	Rolled Homogeneous Armour
R H A G	Rotary Hydraulic Arresting Gear
R H A W S	Radar Homing And Warning System
R H C S A	Regional Hospitals Consultants and Specialists Association
R H E E D	Reflection High-Energy Electron-Diffraction
R H E L	Rutherford High Energy Laboratory (of the SRC) (now The Rutherford Laboratory)
R I	Radar Index
	prefix to numbered series of Reports of Investigations issued by Bureau of Mines (USA)
	Retroactive Interference
	Royal Institution of Great Britain
R I A	Radioimmunoassay
	Railway Industry Association of Great Britain
R I A I	Royal Institute of Architects of Ireland
R I B	River Ice Breaker
R I C	Rare-Earth Information Center (Iowa State University (USA))
R I C E	Rationalised Internal Communication Equipment
	Regional Information and Communication Exchange (a library and information network in the Gulf Coast region of USA based on Rice University)
R I C S	Rubber Impregnated Chopped Strands
R I D E	Rail International Design and Environment conference

R I L E M	Reunion Internationale des Laboratoires d'Essais et de Recherches sur les Materiaux et les constructions (International Union of Testing and Research Laboratories for Materials and Structures) (France)
R I L S	Rapid Integrated Logistics System (US Army)
R I M	Rhodesian Institute of Management (Rhodesia)
R I M P A T T	*W. T. Read* Impact Avalanche Transit-Time diode
R I M S	Remote Information Management System
R I N T	Radiation Intelligence
R I N T I N	Radioisotope Instruments and Tracers in Industry
R I O T	Retrieval of Information by On-line Terminal (a project of Culham Laboratory (UKAEA))
R I P	Radioimmunoprecipitation
	Remote Instrument Package
R I S A	Radioiodinated Serum Albumin
R I S C	Redintegrated Somatotyping Curves
R I S D A	Rubber Industry Smallholders Development Authority (Malaysia)
R I S P	Ross Ice Shelf Project
R I S P P	Rhode Island (USA) Statewide Planning Program
R I S T	Radioisotope Tagged Sand Tracer
R I T	Reverse Income Tax
R I T A	Road Information Transmitted Aurally
R I T A D	Radiation-Induced Thermally Activated Depolarization
R I T S	Remote Input Terminal System
R J I S	Regional Justice Information System (County of Los Angeles (USA))
R K H S	Reproducing Kernel Hilbert Space
R K N F S Y S	Rock Information System (of Carnegie Institute of Washington (USA))
R L	Radioluminescence
R L D	Rijksluchtvaartdienst (Netherlands) (Civil Aviation Authority)
R L V	Rauscher Leukaemogenic Virus
R M A	Reliability-Maintainability-Availability
	Retread Manufacturers Association
R M C	Radiation Medicine Centre (of BARC (India))
	Radical-Molecule Complex
	Radio Monte-Carlo (Monaco)
	Regional Meteorological Centre (of WMO (UN))
	Royal Military College of Canada

R M E R C	Rock Mechanics and Explosives Research Center (Missouri University (USA))
R M F	Rockwell Microficial Scale
R M G	Ranging Machine Gun
R M I T	Royal Melbourne Institute of Technology (Australia)
R M L	Regional Medical Library network (of NLM (USA))
R M M	Read-Mostly Memory
R M O S	Refractory Metal Oxide Semiconductor
R M P	Root Mean Power
R M P A	Royal Medico-Psychological Association
R M S	Rotating Mooring System
R M S E	Root Mean Square Error
R M T	Reliability Maintainability Tradeoff
R M V	Remotely Manned Vehicle
R N A V	Area Navigation
R N E C	Royal Naval Engineering College (MOD (N))
R N E S	Royal Naval Engineering Service (MOD (N))
R N P T E	Royal Naval Nuclear Propulsion Test and Training Establishment (MOD (N))
R N S	Residue Number Systems
	Re-usable Nuclear Shuttle
	Royal Numismatic Society
R N U R	Regie Nationale des Usines Renault (France)
R O	Reverse Osmosis
R O A S T	Ring Out And Stress Tester
R O B O T	Record Organisation Based On Transposition
R O C	Required Operational Capability
R O C K E T	*Rand* (Corporation (USA)) Omnibus Calculator of the Kinematics of Earth Trajectories
R O C S	Railroad Operations Control System
	Range-Only Correlation System
R O D S	Real-time Operations, Dispatching and Scheduling
R O G E R	Remotely Operated Geophysical Explorer
R O K A M S	Republic of Korea Army Map Service (Korea)
R O M C O E	Rocky Mountain Center on Environment (USA)
R O P E	Run-Out Production Evaluation
R O P S	Roll-Over Protection Structure
R O S	Read Only Storage
R O S C O E	Remote Operating System Conversational Operating Environment
R O T L	Remote-Office Test Line
R O V A C S	Rotary-Vane Air-Cycle Air-Conditioning and Refrigeration System

R P	*Raynaud's* Phenomenon
	Recommended Practice
	Rotary Piston
R P A	Retarding Potential Analyzer
R P A O D S	Remotely-Piloted Aerial Observation Designation System
R P C	Remote Power Controller
R P D	Respiratory Protective Device
R P E	Rating of Perceived Exertion
R P G	Rocket Propelled Grenade
R P L	Radiophotoluminescence
R P M	Random Phase Modulator
	Retail Price Maintenance
	Revenue-Passenger-Miles
R P O A D S	Remotely Piloted Observation Aircraft Designator System
R P P	Rocket Propellant Plant (of ISRO (India))
R P R	Rapid Plasma Reagin
R P R V	Remotely Piloted Research Vehicle
R P S	Randomized Pattern Search
	Range Positioning System
	Reversed-Phase Series
R P S M	Resources Planning and Scheduling Method
R P V	Reactor Pressure Vessel
	Remotely Piloted Vehicle
R Q	Respiratory Quotient
R Q - Q S O	Radio-Quiet Quasi-Stellar Object
R R	Rate of Return on capital
	Regenerative Repeater
R R B	Radio Regulatory Bureau (Japan)
R R C	prefix to lettered numbered series of reports issued by Radio Propagation Unit, National Physical Laboratory (India)
R R C S	Roll-Rate Control System
R R D C	Railroad Data Center (of Association of American Railroads)
R R D E	Rotating Ring-Disc Electrode
R R I S	Railroad Research Information Service (of Federal Railroad Administration *and* National Academy of Sciences (USA))
R R L	Road Research Laboratory (now Transport and Road Research Laboratory (DOE))
R R M	Rotation Remanent Magnetisation
R R M A	Refractory and Reactive Metals Association (USA)

r R N A	Ribosomal RNA
R R P	Reader and Reader-Printer
	Rotterdam-Rhine Pipeline
R R R V	Rate of Rise of Recovery Voltage
R R S	Radiation Research Society (USA)
R S	The Royal Society of London for the Improvement of Natural Knowledge
R S - T R	prefix to dated-numbered series of Technical Reports issued by Systems Research Directorate, Redstone Arsenal (US Army)
R S A	Rehabilitation Services Administration (of SRS (HEW) (USA))
	Royal Society for the Encouragement of Arts, Manufactures and Commerce
R S C	Relaxation-Sensitive Cell
	Remote Sensing Center (Texas A&M University) (USA)
R S D	Radio Science Division (National Physical Laboratory (India))
R S D A	Road Surface Dressing Association
R S E	The Royal Society of Edinburgh
R S E W	Resistance-Seam Welding
R S F	Rocket Sled Facility (of ISRO (India))
R S F S	Real Scene Focus Sensor
R S I	Refractory Reusable Surface Insulation
R S I S	Reference, Special and Information Section (of the Library Association)
R S J	Resistively Shunted Junction
R S K	Reaktor Sicherheitskommission (Germany) (Reactor Safety Commission)
R S L	Remote Sensing Laboratory (Stanford University (USA))
R S M	Research into Site Management
	Rotating Sample Magnetometer
R S N A	Radiological Society of North America (USA)
R S N Z	Royal Society of New Zealand (New Zealand)
R S P B	Royal Society for the Protection of Birds
R S R A	Rotor Systems Research Aircraft
R S R S	Radio and Space Research Station (of SRC) (now The Appleton Laboratory)
R S S	Relaxed Static Stability
	Ribbed Smoked Sheet
R S T	Reliability Shakedown Test
R S U A	Royal Society of Ulster Architects

R S V	*Rous* Sarcoma Virus
R S V P	Restartable Solid Variable Pulse
R S W	Refrigerated Sea Water
R T	Reaction Time
R T A C	Roads and Transportation Association of Canada (Canada)
R T A F	Royal Thai Air Force (Thailand)
R T C	Real Time Control
R T C M	Radio Technical Commission for Marine Services (of FCC (USA))
R T C P	Real-Time Control Programme
R T D	Rontgen Technische Dienst (Netherlands)
R T E E B	Radio, Television and Electronics Examination Board
R T G	Radioisotope Thermo-electric Generator
R T H	Regional Telecommunication Hub (of WMO)
R T I	Real-Time Interface
	Research Triangle Institute (USA)
R T L	Radio-Tele-Luxembourg (Luxembourg)
	Real-Time Language
	Reference Testing Laboratory (of Cement and Concrete Association)
R T M	Radiodiffusion Television Marocaine (Morocco)
	Real-Time Management
	Register-Transfer Module
R T M O S	Real-Time Multiprogramming Operating System
R T O L	Reduced Take-Off and Landing
R T P	Radiotelevisao Portuguesa (Portugal)
R T P I	Royal Town Planning Institute
R T R	Remote Transmitter Receiver
R T R C D S	Real-Time Reconnaissance Cockpit Display System
R T S	Real-Time System
R T T	Radiodiffusion-Television Tunisienne (Tunisia)
R T X E	Real-Time Executive Extended
R U	Rutgers-The State University, New Brunswick (USA)
R U B B E R C O N	International Rubber Conference
R U D S	Reflectance Units of Dirt Shade
R U F A S	Remote Underwater Fisheries Assessment System
R U I N	Regional Urban Information Network (of Washington DC (USA) Metropolitan Urban Studies Libraries Group)

R U R O S	Research Unit on the Rehabilitation of Oiled Seabirds (University of Newcastle-upon-Tyne)
R U S H	Rudder Shiped Hull
R U S I	Royal United Services Institute for Defence Studies
R U V	Rikisutvarpid-Sjonvarp (Iceland)
R V	Radio Vatican (Vatican State)
	Residual Volume
R V / T L C	Residual Volume Total Lung Capacity ratio
R V A	Rating and Valuation Association
R V C D	Right Ventricular Conduction Defect
R V D P	Radar Video Data Processor
R V H	Right Ventricular Hypertrophy
R V I	Reverse Interrupt
R W M	Read-only Composite Wire Memory
R Y A	Royal Yachting Association
R Z I	Real-Zero Interpolation

S

S	prefix to numbered : dated series of standards on Steel issued by BSI (letter is sometimes preceded by a number)
S A	Sociedad Anonima (Limited Company)
	Societe Anonyme (Limited Company)
	Submerged-Arc
S A - B P L	Sucrose Acetone-Betapropiolactone
S A / O R	Systems Analysis/Operational Research
S A A C I	Salesmen's Association of the American Chemical Industry (USA)
S A A F A R I	*South African Airways* Fully Automatic Reservations Installation
S A A G S	Semi-Automated Artwork Generator System
S A A S	Standard Army Ammunition System (US Army)
S A A T	Society of Architectural and Associated Technicians
S A B A	South African Brick Association (South Africa)
S A B C	South African Broadcasting Corporation (South Africa)
S A B R E	*Singer (Information Services Company)* Accounting and Business Reporting
S A C	Space Activities Commission (Japan)
	Strong Adsorption Capacity

S A C A	Societa per Azioni Costruzioni Aeronavali (Italy)
S A C A C	South African Council for Automation and Computation (South Africa)
S A C A D	Stress Analysis and Computer Aided-Design (a joint unit of the Imperial College of Science and Technology and the Welding Institute)
S A C C H S	Scottish Advisory Committee on the Computers in the Health Service
S A C C S	Schedule and Cost-Control System
	Strategic Air Command Automated Command Control System (USAF)
S A C L A N T	Supreme Allied Commander Atlantic (of NATO)
S A C L O S	Semi-Automatic Command to Line-Of-Sight
S A C P	Selected Area Channelling Patterns
S A C P E	South African Council for Professional Engineers (South Africa)
S A D F	Statistical Analysis of Documentation Files
S A D I	*Sanders Associates* Direct Indexing
S A D I E	Scanning Analog-to-Digital Input Equipment
S A D I M	Societe Anonyme pour le Developpment Immobilier de Monaco
S A D O I	Sociedad Argentina de Organizacion Industrial (Argentina) (Society of Industrial Management)
S A D 69	South American Datum of 1969
S A D T	Self-Accelerating Decomposition Temperature
S A E C A (number)	prefix for designating Copper and Copper Alloys standards recommended by SAE (USA)
S A E C P	Selected Area Electron Channelling Patterns
S A E D	Selected Area Electron Diffraction
S A E D C	Sensory Aids Evaluation and Development Center (Massachusetts Institute of Technology (USA))
S A E I	Service des Affaires Economiques et Internationales (France) (Department of Economics and International Affairs)
S A E S	State Agricultural Experimental Stations (USA)
S A E S A	Servicios Aereos Especiales SA (Mexico)
S A E T	Spiral After-Effect
S A E T A	Sociedad Anonima Ecuatoriana de Transportes Aereos (Ecuador)
S A F	Society of American Foresters (USA)
	Synchronous Auditory Feedback
S A F A	Soluble Antigen Fluorescent Antibody

S A F C A	Safeguard Communications Agency (of USASTRATCOM)
S A F C O	Saudi Arabian Fertilizer Company (Saudi Arabia)
S A F E	San Andreas (USA) Fault Experiment
	Survival and Flight Equipment Association (USA)
S A F E R	Structural Analysis, Frailty Evaluation and Re-design
	Systematic Aid to Flow on Existing Roadways
	System for Aircrew Flight Extension and Return
S A F M A R I N E	South African Marine Corporation (South Africa)
S A F O C	Semi-Automatic Fight Operations Centre
S A F T	Self-Adaptive Forecasting Technique
	Societe des Accumulateurs Fixes et de Traction (France)
S A G E	Systems Approach to a Growth Economy
S A G F R C	South Atlantic - Gulf Fisheries Research Center (of NMFS (USA))
S A G S	Semi-Active Gravity-Gradient Stabilization
S A G W	Surface to Air Guided Weapon
S A H C	Sleep Analyzing Hybrid Computer
S A H S A	Servicio Aereo de Honduras SA (Honduras)
S A I	Singly Auto-Ionizing
S A I A T	Societa Attivita Immobiliari Ausliarie Telefoniche (Italy)
S A I F E C S	SpA Industria Fibre e Cartoni Speciali (Italy)
S A I L	Sea Air Interaction Laboratory
	Steel Authority of India Limited (India) (state owned)
S A I L S	Standard Army Intermediate Level Supply Sub-system (US Army)
S A I M E	South African Institution of Mechanical Engineers (South Africa)
S A I Mech E	South African Institution of Mechanical Engineers (South Africa)
S A I N T	Symbolic Automatic Integration
S A L B	South African Library for the Blind (South Africa)
S A L E S	Savannah (Georgia, USA) Area Law Enforcement System
S A L S	Standard Army Logistics System (US Army)
S A M	Signal Averaging Monitor
	Six-Axis Manipulator
	Sound-Activated Mobile
	Standard Assembly Module

S A M	Subsynoptic Advection Model
	System Analysis Machine
	System Availability Model
S A M A	Shock Absorber Manufacturers Association
S A M A C	Scientific and Management Advisory Committee (of US Army Computer Systems Command)
S A M B	United Kingdom Liaison Committee for Sciences Allied to Medicine and Biology
S A M C A P	Surface to Air Missile Capability
S A M E	Society of American Military Engineers (USA)
S A M M I E	System for Aiding Man-Machine Interaction Evaluation
S A M O S	Stacked-gate Avalanche-injection Metal Oxide Semiconductor
S A M P	Salary Administration and Manpower Planning
S A M S	Six Axis Motion System
	Society for Advanced Medical Systems (USA)
	Standard Army Maintenance System (US Army)
S A M T	Sleds Amphibious Marginal Terrain
S A M T E C	Space And Missile Test Center (USAF)
S A N	Servicios Aereos Nacionales (Ecuador)
S A N B A R	Sanders Barotropic
S A N C W E C	South African National Committee of the World Energy Conference (South Africa)
S A N S	*Sierra (Research Corporation)* (USA) Air Navigation System
S A N Z	Standards Association of New Zealand
S A O A	Semi-Ascending Order Arrangement
S A P	Serum Alkaline Phosphatase
S A P G O	Simultaneous Adjustment of Photogrammetric and Geodetic Observations
S A P H O	SABENA Automated Passenger Handling Operations
S A P H Y D A T A	System for the Acquisition, Transmission and Processing of Hydrological Data (of IHD (UNESCO))
S A R	South African Railways (South Africa)
	Synthetic Aperture Radar
S A R A H	Search And Rescue And Homing
S A R C	Split Armature Receiver Capsule
S A R C O	Saudi Arabian Refining Company (Saudi Arabia)
S A R I E	Semi-Automatic Radar Identification Equipment
S A R I S	Synthetic Aperture Radar Interpretation System
S A R O A D	Storage And Retrieval of Air-quality Data

S A R P	*Signaal (NV Hollandse Signaalapparenten (Netherlands)* Automatic Radar Processing system
S A R S	Search And Rescue Submersible
	Secretary of the Army Research and Study (US Army)
	Support And Restraint System
S A R S I M	Search And Rescue Simulation
S A S	Satellite Applications Section (of the National Hurricane Center (USA))
	SEAL *(Subsea Equipment Associates Limited)* Atmospheric System
	Small Angle Scattering
	Suspended Array System
	Synthetic Aperture System
S A S / C S S	Stability Augmentation System with Control Stick Steering
S A S A	Small Arms Systems Agency (US Army)
S A S H O	Southeastern Association of State Highway Officials (USA)
S A S O L	South African Coal, Oil and Gas Corporation (South Africa)
S A S P	Seismic Array Station Processor
S A S R	Semi-Annual Status Report
S A S S	Standard Army Supply System (US Army)
	Suspended-Array Surveillance System
S A T	underwater telephone cable connecting South Africa to Great Britain via Spain
S A T A	Societe Anonyme de Transport Aerien (Switzerland)
S A T A N	Speed And Throttle Automatic Network
S A T C O	Servicio Aereo de Transportes Comerciales (Peru)
S A T C R A	Stress in Air Traffic Control Research Association (Netherlands)
S A T E N A	Servicio de Aeronavegacion a Territorios Nacionales (Colombia)
S A T F	Strike And Terrain Following radar
S A T I	Selective Access to Tactical Information
S A T I A T E R	Statistical Approach To Investment Appraisal To Evaluate Risk
S A T I N	Strategic Air Command (USAF) Automated Total Information Network
S A T N A V	Satellite Navigation
S A T O	Self-Aligned Thick-Oxide
S A T T	Strowger Automatic Toll Ticketing

S A V A S I	Simplified Abbreviated Visual Approach Slope Indicator
S A V C O	Servicios Aereos Virgen de Copacabana (Bolivia)
S A V E S	Sizing Aerospace Vehicle Structures
S A W	Strike-Anywhere matches
	Submerged Arc Welding
	Surface Acoustic Wave
S A W A	Screen Advertising World Association
S A W G	Salaried Architects Working Group (of RIBA)
S A W R S	Supplementary Aviation Weather Reporting Station (of NWS (NOAA))
S A X S	Small-Angle X-ray Scattering
S B	Sonic Boom (a panel of ICAO)
S B A	Smaller Businesses Association
S B B	Schweizerische Bundesbahnen (Switzerland) (Swiss Federal Railways)
S B C	Single Burst Correction
	Sonic Boom Committee (of ICAO)
S B C C	Southern Building Code Congress (USA) (now part of CABO (USA))
S B D	Saving Bonds Division (of Department of the Treasury (USA))
	Standard Bibliographic Description
S B F	Short Back-Fire antenna
S B I C	A Small Business Investment Corporation
S B L	Structure Building Language
S B M	Single Buoy Mooring
	Syton-Bromine-Methanol
S B N	Strontium Barium Niobate
S B O	Side Band Only
S B P	Steroid Binding Protein
S B P I M	Society of British Printing Ink Manufacturers
S B R	Signal-to-Background Ratio
S B R S	Side and Back Rack System
S B S S	Standard Base Supply System (USAF)
S B X	Sub-sea Beacon/Transponder
S C / B M S	Sub-Committee on Basic Meteorological Services (of ICMS (USA))
S C - R B	Separable Costs - Remaining Benefits
S C A G	Southern California Association of Governments (USA)
S C A L E	Syllabically Companded And Logically Encoded
S C A M	Societe Commerciale d'Applications Mecanographiques (France)

S C A M	System-support Cost Analysis Model
S C A M A	Station Conferencing And Monitoring Arrangement
S C A M P	Small-Caliber Ammunition Program (of US Army)
	Sperry Computer Aided Message Processor
S C A N	Systematic Classification Analysis of Non-verbal behaviour
S C A N I I R	Surface Composition by Analysis of Neutral and Ion Impact Radiation
S C A N S	Spectra Calculation from Activated Nuclide Sets
S C A P	Systems for the Control of Ambulation Pressure
S C A R	Scientific Committee on Antarctic Research (of ICSU)
	Strike Control And Reconnaissance
S C A S	Stability Control Augmentation System
S C A U L E A	Standing Conference of African University Libraries in East Africa (HQ in Ethiopia)
S C A X	Small Country Automatic Exchange
S C B A	Scottish Building Contractors Association
S C C	Standards Council of Canada (Canada)
S C C C U	Single Channel Communications Control Unit
S C C M	Short Circuit Conductance Matrix
S C D	Spreading Cortical Depression
S C D P	Society of Certified Data Processors (USA)
S C E	Saturated Calomel Electrode
	Standard Calomel Electrode
S C E E T	Support Concept Economic Evaluation Technique
S C E H	Society for Clinical and Experimental Hypnosis (USA)
S C E I	Switching Control and Express Interpreter
S C E P	Study of Critical Environmental Problems (sponsored by Massachusetts Institute of Technology (USA))
S C E T	Society of Civil Engineering Technicians
S C E T A	Societe de Controle et d'Exploitation de Transports Auxiliaries (France)
S C F	Seroconversion Factor
S C F C E F	Syndicat des Constructeurs Francaise de Condensateurs Electrique Fixes (France)
S C F G	Stochastic Context-Free Grammar
S C F S	Slip Cast Fused Silica
S C H A	South Carolina Heart Association (USA)

S C I	Seal Compatibility Index
	Shipping Corporation of India (India) (Government-owned)
	Switched Collector Impedance
S C I B P	Special Committee of the International Biological Programme (of ICSU)
S C I D	Small Column Insulated Delay
S C I I A	Sudden Changes in the Integrated Intensity of Atmospherics
S C I R P	Semiconductor Infra-Red Photography
S C I R T	System Control In Real Time
S C K	Studiecentrum voor Kernenergie (Belgium) (Centre for Nuclear Energy Studies)
S C L	Space-Charged-Limited
	Superconducting Levitron
S C L E R A	Santa Catalina (USA) Laboratory for Experimental Relativity by Astrometry
S C L P	Security Command Language Processor
S C M	Society of Coal Merchants
S C M R	Surface Composition Mapping Radiometer
S C N	Static Charge Neutralizer
S C N Q T	Standing Conference for National Qualification and Title (now Engineers Registration Board *and* Standing Conference on Technician Engineers and Technicians)
S C O	Subcarrier Oscillator
S C O E G	Standing Conference of Employers of Graduates (administered at Manchester University)
S C O P E	Scientific Committee on Problems of the Environment (of ICSU)
	Simple Checkout-Oriented Programming Language
	Space-Craft Operational Performance Evaluation
	Special Committee on Problems of the Environment (of ICSU)
	Status Concept of Programme Evaluation
	System and Component Operating Performance Evaluation
	Systematic Control of Periodicals
	System for Capacity and Orders Planning and Enquiries
S C O P W	Self-Consistent Orthogonalized-Plane-Wave
S C O R	Scientific Committee on Oceanographic Research (of ICSU)

S C O R E	System Cost and Operational Resource Evaluation
S C O T	Semi-automated Computer Oriented Text
	Shaken and Circulatory Oxidation Test
S C O T A	Scottish Offshore Training Association
S C O T E C	Scottish Technical Education Council
S C P	Secure Care Property
	Security Control Processor
	Selfconsistent Phonon Theory
	Sodium-Containing Particle
S C P I	Structural Clay Products Institute (USA) (now Brick Institute of America)
S C P K	Serum Creatine Phosphokinase
S C R	Short Circuit Ratio
	Signal-to-Clutter Ratio
	Solar Cosmic Ray
	Strength Count Ratio
S C R A	Single Channel Radio Access
S C R E	Syndicat des Constructeurs de Relais Electriques (France)
S C R E A M	Society for the Registration of Estate Agents and Mortgage Brokers
S C R O L L	String and Character Recording Oriented Logogrammatic Language
S C R T D	Southern California Rapid Transit District (USA)
	Sea Control Ship
S C S	Silicon Controlled Switch
	Speed Control System
	Stimulated Compton Scattering
	Surface-Compression Strengthened
S C S C	Summer Computer Simulation Conference (USA)
S C S D	Satellite Communication Systems Division (of ISRO) (India)
	School Construction Systems Development (USA)
S C S S T	Standing Conference on Schools Science and Technology
S C S T R	Segregated Continuous Stirred Tank Reactor
S C T	Secretaria de Communicaciones y Transportes (Mexico) (Ministry of Communications and Transport)
	Surface-Charge Transistor
S C T E T	Standing Conference for Technician Engineers and Technicians

S C U A S	Standing Conference of University Appointments Services (administered at Manchester University)
S C W	Space Charge Wave
S D	prefix to numbered series of Business Monitors on Service and Distribution issued by DTI
	Sorbital Dehydrogenase
S D A	Soap and Detergent Association (USA)
S D B	Silver-Dye-Bleach
S D C	Space Defense Center (of ADC (USAF))
S D C C U	Synchronous Data Communication Control Unit
S D D L L	Sample-Data Delay-Lock Loop
S D E	Society of Data Educators (USA)
S D I M	System of Documentation and Information for Metallurgy (of the European Communities)
S D L	Space Disturbances Laboratory (of ESSA) (now of NOAA (USA))
S D L C	Synchronous Data Line Control
S D M	Selective Dissemination of Microfiche (now offered by NTIS (Dept. of Commerce (USA))
	Site Defense of *Minuteman*
	Spares Determination Method
	Structural Dynamics and Materials Conference (of AIAA, ASME, and SAE (USA))
S D M A	Space-Division Multiple-Access
S D N F	Shortened Disjunctive Normal Form
S D N M	Sampled-Data Nonlinearity Matrix
S D R	Single-Drift-Region
	Splash Detection Radar
	System Design Review
S D R S	Splash Detection Radar System
S D S	Sodium Dodecyl Sulphate
S D T I	Signal-Dependent Time Interval
S E	Self-Extinguishing
	Sonic Extract
	Systems Engineering
S E A	Servicios Especiales Aereos (Colombia)
	Sudden Enhancement of Atmospherics
S E A C	Support Equipment Advisory Committee (of seven United States airlines)
S E A C O M	South East Asia Commonwealth Cable (submarine telephone cable connecting Australia, New Guinea, Guam, Hong Kong, Malaysia and Singapore)

S E A C O N	Seafloor Construction Experiment (of NCEL (USN))
S E A D U C E R	Steady-state Evaluation and Analysis of Transducers
S E A F	Sveriges El-och Elektronikagenters Forening (Sweden) (Swedish Electrical and Electronics Agents Association)
S E A I S I	South-East Asia Iron & Steel Institute
S E A L	Sea-Air-Land
	Subsea Equipment Associates Ltd. (an international consortium)
S E A M I S T	Seavan Management Information System (US Army)
S E A O S C	Structural Engineers Association of Southern California (USA)
S E A P S	SEATO Publications
S E A R C H	System for Electronic Analysis and Retrieval of Criminal Histories (of Law Enforcement Assistance Administration (USA))
	Systems for Exploring Alternative Resource Commitments in Higher Education
S E A S	SHARE European Association
S E A S S E	Southeast Asian Society of Soil Engineering
S E A S T A G S	SEATO Military Standardization Agreements
S E A T	Societa Elenchi Ufficiali degli Abbonati al Telefono (Italy)
S E B	Societe Electrotechnique Boulogne-Billancourt (France)
S E B C	Section d'Etudes de Biologie et de Chimie (of DTAT (France))
S E C	Securities and Exchange Commission (USA)
S E C - D E D	Single Error Correction and Double Error Detection
S E C A	Societe d'Exploitation de Constructions Aeronautiques (France)
S E C A N T	Separation and Control of Aircraft using Non-synchronous Techniques
S E C B At	Societe Europeene de Construction de l'avion Bregeut
S E C C	Single Error Correction Circuitry
S E C L	Symmetrical Emitter-Coupled Logic
S E C R A C	System Engineering Cost Reduction Assistance Contractor
S E C R E	Societe d'Etudes et de Constructions Electroniques (France)

S E C V	State Electricity Commission of Victoria (Australia)
S E D	Squared Euclidean Distance
S E D A	Safety Equipment Distributors Association (USA)
	Scanning Electron Diffraction Attachment
S E D A M	Societe d'Etudes et de Developpement des Aeroglisseurs Marins, Terrestres et Amphibies (France)
S E D A S	Spurious Emission Detection Acquisition System
S E D E C	Societe d'Edition, de Documentation Economique et Commerciale (France)
S E E	Secondary Electron Emission
	Society of Electronic Engineers (India)
	Small Evader Experiment
S E E D C O N	Software Evaluation, Exchange and Development for Contractors
S E E P	Support Effectiveness Evaluation Procedures
S E E R	Simplified Estimation of Exposure to Radiation
S E F	Study of Educational Facilities
S E F T	Section d'Etudes et de Fabrications des Telecommunications (of DTAT (France))
	Sintered Electrode Fluorescent Tube
S E G S	Selective Glide Slope
S E I E	Submarine Escape Immersion Equipment
S E I N A	Societe Europeenne d'Instruments Numeriques et Analogiques (France)
S E L	Space Environment Laboratory (of ERL (NOAA) (USA))
	Structural Engineering Laboratory (California University (USA))
	Systems Engineering Laboratory (of Michigan University (USA))
S E L C A L	Selective Calling System
S E L C I R	Systems Engineering Laboratory Circuit-drawing programme
S E L E C	Societe d'Etude des Electrocompresseurs (France)
S E L E M O	Selective Level Meter and Oscillator
S E L F	Societe d'Ergonomie de Langue Francaise (France) (a multi-national institute of ergonomics)
S E L F O C	Sheet-Electric Light Focusing
S E L M A	*Systems Engineering Laboratory's* (University of Michigan) Markovian Analyzer

S E M B R A T	Single Echelon Multi-Base Resource Allocation Technique
S E M I	Semiconductor Equipment and Materials Institute (USA)
S E M L A C	South East Midlands Local Authority Consortium
S E M M	Scanning Electron Mirror Microscope
	Societe Europeenne de Materials Mobiles (France)
S E M M S	Solar Electric Multi-mission Spacecraft
S E M O	Societe Belgo-Francaise d'Energie Nucleaire Mosane (France)
S E N B	Single Edge Notched Bend
S E N E L	Single Event Noise Exposure Level
S E O	Synchronous Equatorial Orbiter
S E P	Samenwerkende Electricitaits Productiebedrijven (Netherlands)
	Specific Excess Power
	Stowarzyszenie Elektrykow Polskich (Poland) (Polish Electrical Association)
S E P A K	Suspension of Expendable Penetration Aids by Kite
S E P E	Secretariat pour l'Etude des Problems de l'Eau (France) (Secretariat for the Study of Water Problems)
S E P L	Societe du Pipe-Line Sud Europeen
S E P O D	Submersible Electric Prototype Ocean Dredge
S E P O R	Service des Programmes des Organismes de Recherche (France) (a government liaison Department)
S E P S	Solar Electric Propulsion Stage
S E P S I T	Solar Electric Propulsion Integration Technology
S E P W G	Safety and Environmental Protection Working Group of JANNAF Interagency Propulsion Committee (USA)
S E R	Secondary Emission Ratio
	Smooth Endoplasmic Reticulum
S E R A T	Societe d'Etudes, de Realisations et d'Applications Techniques (France)
S E R C	Structural Engineering Research Centre (India)
S E R C O B E	Servicio Tecnico Comercial de Constructores de Bienes de Equipo (Spain)
S E R D E S	Serializer/Deserializer
S E R D E S C R C	Serializer-Deserializer Cyclic Redundancy Check
S E R F	Studies of the Economics of Route Facilities (a panel of ICAO)

S E R F	System for Equipment Requirements Forecasting
S E R G	Science Engineering Research Group (Long Island University (USA))
S E R H L	South-Eastern Radiological Health Laboratory (of BRH (USA))
S E R N A M	Service National des Messageries (France)
S E R T I	Societe d'Etudes et de Realisation pour le Traitement de l'Information (France)
S E R T O G	Space Experiment on Relativistic Theories of Gravitation
S E R V	Single-stage, Earth-orbital Reusable Vehicle Surface Effect Rescue Vehicle
S E S	Solar Energy Society (USA) (now International Solar Energy Society (Australia))
S E S A	Societe d'Etudes des Systems d'Automation (France) Social and Economics Statistics Administration (USA)
S E S A M	Super Element Structural Analysis programme Modules
S E S A M E	Supermarket Electronic Scanning for Automatic Merchandise Entry
S E S A M I - S E E D	Sporadic E Stimulation by Artificial Metallic Ion Seeding
S E S C	Special Environmental Sample Container (used by *Apollo 14* astronauts)
S E S C A	South Eastern Society of Chartered Accountants
S E S E R	Source of Electrons in a Selected Energy Range
S E S M	prefix to dated/numbered series of reports issued by Structural Engineering Laboratory, California University (USA)
S E S P A	Scientists and Engineers for Social and Political Action (USA)
S E T	Selective Employment Tax (abolished 1973) Single Escape Tower
S E T A	Societa Esercizi Telefonici Ausiliari (Italy)
S E T A C	Sector TACAN
S E T E	Supersonic Expendable Turbine Engine
S E T O L S	Surface Effect Take-Off and Landing System
S E T R A	Service d'Études Techniques des Routes et Auto-routes (France) (Department of Technical Studies on Roads and Motorways)
S E T S	System, Environment and Threat Simulation
S E T U R B A	Societe d'Etudes de l'URBA (France)

S E V	Sample Error Variance
	Surface Effect Vehicle
S E V A L D S	Strategy for Evaluating Design Strategies
S E W T	Simulator for Electronic Warfare Training
S F A	Societe Francaise d' Astronautique (France) (now part of AAAF)
S F A S	Solid Fuel Advisory Service (of National Coal Board together with other organisations)
S F C	Side Force Control
	Sideway-Force Coefficient
	State Financial Corporations (India)
S F C E S	Survivable Flight Control Electronic Set
S F C S	Survivable Flight Control System
S F C W	Sweep-Frequency, Continuous Wave
S F D	Spatial Frequency Diversity
	Structural Frame Design
S F E	Stacking Fault Energy
S F F	Science Fiction Foundation
	Standard File Format
S F H	Standard Fade Hour
S F I B	Syndicat National des Fabricants d'Ensembles de Information et des Machines de Bureau (France) (National Federation of Data Handling Equipment and Office Machines Manufacturers)
S F I C	Small Firms Information Centre
S F L	Symbolic Flowchart Language
S F M	Societe Francaise de Metallurgie (France) (French Society of Metallurgy)
S F M I	Societe Francaise de Moteurs a Induction (France)
S F O M	Societe Francaise d'Optique et de Mecanique (France)
S H	Solid-State Sequencer System
S F P	Screen Filtration Pressure
S F P A	Southern Forest Products Association (USA)
S F P S	Single Failure Point Summary
S F R	Sinking Fund Return
	Spin Flip Raman
S F R A	Science Fiction Research Association (USA)
S F R P	Societe Francaise de Radioprotection (France) (French Radiological Protection Society)
S F S A	Steel Founders Society of America (USA)
S F T S	Synthetic Flight Training System
S F V S C	San Fernando Valley State College (USA)
S G	Sea Grant program (USA)

S G D	Society of Glass Decorators (USA)
S G N	Saint Gobain Techniques Nouvelles (France)
S G O T	Serum Glutamic Oxaloacetic Transaminase
S G P T	Serum Glutamic Pyruvic Transaminase
S G S R	Society for General Systems Research
S G T	Societe des Garde-Temps (Switzerland)
S G T E	Societe Generale de Techniques et Etudes (France)
S G U	Sveriges Geologiska Undersokning (Sweden) (Geological Survey of Sweden)
S G Z	Surface Ground Zero
S H A	Software Houses Association
	Solid Homogeneous Assembly
S H A R	Sriharikota Rocket Range (of ISRO (India))
S H A R E S	Shared Airline Reservation
S H C	Sensitized Human Cell
	Synthesised Hydrocarbons
S H E	Standard Hydrogen Electrode
S H E E D	Scanning High Energy Electron Diffraction
S H H D	Scottish Home and Health Department
S H I P	Simplified-Helmholtz-Integral Programme
S H O C	Submerged Hydrodynamic Oil Concentrator
S H O M	Service Hydrographique et Oceanographique de la Marine (France) (Naval Hydrographic and Oceanographic Service)
S H O R A D	Short-Range Air Defense (a study group of the US Army)
S H R E A D	Share Registration and Dividend Warrants
S H S S	Short-Haul System Simulation
S H W	prefix to numbered series of publications on Safety, Health and Welfare (issued by Ministry of Labour, later Department of Employment and Productivity, and then Department of Employment) (series now entitled ' Health and Safety at Work ')
S I A	Singapore Internation Airlines (Singapore) (National Airline)
	Societe Internationale d'Acupuncture (International Society of Acupuncture)
	Society of Industrial Accountants (Canada)
	Stereo-Image Alternator
S I A C	Shipbuilding Industry Advisory Committee (USA)
S I A D	Society of Industrial Artists and Designers

S I A G L	Surveying Instrument, Azimuth Gyro, Light-weight
S I A M S	Study for Improved Ammunition Maintenance Support (US Army)
S I A R	Societe de la Surveillance Industrielle (France)
S I B	Shipbuilding Industry Board (disbanded 1971)
S I B M A C	Second International Brick Masonry Conference
S I C	Standards Information Center (of NBS (USA))
S I C A	Schizont-Infected Cell Agglutinin
S I C L O P S	Simplified Interpretive COBOL Operating System
S I C O M	State Industrial and Investment Corporation of Maharashtra (India)
S I D	Standard Instrument Departure
	Suprathermal Ion Detector
S I D E	Suprathermal Ion Detector Experiment
S I D P E R S	Standard Installation-Division Personnel System (US Army)
S I E	Societa Italiana di Ergonomia (Italy) (Italian Ergonomics Society)
S I F	Selective Identification Feature
S I F T	Software Implemented Fault Tolerance
S I F T A	Sistema Interamericano de Telecommunicaciones para las Fuerzas Aereas (telecommunications link between the Air Force Commanders of the USA and those of Central and South America)
S I G	Stellar Inertial Guidance
S I G / N P M	Special Interest Group for Non-Print Media (of ASIS (USA))
S I G / T I S	Special Interest Group/Technical, Information, and Society (of ASIS (USA))
S I G / U O I	Special Interest Group/ User On-line Interaction (of ASIS (USA))
S I G M A	System for Interactive Graphical Mathematical Applications
S I G M A L O G	Simulation and Gaming Methods for the Analysis of Logistics
S I I A	Sudden Increase in Ionospheric Activity
S I L S	School of Information and Library Studies (State University of New York (USA))
S I M	Scientific Instrument Module
	Simulated Machine Indexing
	Surface-to-air-missile Intercept Missile
	System Information Management
S I M A	Secondary Ion Mass Analysis

S I M A L	Simplified Accountancy Language
	Simulated All-purpose Language
S I M A L E	Super Integral Microprogrammed Arithmetic Logic Expediter
S I M A N N E	Simulation of Analogue Networks
S I M B A	System of Integrated Modular Breathing Apparatus
S I M C O N	Simulation Control
S I M D	Single-Instruction, Multiple-Data stream
S I M G F	Semi-Invariant Moment Generating Function
S I M O N	Simple Instructional Monitor
S I M P L E	Simulation Programming Language
S I M S	Secondary-Ion Mass Spectrometry
	Scientific Inventory Management System
	Selected Item Management System (US Army)
	Social Science Information Management System
	Subscribers Installation Management Information and Control System (of the Australian Post Office)
S I M S E P	Simulation of Solar Electric Propulsion
S I M S L I N	Safety In Mines Scattered Light Instrument
S I M T O P	Silicon Nitride-Masked Thermally Oxidized Post-Diffused Mesa Process
S I M T O S	Simulated Tactical Operations Systems
S I N	Schweizerisches Institut fur Nuclearforschung (Switzerland) (Swiss Institute for Nuclear Research)
S I N A D	Ratio of Signal plus Noise and Distortion to Distortion and Noise
S I N D	Southern Interstate Nuclear Board (USA)
S I N F D O K	Statens Rad for Vetenskaplig Information och Dokumentation (Sweden) (National Committee for Scientific Information and Documentation)
S I N P	Saha Institute of Nuclear Physics (India)
S I P	Surface Impulsion Propulsion
S I P A R E	Syndicat des Industries de Pieces detachees et Accessoires Radioelectriques et Electroniques (France)
S I P I	Scientists Institute for Public Information (USA)
S I P P S	System of Information Processing for Professional Societies
S I P S	Satellite Instrumentation Processor System
S I Q R	Semi-Inter-Quartile Range

S I R	Societa Italiana Resine (Italy) Symbolic Input Routine System Integration Receiver
S I R A	British Scientific Instrument Research Association (now known as The SIRA Institute)
S I R C E	Societa per l'Incremento Rapporti Commerciali con l'Estero (Italy)
S I R C H	Semi-Intelligent Robot for Component Handling
S I R E	Symbolic Information Retrieval
S I R N E M	Strategic International Relations Nuclear Exchange Model
S I R S	Ship Installed RADIAC System
S I R T I	Societa Italiana Reti Telefoniche Interurbane (Italy)
S I S	Scanning Imaging Spectrophotometer Scientific Information System Seaborne Instrumentation System SEAL (*Subsea Equipment Associates Limited*) Intermediate System Semiconductor-Insulator-Semiconductor Short-Interval Scheduling Societe d'Informatique et de Systemes Compagnie Bancaire (France) Special Industrial Services (of UNIDO) Specification Information System Stall Inhibitor System prefix to numbered series of Standards Information Sheets issued by the Machine Tool Trades Association Surface Indicator Scale (of ACI (USA))
S I S A M	Selective Interferential Spectrometry through Amplitude Modulation
S I S I R	Singapore Institute for Standards and Industrial Research (Singapore)
S I S O	Single-Input/Single-Output
S I S T E L	Sistemi Elettronica (Italy)
S I T	Silicon Intensifier Target Silicon Intensifier Tube Spontaneous Ignition Temperature
S I T - D L	Stevens Institute of Technology - Davidson Laboratory (USA)
S I T A P	Simulator for Transportation and Analysis
S I T B	Societe Industrielle de Travaux de Bureaux (France)

S I T E	Satellite Instructional Television Experiment
S I T E C	Sudden Increase of Total Electron Content
S I T E L E S C	Syndicat des Industries de Tubes Electroniques et Semiconducteurs (France)
S I T P H	Stowarzysznenie Inzynierow i Technikow Przemyslu Hutniczego (Poland) (Association of Engineers and Technicians of the Metallurgical Industry)
S I T P W	Stowarzyszenie Inzynierow i Technikow Przemyslu Wlokienniczego (Poland) (Association of Engineers and Technicians of the Textile Industry)
S I T R A	South Indian Textile Research Association (India) Suomen Itsenaisyyden Juhlavouden Rahasto (Finland) (Finnish Independence Jubilee Fund) (now known as the Finnish National Fund for Research and Development)
S I T S	Systems Integration Test Stand Societa Italiana Telecommunicazione Siemens (Italy)
S I T U M E R	Societe d'Ingeneirie du Tunnel sous la Mer (France)
S J C L	Standardized Job Control Language
S J P	Self-Judgment Principle
S J P E	Symposium on Jet Pumps and Ejectors
S K E A	Signal Known Except Amplitude
S K E M	Spares Kit Evaluator Model
S K I	Station Keeping Indicator
S K K	Stichting Kernvoortstuwing Koopvaardijschepen (Netherlands) (Foundation for Nuclear Propulsion of Merchant Ships)
S K T F	Sveriges Kvalitetstekniska Forening (Sweden) (Swedish Organisation for Quality Control)
S L A	Saturn Lunar-module Adapter Sun-Line Algorithm
S L A E	Standard Lightweight Avionics Equipment
S L A M	Ship-Launched Anti-aircraft Missile Simulation Language for Analogue Modelling Small Low Angular Momentum Stress waves in Layered Arbitrary Media Submarine-Launched Airflight Missile Surface-Launched Air Missile
S L A P	Small-signal Linear Analysis Programme
S L A T	Study of Land/Air Trade-offs

S L B M	Sea *or* Ship *or* Submarine Launched Ballistic Missile
S L C	Sidelobe Clutter
	Sustained-Load Cracking
S L C M	Submarine-Launched Cruise Missile
S L D	Superluminescent Diode
S L D H	Serum Lactic Acid Dehydrogenase
S L E	Superheat-Limit Explosion
	Systemic Lupus Erythematosus
S L E E P	Scanning Low Energy Electron Probe
S L G	Synchronous Longitudinal Guidance
S L I C	Simulator for Linear Integrated Circuits
S L I C E	Southwestern Library Interstate Cooperative Endeavor (Southwestern Library Association (USA))
S L I D	Standard Library of Item Descriptions
S L I M	Single-sided Linear Induction Motor
	Stock Line Inventory Management
	Surface-Launced Interceptor Missile
	System Library Maintenance
S L M	Subscriber Loop Multiplex
S L O	Streptolysin O
S L O T	Sequential Logic Tester
S L P M	Scanned-Laser Photoluminescence Microscope
S L R	Single-Lens-Reflex camera
S L T E A	Sheffield Lighter Trades Employers Association
S L T F	Shortest Latency Time First
S L U F A E	Surface-Launched Unit Fuel Air Explosive
S L U R P	Self Levelling Unit for Removing Pollution
S M	Streptomycin
S M A	Segnalamento Marittimo ed Aereo (Italy)
	Ship Maintenance Authority (MOD (N))
	Singapore Medical Association (Singapore)
	Solder Manufacturers Association (USA)
S M A C	Scene-Matching Area-Correlator
	Simultaneous Multiframe Analytical Calibration
S M A C N A	Sheet Metal and Air Conditioning Contractors National Association (USA)
S M A F	Smooth Muscle-Acting Factor
S M A R A	Servicio Meteorologico de la Armada Argentina (Argentina) (Naval Meteorological Service)
S M A R T	Storage Modification And Retrieval Transaction
	Storno (Denmark) Multichannel Automatic Radio Telephone)
	Supermarket Allocation and Recorder Technique

11*

SMART (continued)

S M A R T	Supervisors Methods Analysis Review Technique
S M A R T S	San Mateo (USA) Automated Rapid Telecommunication System
S M A S	Switched Maintenance Access System
S M A W	Shielded Metal-Arc Welding
S M A W T	Short-range, Man-portable, Anti-tank Weapon Technology
S M B	Single Mouldboard ploughing
S M C	Screened Multilayer Ceramic
	Sheet Moulding Compound
	Small Magellanic Cloud
	Spectacle Makers Company
S M C S	Structural Mode Control System
S M E A	Sheffield Metallurgical and Engineering Association
S M E A C	Science, Mathematics and Environmental Education Information Analysis Center (Ohio State University (USA))
S M E A T	*Skylab* Medical Experimental Altitude Test (of NASA)
S M E D A L	STAG (US Army Strategy and Tactics Analysis Group) Monotone Experimental Design Algorithm
S M E S	Superconducting Magnetic Storage
S M I C	Study of Man's Impact on Climate (sponsored by MIT (USA))
S M I L E	"S" Machine Interpreter Language Emulation
S M L	Semantic Meta-Language
S M L B	Sea-mobile Logistic Base
S M M	Standard Method of Measurement of Building Work (of RICS and NFBTE)
	Systems Maintenance Management
S M O	Synchronized Modulated Oscillator
S M P	Small Metal Particles
S M R	Solid Moderated Reactor
	Super-Metallic Rich
S M R A B	Safety in Mines Research Advisory Board (of DTI)
S M R E	Safety in Mines Research Establishment (of DTI)
S M R L	Sudan Medical Research Laboratories (Sudan)
S M S	Stock Management System
	Synchronous Meteorological Satellite
	System Measurement Software
S M T A	Scottish Motor Trade Association

330

S M T R B	Ship and Marine Technology Requirements Board
S M V	Standard Minute Value
S M W G	Space Shuttle Structures and Materials Working Group (of NASA (USA))
S N	Substantia Nigra
S N A P	School for Nautical Archaeology at Plymouth
	Stereonet Analysis Programme
S N A P S	Switched Network Automatic Profile System (of AUTODIN)
S N A S	Ship Navigation Alarm System
S N A S C	Symbolic Network Analysis on a Small Computer
S N B B	Saskatchewan-Nelson Basin Board (Canada)
S N C F	Societe Nationale des Chemins de Fer Francais (France) (French National Railways)
S N C F A	Societe Nationale des Chemins de Fer Algeriens (Algeria) (Algerian Railways)
S N D V	Strategic Nuclear Delivery Vehicles
S N F	Sampled N-path Filter
S N G	Substitute Natural Gas
	Synthetic Natural Gas
S N I A S	Societe Nationale Industrielle Aerospatiale (France)
S N O E	Smack, Noise Equipment
S N P E	Societe Nationale des Poudres et Explosifs (France)
S N P S	Satellite Nuclear Power Station
S N R	Society for Nautical Research
	Static Negative Resistance
	Supernova Remnant
S N T I T P ch	Stowarzyszenie Naukowo-Techniczne Inzynierow i Technikow Przemyslu Chemicznego (Poland) (Scientific and Technical Association of Engineers and Technicians of the Chemical Industry)
S N T I T P P	Stowarzyszenie Naukowo-Techniczne Inzynierow i Techinkow Przemyslu Papierniczego (Poland) (Scientific and Technical Association of Paper Industry Engineers and Technicians)
S N T I T R	Stowarzyszenie Naukowo-Techniczne Inzynierow i Technikow Rolnictwa (Poland) (Scientific and Technical Association of Engineers and Technicians in Agriculture)
S N U	Solar Neutrino Unit

S N U P P S	Standardized Nuclear Power Plant Syndicate (USA) (a commercial syndicate)
S O A	State of the Art
	Stimulus Onset Asynchrony
S O A C	State-of-the-Art Car (Car here is American term for railway waggon)
S O A E	State Organization for Administration and Employment Affairs (Iran)
S O A P	Silicate-Oxy-Apatite
	Simplify Obscure ALGOL Programmes
	Spectrometric Oil Analysis Programme
S O A R	Shuttle Orbital Applications and Requirements
	Simulation of Airlift Resources
S O C	Severity of Ozone Cracking
S O C A B U	Societe de Caoutchouc Butyl (France)
S O C C	Self-Orthogonal Convolutional Code
S O C E A	Societe Charentaise d'Equipements Aeronautiques (France)
S O C M A	Second Order Coherent Multiple Access
S O C R A T E S	*Scope's* Own Conditioned-Reflex, Automatic Trainable Electronic System
S O C T A P	Sulphur Oxide Control Technology Assessment Panel (USA)
S O D A	Source Data Automation
	Systems Optimization and Design Algorithm
S O D E R N	Societe Anonyme d'Etudes et Realisations Nucleaires (France)
S O D E T	Sound Detector
S O E	Specific Optimal Estimation
S O E C	Statistical Office of the European Communities (Luxemburg)
S O F R E	Societe Francaise d'Etudes (France) (French Consulting Engineers Organisations)
S O F R E C O M	Societe Francaise d'Etudies et de Realisations d'Equipements de Telecommunications (France)
S O F R E G A Z	SOFRE Gaz (France) (French Gas Engineers Consulting Organisation)
S O F R E L E C	SOFRE Electrique (France) (French Electrical Engineers Consulting Organisation)
S O F R E M I N E S	SOFRE Miniere (France) (French Mining Engineers Consulting Organisation)
S O F R E S I D	SOFRE Siderurgique (France) (French Metallurgical Industries Consulting Organisation)

S O G A M M I S	*South Gate* (City) (USA) Municipal Management Information System
S O G E C O R	Societe de Gestion et de Conseil en Organisation (France)
S O G E M	Societe de Gestion Moderne (France)
	Sortie Generation Model
S O G E R M A	Societe Girondine d'Entretien et de Reparation de Materiel Aeronautique (France)
S O G E S C I	Societe Belge pour l'Application des Methodes Scientifiques de Gestion (Belgium) (Belgian Society for the Application of Scientific Methods of Management)
S O I S	Silicon On Insulating Substrate
S O L	Simulation Orientated Language
	System Orientated Language
S O L A R	Shared On-Line Automated Reservation
S O L D	Soft Option in Logic Design
S O L I D	Self-Organizing Large Information Dissemination
S O L M I S	Supply On-Line Management Information System
S O L O	System for On-Line Optimization
S O L R A D	Solar Radiation Monitoring Satellite Program (USN)
S O M	Simulation Option Model
	Small Office Microfilm
	Society of Occupational Medicine
	Space Organization Method
S O M A S E R	Societe Maritime de Service (France)
S O M I R E N	Societa Minerali Radioattivi Energia Nucleare (Italy)
S O M I S A	Sociedad Mixta Siderurgia Argentina (Argentina)
S O N	Supraoptic Nuclei
S O N A C O B	Societe Nationale de Commercialisation des Bois et Derives (Algeria)
S O N A C O M E	Societe Nationale des Construction Mecaniques (Algeria)
S O N A P	Sociedad de Navigacion Petrolera (Chile)
S O N A T I T E	Societe Nationale des Travaux d'Infrastructure des Telecommunications (Algeria)
S O N A T R A C H	Societe Nationale de Transport et de Comercialisation des Hydrocarbures (Algeria)
S O N A T R A M	Societe Nationale de Travaux Maritimes (Algeria)
S O N D E	Society of Non-Destructive Evaluation
S O N I C	Simultaneously Operating Numerical Integration Computer

S O P	Secretaria de Obras Publicas (Mexico) (Ministry of Public Works)
S O R	Successive Over-Relaxation
S O R D	Submerged Object Recovery Device
S O R T	Staff Organization Round Table (of American Library Association (USA))
	Structures for Orbiting Radio Telescopes
S O R T R A N	Syntax Oriented Translator
S O S	Self-shielding Open-arc Stainless
	Silicon-on-Sapphire
	Stabilized Optical Sight
	Statics of Solids
S O S - M E	Silicon-on-Sapphire Memory Evaluator
S O S I	Space Operations and Scientific Investigations
S O S O F T	Software System Oriented to Fuze Testing
S O S T E L	Solid State Electric Logic
S O S U S	SONAR Surveillance System
S O V A L	Single Operator Validation
S O W	Statement of Work
S O Y D	Sum-of-the-Year-Digits
S P	prefix to numbered: dated series of Aircraft construction mechanical parts issued by BSI (letter sometimes preceded by a number)
	Separable Programming
	Staff Paper
S P A	Sea Photo Analysis
	Screen Printing Association (USA)
	Societe Protectice des Animaux (France) (Society for the Protection of Animals)
	Specialised Publications Association (India)
	Statens Provningsanstalt (Sweden) (National Institute for Materials Testing)
S P A	Societa per Azioni (Joint Stock Company)
S P A C E	Settlement, Payment, Accounting, Credit Extension
S P A D A T S	Space Detection and Tracking System (of NORAD)
S P A D E	Single channel per carrier, Pulse code modulation, multiple-Access Demand-assignment Equipment
S P A D E S	Solar Perturbation of Atmospheric Density Experiments Satellite
S P A I S	Suburban Police Automated Information System (Massachusetts (USA))
S P A M	Soil-Plant-Atmosphere Model
S P A N	Social Participatory Allocative Network

334

S P A N	Solar Proton Alert Network (of Space Disturbances Laboratory (NOAA (USA)))
	Solid Phase Alloy Nucleation
S P A N P A C	Sales, Purchases and Nominal Package
S P A R	Solid-state Phased-Array Radar
	Subjective Probability Analysis Routine
S P A R C	Selected Parts Control System
	South Platte Area Redevelopment Council (USA)
	Spectral Analyzer and Recognition Computer
S P A R T	Space Research and Technology
S P A R T A N	Scheduling Programme for Allocating Resources To Alternative Networks
S P A T E	Submersible Position and Tracking Equipment
S P C	Science Policy Committee (of OECD)
	Standard Printing Colour
	Supraventricular Premature Contractions
S P C C	Strength Power and Communications Cable
S P D	Spectral Power Distribution
	Statistical Policy Division (of OMB (USA))
S P D A	Sea Photo Diffraction Analysis
S P D P	Society of Professional Data Processors (USA)
S P D T	Single-Pole Double-Throw
S P E	Solar Particle Event
	Solid Polymer Electrolyte
S P E A R	*Stanford* (University (USA)) Positron-Electron Asymmetric Ring
S P E C	System Performance Evaluation Console
S P E C A	Supplier Performance Evaluation and Corrective Action
S P E D	Supersonic Planetary Entry Decelerator
S P E E A	Seattle Professional Engineering Employees Association (USA)
S P E E D	Systematic Plotting and Evaluation of Enumerated Data
	System-wide Project for Electronic Equipment at Depots (US Army)
S P E E D E X	System Project for Electronic Equipment at Depots Extended (US Army)
S P E E D S	System for Pin-pointed, Exhaustive and Expeditious Dissemination of Subjects
S P E M E L E C	Specialites Mecaniques et Electro-mecaniques (France)

S P E P E	Secretariat Permanent pour l'Etude des Problemes de l'Eau (France) (Permanent Secretariat for the Study of Water Problems)
S P E R	Syndicat des Industries de Materiel Professionnel Electronique et Radioelectrique (France)
S P E S	Section on Physical and Engineering Sciences (of American Statistical Association (USA))
	Simple Plant Economic Simulator
S P F	Solid Phase Forming
	Sveriges Plastforbund (Sweden) (Swedish Plastics Federation)
S P G G	Solid Propellant Gas Generator
S P H I N X	Space Plasma High-voltage Interaction Experiments
S P I	Scatter Plate Interferometer
	Symbolic Pictorial Indicator
	Synthetic Phase Isolator
S P I C A N A D A	Society of the Plastics Industry of Canada (Canada)
S P I C E	Sales Point Information Computing Equipment
S P I D	Seismic Personnel Intrusion Detector
	Submersible Portable Inflatable Dwelling
S P I F	Sequential Prime Implicant Form
S P I L	Systems Programming Implementation Language
S P I N	Searchable Physics Information Notices (of AIP (USA))
S P I N D E X	Selective Permutation Indexing
S P I R A S	Setpoint Precision Infra-Red Angular Scanner
S P L	Signature and Propagation Laboratory (of USABRL)
	Simple Programming Language
	Subrecursive Programming Language
S P L C	Standard Point Location Code (USA, Canada and Mexico)
S P L I C E	Systematic Planning of Logistics for the Introduction of Complete Equipment
S P L I S	Source Programme Library System
S P L M	Space Programming Language Machine
S P M	Solar Proton Monitor
	System Planning Manual
S P M E	Solar Proton Monitoring Experiment
S P N R	Society for the Promotion of Nature Reserves
S P O	Surface Plasmon
	Systems Program Office (USAF)

S P O O F	Structure and Parity Observing Output Function
S P O T	Speed, Position and Track
S P R	Sequential Pattern Recognition
	Sintered Particle Rolling
	Spontaneous Parametric Radiation
S P R A	Special Purpose Reconnaisance Aircraft
S P R I N T	Special Police Radio Inquiry Network
S P R I N T E R	Specification of Profits with Interdependencies
S P R O B	Solid Propellant Space Booster Plant (of ISRO (India))
S P R O G S	SD4020-PDPI5 Rapid Output of Graphics System
S P R O S S	Simulation Programme for Sequential Systems
S P R P	Signalling Preprocessing Programmes
S P R U	Science Policy Research Unit (Sussex University)
S P S	Society of Physics Students (USA)
	Submerged Production System
	Super Proton Synchroton
S P S G	Spin Period Sector Generator
S P S P	Signalling Postprocessing Programmes
S P S S	Sodium Polystyrene Sulphonate
	Statistical Package for the Soil Sciences
S P S T	Single-Pole Single-Throw
S P T	Standard Penetration Test
S P U R	System for Project Updating and Reporting
S P U R T	Simulation Package for University Research and Teaching
S P U R V	Self-Propelled Underwater Research Vehicle
S P V	Surface Photovoltage
S P W L A	Society of Professional Well Log Analysts (USA)
S Q	Stereo Quadraphonic
Sq D M	Sequency Division Multiplexing
S Q U A N K	Simpson Quadrature Used Adaptively - Noise Killed
S Q U I D	Superconducting Quantum-mechanical Interference Device
S R	Scanning Radiometer
	Sveriges Radio (Sweden)
S R A	Systems Requirements Analysis
S R A A M	Short-Range Air-to-Air Missile
S R A C	Safety Research Advisory Committee (of SAE (USA))
S R A D	Steerable Right Angle Drive

S R A E N	Systeme de Reference pour la determination de l'Affaiblissement Equivalent pour la Nettete (of CCITT) (Reference System for Determining Articulation Ratings)
S R A T S	Solar Radiation and Thermospheric Structure Satellite
S R B	Statens Rad for Byggnadsforskning (Sweden) (National Council for Building Research)
	Sulphate Reducing Bacteria
S R B D M	Short-Range Bomber Defence Missile
S R C	Saskatchewan Research Council (Canada)
	Solvent Refined Coal
	Submarine Rescue Chamber
	Survey Research Center (California University (USA))
S R C U	Shared Remote Control Unit
S R D	Safety and Reliability Directorate (of UKAEA)
S R D M	prefix to numbered series of Memoranda issued by SRD (UKAEA)
S R D R	prefix to numbered series of Reports issued by SRD (UKAEA)
S R E	Society of Relay Engineers
S R F	Secondary Refrigerant Freezing
	Station de Recherches Forestieres (Morocco) (Forestry Research Station)
	Strength Reduction Factor
S R I	Soil Research Institute (Ghana)
S R L	Science Reference Library (a part of the British Library)
	Systems Research Laboratory (University of Michigan (USA))
S R M	Society for Range Management (USA)
	prefix to series of Research Memoranda issued by NPTRL (previously NPRA (USN))
S R O B	Short Range Omni-directional Beacon
S R P	Seismic Reflection Profiling
	Self-Recording Penetrometer
	Stationary Random Process
	System Response Patterns
S R R	System Requirements Review
	prefix to series of reports issued by NPTRL (previously NPRA) (USN)
S R S	Social and Rehabilitation Service (of HEW (USA))
	Systems Reliability Service (of UKAEA)

S R T S	System Response Time Simulator
S R V	Styling Research Vehicle
	Surface Recombination Velocity
S S	Starlight Scope
S S A	Seismological Society of America (USA)
	Smallest Space Analysis
	Social Security Administration (of HEW (USA))
	Sulphosalicylic Acid
S S A C V	Semi-Submerged Air Cushion Vehicle
S S A D H	Succinic Semialdehyde Dehydrogenase
S S A P	Survival Stabilator Actuator Package
S S B	Salvo Squeezebore
	Space Science Board (of National Academy of Science (USA))
S S C	Sector-Switching Centre
	US Army Telecommunications Software Support Center (of STRATCOM) (US Army))
	Summer Simulation Conference (USA)
S S C A	Southern Society of Chartered Accountants
S S C C	Spin-Scan Cloud Camera
S S C I	Societes de Service et Conseil en Informatique (France)
S S C S	Spatial Spectrum Centre Shifting
S S D	Synthesis, Solute Diffusion
S S D A	Sequential Similarity Detection Algorithm
	Stainless Steel Development Association (disbanded 1973)
S S E O	Seabee Systems Engineering Office (USN)
S S F	Society for the Study of Fertility
S S F C	Sequential Single-Frequency Code
S S G W	Strategic Surface to Surface Guided Weapon
S S H R	Social Systems and Human Resources (a division of the RANN project of NSF (USA))
S S I	Small Scale Integrated
S S I E	Smithsonian Institution's Science Information Exchange (USA)
S S I H	Societe Suisse pour l'Industrie Horlogere (Switzerland)
S S L	Solid State Lamp
	Space Sciences Laboratory (California University (USA))
S S M	Sea Skimmer Missile
	Stochastic Sequential Machine
	Surface-to-Surface Missile

S S M	System-State Model
S S M A	Spread-Spectrum Multiple Access
S S M E	Space Shuttle Main Engine
S S M O	Summary of Synoptic Meteorological Observations
S S O C R	Super-Scale Optical Character Reader
S S P	Schoolhouse Systems Project (USA)
	Scientific Subroutine Package
	Semi-Submerged Platform
	Space Summary Programme
S S P C	Steel Structures Painting Council (USA)
S S P E	Subacute Sclerosing Panencephalitis
S S P I	Sighting System Passive Infra-red
S S P M	System State Phase Modelling
S S P S	Satellite Solar Power Station
	Space Satellite Power Station
S S R	Societe Suisse de Radiodiffusion et Television (Switzerland)
	Solid State Relay
	Switching Selector Repeater
S S S	Self-Shifting Synchronizing
	Small Scientific Satellite
	Systems Safety Society (USA)
S S S M	Subset-Specified Sequential Machine
S S T	Sea-Surface Temperature
	prefix to numbered series issued by Office of Supersonic Transport Division, Federal Aviation Agency (USA) (now Federal Aviation Administration (USA))
	Society of Surveying Technicians
S S T C	Space Science and Technology Centre (of ISRO (India))
S S T M	Solid State Target Monoscope
S S T P	Supersonic Transport Panel (of ICAO)
S S T R	Solid-State Track Recorder
S S T S	Sight Switch Technology System
S S T V	Slow-Scan Television
S S U	Semiconductor Storage Unit
S T	Staphylococcal Toxin
S T A	Service Technique de l'Aeronautique (France) (government establishment for Aerospace Quality Control and Specifications)
	Solution Treat and Aged
S T A B E	Second-Time-Around-Beacon-Echo

S T A E	Second-Time-Around-Echoes
S T A G	Simultaneous Telemetry Acquisition and Graphics
S T A G G	Small Turbine Advanced Gas Generator
S T A I R S	Storage And Information Retrieval System
S T A L O	Stable Local Oscillator
S T A M O	Stable Master Oscillator
S T A N	Sum Total And Nosegear
S T A N - C S	Stanford University, Department of Computer Science (USA)
S T A N A V - FORCHAN	Standing Naval Force Channel (of NATO)
S T A N A V - FORLANT	Standing Naval Force Atlantic (of ACLANT (NATO))
S T A N S I T	Working Group on Methods of Obtaining Statistics on Non-scheduled Air Transport (of European Civil Aviation Conference)
S T A P L	Ship Tethered Aerial Platform
S T A R	Satellite for Telecommunications, Applications and Research (a consortium of European Companies)
	Sequential Talking Audio Response
	Shell Transient Asymmetric Response
	Simple Test Approach for Readability
	Standard Terminal Arrival Route
	String and Array data
	Systems for Telephone Administrative Response
S T A R E C	Societe Technique d'Application et de Recherche Electronique (France)
S T A R S	Silent Tactical Attack Reconnaissance System
S T A R T	Spacecraft Technology and Advanced Re-entry Tests
	System of Transportation Applying Rendezvous Technology
S T A R U T E	Stabilization and Retardation Parachute
S T A T P A C	Statistical Package (of United States Geological Survey)
S T A T P K	Statistical Package
S T A T S I M	Statistical Simulation
S T B	Singapore Telephone Board (Singapore)
	prefix to dated-numbered series of Technical Bulletins issued by NPTRL (USN)
S T C	Short-Title Catalogue
	Society for Technical Communication (USA)

S T C	Solid Tantalum Capacitor
	State Trading Corporation (India)
S T C A N	Service Technique des Constructions et Armes Navales (France)
S T D	Solid Track Detector
	Stream Tree Data
	Subscriber Toll Dialling
S T D M	Synchronous Time-Division Multiplexing
S T D M A	Space-Time-Division Multiple Access
S T E A M	Stochastic Evolutionary Adoption Model
S T E C	Solar to Thermal Energy Conversion
S T E E L	Societe de Travaux d'Electricite et d'Electronique du Languedoc (France)
	Structural Engineers Easy Language
S T E L L A	System Ten European Language Ledger Accounting
S T E M	Scanning Transmission Electron Microscope
	Shaped-Tube Electrolytic Machining
	Social/Technological/Economic/Military
S T E P	Science Teacher Education Project (sponsored by the Nuffield Foundation)
	System Three Emulation Programme
S T E T	Societa Finanziaria Telefonica (Italy)
S T E X	Static Test and Evaluation Complex (of ISRO (India))
S T F	Square Wave Transfer Function
	Svenska Teknologforeningen (Swedish) (Swedish Technical Association)
S 3	Semi-Submerged Ship
S T I	Scientific and Technical Information
	Shear Thinning Index
	Steel Tank Institute (USA)
S T I L	Statistical Interpretive Language
S T J	Subtropical Jet stream
S T M	Short-Term Memory
S T N A	Service Technique de la Navigation Arienne (France)
S T O A	Solution Treatment and Over Aging
S T P	Source Term Programme
	prefix to numbered series of Special Technical Publications issued by ASTM (USA)
S T P C	Society of Technical Publications Contractors (now Society of Technical Presentation and Communication)

S T P D	Standard Temperature and Pressure, Dry
S T P G	Sequential Test Plan Generator
S T P O	Science and Technology Policy Office (of NSF (USA))
S T R A C S	Surface Traffic Control System
S T R A I N	Structural Analysis-Interactive
S T R C	Scientific, Technical and Research Commission (of Organization of African Unity) (Nigeria)
S T R E A M	Standard Tensioned Replenishment Alongside Method
S T R I P E	Stress Induced Pseudoelasticity
S T R U M S	Structural Modelling System
S T S	Consorzio per Sistemi di Telecomunicazioni via Satelliti (Italy)
	Selective Two-Step
	Sequential Transistor Switch
	Space Transportation System
	Surface-to-Surface
S T T	Single-Transition-Time
S T U	Styrelsen for Teknisk Utveckling (Sweden) (Board for Technical Development)
S T U C	Scottish Trade Union Congress
S T U V A	Studiengesellschaft fur Interidische Verkehrarlagen (Germany) (Research Association for Vehicle Tunnels)
S T V	Steerable Low Light Level Television
S U	Syracuse University (USA)
S U - D M S	Stanford University, Department of Materials Science (USA)
S U - S E L	Stanford University, Stanford Electronics Laboratories (USA)
S U A W A C S	Soviet Union Airborne Warning and Control System
S U B - I C E	Submerged Ice Cracking Machine
S U B I C	Submarine Integrated Circuit
sub I R S	Submarine Installed Radiac Systems
S U B T R A P	Submersible Training Platform
S U C E S U	Sociedade de Usuarios de Computadores Eletronicos e Equipmentos Subsidiaros (Brazil) (Society of Users of Electronic Computers and Ancillary Equipment)
S U F F E R	System Utility Facility For Easy Recovery
S U I S	Ship Upkeep Information System (MOD(N))
S U I T	Sight, Unit, Infantry, Trilux

S U L I S	*Sulzer* Literature distribution and Sorting
S U M	School of Underwater Medicine (Royal Australian Navy)
	System Utilization Monitor
S U M C	Space Ultrareliable Modular Computer
S U M M A C	*Stanford University* (USA) Modified Marker and Cell method
S U M S	*Sperry/UNIVAC* Material System
S U N	Scientific Users of 1900s (computers)
S U N A M A M	Superintendencia Nacional da Marinha Mercante (Brazil) (National Controller of the Mercantile Marine)
S U N Y - B C N	State University of New York (USA) Biomedical Communication Network
S U N Y A B	State University of New York at Buffalo (USA)
S U P	Solid Urethane Plastic
S U P A R S	Syracuse University (USA) *Psychological Abstracts* Retrieval Service
S U R F A I R	International Congress on Surface Treatments in the Aerospace Industry
S U R G E	Colorado State University Research in Graduate Education system (USA)
S U T	Sandvik-Universal Tube GmbH (Germany) (a company shared by Federal Republic of Germany, the United States of America and France)
S V	Selector Vision
	Slope and Voltage
	Stifterverband fur die Deutsche Wissenschaft (Germany) (Donors' Association for Promoting Arts and Sciences)
S V A	Slowly Varying Absorption
S V D	Swine Vesicular Disease
S V I M	Sociedad Venezolana de Ingenieros de Minas y Metalurgicos (Venezuela) (Venezuelan Society of Mining and Metallurgical Engineers)
S V F R	Special Visual Flight Rules
S V S	Suspended Vehicle System
S W	prefix to numbered-letter series of publications on Solid Waste Management issued by EPA (USA)
	Stud Welding
S W A	Steel Window Association
S W A C	Specification Writers Association of Canada (Canada)
S W A M I	Soft-Ware Aided Multi-font Input

S W A P	Stress Wave Analysing Programme
	Switching Assembly Programme
S W A P S	Standing-Wave Acoustic Parametric Source
S W A T H S	Small Waterplane Area Twin Hull Ship
S W C	Skywave Correction
	Soil and Water Conservation Research Division (of Agricultural Research Service (USDA))
	Submerged Work Chamber
S W C D	Solar Wind Composition Detector
S W C E	Solar Wind Composition Experiment
S W D	Surface-Wave Device
S W D L	Surface Wave Delay Line
S W E	Stress Wave Emission
S W E R	Single Wire Earth Return
S W F	Short Wave Fade-out
S W I F S	Surface Wave Integratable Filters
S W I F T	Society for Worldwide Inter-bank Financial Tele-communication
S W I M	Surface Wave Interference Modulator
S W I R	Short Wave Infra-red
S W I S S A I R	Schweizerische Luftverkehr AG (Switzerland)
S W M O	Solid Waste Management Office (of EPA (USA))
S W M P O	Solid Waste Management Programs Office (of EPA (USA))
S W O P S I	*Stanford University* (USA) Workshops on Social and Political Issues
S W R	Standing-Wave Ratio
S W R H L	Southwestern Radiological Health Laboratory (of PHS (USA))
S W R I	Southwest Research Insitute (USA)
S W R I - A R	Southwest Research Institute, Department of Automotive Research (USA)
S W R S I C	Southern Water Resources Scientific Information Center (of University of North Carolina and North Carolina State University (USA))
S W S	Saturn Workshop
S W T L	Surface-Wave Transmission Lines
S X	Sheet Explosive
	Starch Xanthide
S Y B A N	Syndicat Belge d'Assurances Nucleaires (Belgium)
S Y B E S I	Syndicat Belge pour le Seperation Isotopique (Belgium)
S Y M A P	Symbol Manipulation Programme
	Synagraphic Mapping

345

S Y M A T E X	Syndicat des Constructeurs Belges de Machines Textiles (Belgium)
S Y M B I O S I S	System for Medical and Biological Sciences Information Searching (of SUNY (USA))
S Y M B O L	System for Mass Balancing On/Off Line
S Y M B U G	Symbolic Debugging
S Y M E S	Systematic Machinery and Equipment Selection
S Y M P L E	Syntax Macro Preprocessor for Language Evaluation
S Y N A M E	Syndicat National de la Mesure Electrique et Electronique (France)
S Y N C O N	Syntax Conversion language
S Y N S P A D E	Symposium on the Numerical Solution of Partial Differential Equations
S Y P	Society of Young Publishers
S Y Q I	System Image Quality Indicator
S Y S C A P	System of Circuit Analysis Programmes
S Y S E X	System Executive
S Y S T I D	System Time-Domain Simulation programme
S Y S T I M	Systematic Interaction Model
S Y T A	Sustained-Yield Tropical Agroecosystem

T

T	prefix to numbered : dated series of Tubes standards issued by BSI
T & R I	Training and Research Institute (of the American Foundrymen's Society (USA))
T / A M	prefix to numbered series of reports issued by Department of Theoretical and Applied Mechanics, University of Illinois (USA)
T / E L	Test and Evaluation Laboratory (of National Weather Service (NOAA) (USA))
T A	Technology Assessment
	prefix to numbered : dated series of Titanium and Titanium Alloys standards issued by BSI
T A A	The Aluminium Association (USA)
	Thioacetic Acid
T A A M	Terminal Area Altitude Monitoring
T A B	Technology Assessment Board (of OTA (US Congress))
T A B V E E	Theater Air Base Vulnerability
T A B A	Transportes Aereas de Buenos Aires (Argentine)

TABTRAN	Table Translator
TAC	Television Advisory Committee (of the Ministry of Posts and Telecommunications)
	Thyristor-Assisted Commutation
	Transistorised Automatic Computer
	Turbo-Alternator-Compressor
TACASA	Tactical ADP Support System of the Army Security Agency (US Army)
TACCAR	Time Average Clutter Coherent Airborne Radar
TACDEW	Tactical Advanced Combat Direction and Electronic Warfare
TACLAND	Tactical Landing
TACMA	The Association of Control Manufacturers
TACMOD	Tactical Modular Display
TACOR	Threat Assessment and Control Receiver
TACRAC	Tactical Warfare Research Advisory Committee (of government, industry and Armed Forces (USA))
TACRV	Tracked Air Cushion Research Vehicle
TACS	Television Automatic Control System
	Thruster Attitude-Control System
TACSAT	Tactical Communications Satellite
TACT	Transonic Aircraft Technology
TACTICS	Technical Assistance Consortium to Improve College Services (a program of USOE (USA))
TACV	Transportes Aereos de Cabo Verde (Cape Verde Islands)
TACV/LIM	Tracked Air Cushion Vehicles powered by Linear Induction Motors
TAD	Technical Analysis Division (of NBS Institute for Applied Technology (USA))
TADJET	Transport-Airdrop-Jettison
TADS	Tactical Air Defence System
	Tactical Automatic Digital Switches
	Transportable Automatic Digital Switches
TAEC	Thai Atomic Energy Commission for Peace (Thailand)
TAF	Tumor-Angiogenesis Factor
TAFI	Turn-Around Fault Isolation
TAFSEG	Tactical Air Force Systems Engineering Group (USAF)
TAG	Thrust Alleviated Gyroscope
	Trans-Atlantic Geotransverse

T A G A	Technical Association of the Graphic Arts (USA)
T A G P	Transportes Aereos da Guine Portuguesa (Portuguese Guinea)
T A I R	Terminal Area Instrumentation Radar
T A L	Terminal Application Language
T A L I S S I	Tactical Light Shot Simulator
T A L K	Teletype Access to the Link at *King's* (College, London)
T A L O N	Texas, Arkansas, Louisiana, Oklahoma and New Mexico (USA)
T A L O N S	Tactical Airborne LORAN Navigation System
T A M	The Access Method
	The Assistant Mathematician
	Trajectory Application Method
	Transportes Aereo Militar (Paraguay) (Transport Branch of the Military Air Force)
T A M E	Transportes Aereos Militares Ecuatorianos (Ecuador) (Transport Branch of the Military Air Force)
T A M M S	The Army Maintenance Management System (US Army)
T A M U	Texas A and M University (USA)
T A M U - S G	prefix to dated-numbered series of reports issued by Texas A and M University (USA) Sea Grant Program
T A M V E C	Texas A&M (University (USA)) Variable Energy Cyclotron
T A N E S C O	Tanzania Electric Supply Company (Tanzania) (State owned)
T A N S	Tactical Air Navigation System
T A P	Time-sharing Accounting Package
T A P S	TERCOM Aircraft Positioning System
	Trans-Alaska Pipeline System
T A R	Transporte Aereo Rioplatense (Argentina)
T A R A N	Test and Repair as Necessary
T A R C	Government/Industry Transport Aircraft Requirements Committee
T A R C - O A	Tactical Air Reconnaissance Center, Office of Operations Analysis (USAF)
T A R E	Telegraph Automatic Relay Equipment
T A R E N A	Tallares de Reparaciones Navales (Argentina)
T A R E W S	Tactical Air Reconnaissance and Electronic Warfare Support

T A R G E T	Team to Advance Research for Gas Energy Transportation (a project supported by a number of public utility companies in the USA)
T A R I F	Telegraph Automating Routeing In the Field
T A R P S	Transportation Auditing and Reporting System
T A S	True Air-Speed
T A S C	Training Assistance in Small Companies (a division of RTITB)
T A S C O M	Theater Army Support Command (US Army)
T A S I C	Thermal Analysis of Substrates and Integrated Circuits
T A S M A N	submarine telephone cable between Australia and New Zealand
T A S S	Tactical Automatic Switching System
	Talent Attraction Selection System
	Towed Array Surveillance System
T A S S T	Tentative Airworthiness Standards for Supersonic Transports (issued by FAA (USA))
T A T	Tactical Armament Turret
	Thematic Apperception Test
T A Z A R A	Tanzania-Zambia Railway Authority
T B A	Thermobarometric Analysis
	Thiobutyric Acid
T B C	Tertiary Butyl Catechol
T B E	Tetrabromoethane
T B E A	Truck Body and Equipment Association (USA)
T B G	Thyroxin Binding Globulin
Tb I G	Terbium Iron Garnet
T B M	Trillion Bit Memory
	Tunnel Boring Machine
T B N	Total Base Number
T B P	Tetrabenzporphin
	Trigonal Bipyramid
	True Boiling Point
T B P A	Thyroxin Binding Prealbumin
	Torso Back Protective Armour
T B R C	Top Blown Rotary Convertor
T B S	Tokyo Broadcasting System (Japan)
T B S T	Triple Bituminous Surface Treatment
T C	Taenia Coli
	Tetracycline
	Time Constant
	Total Cholesterol

T C A	Tile Council of America (USA)
	Time of Closest Approach
	Trichloracetic Acid
T C A M	Telecommunications Access Method
T C A R	Technical Committee on Automotive Rubber (of SAE and ASTM (USA))
T C A R S	Test Call Answer Relay Set
T C C	Thermal Control Coatings
T C C A	Technical Committee on Computer Architecture (of IEEE Computer Society (USA))
	Tin Container Collectors Association (USA)
T C C L	Transport Co-ordinating Council for London
T C E	Trichtoroethanol
T C M L	Target Map Co-ordinate Locator
T C N Q	Tetracyanoquinodimethane
T C O A	Transvaal Coal Owners Association (South Africa)
T C P	Technology Coordinating Paper
	Tetrachlorophenol
	Texaco Combustion Process
	Tropical Canine Pancytopenia
T C Q N	Tetracyano-quinodimethane
T C R C	Telecommunication Research Centre (India)
T C S	Terylene/Cotton Core-spun Canvas
T C S P	Tandem Cross Section Programme
T C T	Total Circular Triad
	Transverse Current Tube
T C V	Tracked Cushion Vehicle
T C Z D	Temperature Compensated Zener Diode
T D	Topographic Division (of USGS (USAA))
T D A	Tax Deposit Account
	Trade Development Authority (India)
	Transmission and Distribution Association (a section of British Electrical & Allied Manufacturers Association)
	Transportation Development Agency (Canada)
	Tube Deviation Analyzer
	Tunnel Diode Amplifier
T D C	Thermal Diffusion Column
	Through-Deck Cruiser
T D C B	Tapered Double-Cantilever Beam
T D C C	Transportation Data Coordinating Committee (USA)
T D F	Tape Data Family

T D F	Two-Degree-of-Freedom
T D H S	Tactical Data Handling System
T D I	Toluene Diisocyanate
T D L	Tapped Delay Line
	Technical Development Laboratories (of NCDC (USA))
T D N	prefix to numbered series of Technical Data Notes issued by the Department of Employment
T D P A C	Time-Differential Perturbed Angular Correlations
T D P I	Two-Dimensional Probabilistic Image
T D S	Thermal Diffuse Scattering
	Time Domain Spectroscopy
T E A	Texas Electronics Association (USA)
	Transferred Electron Amplifier
	Transportation Engineering Agency (US Army)
	Transverse Electrical-discharge Atmospheric-pressure
	Triethylammonium
T E A M	Telecommunications, Electronique, Aeronautique et Maritime (France) (a company)
	Thames (*Case Ltd.*) Evaluation of Alternative Methods
	Thermal Energy Atomic and Molecular
T E C	Technician Education Council
	Thermal Energy Converter
	Three-dimensional Epitaxial Crystallites
	Total Electron Content
T E C E	Trans-Europe Container Express
T E C H N I O N	Israel Institute of Technology (Israel)
T E D	Transferred Electronic Device
	Transmission Electron Diffraction
T E D S	Tactical Expendable Drone System
T E E	Tubular Extendible Element
T E F	Tilted Electric Field
T E F O	Textilforskningsinstitutet (Sweden) (Textile Research Institute)
T E F S	Transportable Electromagnetic Field Source array
T E G	Thromboelastograph
T E G A S	Test Generation and Simulation
T E G D N	Triethylene Glycol Dinitrate
T E G I	Train-Elevated Guideway Interaction
T E I	Triethylindium
T E K	Turkiye Elektrik Kurumu (Turkey) (Turkish Electricity Authority)

T E L C O	Tata Engineering and Locomotive Company (India)
T E L E C O M	Empresa Nacional de Telecommunicaciones (Colombia) (State Telecommunications Authority)
T E L L	Teacher-aiding Electronic Learning Links
T E M A	Telecommunications Engineering and Manufacturing Association
T E M M A	Transmission Electron Microscopy and Microprobe Analysis
T E O	Transferred Electron Oscillator
T E O S	Tetraethyl Orthosilicate
T E P	Thermo-Electric Power
T E P A	Tetra-ethylene Pentamine
T E P O P	Tracking Error Propagation and Orbit Prediction Programme
T E P P	Tetraethyl Pyrophosphate
T E R	Transverse Electro-Reflectance
	Triple Ejection Rack
T E R C O M	Terrain Contour Matching Guidance System
T E R E C	Tactical Electronic Reconnaissance
T E R L S	Thumba Equatorial Rocket Launching Station (of ISRO (India))
T E R M S	Terminal Management System (DOD (USA))
T E R P	Turbine Engine Reliability Programme
T E S A	Television Electronics Service Association (Canada)
T E S A T	Teaching Sample Tables
T E S E	Tactical Exercise Simulator and Evaluator
T E S S A R	Test Event Sequencing, Simulating and Recording system
T E S T	Technical Evaluation of Solid-State Technologies
T E T	Turbine Entry Temperature
T E T A	Triethylenetetramine
T E T O C	Council for Technical Education and Training for Overseas Countries
T E T R	Test and Training satellite
T E T W O G	Aircraft Turbine Engine Testing Working Group (USA)
T E U R	Tariffs-Europe (a joint working party of CCITT)
T E X	Temperature Excess
T F	Technological Forecasting
	Thermal Feedback
	Toroidal Field

T F / D	Time and Frequency Dissemination
T F A	Trifluoroacetic Acid
	Trifluoroacetyl
T F D	Target Film Distance
T F E	Thermionic Fuel Element
T F G	Thrust Floated Gyroscope
T F O	Thin Fuel Oil
T F P A	Torso Front Protective Armour
T F P M S	Trifluoropropmethylsiloxane
T F R A N	*Toshiba* Framed Structure Analysis Programme
T F S	Tin-Free Steel
T F S - C T	Tin-Free Steel Chromium-Type
T F S F	Time to First System Failure
T F S O	Tonto Forest Seismological Observatory
T F T A	Tetraformal Trisazine
T G A	Toilet Goods Association (USA)
T G D	Triggered Discharge Gauge
T G F B	Triglycine Fluoberyllate
T G M	Training Guided Missile
T G S	Triglycine Sulphate
T G S M	Terminally Guided Sub-Missile
T G T	Thromboplastin Generation Test
T H	Tyrosine Hydroxylase
T H A D	Terminal Homing Accuracy Demonstrator
T H B	Temperature-Humidity-Bias
T H C	Tetrahydrocannabinol
T H E	Technical Help to Exporters (section of British Standards Institute)
	Technical Help to Exporters (a service of ANSI (USA))
T H E B R A I N	The *Harvard* (*University* (USA)) Experimental Basic Reckoning And Instructional Network
T H E R P	Technique for Human Error Prediction
T H F A	Thermal Hartree-Fock Approximation
T H G	Third Harmonic Generation
T H K	Turk Hava Kuvvetleri (Turkey) (Military Air Force)
T H M	Travelling Heater Method
T H P	Tetrahydropapaveroline
T H V	Tracked Hover Vehicle
T I A C	Transport Industries Advisory Council (Australia)
T I B	Technische Informationbibliothek (Germany) (Technical Information Library)
	Transparent Interleaved Bipolar

353

12

T I C	Tantalum Integrated Circuit
	Technical Information Center (USAEC)
	Total Ion Current
	Trypsin Inhibitor Capacity
T I C C I T	Time-shared, Interactive Computer Controlled Information Television
T I C E S	Type-In Coding and Editing System
T I C S	Terminal Interface Control System
T I C U S	Tidal Current Survey (of NOAA (USA))
T I D	Tactical Information Display
T I D A S	Totally Integrated Data System
T I D F	Triple Input Describing Functions
T I D P	Telemetry and Image Data Processing
T I E S	Total Integrated Engineering System
T I L T	*Texas Instruments* Language Translator
T I M	Technical Information on Microfilm
T I M A R C	Time Multiplexed Analogue Radio Control
T I M I C	Time Interval Modulation Information Coding
T I M I S	Totally Integrated Management Information System
T I M O C	Time Dependent Monte Carlo Code
T I N	Temperature Independent
T I N C	Theory of Interacting Continua
T I N T S	Turret Integrated Night Thermal Sight
T I O A	Triisooctylamine
T I O S	Tactical Information Organization System
T I P	Time to Initial Precipitation
	Toxicology Information Program (of National Library of Medicine (USA))
	Tracking and Impact Prediction
	Translation Inhibitory Protein
	Traversing In-core Probe
T I P I	Tactical Information Processing and Information
T I P I S P O	Tactical Intelligence Processing and Interpretation System Program Office (USAF)
T I P S	Tactical Information about Perilous Situations
T I R	Target Illuminating Radar
	Thermal Infra-Red
T I R A S	Technical Information Retrieval and Analysis System
T I R C	Toxicology Information Response Center (of Oak Ridge National Laboratory (USAEC))
T I R I S	Traversing Infra-Red Inspection System
T I R K S	Trunks Integrated Records Keeping System

T I S	Total Information System
	Transportation Information System
T I S A B	Total Ionic Strength Adjustment Buffer
T I S C	Tire Industry Safety Council (USA)
T I S C O	Technical Information Systems Committee (of FSPT (USA))
T I S E O	Target Identification Sensor Electro-Optical
T I T A N	*Teamster* (International Brotherhood of Teamsters (USA)) Information Terminal and Accounting Network
T K M	Tonne-Kilometres
T K O	Trunk Offering
T L	Thermoluminescence
T L A	Thai Library Association (Thailand)
T L C	Total Lung Capacity
T L D	Thermoluminescent Disc
T L E	Target Logistic Effect
T L M A	Truck and Ladder Manufacturers Association
T L P	Transient Lunar Phenomena
T L S	Tactical Landing System
	Trans-Lunar Shuttle
T M	Tantalum-Metal
	Transverse Mercator
T M A	Terminal Movement Area
	Trimethyl Aluminium
	Trimethylamine
	Trimethylammonium
T M C	Tata Memorial Center (India)
T M D P	Training Master Datum Plane
T M E L	Trimethylethyl Lead
T M F	Third Moment of Frequency
T M G	Thermal and Meteoroid Garment
	Trimethylgallium
T M I	Tri-monoiodide
T M M	Tantalum-Manganese Oxide-Metal
T M P	Thermo-Mechanical Processing
	Time to Maximum Precipitation
	Transversely Magnetized Plasma
T M P D	Tetramethylparaphenylenediamine
T M P T	Trimethylphosphorothionate
T M S A	Trainer Mission Simulator Aircraft
T M S O	Tetramethylene Sulphoxide
T M T	Thermo-Magnetic Treatment
	Thermo-Mechanical Treatment

355

T M T U	Tetramethylthiourea
T M X O	Tactical Miniature Crystal Oscillator
T N	Toxin-Neutralization
T N A	Transient Network Analyzer
T N C	Tetranitrocarbazole
T N F	Toxin-Neutralizing Factor
T N M	Tetronitromethane
T N P G	The Nuclear Power Group (partly Government owned)
T N R I S	Transportation Noise Research Information Service (of Highway Research Board, National Academy of Sciences (USA))
T N T	Trinitrotoluene
T O A	Total Obligational Authority
T O A / D M E	Time-of-Arrival/Distance Measuring Equipment
T O A S T	Tests, Observe, Analyse, Split, Tests
T O B	Technical Operations Board (of the Engineering Institute of Canada)
T O C	Target Optimization Control
T O C S	Terminal Operations Control System
T O D	Theoretical Oxygen Demand
T O D A	Take-Off Distance Available
T O F M S	Time Of Flight Mass Spectrometer
T O G W	Take-Off Gross Weight
T O L	Test Oriented Language
T O L A	Take-Off and Landing Analysis
T O L T S	Total On-Line Testing System
T O M M S	Terminal Operations and Movements Management System (US Army)
T O N	Threshhold Odour Number
T O O L	Test Oriented Onboard Language / Test-Oriented Operator Language
T O P I C S	Traffic Operations Program to Increase Capacity and Safety (of Federal Highway Administration (USA))
T O P O	Trioctylphosphine Oxide
T O P O C O M	Topographic Command (US Army) (now Defense Mapping Agency Topographic Center)
T O P S	Thermoelectric Outer Planet Spacecraft / Training Opportunities Scheme (of the Department of Employment)
T O P S E P	Targeting/Optimization for Solar Electric Propulsion

T O P S Y	Time-sharing Operation of Product Structure Directory System
T O R A	Take-Off Run Available
T O R C O	Treatment of Refractory Copper Ores
T O R V A P - A	Torsional Vibration Analysis Package - A
T O S	Transverse Open Stoping
T O S C A	Test of Containerized Shipments for Ammunition (US Army)
T O U R S	Tourist Observation and Underwater Research Submarine
T P	Thermoplastics
	Thermosets
T P - T	Target Practice - Tracer
T P A	Technical Publications Association (now part of Institute of Scientific and Technical Communicators)
	Thiopropionic Acid
	Triphenylamine
T P A R	Tactical Penetration Aid Rocket
T P B V	Two-Point Boundary Value
T P B V P	Two-Point Boundary Value Problem
T P C	Technical Practices Committee (of NACE (USA))
T P C V	Turbine Power Control Valve
T P D	Technical Data Package
	Technology Planning Document
T P F	Trigonometric Product Function
	Two-Photon Fluorescence
T P I	Tropical Products Institute (of ODA)
	Town Planning Institute (now Royal Town Planning Institute)
T P I C	Thermophysical Properties Information Center (Purdue University (USA))
T P L	Teacher Programming Language
	Telecommunications-oriented Programming Language
T P N H	Triphosphopyridine Nucleotide
T P P	Total Package Procurement
	Triphenylphosphine
T P R	Terrain Profile Recorder
	Thermoplastic Rubber
	Transportation Programs Report (of Applied Physics Laboratory, Johns Hopkins University (USA))
T P R E	Twin Plane Re-entrant Edge

T P R I	Tropical Pesticides Research Institute (Tanzania)
T P S	Telecommunications Programming System
	Thermal Power Station
	Thermal Protection Systems
T P X	Transportation Problem Extended
T R A	Tea Research Association (India)
	Thrust Reversers Aft
	Tire and Rim Association (USA)
T R A C	Train Regulation Advisory Control
T R A C E	Time Repetitive Analog Contour Equipment
	Transaction, Accounting, Control and Endorsing
	Tree Analysis Code
T R A C I S	Traffic Records And Criminal Justice Information System (Iowa (USA))
T R A C O N	Terminal Radar Approach Control
T R A C T I O N E L	Societe de Traction et Electricite (Belgium)
T R A C Y	Technical Reports Automated Cataloguing - Yes
T R A D E S	Transaction Reporting, Analysis, Documentation and Evaluation System
T R A D O C	Training and Doctrine Command (US Army)
T R A G	Transport Research Assessment Group (of Joint Transport Research Committee)
T R A I N	TeleRail Automated Information Network
T R A M	Target Recognition Attack Multi-sensor
T R A M M S	Transportation Automated Materiel Movements System (US Army) (now known as TOMMS)
T R A M P S	Text Information Retrieval and Management Programme System
T R A N S	Traffic Network Simulator
T R A N S L O C	Transportable LORAN-C
T R A N S M A R K	Transportation Systems and Market Research (a consultancy service of the British Railways Board)
T R A P	Tape Recorder Action Plan (a committee of NASA and AF (USA))
T R C	Technology Reports Centre (Dept. of Trade and Industry) (formerly of MINTECH)
	Tekniska Rontgencentralen (Sweden)
	Telecommunications Research Centre (of Posts and Telegraph Department (India))
T R C L	The Radiochemical Centre Limited (a public company)
T R D I	Technical Research and Development Institute (of Japan Defence Agency)

T R E E S	Tree-Structured
T R E F	Transient Radiation Effects Facility (of AFWL (USAF))
T R E X	Thermionic Reactor Experiment
T R F	Thyrotropin Releasing Factor
T R F C S	Temperature Rate Flight Control System
T R H	Thyrotropin-Releasing Hormone
T R I - T A C	Tri-Service Tactical Communications (USDOD)
T R I A	Tracking Range Instrumented Aircraft
T R I A D	Three Rivers Improvement and Development Corporation (USA) (non-profit corporation)
T R I C A P	Triple Capability
T R I C O N	Tri-Container
T R I E A	Tea Research Institute of East Africa (Kenya)
T R I M	Task Related Instructional Methodology
	Technique for Responsive Inventory Management
T R I P	Total Replenishment Inventory Programme
	Trajectory Integration Programme
	Truck Routing Improvement Procedure
T R I P S	*Talon* (USA) Reporting and Information Processing System
T R I S	Transportation Research Information Service (of Highway Research Board and Dept. of Transportation (USA))
tR N A	Transfer Ribonucleic Acid
T R O I D	Teesside Regional Organization for Industrial Development
T R O P E X	Tropical Atlantic Experiment
T R O P I C S	Tour Operators Integrated Computer System
T R R	Technical Research Report
T R R L	Transport and Road Research Laboratory (of DOE)
T R R R	Trilateration Range and Range Rate
T R S	Torry Research Station (transferred from DTI to MAFF, April 1972)
T R T	Traffic Route Tester
	Turkiye Radyo-Televizyon Kurumu (Turkey)
T R T A	Tasmanian Road Transport Association (Tasmania)
T R U N K S	Tour Reservation United Kingdom System
T R U S T	Tamper-Resistant Unattended Safeguards Techniques
	Television Relay Using Small Terminals
T R V	Transient Recovery Voltage

T S A	Trypticase Soy Agar
TS A O	Tsentral'nyy Aerologischeskaya Observatoriya (USSR) (Central Aerological Observatory)
T S C	Thermally Stimulated Conductivity
	Thermally Stimulated Current
	Transportation Systems Center (of DOT (USA))
T S D	Theory of Signal Detectability
	Towed Submersible Dry-dock
	Traffic and Safety Division (Michigan Department of State Highways (USA))
T S D A	Thermal Single-Determinant Approximation
T S E	Transmission Secondary Electron Emitters
T S E E	Thermally Stimulated Exoelectron Emission
T S F	Ten Statement FORTRAN
T S F E	Thermally Stimulated Field Emission
T S I A	Titanium Substrate Insoluble Anode
T S L	Tree Searching Language
T S L S	Two-Stage Least-Square
T S N	Thermal Severity Number
TS N I I G Ai K	Tsentral'nyy Nauchno Issledovatel'skiy Institut Geodezii Aeros'yemk i Kartografii (Central Scientific Research Institute of Geodesy, Aerial Photography and Cartography (USSR))
T S O	Technical Standards Orders (of FAA (USA))
	Time Sharing Option
T S P	Terminal Support Processor
	Travelling Salesman Problem
	Triple Super Phosphate
T S P E	Texas Society of Professional Engineers (USA)
T S P R T	Truncated Sequential Probability Ratio Tests
T S P R T R	Truncated Sequential Probability Ratio Tests for Reliability
T S P S	Traffic Service Position System
T S R S	Time Synchronized Ranging System
T S T	Truncated Sequential Test
T S T A	Tumour Specific Transplantation Antigens
T S T C	Tri-State Transportation Commission (New Jersey, New York, Connecticut (USA))
T S X	Time Sharing Executive
T T C	Toronto Transit Commission (Canada)
	Total Trichlorocompounds
	Tracking, Telemetry and Command
	Trunk-Telephone Centre
T T F - T C N Q	Tetrathiofulvalene Tetracyanoquinodimethane

T T F C	Textile Technical Federation of Canada (Canada)
T T L I C	Transistor-Transistor Logic Integrated Circuit
T T S C	Transportation and Traffic Safety Center (Pennsylvania, USA)
T T T	Time-Temperature Transformation
T T U	Texas Technological University (USA)
T T U C S	Through-Transmission Ultrasonic C-Scan
T T W S	Trunk Telecommunication Waveguide System
T T X	Tetrodotoxin
T T Y	Telephone-Teletypewriter
T U A C	Trade Union Advisory Committee (of OECD)
T U C C	Transport Users Consultative Committee
	Triangle Universities Computation Center (of Duke University, North Carolina State University and North Carolina University (USA))
T U C S I C C	Trades Union Congress Steel Industry Consultative Committee
T U E P	Tokyo University of Education, Department of Physics (Japan)
T U F	Time of Useful Function
T U L I P S	Telemetered Ultrasonic Liquid Interface Plotting System
T U P	Technology Utilization Program (of NASA (USA))
	Transfer-Under-Pressure
T U P C	Transfer-Under-Pressure Chamber
T V A - O H E S	Tennessee Valley Authority, Office of Health and Environmental Science (USA)
T V B S	Television Broadcast Satellite
T V D	Traumatic Vasospastic Disease
T V E	Television Espanola (Spain)
T V M	Track-Via-Missile
T V N	Total Volatile Nitrogen
T V O	Teollisuuden Voima Oy (Finland) (a consortium of industrial enterprises and public utilities)
T V P	Time-Varying Parameter
	True Vapour Pressure
T V R O	Television Receive Only
T V S	Transparent Fused Silica
	Triangular Voltage Sweep
	Tube Vehicle Systems
T W	Thermit Welding
T W D	Touch Wire Display
T W E R L E	Tropical Wind Energy Conversion Reference Level Experiment (of NASA (USA))

T W L C	Two Way Logic Circuits
T W S	Track While Scan
T W T	Translator Writing Tools
T W X	Teletypewriter Exchange Network *or* Service
T Y M V	Turnip Yellow Mosaic Virus

U

U - M L S	Universal Microwave Landing System
U A	Unit of Account (of EEC for the expression of monetary values)
U A C L	United Aircraft of Canada Limited (Canada)
U A H	University of Alabama in Huntsville (USA)
U A L	User Adaptive Language
U A R C	Upper Atmosphere Research Corporation (a consortium of certain universities in Canada and USA)
U A R E P	Universities Associated for Research and Education in Pathology (USA)
U A R I	University of Alabama Research Institute (USA)
U A R S	Unmanned Arctic Research Submersible
U A S	Upper Airspace
U A T S	Universal Assembly Translator System
U B C	Universal Bibliographical Control
U C A	Underground Contractors Association (USA)
U C A R	University Corporation for Atmospheric Research (USA)
U C A T	Ultra-Compact Airport Terminal
U C B	University of California, Berkeley (USA)
U C C	Universal Copyright Convention
U C E E R	Universities Council for Earthquake Engineering Research (USA)
U C I L	Uranium Corporation of India Ltd. (of Dept. of Atomic Energy (India))
U C L A - E N G	prefix to numbered series of reports issued by University of California, Los Angeles, School of Engineering and Applied Science (USA)
U C N	Ultra-Centrifuge Nederland (Netherlands)
U C N I	Unified Communications, Navigation and Identification
U C N W	University College of North Wales

U C R	University, College and Research Section (of the Library Association)
U C S	Unconfined Compress Strength test
	Underwater Combat System
	Union of Concerned Scientists (USA)
U C S B	University of California at Santa Barbara (USA)
U C S B - M E	University of California, Santa Barbara - Department of Mechanical Engineering (USA)
U C S E S M	University of California, Division of Structural Engineering and Structural Mechanics (USA)
U C S T	Upper Critical Solution Temperature
U D A T S	Underwater Damage Assessment Television System
U D C	Urban Data Center, Washington University (USA)
U D D S	Urban Dynamometer Driving Schedule (of EPA (USA))
U D E A C	Union Douaniere et Economique de l'Afrique Centrale (Central Africa Customs and Economic Union)
U D E A O	Union Douaniere des Etats de l'Afrique de l'Ouest (West African Customs Union)
U D R	Universal Document Reader
U D S	Universal Data Set
U D T	Uni-Directional Transducer
U E C	Union Europeenne des Experts Comptables Economiques et Financiers (European Union of Chartered Accountants)
U E G	Underwater Engineering Group (of CIRIA)
U E G G S P	Union Europeenne des Groupements de Grossistes Specialises en Papeterie (European Union of Groups of Wholesalers Specialising in Papermaking)
U E R S	Universal Event Recording System
U E S A	Union Electrica SA (Spain)
U E T E	Usinas Electricas y Telefonos del Estado (Uruguay)
U F	University of Florida (USA)
U F E M A T	Union des Federations Nationales des Negociants en Materiaux de Construction de la CEE (Union of National Federations of Building Materials Merchants in the EEC)
U F I	Union des Foires Internationales (France) (International Trade Fair Organisers)
U F L	Upper Flammable Limit

U F S	Ultimate Flexural Strength
U G A	University of Georgia (USA)
U G A L	Union des Groupements d'Achats de l'Alimentation (Union of Food Purchasing Groups)
U G S	Unattended Ground Sensor
U H C	Unburned Hydrocarbons
U H E L P	*University of Houston* (USA) Easy Linear Programming
U H F	Unrestricted *Hartree-Fock*
U H F M	*University of Houston* (USA) Formula Manipulation
U H M W	Ultra-High-Molecular-Weight
U H T S S	*University of Hawaii* Time-Sharing System
U H V	Ultrahigh Vacuum
U I	University of Iowa (USA)
U I C	Union Internationale des Chemins de fer (France) (International Union of Railways)
U I C C	Union Internationale Contre le Cancer (Switzerland) (International Union Against Cancer)
U I D A	Union Internationale des Organisations de Detaillants de la Branche Alimentaire (Switzerland) (International Union of Organisation of Retailers of Food)
U I E	UNESCO Institute for Education
U I J C	Universities and Industry Joint Committee
U I L I	Union Internationale des Laboratoires Independants (England) (International Union of Independent Laboratories)
U I L U	University of Illinois, Urbana (USA)
U I L U - E N G	prefix to dated-numbered series of reports issued by University of Illinois, Urbana - Coordinated Science Laboratory (USA)
U I L U - W R C	University of Illinois, Urbana, Water Resources Center (USA)
U I M	Ultra-Intelligent Machine
U I T	Unified Income Tax
U I T P	Union Internationale des Transports Publics (Belgium) (International Union of Public Transport)
U I U C D S	University of Illinois, Urbana - Department of Computer Science (USA)
U K	University of Kentucky (USA)
U K O O A	United Kingdom Offshore Operators Association
U K S A T A	United Kingdom South Africa Trade Association
U K Y	University of Kentucky (USA)

U L C S	Uniform Lightness and Chromaticity Scale
U L E	Ultra-Low Expansion glass
U L I N C	Underwater Laboratories Incorporated (USA)
U L L A	Ultra Low Level Air Dropping System
U L M S	Office of University Library Management Studies (of Association of Research Libraries (USA))
	Undersea Long-range Missile System (now known as Trident)
U L P	Universal Logic Primitive
U L T C	Urban Library Trustees Council (USA)
U M	University of Massachusetts (USA)
U M - H S R I	University of Michigan, Highway Safety Research Institute (USA)
U M - P	prefix to dated/numbered series of reports issued by University of Melbourne School of Physics (Australia)
U M C	University of Missouri-Columbia (USA)
U M E R	Ultrasonically Modulated Electron Resonance
U M I C H	University of Michigan (USA)
U M L E R	Universal Machine Language Equipment Register
U M M I P S	Uniform Materiel Movement and Issue Priority System (USDOD)
U M P	Uniformly Most Powerful
U M R	Uniform Modular Realization
U M R E C C	University of Manchester Regional Computer Centre
U M S	Undersea Medical Society (USA)
U N	The United Nations
U N A C O M A	Unione Nazionale Costruttori Macchine Agricole (Italy) (National Union of Agricultural Machinery Manufacturers)
U N C - W	University of North Carolina at Wilmington (USA)
U N C H E	The United Nations Conference on the Human Environment (the Stockholm Conference)
U N C L	Unified Numerical Control Language
U N D	Uniformly Negative Definite
	University of Notre Dame (USA)
U N F P	United Nations Environment Programme
U N E S A	Unidad Electrica SA (Spain)
U N E S C O	United Nations Educational, Scientific and Cultural Organisation (France)
U N E U R O P	European Economic Association (Switzerland)
U N E X S O	International Underwater Explorers Society

UNFPA	United Nations Fund for Population Activities (of UN)
UNH	University of New Hampshire (USA)
UNI	Ente Nazionale Italiano di Unificazione (Italy) (Italian Standards Association)
	User Node Interface
UNICCAP	Universal Cable Circuit Analysis Programme
UNICE	Union des Industries de la Communaute Europeene (National Confederation of Employers Associations of the EEC)
UNICHAL	Union Internationale des Distributeurs de Chaleur (Germany) (International Union of Heating Distributors)
UNIHEDD	Universal Head-Down Display
UNINSA	Union de Siderurgicas Asturianas SA (Spain)
UNIQUE	Unified Command Interface with a Queued User Job Environment
UNISIST	UNESCO/ICSU World Science Information System
UNISOR	University Isotope Separator - *Oak Ridge* (USA)
UNISTAR	User Network for Information Storage, Transfer, Acquisition and Retrieval
UNISURV	prefix to numbered series of reports issued by the School of Surveying, University of New South Wales (Australia)
UNOLS	University-National Oceanographic Laboratory System (USA)
UNOTC	United Nations Office of Technical Co-operation (UN)
UNREP	Underway Replenishment
UNRWA	United Nations Relief and Works Agency (of UN)
UNTS	Undergraduate Navigator Training System (USAF)
UOMC	University of Oklahoma Medical Center (USA)
UPACS	*Univac* Patient Accounting and Control System
UPD	Uniformly Positive Definite
UPIC	Universal Personal Identification Code
UPL	Universal Programming Language
UPPS	Unified Pilot Publication System (of Chemical Abstracts Service of the American Chemical Society (USA))
UPRICO	University of Puerto Rico
UPS	Underwater Physiology Sub-committee (of the Royal Naval Personnel Research Committee)
	Unidirectional Point Source
UPSD	Uniformly Positive Semi-Definite

U P U	Universal Postal Union (Switzerland) (of UN)
U R A N I T	Uran-Isotopentrennungs-Gesellschaft (Germany)
U R D	Underground Residential Distribution
U R E N C O	Uranium Enrichment Company (shareholders are United Kingdom, Netherlands and Federal Republic of Germany)
U R E S	University Residence Environment Scale
U R G	United Reprocessors GmbH (Germany) (a company with share capital provided by United Kingdom, France and Federal Republic of Germany)
U R I S	Universal Resources Information Symposium
U R I S A	Urban and Regional Information Systems Association (USA)
U R M	Uniform Reflectivity Mirror
U R M S	Universal Reproducing Matrix System
U R S I	Union Radio-Scientifique Internationale (of ICSU) (International Scientific Radio Union)
U R S I E S	Ultravariable Resolution Single Interferometer Echelle Scanner
U R T	Underground Residential Transformer
U R T I	Universite Radiophonique et Televisuelle Internationale (France)
U R T N A	Union of National Radio and Television Organizations of Africa
U R V	Underwater Research Vehicle
U S A A A	United States Army Audit Agency
U S A A A V S	United States Army Agency for Aviation Safety
U S A A M R D L	United States Army Air Mobility Research and Development Laboratory
U S A A R D C	United States Army Aberdeen (Maryland) Research and Development Center
U S A A R L	United States Army Aeromedical Research Laboratory
U S A A S L	United States Army Atmospheric Sciences Laboratory
U S A A S O	United States Army Aeronautical Services Office
U S A A S T A	United States Army Aviation Systems Test Activity
U S A A V A	United States Army Audio-Visual Agency
U S A A V S C O M	United States Army Aviation Systems Command
U S A B E S R L	United States Army Behavioral Science Research Laboratory (now part of ARI (US Army))
U S A C C	United States Army Communications Command

USACCS	United States Army Chemical Center and School
USACEEIA	United States Army Communications-Electronics Engineering Installation Agency
USACRREL	United States Army Cold Regions Research and Engineering Laboratory
USACSSEC	United States Army Computer Systems Support and Evaluation Command
USAFE	United States Air Forces in Europe
USAFETAC	United States Air Force Environmental Technical Applications Center
USAFSS	United States Air Force Security Service
USAICA	United States Army Inter-agency Communications Agency
USAISR	United States Army Institute of Surgical Research
USALMC	United States Army Logistics Management Center
USAMBRDL	United States Army Medical Bioengineering Research and Development Laboratory
USAMBRL	United States Army Medical Biomechanical Research Laboratory
USAMECOM	United States Army Mobility Equipment Command
USAMMAE	United States Army Material Management Agency
USAMRDC	United States Army Medical Research and Development Command
USAMRIID	United States Army Medical Research Institute of Infectious Diseases
USAMRRDC	United States Army Manpower Resources Research and Development Center
USAMSSA	United States Army Management Systems Support Agency
USARBCO	United States Army Base Command
USAREUR-MATCOM	United States Army, Europe, Materiel Command
USARP	United States Antarctic Research Program (of NSF (USA))
USASAFS-COM	United States Army Safeguard Systems Command
USATOPO-COM	United States Army Topographic Command
USATTC	United States Army Tropic Test Center
USAWECOM	United States Army Weapons Command
USB	Unified S-Band

U S B	Upper Sideband
U S B A	United States Brewers Association (USA)
U S B R	United States Bureau of Reclamation (of Dept. of the Interior)
U S C	Underwater Systems Center (USN)
U S C A E	University of Southern California, Department of Aerospace Engineering (USA)
U S C A R	United States Civil Administration, Ryukyu Islands
U S C E E	University of Southern California, Electronic Sciences Laboratory (USA)
U S C G S	United States Coast and Geodetic Survey (of NOAA (USA))
U S C O N A R C	United States Continental Army Command
U S C S C	United States Civil Service Commission
U S D A - A P H I S - P P / Q	United States Department of Agriculture, Animal and Plant Health Inspection Service, Plant Protection and Quarantine Programs (USA)
U S D A - F S	United States Department of Agriculture - Forest Service (USA)
U S D A - R E A	United States Department of Agriculture - Rural Electrification Administration (USA)
U S F S	United States Forestry Service (USA)
U S G W	Underwater Launched Anti-Surface Ship Guided Weapon
U S I A S	Union Syndicale des Industries Aeronautiques et Spatiales (France) (Aerospace Industries Association)
U S I T A	United States Independent Telephone Association (USA)
U S I T E	United States International Transportation Exposition (USA)
U S L	Underwater Sound Laboratory (USN) (now Naval Underwater Systems Center)
	University of Southwestern Louisiana (USA)
	Urban Systems Laboratory (Massachusetts Institute of Technology (USA))
U S M C E B	United States Military Communications Electronics Board (USA)
U S N A	United States Naval Academy (USN)
U S N A V E U R	United States Navy - Europe
U S N D C	United States Nuclear Data Committee (of USAEC)
U S N T P S	United States Naval Test Pilot School (USN)

U S P	Ultra-Short Pulses
U S P O	United States Patents Office (USA)
U S P S	United States Postal Service (USA)
	United States Power Squadrons (USA)
U S R D	Underwater Sound Reference Division (of Naval Research Laboratory (USN))
U S S	Unsmoked Sheets
U S S A	Unified Systems Safety Analysis
U S V R U	Ultra-Stable Voltage Reference Unit
U S W	Ultra-Sonic Welding
U S Y M	Universal Sequential Synchronous Machine
U T	Universal Time
U T - G S B S	University of Texas - Graduate School of Bio-medical Sciences (USA)
U T - L C P	University of Texas Laboratory of Comparative Pharmacology (USA)
U T C	Urban Technology Conference (USA)
U T C S	Urban Traffic Control System
U T D	University of Texas at Dallas (USA)
U T E	Union Technique de l'Electricite (France) (Technical Union of Electricity)
	Usinas Electricas y Telefonos del Estado (Uruguay) (Uruguay Communications Agency)
U T M U	University of Tennessee, Medical Units (USA)
U T R A O	University of Texas Radio Astronomy Observatory (USA)
U T U	Universidad del Trabajo del Uruguay (Uruguay) (Technical University)
U T X - A / P	prefix to dated-numbered series of reports issued by University of Texas Antennas and Propagation Laboratory (USA)
U U M	Unification of Units of Measurement (a panel of ICAO)
U U M P	Unification of Units of Measurement Panel (of ICAO)
U U P I	Ultrasonic Under-carriage Position Indicator
U U T	Unit Under Test
U V A S	Unmanned Vehicle for Aerial Surveillance
U V L	Ultra-Violet Laser
U V M	University of Vermont (USA)
U V M - T I C	University of Vermont Technical Information Center (USA)
U V S	Ultra-Violet Spectrometer
U V S C	Ultra-Violet Solar Constants

U W	Upset Welding
U W D O B E R	University of Wyoming, Division of Business and Economic Research (USA)
U W I	University of the West Indies (Jamaica)
U W I / C C	University of the West Indies Computing Centre
U W I S	University of Wisconsin (USA)
U W I S - D S	University of Wisconsin - Department of Statistics (USA)
U W O	University of Western Ontario (Canada)
U W T V	Under-Water Television

V

V - C M	Visual Counter Measures
V A	Visual Aids (a panel of ICAO)
	Viterbi Algorithm
V A A C	Vanadyl Acetyl Acetonate
V A B	Vehicle Assembly Building (John F. Kennedy Space Center, NASA (USA))
V A B M	Value Added By Manufacturer
V A C	Volt-Ampere Characteristics
V A D	Variable Abbreviated Dialling
	Velocity-Azimuth Display
V A D S	*Vulcan* Air Defence System
V A G E S	Variable Geometry Simulator
V A I	Video Assisted Instruction
V A K U M E	Visual Audio Kinetic Unit: Multiples and Environments
V A L U E	Validated Aircraft Logistics Utilization Evaluation
V A M	Vinyl Acetate Monomer
	Virtual Access Method
	Visual Approach Monitor
V A M F O	Variable Angle Monochromatic Fringe Observation
V A M P	Value Analysis of Management Practices
V A M S	Vector Airspeed Measuring System
V A N D A	Vision And Audio
V A P	Video-Audio-Participative
	Visual Aids Panel (of ICAO)
V A P I	Visual Approach Path Indicator
V A R	Vacuum-Arc Remelting
	Visual-Aural Range

V A R I G	Empresa de Viacao Aerea Rio Grandense (Brazil)
V A R S D A	Vehicular Actuated Road Signal Development Association
V A S	Virginia Association of Surveyors (USA)
V A S P	Viacao Aereo Sao Paulo (Brazil)
V B B	Vattenbyggnadsbyran (Sweden)
V B D	Veterinary Biologics Division (of ARS (USDA))
V B O	Vsesoyuznyy Botanicheskoye Obshchestvo (USSR) (All-union Botanical Society)
V C	Vanadium Carbide
V C G	Vector Cardiogram Voltage-Controlled Generator
V C M	Verification Comparison Matrix Vinyl Chloride Monomer
V C O A D	Voluntary Committee on Overseas Aid and Development
V C R	Variable-Compression-Ratio Video Cassette Recorder *or* Recording Voltage Coefficient of Resistance
V C S	Voter-Comparator Switch
V C T S	Variable Cockpit Training System
V C V S	Voltage Controlled Voltage Source
V D A L	Variable Datalength Assembly Language
V D M	Vector Dominance Model Vector Drawn Map
V D M A	Variable Destination Multiple Access
V D N C S	Vapour Deposited Non-Crystalline Solid
V D P	Verband Deutscher Papierfabriken (Germany) (German Papermaking Association)
V D P I	Verband der Deutschen Photographischen Industrie (Germany) (Association of the German Photographic Industry)
V D R	Voltage-Dependent Resistor
V D R / E D C	Economic Development Committee for Vehicle Distribution and Repair
V D T	Variable Deflection Thruster
V D W	Verein Deutscher Werkzeugmaschinenfabriken (Germany) (Association of German Machine-Tool Manufacturers)
V E A	Virginia Electronic Association (USA)
V E B	Volkseigener Betrieb (People's Concern)
V E C	Ventricular Ectopic Complex
V E C O R	Vanderbijl Engineering Corporation (South Africa)

V E D C	Vitreous Enamel Development Council
V E E	Venezuelan Equine Encephalomyelitis
V E M G	Vector Electro-myography
V E N U S	Vertical alignment design by the Nodal-tangent and Undulation System
V E O	Verband der Elektrizitatswerke Osterreichisches (Austria)
V E P	Visual Evoked Potential
V E R	Visual Evoked Response
V E R A	Variable Eddington Radiation Approximation
V E R A S	Vehicle for Experimental Research in Aerodynamics and Structures
V E R B	Visual Electronic Remote Blackboard
V E R S A	Vehicle Routing and Scheduling Algorithm
V E R T R E P	Vertical Replenishment
V E S P E R	Vehicles and Equipments Spare Parts Economics and Repair
V E T R A S	Vehicle Traffic Simulator
V F	Voice Frequency
V F A	Volatile Fatty Acids
V F C T	Voice Frequency Carrier Telegraphy
V F M E D	Variable Format Message Entry Device
V F T	Voice-Frequency Telegraph
V F V C	Vacuum-Freezing Vapour-Compression desalting process
V G I	Vertical Gyro Instrument
V G P	Virtual Geomagnetic Poles
V H F R T	Very High Frequency Radio Telephony
V H R C	Virginia Highway Research Council (USA)
V H R R	Very High Resolution Radiometer
V I	Voltage and Inductance
V I A S A	Venezolana Internacional de Aviacion SA (Venezuela)
V I B A C	Vehicle Ice-Breaking - Air Cushion
V I B A N K	computerised information retrieval system on Mechanical Vibration (University Laval (Canada))
V I C C	Visual Information Control Console
V I C O M	International Association of Visual Communications Management
V I C S	Vehicles In Confined Spaces
V I D - R	Visual Information Display and Retrieval system

V I D A	Ventricular Impulse Detector and Alarm
V I D E C	Vibration and Deviation Concept
V I D E O	Visual Inspection of Defects Enhanced by Optics
V I D P I	Visually Impaired Data Processors International (USA)
V I E	Vacuum Insulated Evaporator
V I E W	Video Information Exchange Window
V I F	Visible Index File
V I F F	Vectoring In Forward Flight
V I M	Vacuum Induction Melting
V I M S	Versatile Interior Multiplex System
	Virginia Institute of Marine Sciences (USA)
V I N S	Very Intense Neutron Source
V I P	Verifying Interpreting Punch
V I R	Vertical Interval Reference
V I S Q I	Visual Image Quality Indicator
V I S S R	Visible Infra-red Spin-Scan Radiometer
V I T A	Volunteers for International Technical Assistance (USA)
V I T A L	VAST Interface Test Application Language
V I T E A C	Video Transmission Engineering Advisory Committee (USA)
V I T M	Visvesvaraya Industrial and Techological Museum (India)
V L B C	Very Large Bulk-cargo Carrier
V L C C	Very Large Crude-oil Carrier
V L E D	Visible Light Emitting Diode
V L O O C	Very Large Ore-Oil Carrier
V L P	Video Long Playing records
V M A	Vanillylmandelic Acid
	Virginia Microfilm Association (USA)
V M H	Video Graphics System Message Handler
V M I	Variable Moment of Inertia
V M O S	Virtual Memory Operating System
V M R C	Veterinary Medical Research Council (University of Missouri (USA))
V M S	Vertical Market Structure
V M V	Ventromedial Nucleus
V N	Virus Neutralising
V N I I K I	Vsesoyuznyy Nauchno Issledovatel'skiy Institut Tekhnicheskoi Informatsii i Kodirovaniya (USSR) (All-Union Scientific Research Institute of Technical Information, Classification and Coding)

V N I I M I	Vsesoyuznyy Nauchno Issledovatel'skiy Institut Meditsinskoy i Medikotekhnichesoy Informatsii (USSR) (All-Union Scientific Research Institute of Medical and Medico-technical Information)
V N I I S	Vsesoyuznyy Nauchno Issledovatel'skiy Institut Standartizatsii (USSR) (All-Union Scientific Research Institute of Standardisation)
V O D	Vertical Onboard Delivery
V O M	Volt-Ohm-Milliameter
V O R	Very - high - frequency Omni - directional Radio Range
V O R T A C	Visual Omni-Range Tactical radar
V O R T E X	*Varian (Data Machines)* Omnitask Real-Time Executive
V O S C	VAST Operating System Code
V P A	Variance Partition Analysis
V P B	Ventricular Premature Beat
V P C	Ventricular Premature Contractions Vertical Path Computer
V P I	Vacuum-Pressure Impregnation Vertical Position Indicator
V P I - W R R C	Virginia Polytechnic Institute - Water Resources Research Center (USA)
V P T A R	Variable Parameter Terrain Avoidance Radar
V R A	Value Received Analysis Voltage Regulating Amplifier
V R C	Versatile Remote Copier Visible Record Computer
V R C C C	Vandenberg Range Communications Control Center (USAF)
V R D U	Variable Range Delay Unit
V R I	Vehicle Research Institute (of SAE (USA))
V R M	Variable Reflectivity Mirror
V S A M	Vestigial Sideband Amplitude Modulation
V S C	Video Scan Converter
V S D	Voter-Switch-Disagreement Detector
V S F	Volume Scattering Function
V S I	Vapour Space Inhibiting
V S P X	Vehicle Scheduling Programme Extended
V S S	Variable-Structure System Video Supervision System
V S S C	Vikram Sarabhai Space Centre (of ISRO (India))
V S T	Variable Stability Trainer
V S T A	Virus-Specified Tumour Antigens

V S V	Vesicular Stomatitis Virus
V T A	Vapour Trace Analyzer
V T A M	Virtual Telecommunications Access Method
V T A S	Visual Target Acquisition System
V T C	Vibratory Torque Control
V T E	Vertical Tube Evaporator
V T G	Volume of Thoracic Gas
V T M	Versatile Tracking Mount
V T M S	Vinyltrimethylsilane
V T O V L	Vertical Take-Off and Vertical Landing
V T P	Verification Test Plan
V T P R	Vertical Temperature Profile Radiometer
V T S	Vessel Traffic System
V U E C	Variable Underwater Experimental Community
V U P C H	Vyzkumny Ustav Prumyslove Chemie (Czechoslovakia) (Research Institute for Industrial Chemistry)
V W F	Vibration-induced White Fingers
V W R S	Vibrating Wire Rate Sensor

W

W / C	Water/Cement ratio
W A	Widescreen Association
W A A C	Western Australian Chamber of Commerce (Australia)
W A A S	World Academy of Art and Science (Israel)
W A C	Women's Advisory Committee (of BSI) (now Consumer Standards Advisory Committee)
W A C A	World Airline Clubs Association
W A C C	World Association for Christian Communication
W A I M	Wide-Angle Impedance Matching
W A I S	Wechsler Adult Intelligence Scale
W A I T	Western Australia Institute of Technology (Australia)
W A I T R O	World Association of Industrial and Technological Research Organizations (Canada)
W A L R U S	Water and Land Resource Utilization Simulation
W A M F L E X	Wave Momentum Flux Experiment
W A M I	Wide-Angle Michelson Interferometer
W A M L	Western Association of Map Libraries (USA)
W A M R A C	World Association of Methodist Radio Amateurs and Clubs (England)

W A M S	Weapon Aiming Mode Selector
W A N D	*Westinghouse* Alpha-Numeric Display
W A N D A	Water Network Distribution Analyser
W A N D E R E R	*Paul S-H Wang's* Definite Integral Evaluator
W A R C - S T	World Administrative Radio Conference for Space Telecommunications (of ITU)
W A R D E N	*Warwick* (University) Data Engineering system
W A R P A T H	Wadkin Automatic Remote Processor Accessed via Terminals
W A R S	Warfare Analysis and Research System
	Western Agricultural Research Station (Kenya)
	Worldwide Ammunition Reporting System (US Army)
W A S A L	Wisconsin Academy of Sciences, Arts and Letters (USA)
W A S A R	Wide Application Systems Adapters
W A S H O	Western Association of State Highway Officials (USA)
W A S P	Waveform And Spectral-analysis Programme
	Williams (Research Corporation) (USA) Aerial Systems Platform
W A T F I V	*Waterloo* (University) (Canada) FORTRAN IV
W A W F	World Association of World Federalists
W B	Weather Bureau (formerly of ESSA now of NOAA (USA))
	Women's Bureau (Dept. of Labor (USA))
W B A A	Wholesale Booksellers Association of Australia (Australia)
W B C	White Blood Cell
W B O	Wien Bridge Oscillator
W B G T I	Wet Bulb Globe Temperature Index
W B N M M U M A	West Bengal Non-ferrous Metal Merchants and Utensils Merchants Association (India)
W B P T	Wet-Bulb Potential Temperature
W B T M	Weather Bureau (formerly of ESSA now of NOAA (USA)) Technical Memoranda
W B T M - E D	prefix to series of numbered Technical Memoranda issued by Weather Bureau, Equipment Development Laboratory (formerly of ESSA now of NOAA (USA))
W B T M - E R	Weather Bureau Technical Memoranda - Eastern Region (formerly of ESSA now of NOAA (USA))

W B T M - N M C	prefix to numbered series of Technical Memoranda issued by the National Meteorological Center of the Weather Bureau (formerly of ESSA now of NOAA (USA))
W B T M - P R	prefix to numbered series of Technical Memoranda issued by Weather Bureau, Pacific Region (formerly of ESSA now of NOAA (USA))
W B T M - S R	prefix to series of numbered memoranda issued by the Weather Bureau, Southern Region (formerly of ESSA now of NOAA (USA))
W B T M - T D L	prefix to numbered series of Technical Memoranda issued by the Weather Bureau Techniques Development Laboratory (formerly of ESSA now of NOAA (USA))
W B T M - W R	prefix to numbered series of Technical Memoranda issued by the Weather Bureau, Western Region (formerly of ESSA now of NOAA (USA))
W B V T R	Wideband Video Tape Recorder
W C C F	West Coast Cancer Foundation (USA)
W C E E	World Conference on Earthquake Engineering
W C G	Water Cooled Garment
W C P T	World Confederation of Physical Therapy
W C Q L	Worst Cycle Quality Level
W C S	Water Colour Spectrometer
	Waveguide Communication System
	Writeable Control Store
W D	Working Document
W D E L	Weapons Development and Engineering Laboratories (US Army)
W D F M	Wright Dust Feed Mechanism
W D P C	Western Data Processing Center (University of California (USA))
W D R	Westdeuscher Rundfunk (Germany)
W D S	Wavelength Dispersive Spectrometer
W E A A	Western Europe Airport Association
W E C	World Energy Conference
W E D S	Weapons Effects Display System
W E E	Western Equine Encephalitis
W E I S	World Event/Interaction Survey
W E M T	West European Conference on Marine Technology
W E S	Welding Engineering Society (Japan)
W E S D A C	*Westinghouse* Data Acquisition and Control
W E S D E X	Western Design Engineering Exposition (USA)

378

W E S T A R	*Western Union* (*Telegraph Company*) (USA) domestic satellite communications system
W E S T E C	Western Metal and Tool Exposition and Conference (USA)
W E T S	West European Triangulation Subcommission (of International Association of Geodesy)
W F D	World Federation of the Deaf
W F M U	Weather and Fixed-Map Unit
W F O T	World Federation of Occupational Therapists
W F S	Waterborne Feeder Services
W F S A	World Federation of Societies of Anaesthesiologists
W F T	Walsh-Fourier Transform
W F U N A	World Federation of United Nations Associations
W G A	Wheat Germ Agglutinin
W G N	White Gaussian Noise
W H A	World Health Assembly (of WHO (UN))
W H C A	*White House* Communications Agency (USA)
W H O	World Health Organisation (of UN) (Switzerland)
W H T	Walsh-Hadamard Transform
W I A S	West Indies Associated States
W I C H E	Western Interstate Commission on Higher Education (USA)
W I H C	Western Industrial Health Conference (USA)
W I M	Weight-In-Motion system
	Wirtschaftsvereininigung Industrielle Meerestechnik (Germany) (Industrial Ocean Technology Association)
W I N C O N	Aerospace & Electronics Systems Winter Convention (of IEEE (USA))
W I N D E E	Wind Tunnel Data Encoding and Evaluation
W I P O	World International Property Organisation (Switzerland)
W I R A	Wool Industries Research Association (now known as Wira)
	Wool Institute Research Association (USA)
W I S - S G	prefix to dated-numbered series of reports issued by Wisconsin University, Sea Grant Program (USA)
W I S D O M	*Wall's* (T. Wall & Sons (Ice Cream Ltd.) Information System from Depot Order Mechanisation

W I T C H	*Wolverhampton (Polytechnic)* Instrument for Teaching Computation from Harwell (a computer now in the Birmingham Museum of Science and Industry)
W I T S	*University of Waterloo* (Canada) Interactive Terminal System
W M A	World Medical Assembly
W M C	World Meteorological Centre
W M O	World Meteorological Organisation (of UN) (Switzerland)
W M R G	Water Management Research Group (of OECD)
W M S	World Magnetic Survey (of ICSU)
W M S C	Weather Message Switching Center (of FAA (USA))
W M T R	Wheeled Mobility Test Rig
W N A R	Western North American Region of the Biometric Society
W N T V	Western Nigerian Television (Nigeria)
W P	White Phosphorus
W P I	Whey Products Institute (USA)
W P L	Wave Propagation Laboratory (formerly of ESSA now of NOAA (USA))
W P O	Water Programs Office (of EPA (USA))
	World Packaging Organization (England)
	World Ploughing Organisation
W P R L	Water Pollution Research Laboratory (formerly of MINTECH transferred to DOE, 1971)
W P R S	prefix to dated/numbered series of World Power Reactors Summaries issued by AEEW (UKAEA)
W Q O	Water Quality Office (of EPA (USA)) now (Water Programs Office)
W R A	Wool Research Association (India)
W R A P S	Workload and Repair Activity Process Simulator
W R B	Water Resources Board
W R C	Water Resources Center (Illinois University (USA))
W R K	Westdeutsche Rektorenkonferenz (West German Rectors Conference)
W R L	Willow Run Laboratories (Michigan University (USA))
W R M	prefix to dated-numbered series of reports issued by Naval Personnel Research and Development Laboratory (USN)
W R R C	Water Resources Research Center (Minnesota University (USA))

W R R I	Water Resources Research Institute (Clemson University (USA))
W S	Watershed
W S A	Weapon System Automation
W S E C	Washington State Electronics Council (USA)
W S I M	Water Separation Index, Modified
W S L	Warren Spring Laboratory (formerly of MINTECH now of DTI)
	Weldbund zum Schultze des Lebens (World Union for the Protection of Life)
W S P	Wheel Slide Protection
W S R N	Western Satellite Research Network (USA)
W S T I	Welded Steel Tube Institute (USA)
W S U	Washington State University (USA)
W S U - S D L	Washington State University - Shock Dynamics Laboratory (USA)
W T O	World Tourism Organization
W V A L S	West Virginia Association of Land Surveyors (USA)
W V T R	Water Vapour Transmission Rate
W V U	West Virginia University (USA)
W W E M A	Water and Waste-water Equipment Manufacturers Association (USA)
W W F	World Wildlife Fund
W W P	World Weather Programme
W W P T	Welded Wide-Plate Tests
W W S C	World Wide Soundings Committee
W W W	World Weather Watch (of WMO (UN))

X

X D U P	Extended Disk Utilities
Xe C F	Xenon Collateral Flow
X E L E D O P	Transmitting Elementary Dipole with Optional Polarization
X E R B	Experimental Environmental Reporting Buoy
X L D	Experimental Laser Device
X L T	Experimental Lunar Tyres
X M C	Experimental Magic Carpet
X R C	Extended Response Colour
X R D	X-Ray Diffractometry
X R E D	X-Ray Analysis by Energy Dispersion
X R F / N A A	X-Ray Fluorescence Neutron Activation Analysis

X R T	X-Ray Topographical
X S T D	Expendable Ocean Salinity, Temperature, Depth Measuring system

Y

Y C F	Yacimientos Carboniferos Fiscales (Argentina)
Y D T	Yttria-Doped Thoria
Y L S	Yale Legislative Services (Yale University (USA))
Y P F	Yacimientos Petroliferos Fiscales (Argentina)
Y P F B	Yacimientos Petroliferos Fiscales Bolivianos (Bolivia) (State Oil Organisation)

Z

Z A B	Zinc-Air Battery
Z A M	Zinc, Aluminium, Magnesium
Z A M S	Zero-Age Main-Sequence
Z D D P	Zinc Dialkylidithiophosphate
Z D F	Zweites Deutches Fernsehen (Germany)
Z D M D C	Zinc Dimethyldithiocarbamate
Z D P P	Zinc Di-alkyl/aryl Dithiophosphates
Z D T	Zero-Ductility Temperature
Z F M A	Zip Fasteners Manufacturers Association (India)
Z I M C O	Zambian Industrial and Mining Corporation (Zambia) (state owned)
Z I P	Zone Improvement Plan (USA)
Z M B T	Zinc Benzothiazolyl Mercaptide
Z M C	Zero-Magnetostrictive Composition
Z N R	Zinc-oxide Non-linear Resistor
Z O L D	Zeroth Order Logarithmic Distribution
Z R B S C	Zirconium Boride Silicon Carbide
Z S O B	Zinc-Silver-Oxide Battery
Z V L	Zentrale Verkaufsleitung (of DB (Germany)) (Central Marketing Department)

Chemistry
ABA, ADA, AGD, AHH, AIC, AUCET, CCL, CEPACC, CID, CLAQ, CMC, CROSSBOW, CS, CSCE, CSMCRI, EDC, FACSS, FECS, IDC, IPC, IPCR, IUPAC, KNCV, LIS, LNEC, LSR, MCC, NChemL, NCL, NCML, NCRL, NRCC, NZIC, OKhN, PCIC, RACI, THFA, TPRE, TSDA, VTA

Chromatography
GC, GCDC, GZC, HPLC, ITLC, LC, LLC, LSC, LXC, LZC, PGC

Civil engineering (see also Building, Structural engineering)
BACEA, CEPA, CESL, COBRA, COHART, CRAM, CSCE, ISTRAN/PL, JSCERDGG, LUCID, NAMC, NTCA, POLO, SCET, SPT, STRAIN, TFRAN

Clocks and watches
AWI, JWCA

Coal and coke
ACIRL, BCCL, BCURA, CEDOCOS, CIS, HSC, NCDC, SASOL, SCM, SFAS, TCOA

Coating
CCA, CCL, CSCR, MDR, MIDOC, NPCA, TCC

Cocoa
CRIN

Coffee
ACICAFE, ASIC

Colour
AIC, MCCA

Combustion engineering
ECPE

Commerce see Trade

Computers see Data processing

Concrete
AC, ASCC, BFL, CAI, CCRL, CMP, CPA, CPP, CPV, GRC, MPCA, NCMA, PCC, PUNDIT, RTL

Construction (see Building, Civil engineering, Structural engineering)

Consumer organisations
ACA, ACAP, CPA, CPEHS, CPICC, CPSC, CSAC, IOCU, ISCA, NBCCA, WAC

Containerisation see Packaging

Contamination (see also Pollution)
ICCCS

Control engineering
CAMA, CAMAC, INAP, JACC, TACMA

Copper
CDA, CIPEC, HCL, INCRA, SAE CA, TORCO

Corrosion
ACA, BJCG, CAPA, CAPAC, CASS, CCOH, CEFRACOR, CETA, ICCP, ICT, ISPCC, KI, NCCS, NKF, PSCLC, TPC, VSI

Cosmetics
IFSCC

Cotton see Textiles

Cranes (see also Materials handling)
CMMA

Cryogenics
BCC, CDC, CSA, CSS

Cybernetics
AIC, ASC, CERCI, CS, IAC

Cyclones
ISU-CCL

CUMARC, CUPID, CVS, DACC, DACE, DAD, DADC, DADEC, DADIOS, DAD-PTC, DADS, DAI, DAISY, DAMID, DAMN, DAMUSC, DAPR, DARA, DARE, DART, DASD, DASYS, DAT, DATAS, DATGEN, DAWNS, DBBOL, DBDL, DBL, DBMS, DBOS, DBTG, DCOL, DCPL, DCRT, DCS, DDF, DDL, DDLC, DEEP, DELDIS, DELIMITER, DEMON, DEMOS, DEPLOC, DES, DEVIL, DFLD, DI, DIAL, DIALATOR, DIALS, DIC, DICAP, DIDO, DIECAST, DIME, DIMES, DIRAC, DISCOP, DISCUS, DISFP, DISSPLA, DLP, DLS, DMAC, DMACS, DML, DMTG, DMTS, DNC, DOCS, DOCTOR, DOLAN, DOMEX, DORIS, DPS, DRESS, DRIFT, DRL, DRUGR, DSL, DSO, DSS, DTC, DTOL, DTSS, DUAL, DUNMIRE, DYDE, DYNAMO, DYNASAR, DYNSYS, EARL, EARS, ECAM, ECCP, ECIP, ECMA, ECODU, ECSL, ECSS, EDC, EDINET, EDMF, EDP, EDRS, EFOP, EICON, EIS, ELAMP, ELAS, ELCA, ELECSYS, ELMS, ELRAFT, ELSA, EMAS, EMMA, EMOS, EMPHASIS, ENCORE, EPIC, EPSS, ERAP, ERB, ERIA, ERNIE, ESAR, ESCANT, ESDL, ESF, ESP, ESS ADF, ETA/MDUSAS, ETA/NAME, ETC, ETNS, ETS, EUCLID, EX-APT, FACEL, FACT, FACTAN, FADES, FAMS, FAMSNUB, FAPS, FARS, FAST, FATAL, FCCTS, FDEP, FDP, FDS, FEABL, FEASIBLE, FEEDBAC, FEFI, FESS, FETE, FGRAAL, FICO, FINDER, FIPS-PUB, FLAG, FLAMES, FLEXMIS, FM, FMR, FNAP, FOCAL, FOCAS, FOCS, FOCUS, FOPS, FOREM, FORMAL, FORMS, FOSIL, FPS, FRACAS, FRAT, FRED, FRELIS, FTR, FTS, FURST, FUS, GAATS, GAP, GBRP, GCCA, GCOS, GCSC, GDMS, GEA, GEMCS, GEMS, GENE-SES, GENIRAS, GEO, GESPL, GFI, GINA, GINO, GINO F, GIPSY, GISP, GLIM, GLOL, GLOPR, GLP, GMD, GMS, GNATS, GOD, GOLD STAR, GOS, GOSS+P, GOSSIP, GPAP,

GPDL, GPLS, GPP, GPYS, GRAFLAN, GRAID, GRAPHIDI, GRAPHSYS GRASS, GREAT, GRIND, GRIPS, GRS, GTOL, GUERAP, GUTS, HADIOS, HAISAM, HASP/RJE, HCSS, HDAS, HDB, HEALS, HECAD, HECB, HELP, HIDECS, HIS, HLS, HNR, HOPS, HSL, HUW, HYDAS, IAF, IAG, IAL, IAM, IATAE, IBI-ICC, IBIS, IBSAT, ICA, ICADS, ICAM, ICC, ICCC, ICCP, ICELA, ICR, ICRMS, ICSL, IDA, IDADS, IDAPS, IDEA, IDIIOM, IDTS, IECCA, IEDS, IFA, IFAM, IFAPT, IFL, IGTS, IMCAS, IMD, IML, IMMAC, IMP, IMPACT, IMPICS, IMS, IMTRAN, INAP, INCRAPLAN, INFLO, INFO, INFORMAC, INFOR-MAP, INGA, INSIGHT, INSPECT, INTASS, INTIME, IOP, IPAD, IPARS, IPM, IPS, IPSJ, IPSO, IRIA, IRL, IRMA, ISDOS, ISDS, ISFMS, ISIJU, ISIS, ISL, ISM, ISMAP, ISODATA, ISP, ISPA, ISPICE, ISPL, ISTRAN/PL, ISU-CCL, ITF, ITMC, IVCS, JCL, JCUDI, JCVS, JECC, JETS, JPL-STAR, JSS, JUSSIM, KOS, LABORIA, LAL, LAMBDA, LASAR, LBJCC, LCCP, LDL, LDOS, LEAF, LEAP, LEAPS, LEEP, LEMRAS, LERSC, LESA-A-A, LFRAP, LIDIA, LIL, LINCO, LINCS, LIS, LISP, LISTAR, LITE, LITS, LMICS, LMIS, LOGMIS, LOLA, LOLITA, LOPAC, LORA, LOS, LPS, LSNLIS, LSP, LUCID, LUCS, LUST, LVRCN, LWSS, M&FCS, MABUS, MACDAC, MACE, MADARS, MAGEN, MAGIC, MAGPIE, MAI, MAO, MAP, MAPLE, MAPS, MARC, MARCS, MARS, MAS, MASC, MASH, MASSOP, MATE, MATPS, MATS, MBASIC, MCAP, MCC, MCIS, MCL, MCU, MDS, MDTS, MECA, MEDALS, MEDHOC, MEDIS, MEDISTARS, MEDLINE, MEMBERS, MENDAP, MERIT, MFCS, MGRL, MIAS, MIDAS, MIDS, MIF, MINCIS, MIND, MINDEN, MINERVA, MINTS, MIPAS, MIS, MISAR, MISTRESS, MLAB, MMIS, MOBSSL-UAF, MOCA,

MODAPS, MODCON, MODS, MOFACS,
MOLE, MOMS, MOPS, MOSAICS,
MOST, MPDS, MPIS, MPL, MPSX,
MPX, MRIS, MRMS, MRPPS, MSIS,
MTC, MTMT, MTS, MULTIPAC,
MUMPS, MURS, MUSE, MUT, MUX,
NACTAC, NASDAQ, NASIS, NCCDPC,
NCECS, NCP, NCPI, NCS, NELAPT,
NFLDS, NIMMS, NIMROD, NIPS,
NOAH, NOLAP, NSFORT, NST,
NUCOL, NUMEPS, NUSLIP, NUTS,
NYSIIS, NYSPIN, OBAR, OPB, OCAS,
OCRUA, OCS, ODIN, ODPCS, OLDAP,
OLEP, OLPARS, OLSASS, OMP, OMR,
OMRS, OPERUN, OPINS, OPSA,
OPTNET, ORACLE, ORDEAL, ORE,
OROS, ORVID, OS/MVT, OSR, OSS,
OSSL, PABLOS, PAC, PACE, PACT,
PACTS, PAD, PADDS, PADEL, PADS,
PAGOS, PAID, PAL, PALC, PAMD,
PAMM, PAP, PARIS, PARS, PARTAN
SD, PATRIC, PATROL, PCMR, PCOS,
PCP, PCS, PDS, PEARL, PEDANT,
PEM, PEP, PEPE, PEPPER, PERCY,
PEST, PGS, PHAROS, PHASE, PHIL-
CON, PICASSO, PICLS, PICS, PIFAL,
PILAR, PIMISS, PIPS, PLANET,
PLANS, PLC, PLOT, PLUM, PLUTO,
PMACS, PMI, PMIS, PMS, PM3,
PNP, POEM, POLAR, POLLS, POLO,
POLYP, POLYPAGOS, POWER, PPE,
PREP, PRESAGE, PRIDE, PRISE,
PRISM, PROD, PROF, PROFACTS,
PROMIS, PROMISE, PRONTO, PRTB,
PSG, PT, PTL, PTLS, PULSE, QDGS,
QE/C, QEEL, QL, QSAM, QTAM,
QUEST, QUIP, QUOBIRD, RACE,
RACMAP, RACSS, RADDS, RAGS,
RAL, RAMP, RAMUS, RAPID, RASB,
RASCAL, RBM, RBT, RCS, REACT,
REL, RELCOMP, RETAIN, RIMS,
RIOT, RITS, RJIS, ROBOT, ROCS,
RODS, ROS, ROSCOE, RPSM, RRDC,
RTCP, RTI, RTL, RTM, RTMOS, RTS,
RTXE, SAAFARI, SAAGS, SABRE,
SACAC, SACAD, SACCHS, SADI,
SAFER, SAHC, SAILS, SAINT, SALES,
SAM, SAMMIE, SAPGO, SAPHO,

SARSIM, SATI, SAVES, SBL, SCAMP,
SCDP, SCOPE, SCOT, SCROLL, SDE,
SDLC, SDM, SEADUCER, SEAMIST,
SEARCH, SEAS, SEEDCON, SEER,
SELCIR, SELMA, SERF, SESAME,
SFD, SFF, SFL, SHA, SHARES,
SHIP, SHREAD, SICLOPS, SIGMA,
SIGMALOG, SIM, SIMAL, SIMALE,
SIMANNE, SIMCON, SIMD, SIMON,
SIMPLE, SIMS, SIMSEP, SIR, SIRE,
SIRNEM, SIS, SJCL, SLA, SLAM,
SLAP, SLIC, SLIM, SLOT, SMART,
SMARTS, SMEDAL, SML, SMM,
SMS, SNAP, SNASC, SOAP, SODA,
SOGAMMIS, SOL, SOLAR, SOLD,
SOLID, SOLMIS, SOLO, SOM, SONIC,
SORTRAN, SOS, SOSOFT, SOVAL,
SPACE, SPAIS, SPANPAC, SPARC,
SPDP, SPEED, SPICE, SPIL, SPL,
SPLC, SPLIS, SPRINT, SPROGS,
SPROSS, SPSS, SPURT, SRCU, SSC,
SSOCR, SSP, SSTS, STAG, STAIRS,
STAR, STATPAC, STATPK, STEEL,
STELLA, STEP, STIL, STP, STPG,
STRACS, STRAIN, STRUMS, SUCE-
SU, SUFFER, SUIS, SUM, SUMC,
SUMMAC, SUMS, SUN, SUPARS,
SWAMI, SWAP, SYMAP, SYMBOL,
SYMBUG, SYMPLE, SYNCON, SYS-
CAP, SYSEX, SYSTID, TABTRAN,
TAC, TACASA, TADS, TAFI, TAL,
TALK, TAM, TAP, TARPS, TASIC,
TCAM, TCCA, TCSP, TEAM, TEGAS,
TEGI, TEPOP, TERP, TESAT, TES-
SAR, TFRAN, THE BRAIN, TIB,
TICCIT, TICES, TIDAS, TIES, TILT,
TIMIS, TIP, TIRKS, TIS, TITAN,
TOAST, TOCS, TOL, TOLA, TOLTS,
TOOL, TOPSET, TORVAP-A, TPL,
TPLI, TRACE, TRACIS, TRADES,
TRAIN, TRAMPS, TRANS, TRIM,
TRIP, TROPICS, TRUNKS, TSF, TSL,
TSO, TSP, TSX, TWT, UAL, UATS,
UDR, UDS, UHELP, UHFM, UHTSS,
UMLER, UMRECC, UNCL, UNICAPP,
UNIQUE, UPACS, UPL, USACSSEC,
UTCS, VAI, VAM, VCS, VDAL,
VENUS, VERA, VERSA, VICC, VIDEC,

VIDPI, VIEW, VIP, VITAL, VMH, VMOS, VORTEX, VOSC, VRC, VSPX, VTAM, WANDA, WANDERER, WARDEN, WARPATH, WASP, WATFIV, WCS, WEDS, WESDAC, WIM, WINDEE, WISDOM, WITCH, WITS, XDUP

Dentistry
AADS, ACD, FIDE, GDPA, NDS

Desalination see Water

Design
COID, DORIS, DPS, ICSID, JIDA, NMG, NUSLIP

Detergents
AIS, SDA

Diesel engines
ASR, ATR, BERSAFE, DEUA, DG

Documentation
ABLS, ADRES, ADSATIS, AGRIS, AID, AIDS, AIM-TWX, APAIS, ASIDIC, ASIN ASSASSIN, BANSDOC, BASIS, BCN, BMDC, BPDA, CAIC, CAIN, CAIS, CAMP, CAN/SDI, CATNIP, CC, CCR, CDICP, CDM, CDS, CDVTPR, CEDOCOS, CFSTI, CI, CIDHEC, CIG, CILG, CINDA, CIP, CIRCA, CIRK, CIS, CNK, COBSI, COIN, COMMANDS, COSTAR, COSTI, CROSSBOW, CSMS, CUMARC, DAIRI, DDC, DESIDOC, DEVIL, DGD, DIRAC, DOCTOR, DRIC, DRL, DSIS, DZW, EARS, EDRS, EICON, ERIC/CLIS, ERISTAR, ETK, EUDISED, EURIM, EUSIDIC, FACT, FAIRS, FAS, FIDRRS, FIRST, FNIC, GATTIS, GIPSY, GITIS, HICLASS, HRMR, ICSSD, IDC, IDCHEC, IDW, HS, ILACS, IMAC, INFIRS, INI, INSPEC, INTIME, IPSJ, IRADES, IRANDOC, IRL, ISBD, ISDG, ISDS, ISIS, ISMEC, ISORID, ISSN, KLIC, KWAC, KWIP, LEADERMAR, LEEP, LISTAR, MAI, MASS,

MCC, MEDHOC, MEDLINE, MIC, MIND, MINICS, MRIS, MUMS, NCMHI, NIDER, NIRC, NLM-BCM, NSTIC, NTIS, OCCI, OIBF, ORCHIS, OSTI, PNBC, PRECIS, QUIS, QUOBIRD, QUODAMP, RADIR, RAIDS, RAPID, RB, RDC, RECON, RIMS, RIOT, SAROAD, SDIM, SIM, SINFDOK, SIPPS, SOLID, SPINDEX, STC, SULIS, SUNY-BCN, SUPARS, SYMBIOSIS, TESAT, TRACY, TRAMPS, TRC, TRIPS, UNISIST, UNISTAR, UPPS, VNIIMI

Doors
DSA

Dowsing
BSD

Dredging
CLB, INC, SEPOD

Drugs see Medical science, Pharmaceutical chemistry

Earthquakes
CCEP, EERC, EML, EPOC, ERA, ERI, NCER, NISEE, SAFE, UCEER, WCEE

Ecology (see also Environment)
CHEC, IAIE, INTECOL

Economics
AsDB, BIPE, BTE, CABEI, CBEUS, CBIS, CEC, CEP, CESI, CIES, CIPE, EDA, EDA-DER, EDRC, EGC, EPA, EPC, EPL, ER, ERFA, IA-ECOSOC, IAECOSOC, IFA, IFC, IFCI, IFE, IIC, IIPF, IMF, ISIC, JERC, JTES, KFC, LOS, LSE, MOLE, NABE, NACE, NCAER, NNP, NPVH, NZIER, OBE, OEC, OER, SAEI, SAGE, SESA, UA, UNEUROP

Education and training
ABAE, ACTIVE, AHFITB, AHME, AnCO, APLET, APT, ASME, ASSIST, ATM, ATPM, ATTITB, AUCET, BABW,

BAK, BAT, BEAMS, BMWB, BTSD, CACHE, CAI, CAINS, CAPE, CAPITB, CAPLIN CATALYST, CBAE, CEC, CEDO, CEPACC, CERL, CERT, CETT, CLW, CMI, CMT, COTI, CQA, CSCFE, CTC, DBR, DRIFT, EAESP, ECCP, ECFMG, EDINET, EDRS, EDSAT, EEA, EFMD, EMAC, ENA, ENAC, ENAP, ENSAE, ENSAIS, ENSB, ERIC/CRESS, ESM, ETRAC, ETS, EUDISED, FDTI, FEF, FIT, FITAC, FOPERPIC, FTITB, FUSE, GATB, GENESYS, GFA, HV, IATLIS, IBE, ICCE, ICEM, ICMI, IERF, IEASA, IESE, IGAEA, IITC, IMEDE, INACAP, INSIGHT, ISTC, ITFS, ITO, ITS, KMK, LEEP, LISE, LORA, LVRCN, MBS, MERIT, MIECC, MOTEC, NABT, NACAE, NAEE, NBME, NCECS, NCTJ, NCTM, NIE, NITIE, OJE, OPTA, OTTS, PITAS, PPITB, PRISE, PSI, RADOT, RASCAL, SCOTA, SCOTEC, SDE, SIMON, SITE, STEP, SURGE, T&SI, TACTICS, TASC, TEC, TETOC, TIC-CIT, TOPS, TRIM, UIE, WICHE, WRK

Electrical engineering

AEDS, AFRC, ALFC, ANT, ASINEL, AVI, BEAMI, BECSM, BESA, BHEL, CADICS, CAPICS, CEA, CEMA, CENEL, CENELEC, CERL, CESP, CIAME, CIGRE, CIMEC, CIRED, CNE, CNSEE, CONSUEL, COSINE, CTC, DATE, DESU, DSLIM, DWR, EERA, EGAT, EHN, EIEMA, ELCB, ENDESA, ENEL, EPRI, EPSEL, ESAA, GESA, GFCI, HGEEA, HIA, HSEB, HVAC, HVDC, IAEI, ICE, ICEL, IEC, IEEE-PES, IEMA, IREDA, ISES, ISPE, KECO, LAB, LABORELEC, LFC, LIMRV, MEA, MEPP, NCB, NECA, NEF, NEMKO, NETA, NGEF, NST, NZED, OVF, PCEA, PEA, PEHLA, PEON, PES, PITB, PWMI, RDOEI, RODS, SCN, SCR, SEAF, SECV, SEP, SLIM, SOFRELEC, SVER, TACV/LIM, TANESCO, TDA, TEK, TNA, TRV, URD, URT, UTE, ZAB, ZSOB

Electro-chemistry

CECRI, CITCE, ECS, ED, ICETK, ISE, RGRDE, SCE, SHE

Electro-magnetism

ARES, COSAM, EMCDAS, EME, EM-PASS, EMPRESS, EMR, EMS, ERMAC, ESP, GECCMSEF, HEM, IEMP, LM-MHD, NECAF, TEFS

Electronics (see also Radar, Telecommunications)

AABNCP, AANCP, AAT, ABE, ACT, ACU, ADATE, ADR, AEDCAP, AEEC, AEI, AEU, AFDEC, AIDE, AIDS, AILS, AIMS, ALEC, ALMS, ALU, AMCAP, AMPS, AMUX, ANIE, APCM, APD, APLL, ARM, AROM, ASE, ASEA, ASESA, ATCAP, ATEC, ATF, ATTO, AUD, BACE, BARITT, BBD, BDI, BEAMA, BEL, BET, BIGFET, BJT, BMRA, BROM, BTB, CACA, CADCOM, CADEP, CADLIC, CADOPCART, CALD, CANCER, CAPARS, CAPP, CASCADE, CATE, CCD, CCNR, CDMLS, CEADI, CECC, CEEIA, CEEIA-WH, CEMAC, CENEL, CENELEC, CENET, CIAME, CIC, CIGFET, CIMEC, CLIM, CMOS, COD, COED, COHO, COMSAP, COM-SEQIN, COS/MOS, COSMOS, COURT, CP, CPC, CPEA, CROM, CRR, CRT, CSEA, CSERB, CSIO, CTD, CTE, CTM, CUERL, CUJT, CVR, DAC, DACE, DAD, DAIS, DATE, DCFP, DCGFF, DCRP, DCSM, DDR, DDS, DECM, DEMON, DEPICT, DESC, DF, DFET, DFTI, DIL, DIR, DISCOLA, DLA, DLFET, DLS, DMA, DMAC, DMOS, DMOST, DORIS, DOT, DOTRAM, DPM, DSA, DSDT, DSTL, DSUCR, DTM, DVCCS, DYNFET, EAA, EAEM, EEROM, EARS, EBIRD, EBMLM, EBS, ECIL, ECM, ECP, ECQAC, EDE, EEPAC, EERA, EFC, EFCIS, EFL, EIA-J, EIAC, EIAJ, EIPC, ELAB, ELCA, ELECSYS, ELIPS, ELSI, ELSIE, EMMA, EMU, END, EPIC, EPID, EPSS, ER, ESC, ESD, ESDERC, ESFI, ESONE, ESR,

ESSDERC, ESTA, ETL, EUROCAE, EVS, EXACT, FACT-AID, FACT-LIFT, FACT-QUIC, FAM, FAMOS, FAPEL, FBB, FCC, FEC, FEDIS, FEM, FETC, FIC, FID, FIET, FIMS, FIR, FIT, FNAP, FPN, FRED, FT, FTDAS, FTLO, FWHM, GAREX, GATT, GCB, GCUGA, GEEIA, GEISHA, GFAE, GPLS, GPMG, GVUGA, HCD, HDF, HELP, HEMAC, HERPES, HFD, HLSI, HTL, IBS, ICC, ICFET, ICMS, ICU, IDA, IDIIOM, IEEE, IEN, IESA, IEVD, IHTS, IIPACS, IIR, ILO, IMPATT, INAP, INCA, IR, IREE, ISPICE, ISSCC, ITEC, JETDS, JFETT, JSEP, KCL, KEA, KETA, KVL, LABEN, LAHA, LATRIX, LCD, LCR, LEF, LEOK LEP, LITES, LLFET, LLL, LOCOS, LSC, LVR, MACE, MADGE, MAGFET, MAGIC, MAMS, MAPS, MARS, MAS, MATE, MCAP, MCP, MDS, MDSIC, MECA, MEG, MEMBRAIN, MESFET, META, MEWS, MGOS, MIC, MICOS, MINDEN, MLB, MLIS, MMIC, MNG, MNOS, MOM, MOSASR, MOV, MPS, MRCD, MS, MSIS, MSM, NATESA, NAVWAS, NDC, NDR, NEA, NERAM, NESA, NESC, NETRS, NISM, NOLAP, NRJ, OXIM, ORDEAL, ORELA, OSI, OXIM, PABLOS, PAD, PAF, PAFAM, PANDA, PANEES, PATT, PBT, PC, PCP, PCT, PEK, PEM, PI-FET, PLA, PLANET, PMC, PPG, PREP, PROM, PSC, PTCR, PTE, PULSE, PWC, QNF, RAC, RADDS, RADLE, RALU, RAM, RAT, RATEN, RC, RCT, REMCAN, RGF, RGPO, RIMPATT, RMM, RMOS, RPC, RTRCDS, RWM, SAAGS, SAMOS, SATO, SAW, SCI, SCO, SCS, SCT, SCW, SDR, SEAF, SECL, SEE, SELCIR, SEMI, SIMTOP, SIR, SIS, SIT, SLAE, SLAP, SLD, SLEEP, SLIC, SMC, SMES, SMO, SNASC, SNF, SNR, SOIS, SOS-ME, SPEED, SPI, SPOOF, SPROSS, SPST, SROB, SSI, SSR, SSU, STC, STS, STT, SV, SWIF, SWR, SYNAME, SYSCAP, TAC, TACMOD, TASIC, TASS, TCT, TCZD, TDA, TEA, TED, TEO, TEREC, TEST, TF, THB, TIC, TIN, TMT, TMXO, TTLIC, TVS, TWLC, USA-CEEIA, USMCEB, USVRU, VAC, VCG, VCVS, VDR, VEA, VIDA, VIDEO, VIMS, VLED, WAND, WASP, WSEC, ZNR

Electroplating
JES, MEPA

Engineering (General)
ACEC, AEAI, AICE, CCESP, CCPE, CEC, CEC/PA, CES, EIZ, ERB, ERC, ERI, ESP, EUSEC, FAOE, FEANI, FIDIC, FSPE, HEC, ICMEE, IE(I), IEAust, IME, IVA, LEA, NIS, NZIE, PEJC, PEPP, PSEF, SACPE, SAME, TSPE

Environment (see also Ecology, Air pollution, Pollution)
CEQ, CERE, CESE, CIDHEC, COEnCO, CPEHS, DOE, EA, ECB, ECOSEC, EDF, EDS, EDSTM, EHL, EHS, ENDEX, ENPOCON, ENVITEC, EPA, ERC, ERL, ERLUA, ESAC, ESIC, FIANE, FOE, GCEP, GEMS, GSF, IAMFES, IDCHEC, IIEQ, IUCN, MDPNE, MECCA, NAEE, NAS/NAE-ESB, NEEDS, NEHA, NERC, NESC, NESS, NIEHS, NOISE, OHES, PCUE, PICC, PIECE, PROCON, PROTECNA, ROMCOE, SCEP, SCOPE, SEL, SEPWG, TVA-OHES, UNCHE, UNEP

Ergonomics
EMMA, HECAD, ICE, NVE, SAMMIE, SELF, SIE, SIFT

Explosives
APFSD, APHE, API, API-T, APSA, APT, CE, CUE, EERL, EERO, EOD, ERDE, ERDL, ERR, FAE, GECCMSEF, HEI-T, HEIT, HOBO, HOBOS, HSDD, ISES, LBLG, LEDC, LRGB, MSDD, RPG, SLU FAE, SNPE, SOSOFT, SSB, SX, TNT

Groundnuts
GEEDA

Health see Medical science

Heating
DHA, NAPHCC, RFDMA, UNICHAL

Helicopters
AAH, AARV, AMES, ARAAV, ARV,
BHAB, BIM, CAC, CCR, CONFICS,
FSAS, HASTE, HCGB, HELMS, HEL-
NAVS, HGMS, HLH/ATC, ICU, ISIS,
LOTAWS, LTTAS, MAST, MATCH,
MTH, OGE, PHS, RSRA, SCAS, VDT,
VERTREP, VOD

Herbicides
HAC

*Highway engineering see Roads
and Road transport*

Horology see Clock and watches

Horticulture
AHFITB, AIPH

Hotels
CERT

Housing see Building

*Hovercraft see Air cushion
vehicles*

Hurricanes
NHC, NHRL, SAS

Hydraulics
APHA, HEL, HRS

Hydrography and hydrology
DMAHC, IAHS, IHB, IHO, SAPHY-
DATA, SHOM

Hygiene see Medical science
396

Illumination
DLMA, IES, IESA, IllumES, LIF,
LLG, MSCP

*Industrial relations see Manage-
ment*

*Information science see Docu-
mentation, Libraries*

Infrared (see also Radiation)
ACSTIS, CAIR, CIRM, DRI, DRIR,
FAC/SCAR, GLAADS, HIPERFLIR,
HRSCMR, IBIS, IHR, ILAMS, IR-NDT,
IRGA, IRIE, IRISH, IRLS, IRMA,
IRNDT, IRT, IRTS, IRTTD, ITPR,
LIRTA, LOPAIR, MAFLIR, MATS,
MIRA, NEI, NODLR, OASIS, SCIRP,
SPIRAS, SSPI, SWIR, TINTS, TIR,
TIRIS, VISSR

Innovation
CSII

Inspection, see Testing, Quality

Instruments
BCS, BSIRA, CIAME, CIMEC, CIMO,
CSIO, EDS, IRDE, JEMIMA, NINA,
NOIC, OIP, RINTIN, SIRA

Insurance
CII, FCIA, FIA, FOC, IITC, IUAI,
NIASA

Inventions
AAII, IPB

Inventory control
IMMAC, IMP, MCIS, SIMS, SLIM,
SMART, SPARC, TRIM, TRIP

Ionosphere
AIO, IBS, IRL, ISS, NAIC, ORBIS
CAL, PUS-IRL, QUIPS, SESAMI-
SEED, SIIA, SITEC

ICLG, IEAB, ILR, INFORM, IPLO, IRLA, JNUL, KOMRML, LAD, LARC, LARSIS, LASER, LIBER, LINK, LISE LLA, LOLITA, MELA, MINTEX, MIS-LIC, MLA, NAL, NAPL, NCLIS, NEILC, NLL, NLLST, NLM, NRL, NYLA, OCLC, OOKDK, PLRG, RAILS, RB, RECON, RML, RSIS, SALB, SCAULEA, SLICE, SORT, SPEEDS, TIB, TLA, UCR, ULMS, ULTC

Lighting see Illumination

Local government
IMBM, IME, IMPC, IMSO, IMTA, JACLAP, LAMIS, LBJCC, LBMSU, LGORU, LHS, LOLA, MHLG, POLLS, RDCA, RICE, SEMLAC, SILS, SRL, WAML

Locusts
DLCO-EA, IRLCS

Logistics
ABLE, ALA, ALMSA, ALPC, ALPHA, ALS, CCMIS, COSMOS, CS3, DLOGS, DSA, FILES, IBMIS, ISSMIS, LASS, LCOM, LDSRA, LEA, LMI, LMICS, LMIS, LOGCOST, LOGMAP, LOGMIS, LOGPLAN, LPI, LSPC, MAWLOGS, MECHTRAM, MLE, OMLRS, RILS, SAAS, SAILS, SALS, SEAMIST, SIG-MALOG, SMLB, SPEED, SPLICE, TLE, TOMMS, TRAMMS, UNREP, USALMC, VALUE

Lubrication (see also Tribology)
EHL, IPF

Machinery
ACIMIT, ACMC, AMTDA, BCPMMA, BPMMA, CPA, EUMABOIS, EUMA-PRINT, FMA, JMMII, JSMEA, MDNA, NTML, PAMM, PMMA, SYMATEX, UNACOMA

Machining and machine tools
ABC, AC, AGIPAC, APT, ARELEM,

AUTOPOL, AUTOSPOT, BWTA, CIM-AF, CINAP, CLDATA, CMTI, CNC, COMSEQIN, DNC, ESCAWT, EXAPT, FAST, FMA, GEM, GWF, HMT, IAMA, IFAPT, IMTMA, MAMC, NCADS, NCS, NELAPT, NRS, NTDPMA, NUCOL, NUMEPS, OS, PHILCON, PNP, PRONTO, SBRS, STEM, UNCL, VDW, WARPATH

Magnesium
MIC

Maintainability see Quality and reliability

Maintenance
BCMA, CAMP, CAMS, CCMA, CLAMP, COAMP, DEQMAR, DMRC, EFNMS, EMMA, FIMS, FMR, HMI, MAC, MEAPS, MMIS, MRSM, NAMSO, OCM, OMLRS, RAFM, TAMMS

Management
AAA, AAS, ACC, ACP, ACTU, ADSE, ADSG, AICD, AIM, AIMC, AIMO, AITUC, APP, AUTONET, BIAC, BPICS, BRLT, C/SCSC, CAMC, CAN, CAPER, CBR, CCA, CDICS, CDPI, CEA, CEMIS, CENIP, CFA, CIFC, CIM, CIR, CIRP, CLASS, CMIS, CMSR, CNP, CNPF, COMPACE, COPICS, COPRAI, CORFO, CORPORAL, COURT, CPR, CSD, DEPICT, DGB, DISCLOSE, DITA, DOCS, DOM, DONA, EAESP, EAMTC, ECS, EFMD, EGCM, EM-PHASIS, ENA, ENAP, ERB, FIFI, FOPSA, FPIS, FPS, FTC, GFA, GIMPA, IAM, ICEP, ICFTU, ICTU, IDE, IDEA, IESA, IESE, IFAP, IIMA, IIRA, ILO, IMA, IMAC, IMAM, IMEDE, IMPACT, INAD, INCAE, IN-COLDA, INPC, INSORA, INTERNET, IOE IPADE, IPAE, IPL, IPM, IPSO, IRGOM, IRRU, IT, IVF, JAR, JIBA, JPC, JRBAC, LAMBDA, LAMIS, LBMSU, LDR, LMSA, MAPLE, MAPS, MBS, MCE, MCP, MCSIB, MDPI,

COMPSY, COS, CPEHS, CPHA, CPHERI, CPI, CPRI, CRC, CRF, CRHL, CRSS, CS, CSF, CSL, CSP, CUPID, CVD, CVSF, DAF, DCIEM, DDDIC, DHSS, DIC, DRMP, DRR, DRUGR, EAMIR, EARLC, EAMRC, EAMVD, EARS, EATIC, EBAA, ECFMG, ECHO, EHAA, EHL, EHS, EMA, EMAS, EMRO, ENMG, EPP, EPR, EPSP, ERCP, ERV, ESCI, ESG, ESR, ETR, FAA-AM, FAE, FEV, FIGO, FNS, FPA, FR, FRAME, FVC, GVH, HA, HAA, HAFOE, HAI, HANE, HAS, HASTE, HBAb, HBAg, HCSS, HFAK, HGH, HIPH, HIS, HLV, HMOS, HPNS, HPS, HS, HSMHA, HSRD, IAGEBS, IARC, IASSMD, IBE, IBRO, IBT, IC, ICD, ICDA, ICH, ICMPH, ICMR, ICN, ICP, ICPM, ICRC, ICRF, ICS, IFA, IFT, IGA, IgM, IGS, IHBTD, IHEA, IHF, IIEM, IMA, IMBI, IMBLMS, IMIS, INFORM, INMAS, IOA, IOTT, IPM, IPPR, IRP, ISCTR, ISGSH, ISGP, ISHC, ISR, ISS, IUAT, IV, IVP, JCAP, JCHST, JE, JEV, KCCT, KOMRML, LAIR, LATG, LCM, LEMAG, LERSC, LH, LH-RH, LMG, LMSA, LNP, LORCS, LP, LSHTM, LVH, MAACL, MACDAC, MAE, MANZ, MAS, MASA, MAST, MAVIS, MBPO, MCAP, MCHR, MDCC, MDS, MEDIHC, MEDIS, MEDISTARS, MEFR, MESA, MFCS, MHTC, MIOR, MIRU, MIS, MISAR, MLD, MLV, MMF, MMR, MRF, MRMS, MSA, MUMPS, NAMCW, NAMH, NAMRL, NAPAN, NBME, NCCMT, NCDC, NCHSRD, NCMHI, NEHA, NEI, NERHL, NGF, NHLI, NHW, NIAAA, NIAMDD, NICHD, NIEHS, NIMH, NIMR, NINDS, NIOSH, NITR, NLM-BCN, NMA, NNMC, NOTBA, NSMRL, NSPB, NTRDA, NTS, NTTRL, NYHA, NZIMP, OAA, OAM, OCCGE, OCEAC, ODC, OHES, OMGE, OOKDK, ORO, ORVID, OSHA, OSHRC, PAHEF, PBI, PCI, PCM, PCMR, PCRI, PEF, PEFR, PGM, PHLS, PHS, PIRP, POMR, PTA, PTB, PTT, PVC, PVT, PAOO, QUARK,

RA, RACP, RACS, RASMP, RBC, RCP, RCPA, RCPath, RCPed, RCPI, RC-Psych, RCS, RCS(C), RCSed, RES, RHCSA, RISA, RISC, RMC, RML, RMPA, RP, RPE, RQ, RV, RV/TLC, RVCD, RVH, SACCHS, SACCS, SAET, SAHC, SAMB, SAMS, SCAP, SCD, SCEH, SCHA, SERHL, SFP, SHHD, SIA, SLE, SMA, SMAF, SMEAT, SMRL, SN, SOM, SPAR, SPC, SSPE, SUM, SUNYBCN, SWRHL, SYMBIOSIS, TAF, TC, TGT, TLC, TMC, TRIPS, TVA-OHES, UAREP, UICC, UMS, UOMC, UPC, USAARL, USAISR, USAMBRL, USAMRIID, VCG, VEMG, VER, VIDA, VNIIMI, VPB, VPC, VSV, VTG, VWF, WBC, WCCF, WCPT, WFOT, WFSA, WHO, WIHC, WMA

Metal finishing (see also Electroplating)
BMFSA, MFF, MMFANE

Metallurgy
ABM, AIMMPE, CESME, CIM, CODA, CRSS, CSM, CVN, DMIC, DMRL, GYFM, HAC, HB, HSC, IM, LEFM, LTMT, MTT, NCML, NIM, NML, PTC, Q&T, SDIM, SFE, SFM, SITPH, SLC, SMEA, SOFRESID, SPAN, STRIPE, SVIM, TMT, TTT

Metals
IOM, ISME, JMMII, MCIC, MFI, MMTC, MPC, MTIA, NAAMM, ORGA-LIME, RRMA, SMACNA

Meteorology
ADC, ADWS, AEROS, AFGWC, AIV, AMOS, AOML, ATDL, AWRS, BAL-THUM, CAgM, CARP, CAS, CAVU, CCl, CCN, CEC, CEMS, CIAP, CIB, CIMO, CIT, COMESA, COVOS, CSM, CWC, DALR, DAO, DAPP, DRI, EAMD, ECMWF, EMOS, EROWS, ESSA, FCM, FGGE, FIDO, GDPS, GMS, GMTS, GOS, GTS, GUGMS, HATRACK, HUR-RAN, IAMAP, ICMS, ICPM, IMD, IPM,

IPS, IRATE, ISMG, ITM, ITPR, JMSPO, KHI, LAWS, LFM, LRIE, LRIR, MADS, MATE, MESONET, MIRT, MOTNEG, MPI, MRF, NCC, NHC, NLC, NMC, NMS, NOAA, NOMSS, NORPAX, NSSFC, NSSL, NWS, OSV, PEATMOS, PEM, POP, PWC, RAREPS, RI, RMC, RTH, SAM, SANBAR, SAWRS, SC/BMS, SMARA, SMIC, SMS, SR, SSMO, STJ, T/EL, TIP, TMP, TWERLE, USATTC, VHRR, VISSR, VTPR, WAMFLEX, WMC, WMO, WMSC, WWP, XERB

Metrology
ASMO, BIML, BNM, CIML, MC, PMEL

Microbiology
IAMS, ICNB, ICSB

Microform
AMSR, CAMP, CATS, CIM, COM, CPM, FISHROD, IMAC, INPLAY, MASPAC, MCRS, MIDAS, MIRS, MMF, MOST, POM, RRP, SDM, SOM, TCML, TIM, VMA

Microscopy
CESEMI, EMAG, EMCON, EMM, EM-MA, EMSA, FIM, HVEM, IAM, JMMA, MEM, NYMS, SEMM, SLPM, STEM, TEMMA

Mining
AIMMPE, BRPM, CALM, CIM, CMRS, CSM, DNPM, EMR, IAGOD, IBM, ICAMC, IMPC, JMIA, MAMC, MIN-ECO, MRDE, NOMES, NUTMAQ, OMA, ORE, PMSRC, SIMSLIN, SMRAB, SMRE, SNAP, SOFREMINES, SIV, TOS, ZIMCO

Missile technology (see also Rockets)
ACLOS, ADSM, ALI, ALVRJ, ASGW, ASMD, ASTP, ATGW, ATIGS, ATS, ATSM, CAMS, CASM, CEL, CLOS, CRMS, DCTM, G/MFCS, GMLS, HARM, HAST, HITS, HOGS, ISM, ISMAP, ISSM, LABP, MACOM, MATS, MAWA, MCLOS, MEMO, MFCS, MHV, MIF, MPM, MPMS, MRAM, NSMSES, PARM, PARS, PEPE, PRESAGE, QRI, RAM, SACLOS, SAGW, SAMCAP, SAMTEC, SDM, SDR, SDRS, SEE, SIM, SLAM, SLCM, SLIM, SMAWT, SRAAM, SRBDM, SSGW, SSM, STS, TERCOM, TGM, TGSM, THAD, ULMS, USGW, VADS

Moon (see also Aeronautics and astronautics
LAC, LACE, LAD, LCRU, LEAM, LFV, LGEC, LID, LIL, LOVER, LPL, LPM, LPO, LRCU, LSG, LSM, LSNLIS, LST, MESA, MET, MLRV, PSE, SESC, XLT

Mycology
NAMA

Naval engineering (see also Marine engineering, Oceanography, Ships)
INSPEAN, IPEN, NSRDL, PANEES, RCNC, SMA, TDC

Navigation
ADRI, AINS, ANDAS, ANT, ATN, BENS, CENA, COCESNA, COGLAD, DNSS, DSNS, GAN, GNC, GPI, GPL, IMPA, INCAS, IPL, MAINS, MAN, MANAV, MASS, MONA, NASS, ONS, PIANC, PNP, R-Nav, RACON, RNAV, SANS, SATNAV, SETAC, SIG, SNAS, SNTA, TALONS, TANS, TFG, TRANSLOC

Newspapers
IENS, NNA, NPA, PNPA

Noise see Acoustics

Nutrition see Food

Observatories
ANRAD, CTIO, ESC, FLO, KGO, NEROC, RGO

Personnel management
EAMP, NPA, PMI, TASS

Pests and pesticides
ALRC, BPCA, COPR, DLCO-EA, EAP-CO, FWGPM, GEFAC, PAC, TPRI

Petrochemicals
EPCA, IVP

Petroleum
AIMMPE, APEA, APOA, BTC, CBMPE, CDICP, CODM, COPM, CORC, COSM, CPA, CRC, ECOPETROL, EGPC, ENAP, EPGA, FCC, FCCU, FFITP, IFP, IPAA, IPCL, IPFF, IPI, JPA, JPDC, LPGITA, NPRA, OAPEC, OPTA, ORI, PEACER, PESA, PESL, PETROBRAS, PETROMIN, PETRONOR, PETROSUL, PFB, PIECE, PILAR, PITAS, PRA

Pewter
ABPC

Pharmaceutical chemistry
AACP, ACA, AMAPI, APA, ASPET, CDRI, CIMPO, CPA, GIIP, IFPMA, NPU, PAA, PDA, UT-LCP

Photogrammetry
ACDPS, EIRA, ICAP, ISSP, SAPGO, TIES

Photography
AFAEP, AHSP, APL, ARPS, ASCS-AP, BCPS, BPEG, BPIA, BSC, BSPA, CPX, ECPS, EPIC, ETC, EUROPHOT, FIAP, FOCIA, IDHEC, IIP, IMBI, IMIS, IPART, IPPA, IRSLL, JCIA, LAPSS, LGEC, NAPL, NPC, NZIMP, PAPE, PDA, PIA, PIC, PPANI, PSA, PTAB, SCIRP, SDB, SLR, SOCRATES, VDPI, XRC

Physics
AA, AAS, ACSAP, BF, BNDC, CAPE, CAPLIN, CLAF, CLASP, COMPAS, CPA, CPAA, CPB, CBM, CPSA, CPT,

CTC, DNPL, EDS, ESSDERC, FAPS, FZP, HPS, ICPEAC, IMTRAN, INFN, InstPhys, IN2P3, IOP, IPCR, IPP, IPPS, ISPP, ITEF, ITP, JSAP, LEP, MOC, MODR, NISPA, NPL, PENDOR, PNACP, PPIP, PPL, PTB, QUIPS, QUODAMP, RCPG, RSJ, SCS, SEE, SINP, SOS, SPO, SPS, SWAP, THG, TMP, VERA

Plastering
NFPC

Plastics see Rubbers and plastics

Plumbing
ASPE, NAPHCC

Pneumatics
APHA

Pollution (see also Air pollution)
ADAPTS, ASIWPCA, CEPEX, CRISTAL, DIP, ENPOCON, FOE, GESAMP, GIPME, HPS, IAPC, IAWPR, ISIMEP, MPCA, NIPCC, OHMSETT, OWPCB, PGMOT, PIP, SHOC, SLURP, WPRL

Population
IUSSP

Porcelain
FEPF

Pottery
FEPF

Postal services
AFPU, AOPU, APO, BPOC, CEPM, CSOCR, EAPT, INTP, LMCSS, MINPOSTEL, MLO, MPT, PARIS, POMP, POUNC, PTTI, UPU, USPS, ZIP

Powder metallurgy
APMI, BMSA, DPR, DS, HIC, HIP, HPR, MPIF, P/F, P/M, PM

Power presses
EPPMP

PTLS, RACE, RDSO, RFFSA, RIA, RIDE, ROCS, RRDC, RRIS, SAR, SBB, SERNAM, SNCF, SNCFA, SOAC, START, TAZARA, TECE, TEGI, TRAC, TRAIN, TRANSMARK, UIC, UMLER, ZVL

Refrigeration
AEEF, DORDEC

Reliability see Quality and reliability

Remote sensing
RSC, RSL

Roads and road transport
ADH, ADT, ATFC, AVI, AZHD-EPD, BMCS, BPA, BRRI, CAPS, CARS, CITRAC, CMS, CRRI, CVS, DBST, DNER, FHWA, FLASH, HECB, HOPS, HRIS, HUF, IDBRA, IMPC, IRTDA, JHRP, MESL, MINERVA, MOTEC, NCHRP, NHSB, NHTSA, NOAH, NRMA, ONSER, PAVM, PETA, PSSM, RATTLE, RITA, RRL, RSDA, RTAC, SAFER, SASHO, SCETA, SETRA, SKI, SLG, TASC, TBST, TIES, TOPICS, TRIP, TRRL, TRTA, TSD, UCS, UM-HSRI, VARSDA, VENUS, VERSA, VHRC, WASHO, WIM

Rockets (see also Missile technology)
ANSSR, ATR, ATRL, GCNR, GLOW, GNR, HAEC, HAT, LAR, LARS, LTTA, LTTAD, LTTAT, MAR, POHWARO, RFF, RPP, RSF, SHAR, STEX, TPAR

Ropes
OIPEEC, OITAF

Rubbers and plastics
ACB, ADICEP, ADN, AIPMA, ANRPC, ARG, ASSOGOMMA, BD, BFRP, BMC, CA, CASING, CCD, CDVTPR, CLD, CNR, CPE, CPVC, CSM, CSP, CSR, CTPIB, CV, DGEBA, DRPG, EPPMA,

ETU, GKV, GRPP, GRTP, HDPE, HPC, HTPIB, IB, IIR, IKV, ILD, IPC, IPN, IRB, IRIA, ISAF, ISPF, LaSS, LCM, LPF, MCS, MEU, MRI, NBR, OESBR, OESR, OKI, PCA, PINTEC, PMRN, PNC, PPL, PPS, PSCC, PSF, PTMT, PVI, QRPG, RICS, RISDA, RUBBER-CON, SIS, SMC, SPF, SPI CANADA, SPSS, SUP, TCAR, TP, TPR, USS

Safety (see also Fire protection)
ACIR, ADR, AFFSCE, AFISC, AHSB, ASAP, ASRDI, BEAB, BMCS, BPS, CISA, CONSUEL, CPSC, ENPI, HUF, IAEI, IMSO, IOHC, IORS, IOTTSG, IRS, IS(PE)MA, ISA, ISHC, ISPEMA, MCAP, MVPCCS, MVSS, NEISS, NHSB, NHTSA, NIOSH, NMVSAC, NSC, NTSB, ONSER, OPS, OSAHRC, OSHA, OSHRC, PMSRC, RAIDS, RASMP, SARS, SEDA, SEPWG, SIM-SLIN, SKI, SMRAB, SMRE, SRAC, SRD, THERP, TISC, TTSC, UM-HSRI, USAAAVS

Sanitation
CCSE

Satellites see Aeronautics and astronautics

Scaffolding
NASC

Science fiction
SFF, SFRA

Seismology
ASE, CSO, CSP, DSID, DSS, IASPEI, ISC, NORSAR, OBS, PDE, SASP, SLAM, SSA, TFSO

Sericulture
CSRS

Sewage
AAWSA, BWETPA, CORPOSANA, EWAC, INAPA, KASP

SELECTIVE SUBJECT INDEX

Ships and shipping (see also Marine engineering, Naval engineering)

AALC, ABS, ABSTECH, AIMS, APU, ASCM, ATN, BACAT, CAPAC, CENSA, CES, CGT, CMI, COGAP, COGLAD,, COMLOSA, COMMODORE, CONCAT, CPIC, CSUK, CTA, DEMS, DnV, DSF, EBCS, EMPASS, EMPREMAR, EM-PRESS, FLOCON, FPB, FRELIS, FSPS, GRT, IACS, ICPL, INCAS, IOTTSG, ISES, ISF, ISG, ISPCC, ITESC, JSEA, JSMEA, KNSM, LARC, LBP, LCL, LOA, LOT, LPD, LWP, MCMV, MERSAR, MLB, MPS/MMS, MTB, NSB, NSMB, OBO, OSDOC, RAS, REMCALC, RIB, RTCM, SMB, SCI, SIAC, SIB, SIP, SIRS, SMTRB, SNAP, SNAS, SNR, S3, STREAM, SUIS, SUN-AMAM, SWATHS, SYMES, TARPS, UNREP, VERTREP, VLBC, VLCC, VLOOC, VOD, WFS

Shock absorbers
EUSAMA, SAMA

Shoes
ANCI, BFMF, CODIFAC

Shutters
DSA

Soap
AIS, SDA

Soil
CSMRS, SRI, SRP, SWC

Solar energy
FRUSA, GOD, ISES, SEMMS, SEPS, SEPSIT, SES, SIMSEP, STEC, TOP-SEP

Solder
BABS, SMA

Spectrometry and spectroscopy
AFS, AS, CAMSPEK, CARIS, FACSS, HEAPS, HEPS, IMMS, ISS, IUCS,

MSS, PES, PESIS, PESOS, PIS, QMS, SIMS, SISAM, SOAP, TDS, UVS, WCS, WDS

Standards
A, AGS, ASAC, ASCS-AP, ASESA, ASI, ASMO, BNA, C, CECC, CEN, CENEL, CENELEC, CERTICO, CSAC, DBS, DC, DD, DEF(AUST), DIS, DMSC, DTD, EXCO, F, FIPS-PUB, FNKe, FNR, G, HC, HR, ICONS, ICSHB, INFOTERM, ISCA, ISO, JETDS, L, LESL, LORCO, M, MA, MPS, MSS, MVSS, N, NCSBCS, NETR, NETRS, NIBSC, NIS, NMAS, NZS, PAS, PASC, PHILSA, PL, PLACO, PSST, PTAB, RDSO, S, SANZ, SCC, SEASTAGS, SIC, SIS, SISIR, SP, SPIN, STA, SWAC, T, TA, TASST, THE, TSO, 2HR, ULINC, VNIIS, WAC

Stationery
ESMA, NBFA

Statistics
ABLE, AOV, ARMA, ASI, ASRL, ATEV, BLUE, BPME, BPRE, BRDT, BSO, CCBV, CCSS, CDF, CDSU, CLUSAN, COCAAHOS, COINS, COPSS, CSO, CSPRT, DBS, DCS, EIWLS, EUROSTAT, FACTAN, FAMS, FSD, GLSE, GRASS, IARS, IASA, IASI, IASS, IDSC, IMS, IMSE, IPDF, ISE, ISI, ITSE, IWLS, LIL, LMS, LSD, MAP, MBPRE, MDS, MEP, MINQUE, MISER, ML, MMS, MRA, MRL, MSE, MSEP, MVLUE, MVU, MVUE, NIP-ALS, OLS, OSCAS, PASS, PDF, PEATMOS, PMP, PSPRT, QS, RKHS, SELMA, SESA, SEV, SOEC, SPD, SPES, STANSIT, STATPK, STATSIM, STEAM, STIL, STPG, TDPI, TSLS, TSPRT, TSPRTR, TST, WNAR

Steel see Iron and Steel

Structural engineering (see also Building, Civil engineering)
ADSTEEL, BAPS, CACCI, CISC, CISE,

406

SATT, SBC, SBF, SBO, SCALE, SCAMA, SCAMP, SCAX, SCRA, SCSD, SDCCU, SDDLL, SDM, SDMA, SEA-COM, SELCAL, SIFTA, SIMS, SINAD, SKEA, SLM, SMART, SMARTS, SMAS, SOCC, SPADE, SPSP, SqDM, SRAEN, SSC SSFC, SSMA, SSR, STB, STD, STDM, STDMA, SWAP, SWC, SWD, SWIFT, TADS, TARE, TARIF, TAS-MAN, TCAM, TCARS, TCRC, TCSP, TDL, TELECOM, TEMA, TESSAR, TEUR, TIRKS, TKO, TPLI, TRC, TRT, TSPS, TTC, TTWS, UNICCAP, USACC, USACEEIA, USB, USITA, UTE, VAD, VDMA, VF, VFCT, VFT, VHFRT, VSAM, VSS, WAIM, WARC-ST, WCS, WESTAR, XELEDOP

Telemetry
APT, ARAPT, ART, ATS, NTC, RAMS, STAG, TIDP, TTC

Telephony see Telecommunications

Television (see also Broadcasting)
CARS, CATS, CATV, CCFF, CCTA, CCTV, CINTEL, CONART, CRTC, CRTPB, CTV, ETRAC, FACTS, FOR-TRA, GENESYS, ICAT, IFTC, ITA, ITCA, ITFS, ITS, LLL, LLTV, MTTSA, NATESA, NCTA, OIT, ORACLE, OTSA, RATEKSA, SIT, SITE, SSTV, STV, SURGE, TAC, TESA, TICCIT, TRUST, TVBS, TVE, TVRO, UDATS, VIR, VITEAC, WVTV

Testing (see also Materials—research and testing)
ADTU, AEM, AET, AIS, AIT, ALT, APTE, ASTP, ATEC, ATSJEA, AUT, BBOL, BEA, BETA, CAEND, CASS, CATE, CEOC, CESME, COBRA, COM-AD, CSNDT, CTA, CUDAS, DAF, DBBOL, DCOL, DEE, DGZfP, DME, DOBETA, DRME, DT, DTOL, DW, EBM, EPMS, EWGAE, FLT, FRAM, GMTO, IDA, IR-NDT, IRNDT, IRSA, ISI,

ITEM, KET, LASAR, LATS, MART, MASS, MATE, MCF, MELETA, MOAT, MODAPS, MRI, NDA, NDAT, NDE, NDTS, NEMKO, NETA, NNDTU, NTTS, ORTS, PAMM, PATT, PEHLA, PERCY, PUNDIT, QUALTIS, RILEM, RMF, RTL, SAMTEC, SCOPE, SCOT, SITS, SONDE, SPA, SWE, TDA, THB, TIRIS, TOAST, TOL, TOLTS, TOOL, UCS, VIDEO, VITAL, VOSC, WWPT

Tetralogy
ETS

Textiles
AATT, ACIMIT, AERTEL, ATI, ATIRA, CCI, CITTA, CMP, CRC, CSP, CTRL, EUROCOTON, FEBELTEX, GEDRT, ICDC, IIC, ITT, IVT, JCPI, LRA, NTC, SCR, SITPW, SITRA, SYMATEX, TEFO, TTFC

Tiles
AVATI, TCA

Timber
BWTA, CFI, COFI, CPA, FEBELBOIS, FEIC, FTITB, GLULAM, IAWA, IPIRA, KAR, PRL

Tobacco
FDTI

Town planning
CIDHE, CLUSTER, ISM, ISOCARP, RTPI, TPI

Toxicology
TIP, TIRC

Trade
ASSOCOM, BDC, BEB, BFEC, BIC-CID, BIMA, BJCC, BNEC, BOT, BOTB, BOTGI, BPEG, BPIA, BSCC, BTANZ, BTI, CAFEA-ICC, CCI, CCT, CEAO, CELA, CELAC, CEMI, COMET, CON-CANACO, CONCEX, CRE, DITC, DTI, ECGD, ECM&MR, ECMRA, EDB,

EEPC, EIS, ESD, EVAF, FICCI, FIEO, FMG, GEEDA, IBCC, ICC, IEX, IM, IMIS, IMRA, KNTC, LTFV, M, MMTC, MPDS, NAAG, NAFTA, NCITD, NCT, NCTRU, NIMEX, STC, TDA, UKSATA, WAAC

Training see Education and training

Transport and transportation (see also Aeronautics, Railways, Roads, Ships)
ABTM, ACCESS, ADR, ASTI, ASTRO, ATT, BTE, CACTQ, CART, CIT, CTC, CTCC, DOT-HS, HEART, HSB, IGTS, IMAT, IRT, ITA, ITE, ITRDC, ITTE, LTE, MEL, MOT, MT, NECTP, NTSB, OST, OTTS, PANCAP, PRT, PTRAC, RATP, RECAT, SCRTD, SPLC, SVS, TARGET, TCCL, TDA, TDCC, TEA, TIAC, TNRIS, TRAG, TRANS, TRIS, TRRL, TSC, TSTC, TTC, TTSC, TUCC, TVS, UITP, USL, UTCS

Translations
JPRS, NTC, TWT

Tribology (see also Lubrication)
ESTL, NCT

Tunnelling
STUVA, TBM

Turbines
AGT, ATEGG, FAST, GTRE, JIC, NXSR, SETE, STAGG, TERP, TETWOG

Tyres
ASPA, ITSC, NDCC, NDMS, NDTA, RICS, TISC, TRA, XLT

Varnish
NPVLA

Vegetables
NVRS

Veterinary science
CMT, EAVRO, FDVR, FVR, ICVAN, VBD, VMRC

Ventilation
RFDMA

Volcanoes
IAVCEI

Warehousing
IFPWA

Waste
ISWM, NAWDC, NSWMA, SW, SWMO, SWMPO

Waste Collection
RAGS

Watches see Clocks and watches

Water
AAWSA ACCC, ASIWPCA, AWRC, BSBG, BWETPA, CAWC, CBCC, CCIW, CFE, CONCAWE, CORPOSANA, CRWR, CSSE, CWA, CWAC, CWPRS, CWRA, DO, DOM, DRBC, DVGW, DZW, ESCOW, EWAC, FWPCA, FWQA, IAWPR, IBWC, ICWP, INAPA, INERHI, ISWRRI, ISWS, IVL, IWA, IWE, IWR, IWRA, KOWACO, ME, MGD, NERBC, NWC, OSC, OSW, OWP, OWPCB, OWRB, OWRC, PPWB, RO, RSW, SEPE, SLURP, SNBB, SPEPE, SWC, SWRSIC, TOD, VFVC, VPI-WRRC, VTE, WALRUS, WANDA

Weights and measures
BIPM

Welding
BWSTMA, CAW, CCIIW, CEMSE, CSW, CVL, CW, DFW, EBW, EW, EXW, FCAW, FOW, FRW, FW, GMA, GMAW, GSSW, GTAW, HDW, HIP, IW, LACD, LBW, MFUW, NIL, NTW, NVL, NWH, OAW, OHW, PAW, PEW, PGW, PIGMA, PTW, PVRC, PWHT,